WAR LETTERS

WAR LETTERS

TO A WIFE

FRANCE AND FLANDERS, 1915–1919

BY

ROWLAND FEILDING

LONDON
THE MEDICI SOCIETY, LTD.

First Published, October 1929
Second Impression, November 1929
Third Impression, December 1929

PRINTED AND BOUND IN GREAT BRITAIN BY
ANTONY ROWE LTD, EASTBOURNE

TO MY WIFE

PREFACE

IT is well to explain—in case the criticism may be made that the letters which follow show a defiance of the censorship—that the originals contained no place names or other indiscretions. These have been added from the writer's diary.

The letters were written while the events described were fresh in mind—often actually on the battlefield or in the trenches. That is their claim to interest, coupled with the extraordinary luck which permitted an individual to survive so long in the front line. Such an experience was allowed by Fate to very few.

LIST OF ILLUSTRATIONS

FRONTISPIECE

INTRODUCTION

BY

MAJOR-GENERAL SIR JOHN PONSONBY, K.C.B., C.M.G., D.S.O.

THIS book contains letters written by a soldier to his wife during practically the whole period of the European War.

They are written by Colonel Rowland Feilding, and give us a very vivid picture of the life of a regimental officer on active service. No family has been more closely identified with the Coldstream Guards than the Feildings, and it was only natural that Rowland Feilding should have been posted to the regiment where so many of his family have served with great distinction. He was appointed Captain in the 3rd Battalion Coldstream Guards in 1915, and was subsequently transferred to the 1st Battalion, which I had the honour to command.

Rowland Feilding soon proved himself to be a keen and capable officer, and I can add from personal observation, an officer in whom all ranks had the greatest confidence.

Perhaps, as Colonel Guy Baring expressed it, he was "too brave"; but the real truth was that Rowland Feilding could not bear giving orders to a subordinate officer to carry out any dangerous duty, and always applied to carry out the duty in question himself. How he managed to survive the War will always remain a mystery to me and many others.

Eventually Rowland Feilding was strongly recommended for the command of a battalion of the New Army, and it was decided by Army Head-quarters that an officer of his age, ability and experience, would be a great asset to a newly formed battalion. He was therefore in 1916 given command of the 6th Battalion Connaught Rangers.

This regiment and, later, the 1st Civil Service Rifles he led with conspicuous success till the conclusion of the War.

It is given to very few to be able to write letters so full

of interest, so free from criticism of his senior officers, so free from exaggeration, and so modest and unassuming.

These letters will be read with great interest by Rowland Feilding's brother officers, who will always remember how "Snowball," by which name he was affectionately known by all ranks, carried on the high traditions of his regiment and family.

JOHN PONSONBY

FOREWORD

"In the end of ends, infantry is the deciding factor in every battle . . . (it) bears the heaviest burden of a battle and requires the greatest sacrifice. . . .

"They have to endure the heaviest bombardments of the enemy, lying quietly in dirt and mud, in damp and cold, hungry and thirsty, or huddled in dug-outs, holes, and cellars, they must await the overpowering assault, until, leaving the safety of their shelters, face to face with death, they must rise to meet the destroying storm. Such is their life. It can be endured only when discipline has prepared the way, and when a deep love of the Fatherland and an imperative sense of duty fill the heart. . . .

"Those who have stayed at home cannot picture it to themselves too often. Before such heroism they must bow the head in silence—and not talk."

Ludendorff.

"We owe these victories . . . to the perfect co-operation of all arms, and, most, perhaps, of all, to the immortal valour of our noble infantry, which continues to bear the greatest burden in the fight, and has once more won imperishable renown. Without it all the labours of other arms would be in vain. It is the infantry with rifle, bomb, and bayonet that both takes and holds, endures the greatest and the longest strain, and suffers by far the heaviest losses. Few lookers-on witness its deeds of valour, but, if we were just, we should distinguish its incomparable gallantry by granting it in future the precedence over all other arms, which it has fairly won by its devotion and its sacrifices."

"The Times" Military Correspondent, June 25, 1917.

"The poor b—— infantry."

British Soldier.

WAR LETTERS TO A WIFE

April 29, 1915. *Harfleur.*

We left Windsor the day before yesterday—a draft of 12 officers and 250 men. The regimental band led the way to the station at the foot of the hill, playing lively airs, as is the custom when troops are leaving for the front. A crowd followed, and men and women pressed forward to shake hands with their friends among the men. The latter seemed very cheerful and sang lustily as they marched along.

We left Southampton for Havre at 9 p.m. and berthed at 6.30 yesterday morning. Leaving the docks at 8.10 we marched about 5½ miles to the Reinforcement Camp, where we now are. It was very hot, and after a rough crossing, I think most of the draft found the march rather trying, being, as they were, in heavy marching order. As for myself, it was the first time I had ever carried a pack, and it felt as if it was filled with lead before we reached Harfleur. I am glad to learn that, as a Captain, it is not likely that I shall have to carry one again.

May 3, 1915. *Le Préol.*

On May 1 I left the Base with Geoffrey Fildes, in charge of drafts for three line battalions, and reached Chocques, where we detrained at one o'clock yesterday (Sunday) afternoon.

On marching my draft to the village where the battalion to which it was consigned was billeted, I found that, by a coincidence, the latter was being relieved by the 1st Batt. Coldstream Guards, who were preparing to go into the trenches as I arrived. Arthur Egerton and the two other officers of his Company were just sitting down to tea and eggs and asked me to join them, which I was very thankful to do, since it was my first square meal of the day and I was ravenously hungry. Afterwards, I returned to Chocques, where I was lent a motor-car by a generous staff officer of whom I casually asked the way, which brought me through Bethune to the village of Le Préol, where the 3rd Battalion, to which I have been posted, is billeted.

As I reached the village last evening I met a company of my new battalion returning from the trenches. It is an impressive sight to see for the first time. The men, led by an officer, were marching along the canal bank, the stretcher-bearers with the stretchers bringing up the rear. Their clothes and boots were stained with the clay and dust of the trenches, but the rifles were spotless, as usual, and I thought their faces wore a strained and tired look such as men get when they have been a long time without sleep.

I daresay I shall cease to notice these details when I have been here longer, but I mention them since this—my first direct contact with the war—brought home to me its reality more than anything had done before. I felt I should like those thick-skinned "home-service" young men of ours to see the sight too. It might perhaps bring home to them their duties and responsibilities.

We are 3 miles behind the firing line and, as I write, one of our heavy guns is blazing away every two or three minutes from close by, making the windows rattle and the ground shake. At night the glimmer of the rockets from the trenches indicates the position of the line, from which the sounds of battle come almost continuously:—the intermittent booming of the artillery, and the crack of rifle and machine-gun:—and yesterday, from 4.30 to 9 p.m., there was added the distant roar of a heavy cannonade:—our artillery, we have since learned, firing upon the Germans, who had attempted another attack near Ypres with asphyxiating gas.

The country is looking lovely. All the fruit trees are in blossom and the banks of the railway cuttings are carpeted with primroses and cowslips. Everything looked so peaceful as we came along in the train that it was difficult to realize the war till we came within the sound of the guns. Even in this village the French children play about, apparently unconscious of the proximity of danger, and in the cottage where I am billeted there is a considerable family of them.

Unfortunately for me, Geoffrey [1] had left the battalion just before I joined, having got command of a Brigade. He has been through the recent fighting north of Ypres, and his Brigade is now, I believe, holding the point of the salient. In his place, Torquhil Matheson [2] commands the battalion, and my Company Commander is Vaughan ("Little Man"), while Longueville is in the same Company. Rollo,[3] also, is here, looking very fit and well, in spite of eight months of the trenches.

P.S. I have been watching the bombardment by the enemy of three of our aeroplanes which have been flying overhead. The shooting has been going on for half an hour, over a hundred shells having been fired. The sky is studded with little puffs of smoke from the bursting shells, which look like flecks of cotton-wool. Yet the pilots continue to circle round recklessly, in a manner most contemptuous and admirable.

Later. It is just beginning to get dark, and weird. The sky is lighting up from the star-shells which rise constantly from the trenches.

May 6, 1915.   *Le Préol.*

On Tuesday evening, just a week after leaving Windsor, I went into the trenches for the first time. We left our billets in a heavy thunderstorm and rain and found the trenches in a very sodden condition. Our bit of line ran through the village of Givenchy, practically nothing of which remains now, though the Germans continue to shell it, so that the little that is still standing of the church will soon have disappeared, and even the graves that surround it are giving up their dead.

We relieved the 1st Irish Guards by daylight, my Company being one of the two whose turn it was to man

---

[1] Now Maj.-Gen. Sir Geoffrey Feilding, K.C.B., K.C.V.O., C.M.G., D.S.O.

[2] Now Maj.-Gen. Sir Torquhil Matheson, K.C.B., C.M.G.

[3] Now Lieut.-Col. Viscount Feilding, C.M.G., D.S.O.

the front line. On either side of me I found relations. On my immediate left Percy Clive [1] commanded a company of Grenadiers, and the Coldstream Company on my right was commanded by Rollo. I visited Percy at 4.30 on the morning after our arrival. The last time I had seen him was at dinner at the House of Commons, and I was very glad to meet him again. While I was shaving, Rollo brought Henry Feilding [2] to see me. He is with a squadron of King Edward's Horse, which is acting as Divisional Cavalry to a Territorial Division near here, and was paying a visit to Rollo in the trenches. You will think I have stumbled into a regular family party.

We were relieved, quite unexpectedly, after twenty-four hours, and ordered to a sector a few hundred yards further to the right, on the other side of the canal, and we spent last night at Le Préol, in our former billets.

May 8, 1915.   *Cuinchy Brickstacks.*

At 3.15 on the afternoon of the 6th, we fell in and marched to the Cuinchy Brickstacks. Some of these are held by the enemy and some by us, and our new trenches run between them.

These brickstacks are big cubical heaps of bricks still standing in the position in which they were burnt. Each has a hollow in the centre at the ground level which contained the fire, and there are upward flues through the structure by means of which the fumes escaped. The bricks are packed in such a way that there are minute spaces between each, so that the mass is very elastic, and practically impervious to shell-fire; and therefore a formidable obstacle in attack, as well as an extremely useful shelter in defence.

Since I last wrote I have been transferred from No. 3 to No. 2 Company, which is commanded by Captain Guy Darell. The other officers are Ernest Platt, Lord Ipswich, [3] and Palmer. It was my new Company's turn for the firing line.

[1] Captain Percy A. Clive, M.P. Killed in action April 5, 1918.
[2] Capt. Hon. Henry Feilding, died of wounds October 11, 1917.
[3] Viscount Ipswich, killed in aeroplane accident April 23, 1918.

It is a tricky bit of trench, there being much sapping and mining from both sides. In the Company's section alone we have six saps, three of which are also mined and charged with high explosive, and the German miners, from their side, are suspected of being actually beneath us at one spot.

Two of our saps run to within 5 or 6 yards of a big mine crater, occupied by the enemy, between which and our No. 6 sap a duel of hand grenades took place yesterday morning, supplemented by trench-mortar bombs and rifle grenades. It was a noisy affair that lasted about an hour and a half, but was harmless in so far as we were concerned. It was a blind fight at close range in the dark, so to speak, since neither side could see the other.

Many of the German hand grenades failed to explode, so it was possible to examine them. They are barbarous-looking things—the shape and size of big square hair-brushes—the kind that has a handle, with a long jagged iron bolt wired on at each corner.

The dead that lie unburied between the trenches are becoming a source of trouble now that the hot weather is setting in. Many have lain there for months. At nights such of them as can be reached are fetched in and buried, or in some cases are covered with chloride of lime. Last night I saw it being done. It is a sickening job.

This morning I paid a visit to the French who hold the trenches on our immediate right, and returned to my Company in time to receive my baptism of shell-fire. Thirty-six "Jack Johnsons," spread over an hour and twenty minutes, were dropped upon us. The enemy started with our fire-trench, of which he showed that he had the range, repeatedly *only just* missing it, and obtaining at least one direct hit which blew in 10 or 15 yards of the parapet alongside the spot where Ipswich and I happened to be standing.

I confess the sensation is far from comfortable. You hear the shell from the moment it leaves the howitzer, and you can have no idea of the long time it takes to come, or of the weird scream it makes in doing so. When at last it bursts and you know that the danger is over, at any rate for the moment, there comes a highly satisfactory feeling of exhilaration and relief.

I was covered with showers of earth and dust time after time, and once was hit on the head by a big lump of dry clay. Ipswich, though he was not actually hit, was rather nearer than I to the shell which fell in the trench alongside of us, and has been a good deal shaken by it.

This afternoon, walking along the fire-trench, I came upon one of our bombers on the ground. A bomb had that moment exploded in his hand and blown off both his hands and forearms. He died in about twenty minutes. These bombs explode four seconds after lighting the fuse, and there is a tendency among the men to hold on for a second or two before throwing them, so that they cannot be used by the enemy to throw back again. It is a risky practice.

Later in the afternoon my Company was relieved from the fire-trench, and we moved some 300 yards back into support. Here we received orders for a great combined French and British attack, to be delivered to-morrow.

May 10, 1915.   *Cuinchy Brickstacks.*

The orders for yesterday were that the 1st Division would attack on our left; the French on our right. We (the 4th Guards Brigade) were, at all costs, to hold the intervening sector, where it was considered probable that a counter-attack would be delivered; and we were given to understand that we must rely upon ourselves alone. The artillery was to begin wire-cutting at 4.45 a.m. in co-operation with the machine-guns. Infantry fire was to open at 5.40 a.m.

About 3.30 a.m. an English aeroplane flew very low over our lines and was met by a heavy fusillade of rifle-fire from the enemy, which brought it down between the trenches, close to the Germans. As it crashed, the latter raised a cheer and threw bombs at the machine, which burst into flames, burning the two occupants, who were probably already dead or dying.

Punctually, at 4.45 a.m., our artillery on the left opened fire, and, after two hours or more of continuous bombardment, the British attack was launched.

A battalion of the Rifle Brigade (4th Corps) succeeded in rushing the first German trench and passing beyond it, but, in their impetuosity, they passed over the dug-outs in which many of the enemy were taking shelter.

The latter came out when the first wave had passed over, and succeeded in holding the second wave which was not expecting opposition from this quarter, as well as cutting off the men who had gone forward.

On their right the 1st Division got hung up in the barbed wire, which the preliminary bombardment had failed to cut. Indeed, the shrapnel, which had been chiefly employed for wire-cutting purposes, had proved a hopeless failure, as also had the machine-guns (who could have expected otherwise?), and when our troops reached the wire they found it intact, and the enemy's trenches, which had been steadily reinforced in anticipation of the infantry assault, manned almost shoulder to shoulder.

The attack was repeated in the afternoon in glorious sunny weather after a second bombardment of two hours' duration. On this occasion a Company of the 1st Black Watch reached the German fire-trench, and an officer with a few men got well beyond it, but there was heavy resistance. The survivors had to fall back after severe hand-to-hand fighting, and at the close of the day our line was as it had been in the morning.

The French, simultaneously, made a series of attacks on our right, preceded by a heavy bombardment. In fact, the roar of their artillery continued the whole of yesterday and a great part of last night. The rumour is that they have met with some success, particularly in the neighbourhood of Loos.

May 12, 1915. *La Tombe Willot.*

The battalion was relieved this afternoon by the Gloucesters and marched to La Tombe Willot, a short distance north of Locon, where we are billeted for the night,

7

and shall take off our clothes for the first time for a week and sleep in sleeping-bags. The distance was about 6 miles, and we carried packs!

As we came through Le Préol we passed our 1st and 2nd Battalions. It was the first time in history that the three Coldstream battalions have met together on active service.

May 13, 1915.   *Le Préol.*

Guy Darell (my Company Commander) and I have been transferred to the 1st Battalion, and this morning Darell said good-bye to the Company which was drawn up for the purpose.

As he left, the men gave him three cheers, and then did the same for myself;—which I appreciated very much, having regard to the very short time I had spent with them.

Afterwards, Darell's eldest brother,[1] who is on the Staff of the 7th Division, sent a car for us, which brought us to his Divisional Headquarters at Hinges, where we lunched, and where I sat between General Heyworth[2] and Lord Bury, both of the Scots Guards. The elder Darell then motored us to Beuvry, from which place we walked to Le Préol and joined our new battalion. The latter is commanded by Colonel John Ponsonby.[3]

Each trench at Cuinchy is labelled with the name of some familiar London street, such as Dover Street, Half-Moon Street, Hanover Street, Edgware Road, Marylebone Road, Birdcage Walk. Even Leicester Square is represented. At the cross-roads (or rather cross-trenches) are sign-boards "To London" or "To Berlin" (as the case may be).

Where bricks are procurable—and that is almost anywhere since scarcely a house remains standing—the floors of the trenches have been paved with bricks. Here and there in the sides of the trenches or behind a brickstack—

[1] Now Col. William Darell, C.M.G., D.S.O.

[2] Brig.-Gen. F. J. Heyworth (Scots Guards), C.B., D.S.O., killed in action May 1916.

[3] Now Maj.-Gen. Sir John Ponsonby, K.C.B., C.M.G., D.S.O.

in fact, wherever the situation has been considered suitable
—dug-outs have been made, of varying stability, with roofs,
some of which are strong enough almost to stand a direct
hit from a light shell, while others would scarcely stop a
splinter.

Some of the dug-outs bear fancy names, such as "The
Guards Club," "Sylvan Villa," and so on. Occasionally,
a bit of doggerel, composed by one of the men, has been
pegged up on the parapet. Here is one:

> Kasier (*sic*) Bill
> We're going to kill;
> I'll bet our score
> is four to nil.

And, occasionally, one comes across a grave in the
trench, with a rough pencilled inscription.

There are, or were, numerous villages and farm buildings
scattered about the area where we are fighting. All are
gone now. The churches in particular have been shelled
to ruins. It is curious, nevertheless, how sometimes the
holy statues have survived the wreckage. Two still stand
on their niches in the roofless walls of Cuinchy Church,
and, at a point where the communication trench passes an
old cemetery, the great crucifix which dominates every
graveyard in this part of France still stands intact against
the sky, amid its shattered surroundings. I shall never
forget the first time I saw it. I had plodded along many
hundreds of yards of the communication trench, seeing
nothing but the bricked floor and the clay walls—for there
was nothing else to see. Then something above me caught
my eye and I looked up, and saw this great crucifix towering
above the trench, and facing me.

One of my duties is to censor the men's letters home. It
is a duty I do not like at all, but it gives me an insight into
the simple minds of the great majority of the writers.
There are no heroics. And almost every letter begins
and ends with the same formula: "Dear Sister" (for
example), "I hope this finds you as it leaves me at present,
in the pink"; and, at the end, are numerous children's kisses.

9

May 14, 1915. *Bethune.*

My new battalion was in reserve during the attack of last Sunday, and was lucky in having only twenty-one casualties. It has not always been so fortunate. Indeed, since the war began its casualties have already reached 2,600, or nearly three times the full strength of the battalion. It has been badly cut up on four occasions—on the Aisne in September, at Givenchy in December, at Cuinchy in January, and it was almost annihilated last October at Gheluvelt, in front of Ypres, when, there being no other officer left, Boyd, the Quartermaster, brought the battalion out of action.

It is still very short of officers, and was resting when I joined yesterday. Nevertheless, shortly after my arrival, we got orders to march at 9 p.m. for Bethune, which we reached about 11.30, and from where I write.

May 16, 1915 (*Sunday*). *Sailly Labourse.*

This morning Darell and I rode with the Colonel (John Ponsonby) to reconnoitre the trenches in front of Vermelles, which our Brigade has just taken over from the French. We found the left section manned by the 1st Cameron Highlanders, the centre by the London Scottish, and the right by the 1st Scots Guards. The German trenches are a long way off—quite 500 or 600 yards away, and possibly even more in places.

There seems to have been a sort of tacit "live and let live" arrangement between the enemy and the French, who, as you know, have several hundred miles of battle front to defend, and are probably not sorry when the opportunity occurs to do a bit of it on the cheap. Indeed, it is very necessary. At any rate John Ponsonby told us to-day that the French commander had assured him that it was a quiet sector, and had added, jokingly, "We are very good friends here—the Boche and ourselves. We never shoot at them, and they never shoot at us!" I wonder how long this "Utopia" will last, now that we have come here. Our line, compared with that of the French, is short, and consequently every yard of it is strenuous.

May 20, 1915.   *Le Rutoire.*

Last night after dark we relieved the 1st Scots Guards in the trenches east of Vermelles. This town, or village —through which we had to pass to reach our new position —was captured by the French last December, after desperate street fighting, and it is almost impossible to describe the scene of desolation which it now presents. Not a house has escaped greater or lesser destruction. The church is a ruin, and the little that remains of its walls is so pitted with bullet and shrapnel wounds that it is almost true to say that scarcely a stone has escaped damage. Of the chateau—around which the fighting was chiefly concentrated—nothing remains but a pile of bricks.

My Company is in the reserve trenches for the moment, my headquarters being in a dug-out made by the French.

The exterior construction of this dug-out amounts to nothing, and would not stop anything heavier than a whizz-bang, if that, but much care has been devoted to its interior decoration, which resembles that of a cottage parlour. The French are much more thorough in these matters than we are. It has a door, two windows with muslin curtains, a little fireplace with wax flowers on the mantelpiece, papered walls and ceiling, a boarded floor, a little crucifix, a big looking-glass, and a sketch and poem by a former occupant nailed upon the wall. The former depicts an angel, flying, and blowing the trump of victory. The latter reads as follows:

> O toi qui de ces lieux demain sera le maitre
> Soigne ce cagibi [1] digne un jour de paraitre
> Dans les fastes pompeux de l'immortalité.
> Loin de la marmitaille, [2] loin de l'humidité,
> Tu pourras a ton aise y manger et y boire,
> Et attendre gaiement les lauriers de la gloire.

The name given to this dug-out by the battalion that preceded us is "Some Hut," though it is also known as "Buck House." You must not suppose that all dug-outs

---

[1] Dug-out.

[2] Slang for shells, etc., in the bulk. "Marmite" is the French equivalent for "Jack Johnson."

are like it. Those in the fire-trench are, as a rule, only just large enough for one or two men to crawl into and lie down side by side.

Scattered about us are little graveyards—French and German; and now we are starting on our own. Those of the French are easily recognizable, owing to the custom of placing the dead soldier's cap on his grave or perched above it on a stick. The grass is growing long and is beginning to hide the older graves. It is thick with all the wild flowers of an English spring—dandelions, thistles, daisies and buttercups.

To our immediate right front, and visible over the parapet, lies the French battlefield of Sunday and Tuesday —the 9th and 11th of this month, and it is a saddening sight to look upon, the ground between the trenches being thickly strewn with many dead. Beyond, further to the south, the famous height of Notre Dame de Lorette stands out prominently. Behind it are the Labyrinth, and the villages of Souchez, Carency, and Ablain St. Nazaire.

To-day has been fairly quiet for us, except for some shelling which killed two N.C.O.'s. We also had a man wounded by rifle fire. On our left, however, there was heavy shelling during the late evening.

We heard officially to-day of the Government's decision to retaliate on the enemy with asphyxiating gases. Every first opinion that I have heard is strongly opposed to this on the principle that two wrongs do not make a right, and we should do better to keep our hands clean, and partially I agree.

To-day the weather is beautiful, though lately it has been miserably cold and wet, and we have longed for the sun again. The lilac was lovely till the rain came; the country is full of it.

May 22, 1915.   *Fire-trench in front of Le Rutoire.*

To-night there has been another heavy bombardment on the French sector to our right. It was already dark when it began, and while the firing was at its height a thunderstorm got up, producing an effect that was wonderfully vivid and inspiring. The forks of lightning mingled with the flashes from the guns and bursting shrapnel and the Véry lights, while the roar of the bombardment was punctuated and occasionally drowned by the loud crashes of the thunder. There then followed torrential rain, which soaked the men to the skin.

It is a healthy life and I have never felt better. It is worry that kills, and we have no worry here. We have practically no sickness. Do you remember the outrageous sick-lists at Putney? We have no sick-list here. The men are quite wonderful, always cheerful under the most trying conditions; sleeping, when not in the trenches, crowded in such accommodation as can be got—in a barn, or a cow-stall, or a loft. Sometimes their boots are so bad that their toes stick out, but they just laugh and patch them up with newspaper or cardboard, and carry on.

Our present trenches are largely in chalk—the most fascinating stuff to carve with a jack-knife—and it is like visiting an art gallery to go through them. Model prayer-books and hymn-books and slabs of chalk carved with the regimental crest—the Star of the Garter—and other devices adorn the parapet. There is also much doggerel—too long to quote, and bits of philosophy that show the trend of the men's minds, all written in that purple ink which is produced from a mixture of indelible pencil and spit.

Here are a few examples:

"I have no pain, dear Mother, now, but lummy I do feel dry—so fix me to a brewery and leave me there to die."

"A loaf in the trench is worth ten at the base."

"What doth it profit a man if he gain a tin of biscuits and lose a loaf of bread?"

(The last two have reference to the fact that bread is not always obtainable, and square things like dog biscuits are issued "in lieu.")

"Love your enemy" (with pictures of Dr. Lyttelton and Bernard Shaw hanging from a gallows).

Pat: "What is life?"

Mike: "It's a puzzle."

Pat: "Why?"

Mike: "Because you've got to give it up."

"Abandon hope, all ye who enter here."

Then, a model of an idiot, and underneath:

"After six months in the C.G."

Then, there's the sentimental sort: a picture, for example, of an old woman rushing from her cottage door to meet the postman, labelled:

"A letter from Tommy."

Looking over the parapet, across Noman's Land, we see the German wire, and, a few feet beyond it, an irregular, built-up line of sandbags. That is the German parapet. These German sandbags are conspicuous by the diversity of their colouring. Some are jet-black; others almost snow-white. Some of the material used looks more as if it had been designed for petticoats than sandbags.

You ask me to describe a day in the trenches. If you want an exaggerated but at the same time a very humorous description your request comes very opportunely, for I have just been handed one, written, I believe, by an officer in the Ox. and Bucks Light Infantry, which, after I have given you my own much drier description, I will quote.

Our days vary a lot, and of course depend on the activity of the people over the way, but generally speaking they are something as follows, in a case where the German trenches and ours are close together:

We stand to arms from a quarter to three in the morning till daylight. Then, except the sentries, all sleep till breakfast at about eight o'clock. Then, perhaps, hand bombing or shelling may begin.

If explosives are falling close, of course, it tends to hinder any repair work that may be in progress, but we sandwich in, as best we can, any digging that has to be done. Naturally, only work that does not show above the parapet can be done in daylight. All work on the parapet or outside is done at night.

Lunch at one o'clock. Tea, say, at 4.30. Dinner for the officers at eight.

But, of course, there can be no definite routine. On still nights we are liable to have alarms of asphyxiating gas. I have been through several, but so far they have all been false alarms.

Then, during the night, we send out patrols and digging parties. The former crawl as near as they can to the German trenches to examine the wire and get other information. It is a tricky game. Flares are being sent up all the time, lighting up Noman's Land, and then the patrols lie flat on their stomachs till it is dark again.

The ground between the trenches is strewed with dead. Where possible, during the night, we get these in and bury them. That is a horrible job, as they may have been there for weeks or months.

Every now and then there is a burst of machine-gun fire, and, when the trenches are close, the sentries on both sides keep up an incessant exchange of rifle-shots throughout the night.

Sapping and mining goes on day and night where the trenches are close, and occasionally the monotony is relieved by the exploding of a mine, which shakes the whole earth for miles around.

Now for "one day of crowded joyous life in the trenches (exclusive of Huns, shells, or bullets)."

By an Officer in the Ox. and Bucks L.I.

5 p.m. Arrival in trenches. Temper normal. Half an hour spent trying to appear interested while the outgoing officer explains the enormous amount of work he has done during his time there.

5.30 p.m. Outgoing officer departs. Half an hour spent in commenting with your own officers on the utter and complete absence of any sign of any work whatever having been done since you were there last.

6 p.m. Start your own work for the night.

6.15 p.m. Telephone operator reports that he has got connection with Battalion Headquarters. (N.B. Life in the trenches has now started.)

6.45 p.m.   First instalment of messages handed in to you.
> No. 1.   "You will hold respirator and smoke helmet drills frequently during your tour a.a.a.[1] The signal for respirators to be put on will be two C's on the bugle.   Adjutant."
>
> No. 2.   "Report at once if you have a fully qualified Welsh miner in your company, who can speak French and German a.a.a.   Age not under 18 years.   Adjutant."
>
> No. 3.   "All respirators will be immediately withdrawn a.a.a.   The signal for putting them on will be two blasts of the whistle and not as per the last part of my message No. 1 of this date. Adjutant."
>
> No. 4.   "A French aeroplane with slightly curved wings, giving it the appearance of a German one, is known to be in your vicinity a.a.a.   Use your discretion in accordance with Anti-Aircraft Regulations para 1; section 5.   Adjutant."
>
> No. 5.   "Report at once number of windows of smoke helmets broken since you have been in the trenches a.a.a.   The signal will now be two blasts on a shell gong and not as per my message No. 3 in correction of my message No. 1. Adjutant."
>
> No. 6.   "Re my message No. 4 for the word "French" read "German" and for the word "German" read "French" a.a.a.   You will still use your discretion.   Adjutant."

7.30 p.m.   Messages dealt with.   Dinner.

8.30 p.m.   Arrival of C.O.   Suggests politely that your men would be better employed doing some other kind of work.   Assent enthusiastically.   All working parties changed over to different work.   Temper indifferent.

9 p.m. to 2 a m.   Answer telephone messages.

2.30 a.m.   Stand to arms.   Walk round and survey the

[1] Indicates full-stop.

16

result of the night's work. Find the greater part of it has been blown in by trench mortars in the early morning.

3.30 a.m. Try and sleep.

4 a.m. Wakened up to receive the following messages:

No. 115. "All smoke helmets are to be immediately marked with the date of issue a.a.a. If no date is known no date should be marked and the matter reported accordingly. Adjutant."

No. 116. "R.E. require a working party from your Company to-day from 6 a.m. to 7 p.m. a.a.a. Strength 150 with suitable proportion of N.C.O.'s a.a.a. Otherwise, your work is to be continued as usual. Adjutant."

5 a.m. Wakened up to send in "Situation Report." Report situation "Normal."

8 a.m. Breakfast.

9 to 11 a.m. Scraping off mud in Oxford Street. Removing bits of bacon in Bond Street. Re-burying Fritz who, owing to a night's rain, has suddenly appeared in Regent Street.

11.15 a.m. Arrival of Brigadier-General and Staff. Orders given for everything that has been dug out in the night to be filled in, and for everything that has been filled in to be dug out.

11.16 a.m. Departure of Brigade Staff. Brain now in state of coma. Feel nothing now except a dull wonder. Rest of day spent in eating chocolates, writing letters home to children and picking flowers off the bank. Final message can remember receiving was about twelve noon:

No. 121. "The Brigadier-General and Staff will shortly be round your trenches. Adjutant."

May 30, 1915 (*Sunday*).   *Support Trench, Le Rutoire.*

Out in Noman's Land, close to the German line, grows a tree, which, though small and insignificant considered as such, is the only object in the broad and desolate and otherwise treeless space intervening here between the German trenches and our own.   This tree, therefore, has achieved a notoriety which it most certainly would never have done otherwise.   It is known as the "Lone Tree," and, I daresay, is as famous among the Germans as among our troops. Last night a patrol of No. 1 Company, which was engaged in examining the enemy's wire, bumped suddenly into a hostile advanced post near it, and lost two killed, while a third man was wounded, but was got away.

To-day has been very quiet.   I lunched at Battalion Headquarters in the cellar under the ruins of Le Rutoire farm, and ate plovers' eggs from home.

May 31, 1915.   *Support Trench, Le Rutoire.*
Another quiet day.   We have orders to hand over, to-morrow, to the 140th Brigade (London Territorials), which may perhaps mean that we are to take part in an attack somewhere.   We shall then have been five days in the trenches, and I shall be glad to get my boots off.

June 10, 1915.   *Bethune.*
Ralph Burton was hit by a shell on the evening of the 5th, and Johnston being in England on seven days' leave, I was left without a single other officer, till Woods[1]—a young Canadian who joined the battalion the same afternoon that Burton was wounded—was posted to my Company.

Our withdrawal from the trenches and the subsequent long rest has given rise to many rumours as to our destiny, and has suggested a "fattening for the slaughter," as it is commonly called; in short, that we are to take part in a fresh "push" that is believed to be pending.

The Cuinchy sector, where we are going, is probably the most difficult of the portion of the line to which it belongs.   At any rate it has very evil memories for many of those who have been associated with it.

June 12, 1915.   *Cuinchy.*
On reaching Cuinchy, I found that, since I was here with the 3rd Battalion, last month, the enemy had blown

[1] 2nd-Lieut. J. R. Woods, died of wounds September 16, 1916.

two mines—one alongside the other—under our fire-trench, immediately north of Hanover Street.

When we were here before the German miners could be heard burrowing at this point from one of the underground listening posts. Yet, somehow, they succeeded in getting their mine off first, with a cost to our side of ten miners and a listener killed underground, in addition to the infantry—probably twenty or more—who were manning the trench above.

The external visible result of the explosion is the total extinction of the trench for a length of about 50 yards, and its substitution by an enormous double crater. The incident took place about five days before we took over, since when all endeavours to repair the damage by digging round the lip of the crater have been frustrated, with considerable loss of life, owing to the bombing activity of the enemy, who is not more than 30 yards away.

I must say that I do not think the battalion we relieved was in a condition to take the initiative. It had suffered heavily in the recent attacks, was still only about half-strength, and was commanded by the Adjutant, the Colonel having been killed. In fact, but for the shortage of troops, I feel sure they would never have been put in such a position.

They were considerably dejected when I first saw them, and, together with the battalion on their right, were enduring what must be regarded as heavy casualties in the ordinary routine of trench warfare. The latter had just lost between forty and fifty men in a single day.

Without questioning the gallantry of these battalions, who ought to have been resting after their heavy trials instead of holding a very tricky piece of line, I should say that the enemy had got the upper hand. He was treating them like naughty boys, punishing them immediately and unmercifully for any small liberty they might take by way of retaliation—though such liberties were few—against the annoyances to which they were being subjected. This, according to my observation, was the condition of affairs when our Brigade took over.

After the relief the enemy continued, to begin with, to treat us as he had treated our predecessors, with an almost continuous stream of rifle and hand grenades, shell-fire, and occasional "minerwerfer" bombs, the latter as big as footballs. But the Brigade replied with interest. There were, of course, casualties, and the day after our arrival (yesterday) we were punished for our temerity by a noisy bombardment, which was intermittent throughout most of the day and heavy for a time, and which continued at intervals during the night.

This afternoon again, between one and two o'clock, the bombardment was repeated, and, for an hour, heavy shells fell thick and fast.

June 14, 1915.   *Cuinchy Support Trench.*

Johnston got a stray bullet through the leg last night, (what the men would call a "cushy" or "blighty" one), so I am again with only one subaltern in the Company.

June 15, 1915.   *Cuinchy.*

To-day, at 1.30 p.m., the Company Commanders were sent for by the Commanding Officer to his headquarters in Cambrin village, just behind here, and given preliminary orders for an attack which is to be delivered by the Brigade, though only in the event of the success of an operation (which takes place to-day on the other side of the canal, to our left) involving the capture of the high ground round Violaines.

My Company is to open the Ball for the Brigade by seizing the Railway Triangle; after which the other companies will advance on the right, and capture the brick-stacks, etc. My "jumping off" position will be in the fire-trench facing the Triangle, with my left on the canal —that is to say, in front of the famous "Hollow," where Michael O'Leary won his V.C. This evening I have been looking at the objective with Captain Forrester, of the Black Watch, whose battalion is holding the front line opposite to it.

The bombardment by our artillery preparatory to the attack continued throughout to-day, and at 5 p.m. "Mother,"

20

"Grandmother," and other heavy howitzers and guns concentrated on the Brickstacks in front of us. At the same time our bombardment of the German trenches to the left of the canal became intense, continuing so till six o'clock, when the infantry were timed to go over the top.

The moment of the assault was signalized by the "blowing" of a mine, after which all was hell and fury for two hours, when the firing slackened and continued on a reduced scale throughout the night.

These are thrilling experiences which make all things else fade into insignificance. How the men and masters, who, in spite of the critical times, are striking and squabbling at home, can belong to the same race as these heroic fellows here beats me altogether. Over and over again it is the soldiers' duty to charge against barbed wire into almost certain death. Often no one comes back. Yet there is never any hesitation or questioning. I tell you that, as an onlooker on this occasion, when the guns were lifted, and from the burst of rifle and machine-gun fire I knew that the time had come for the rush over the parapet and across the open, it brought home to me this mighty contrast.

The old garden belonging to the dilapidated ruin which serves as my Company Headquarters is gaily asserting itself, and though thick with weeds and torn with shell-fire, the rose-trees and sweet-williams and other plants are bright with blossom; and Noman's Land is ablaze with scarlet poppies.

June 16, 1915.   *Cuinchy.*

This morning I took Woods, my very gallant young subaltern whose duty it will be to lead the advanced platoons if the attack takes place, my Company Sergeant-Major (Hill), and the platoon sergeants, to reconnoitre—or rather to look over the parapet—at our objective.

On arrival at the front line Company Headquarters the first thing I learnt was that Forrester, who showed me round yesterday, had been killed by a sniper shortly after I left him. I remember his saying, while he was pointing out the features of the Railway Triangle, that it was quite safe to expose oneself while our shells were falling as thick as they were at that time, since the enemy must certainly be taking cover; and he and I, in consequence, stood upright on the fire-step for quite a time.

The more you look at this Cuinchy Triangle the worse it looks. The problem is anything but a joke really, but so hopeless is it universally regarded by those who know the Triangle, that it is treated as a sort of joke, and there is considerable chaff about it. "Nipper" Poynter[1]—a major of the 1st Scots Guards—said to me when the orders first came out: "The only chance *you* have is that the attack on the left of the canal may fail." As a matter of fact it did fail yesterday, but they are going to have another try to-day.

I am told that the Canadians, who made the assault on the immediate left of the canal, captured three lines of trenches, without casualties. Yet, this morning, out of a battalion, there are left only a major and sixty men, the rest having been knocked out during the night by bombs and shell-fire.

Apparently, more than one thing went wrong. The troops on the left of the attack seem to have been hung up, and there was also a hitch about the mine which, as I have described, synchronized with the first forward rush of the infantry.

This mine unexpectedly blew back through the gallery leading to it, at the mouth of which were congregated the bombers as well as their reserve of bombs. All were destroyed, with the result that when the enemy counter-attacked, bombing along the captured trenches, there was no one to meet them except the riflemen, who were rapidly reduced to a negligible quantity, and the few survivors that were left were compelled to fall back.

June 17, 1915. *Bethune.*

The shelling of the German lines to the left of the canal began again yesterday afternoon at 3.30 o'clock. About 4.20 the bombardment became intense, and half an hour

[1] Major A. V. Poynter, D.S.O. (Scots Guards).

later, or less, the guns were lifted, and the attack was repeated. The storm of rifle and machine-gun fire that followed told us that once again the infantry had gone over the parapet and were making their wild rush across the poppies.

Again the attack failed, and as we left the trenches, having been relieved by a territorial battalion of the King's Liverpool Regiment, the small-arms fire was dying away, though the after-shelling continued fast and furious.

Then we marched to Bethune, where we billeted for the night;—the men in the local barracks, and the officers scattered about in different houses. It was a luxury to have one's boots off for the first time for six days and nights, to wash off the dirt, and to sleep in a bed with sheets.

June 23, 1915.   *Bethune.*

We await orders to move, and in the meantime the battalion has been providing digging parties for the new Reserve defences that are under construction.

To-day, I marched a party of my Company which had been detailed for this work to Cambrin, the little village behind Cuinchy, about a mile from the firing line. The village is much battered by shell-fire, but the church—I suppose because it is hidden behind trees—has escaped, except for a couple of shell-holes through the roof. Near the door is posted a notice—in English (!)—which reads as follows:

"Mayoralty, 16*th May.*

"Nothing of the things to this church has been stolen and has been respected since the beginning of the war.

"Everyone is requested to respect the sanctuary, and to use the organs when it is necessary only.

"THE MAYOR. By Order."

In the churchyard I found the graves of Senhouse and Brabazon—both of the Coldstream, who were killed last week.

The fields around are carpeted with cornflowers and poppies and were bathed in sunshine to-day, and as it was quiet in the line everything seemed very peaceful. I wandered backwards and forwards between the different

23

places where the work was going on. In almost any direction one stumbles upon little and sometimes large groups of graves. I was reading the names, to-day, on the wooden crosses of one of these, when four stretcher-bearers brought along a dead soldier of the —— Regiment, to bury him. He had been considerably broken by a shell. He was small, and was covered over all but his legs. You could see just the puttees and part of his trousers and the crinkled-up marching boots as he lay upon his stretcher. It was a simple enough funeral—without parson or prayers or any paraphernalia—but, for all that, coming upon me suddenly as it did, this funeral struck me as more impressive than most that I have seen, and made me feel a great respect for those who have given up their lives in the way that this little man had given his.

June 24, 1915.   *Burbure.*

We were woken up at 6.30 this morning and ordered to new billets at Burbure—some 8 miles further back, and here we are, away from the sound of gun-fire, except for a faint rumbling in the distance. The silence seems quite odd. My Company is lying out in the open, in an orchard, and I am in a cottage beside the road.

June 28, 1915.   *Burbure.*

We were to have marched to-day, but the order was countermanded. As somebody said this morning, "We are like the Children of Israel, wandering in the Wilderness of Sin." We do not know from hour to hour what our next move will be. But there is nothing to complain about. We are having a very easy time. We drill and march and get plenty of amusement out of life.

I overhear many funny conversations as I ride or march in front of the Company, and, though these are not always of the most edifying order, I must write down one. It was raining, and one of the men, feeling very miserable, was holding forth on the hardships of a soldier's life. "I wish my father had never met my mother," he said. There was silence for a moment; then a voice came softly from behind: "Perhaps he didn't" ! !

24

July 11, 1915.   *"Some Hut," Le Rutoire.*

Life has been dull lately. First, we had a long rest
—about three weeks—which is I think very enervating and
bad for everybody, although very necessary after a long
spell in the trenches. Then, for a week, we have been
marching out and digging every night, and sleeping by
day. And, now that we are back in the trenches, we are
still digging every night.

The Company moved back into support to-day. It is
our third night in the trenches, and we have scarcely been
shelled at all.

I am writing this just before starting off for another
night's digging in Noman's Land, and my subalterns are
talking hard in the dug-out. This is the same dug-out I
described in a former letter; now, alas, plundered of its
crucifix and other furnishings by some souvenir-hunting
vandal who has occupied it during our absence. Can you
believe it?

July 13, 1915.   *Vermelles.*

We came out of the trenches a few hours ago, and are
in reserve, among the ruins of Vermelles. My two subalterns and I have just returned from roaming through what
remains of the village. It amuses them (they are *very,
very* young), when they find a wobbly piece of wall still
standing, to push it over, and certainly the game is rather
fascinating, especially when the piece of wall happens to
be high.

We explored the battered skeleton of the old church.
The roof has collapsed and now litters the floor, mixed
with the loose stones from the shattered walls. Strewed
among the debris are broken chairs, and confessionals, and
screens, and pieces of priests' vestments, ragged and rotting.
The Figure of Christ has been shot from the great crucifix
or rood that hung before the sanctuary, and lies in bits
upon the ground. The side altars have been demolished.
The door has been torn from the tabernacle. Every
particle of the church furniture has been gutted. Yet one
thing alone remains intact, or practically so. This is a

recumbent statue in marble of Our Lord which lies beneath the High Altar. Though a shell has actually passed through the centre of the altar that covers it the Figure remains unharmed, except for a tiny fragment chipped from the beard. Even the fingers are perfect.

July 14, 1915. *Vermelles.*

The digging campaign continues—in fact grows, and though it is pouring with rain we are for it again to-night; not myself (it is the first night I have not been up for many nights), since my Company is "in waiting," and I have been called upon for only two platoons.

Most of our digging has been in Noman's Land, which is always interesting, though so far we have been left in peace, which we probably owe to the fact that our enemies are occupied similarly to ourselves, and also do not desire to be disturbed.

I confess that we are getting "fed up" with digging. The men sing about it as they march—to the tune of a well-known hymn—"Digging, digging, digging: always b——well digging." They write about it in their letters home: they talk about it. Yesterday I saw, worked out on the parapet, in pieces of chalk (the material through which we are digging), the following simple inscription— "1st C. Gds—Navvies."

To-day is *the* day. A big German offensive was pro-phesied first for the 7th, then for to-day; and most of this afternoon, perhaps by way of preventive cure, the French on our right have been hard at it—very hard if one can judge by the noise. It must be nasty in this wet.

July 17, 1915. *Right Fire-trench opposite the Lone Tree.*

Though for the moment the sun is shining through the clouds, the weather is beastly, rainy and windy, and most unsuitable for the work upon which we are principally engaged, namely, digging.

After a very wet night's work we again this morning got to bed at about half-past three. It had been rather a jumpy kind of night. It is difficult to describe what I mean. But there are certain times more than others when a

26

man feels the responsibilities of a long stretch of front line for which he is solely responsible. I think this is especially the case after one has been up, night after night, as we have lately, without quite enough sleep.

Yet this is an easy bit of line, and the German trenches are a long way off.

Last night, the wind was blowing directly to us from the German lines, and at just about the right velocity for gassing. On our left the night started with a furious burst of fire, accompanied by a firework display that would have attracted attention even at the Crystal Palace.

The shooting was taken up by the enemy on our immediate front, and flights of their bullets came whistling overhead as I stood on the parapet, setting the men to their digging. It soon died away, but the general eeriness of such a night affects the men. They do not work with their usual vigour. They are wet through and uncomfortable, and they keep glancing over the parapet, while the covering party lying in the long grass in front shoots freely at whatever arouses its slightest suspicion.

July 20, 1915.   *Bethune.*

At ten last night we were relieved and marched to Bethune, where, at 2.30 a.m., I got into an exceedingly comfortable bed in a house with a lovely garden, in which the owner— a kindly old Frenchman—takes the most lively interest. He showed me round the garden this morning. He made it all himself. Even the trees, which now are big, he saw planted fifty years ago.

He has a fascinating outdoor aviary which leans against an angle of the house. In it are quantities of canaries and other birds—Californian partridges, a Cardinal bird, etc.; and in a separate place he has thrushes, caught in the garden, to which he whistles, and which sing to him in return. There are some very ingenious contrivances for feeding the birds and for them to nest in, and there is a curious little passage by which the bantams, of which there are several, can leave the aviary and walk out into the back yard, where they scrape and scratch about.

The Germans have been shelling Bethune daily of late, and heavily. No doubt they would argue that the women and children ought to have been evacuated long ago, and perhaps they ought: but the fact remains that they have not, and it makes my blood boil to see this useless and vindictive shelling of the towns that the enemy has initiated.

This morning, as I looked out of the window, some fifty children were playing on an open space outside. Suddenly, the shells began to fall. There was immediately a general scuttle of the children to their mothers and their homes, but two little ones were killed, so I have since been told. It is dreadful to think that men can drop shells callously on such surroundings.

This afternoon, the shelling was repeated. My host's old wife was out shopping at the time, which naturally made him anxious. I went down and talked to him in the garden, and he took me and showed me a shell crater just over his garden wall, made the day before yesterday.

July 23, 1915. *Bethune.*

Yesterday was a bad day here in Bethune. In the morning, at bombing practice, one of our officers was wounded—slightly. In the afternoon, while practising with a trench mortar, three were killed and four or five wounded, the former including Mitchell, of the Black Watch, who took on Carpentier, the French boxer, last year.

In the evening there were in the town 128 casualties to our troops from shell-fire, including three men of ours. A great many casualties were caused by a shell which burst in the "Ecole des jeunes filles," which we use as a barrack. I passed the door with John Ponsonby as they were bringing them out. Certainly, this place is becoming very unhealthy, and I wish the civilians would clear out. Yesterday, I am told, a woman and two children were killed.

The old man and his wife with whom I am billeted still cling on, though I doubt if they will stand it much longer. The poor old lady—a dear and very fat—sits down palpitating, each time the shells begin to fly, and counts them.

Our artillery has been retaliating pretty severely the last two nights, and to-day nobody would have been surprised at a super-exhibition of "frightfulness," but so far, to-day, the enemy has not fired a shell into the town. In fact, we have been having a boxing competition; and, to-morrow, we have a horse-show.

*   *   *   *   *

August 7, 1915.   *Bethune.*

On my return from leave, on the 5th, I found the battalion just finishing a tour in the trenches in front of Cambrin, immediately south of the La Bassée road.

I therefore spent only one night there, and now am back in my old billet—the house with the aviary.

Two officers had joined during my absence. One— Captain Gregge-Hopwood[1]—had taken over the command of No. 1 Company, whose former commander—Digby[2]—has come to me. The other, Dermot Browne,[3] had been commanding my Company during my absence.

The trenches which the battalion was holding (Cambrin, Z.2) were new to us, and were very lively; and the contrast between the peaceful life I was leading with you and the children last Wednesday and my occupation the following day and night could scarcely have been greater. Nowhere along the whole front are the Germans and ourselves more close together than there. Twelve to fifteen yards was all that separated us in the advanced portions of the trench, and the ground between was a shapeless waste—a mass of mine-craters, including two so large that they are known officially as Etna and Vesuvius.

The ragged aspect of this advanced trench I cannot picture to you. The hundreds of bombs which explode in and around it each day and night have reduced it to a state of wild dilapidation that is indescribable. There is not a sandbag that is not torn to shreds, and the trench

---

[1] Later Major (T/Lt.-Col.) E. B. G. Gregge-Hopwood, D.S.O. ("Bing" Hopwood), killed in action July 20, 1917.

[2] Now Major Lord Digby, D.S.O., M.C.

[3] Hon. M. H. Dermot Browne, killed in action September 29, 1915.

itself is half filled by the earth and debris that have dribbled down. So shallow and emaciated has this bit of trench now become that you have to stoop low or your head and shoulders poke above the parapet, and so near are you to the enemy that you have to move in perfect silence. The slightest visible movement brings a hail of bullets from the snipers, and the slightest sound a storm of hand-grenades.

The conditions are such that you cannot repair the damages as they should be repaired. You just have to do the best you can, with the result that when the tide of war has passed beyond these blood-soaked lines they will soon become obliterated and lost among the wilderness of craters. The tripper who will follow will pass them by, and will no doubt pour out his sentiment on the more arresting concrete dug-outs and the well-planned earthworks of the reserve lines well behind.

I did a bit of bombing myself during the thirty hours I was there—a rather different occupation to our tea-party in the grotto at Rainhill! Who would have imagined, two years ago, that I should actually so soon be throwing bombs like an anarchist?

Tommy Robartes'[1] Company has a band, and, the night before my arrival, being the anniversary of the declaration of war, he tried a "ruse de guerre." The band was posted in a sap leading from the fire-trench, and, at six minutes to midnight, opened with "Die Wacht am Rhein." It continued with "God Save the King" and "Rule Britannia," each tune being played for two minutes. Then, as the last note sounded, every bomber in the battalion, having been previously posted on the fire-step, and the grenade-firing rifles, trench-mortars, and bomb-throwing machine, all having registered during the day, let fly simultaneously into the German trench; and, as this happened, the enemy, who had very readily swallowed the bait, were clapping their hands and loudly shouting "encore."

[1] Capt. Hon. T. Agar-Robartes, M.P.; died of wounds September 30, 1915.

"English treachery!" I feel sure they are saying, but it is only a leaf out of their own book, after all.

On the evening of my arrival I tried to get into conversation with them, as they had been very talkative the previous day, but they were disinclined to be drawn. The experience of the night before had evidently upset them, and we had also given them a severe "strafing" during the day, which did not help matters. And at 10 p.m. No. 2 Company band once more gave a recital. But there were no "encores" this time, and no applause. When the band had exhausted their stock of tunes they sang, but all was unavailing; their efforts were ignored.

Even Chapman—one of the Company wits—failed to get a reply. I tried a London Scottish machine-gunner who spoke German, and he could get no answer till he asked whether they had orders from their officers not to speak to us: when some one answered in a coy kind of way so that we could not hear what he said. My impression was that he had been promptly silenced from behind.

In these conversations the soldiers on both sides address one another familiarly, as "kamarade," or "Tommy" or "Fritz." On thè whole, the remarks made to men of my Company during the three days they were in these trenches were vacuous but rather amusing. Once the Germans called out "Coldstream form fours": so they apparently knew who was opposed to them. Another time one of our men called, "Do you know a man called Cooper?" It was just one of the catch sentences you so often hear out here, but the reply came: "Yes, he's here." One of our men asked: "Aren't you sick of it, Fritz?" and got the answer: "Yes, aren't you?" Another man shouted: "Wouldn't you like to have peace?" to which the reply was: "We aren't ready for peace, but let's have it to-night!"

Then they asked if we had lost a corporal who had been born at ——. This was a corporal of the Scots Guards who had crawled to the edge of one of the craters the night before we relieved his battalion, and had been bombed and killed at a range of two or three yards. His Captain,

Harold Cuthbert, who is a very gallant fellow, had subsequently crawled out and collected some of his private belongings. Drury Lowe, of the same regiment, told me to-day he had heard that the Germans had put up a notice saying that they had buried this man properly. I cannot vouch for this, but the body had disappeared by the time I arrived from the very prominent position it had occupied on the lip of the crater.

And they also put up a notice-board, which I saw, saying, "Warschau is our" (*sic*)—which, I am afraid, is true. The men tried to shoot this down, and, eventually, the rain washed it off.

I enclose some weed which I got among the ruins of Cambrin. I picked it yesterday as I came out of the communication trench, after being relieved. It is "Flos Crucis," or the flower of the Cross, so Egerton [1] has told me. The legend is that it grew beneath the Cross, and the black spots are supposed to represent the stains of our Lord's blood.

August 16, 1915. *Reserve Trenches. Le Rutoire.*

I hope you are not having weather like we have had this afternoon. The rain has been coming down in floods, and the trenches are swilling. Luckily, they do not take long to dry this time of year, once the sun gets up. To-night is my turn in bed. While we are so short we keep only one officer up while in the Reserve trenches.

The Brigadier (General Lowther) turned up suddenly in my dug-out this morning at 8.20. I was in bed, with my feet in sandbags to keep them warm. I had been up during the night. He told me that we are going back to the other side of St. Omer on the 23rd, to form a Guards Division. He also said that the other day the Germans at Givenchy are reported to have called out: "When are you —— blank Guardsmen going to St. Omer? When you do, we are going to have these trenches back."

[1] Major (T/Lt.-Col.) A. G. E. Egerton, killed in action September 29, 1915.

August 26, 1915.   *Lumbres.*

I write from by far the most luxurious billet I have slept in since I came to France; where my hosts, M. and Mme. Avot Pierret, to say nothing of their small son and daughter, are so kind and hospitable that they make me feel like an invited guest rather than a self-imposed one, as in fact I am.

M. Avot is a sous-officier in the French artillery and is at present home on leave. He is the principal owner of the paper-factory which is the mainstay of this village. Digby and I sleep here. You should see our comfortable bed-rooms and the fine linen, and the bathroom, electric-lighted, with the mat and the clean white towels carefully laid out by the neat little French maids each time we have a bath. It is the first time I have washed in a bathroom since I came to the war, and you can imagine the joy of it!

The Company mess is nearly opposite, in the house of a doctor, M. Pontiet, a palæontologist, who has what must be one of the best private Collections in France of relics of the earliest human period. These include numer-ous implements of the Stone Age and the bones and teeth, etc., of the contemporary animals, principally mammoths, a set-up skeleton of a specimen of which towers above us as we sit and eat.

The village, the name of which is Lumbres, is set amid beautiful surroundings in a well-wooded valley, abounding in rich meadows. An ideal trout stream (if it were properly stocked and cared for) winds through it and supplies water and power to the paper-mill. We are far from the bursting shells, almost out of sound of gun-fire, and as the weather is perfect all is very delightful.

We marched from Vermelles on the 22nd, led by the battalion drums and fifes, which played for the first time during the war.

It was our final exit from the 1st Division, and General Rawlinson,[1] the Corps Commander, and other Generals,

---

[1] Afterwards Gen. Lord Rawlinson, G.C.B., G.C.S.I., G.C.V.O., K.C.M.G.; died 1925.

stood by the roadside to see us off. As we passed them the band of the 1st Black Watch, with whom the 1st Coldstream has been brigaded since the war began, played us out. Colonel John fell out as we reached the Corps Commander and waited beside him. He told me later that he had never seen the battalion march past better, though he added: "He didn't say much, d—n him!"

I believe he (Rawlinson) seldom does say much on these occasions.

The heat was oppressive and the march was trying, and the packs are heavy, and the men's feet soft after the trenches. Besides, the boots often do not fit: they are in many cases the re-soled boots of other men. No. 4 Company marched well. The Colonel told me they marched very well. The Company feeling is strong. When they saw others fall out the men cried: "Stick it, No. 4."

What is going to happen next none of us know. There are bound to be lots of changes due to the organization of the new Guards Division. If it is my lot to go elsewhere, I shall be sorry but not surprised. I have already overstayed the average. Before I came, No. 4 Company ran through, I believe, six Captains in six months. Anyhow, whatever happens, it will be nice to remember that I have commanded a company of Coldstreamers for over three months of the war. And they have been very happy months indeed.

At times I have felt some feeling of despondency and isolation, since I am an old man compared to the boys with whom I associate. But I have, I think, got on well with them, and I have had unswerving support from one and all, and there is much satisfaction in that.

August 31, 1915.   *Lumbres.*

More than one surreptitious attempt has been made to oust me from my hospitable quarters by billet-hunting officers of far senior rank to myself, but my kind hostess has firmly refused them on the plea of my priority, and assures me that no one else shall have my room.

Her son Jean, or Johnnie (as she calls him)—a very

attractive little fellow who talks English fluently, having been at school at Margate—has attached himself to me, and follows me about wherever I go on his bicycle.

On our (that is his and my) way home to-day he rode on ahead, and, as I reached his mother's house, he came out to meet me, with a look of extreme dismay upon his face, and the news that a certain General, who had been before but had been persuaded to go away gracefully enough on that occasion, had returned and insisted upon being given accommodation. He had modestly asked for a bedroom, dining-room, rooms for his servants, and an outhouse for his headquarters: and, up to the present, they had more or less satisfied him by evacuating Johnnie from his bedroom (which Johnnie did not object to in itself), and giving this to the General, who had already arrived in the house.

Quite a comedy was in progress. As I entered the door the whole family—father, mother, son, and daughter—all collected round me, and, while the two last intermittently made faces at the General through his closed door, all in one voice assured me that, whatever happened, *I* should not suffer.

So my door (and Digby's: he is home on leave) and our servants' are always to be kept locked, and the keys are to be handed to Georgina—the maid—so that the General and his servants and staff may not see how much better our rooms are than theirs.

I wonder how long it will last.

*   *   *   *   *

September 13, 1915.   *Lumbres.*

Returning from leave, the day before yesterday, they made everybody on the boat wear cork waistcoats, which, from force of habit, the men called "respirators," and which is an innovation, designed of course to combat torpedoes and floating mines.

As usual, we landed at Boulogne, from which place the less experienced among the officers are wont to come up to the line by the night "leave" trains—a very wearisome way of doing the journey, I should imagine, although the orthodox way. We—that is I and my friends—considering ourselves superior to "leave" trains, decided to spend a comfortable night at the Louvre Hotel and to chance finding a car in the morning.

However, though Boulogne literally teems with cars, we had no luck. For some reason or other it is now made almost as difficult to get out of Boulogne as into Berlin. Amongst many others we tried the Red Cross people (where we saw Miss Lloyd George), but the officer in charge, though very friendly, was unable to help.

We then saw the Base Commandant, Colonel Wilberforce, who used to command the Bays. He seemed highly amused at our predicament, but was unable to make any suggestion; till he remembered that Major Sewell (4th Dragoon Guards) was starting off in a car at 10 a.m. But Sewell's car failed, and, in the end, he and Hammersley and Jeffrey Holmesdale [1] and I came up by train after all. The distance by road is not more than 25 miles. Yet it took us till 3 p.m. to get to St. Omer, where we succeeded in borrowing a car from the A.S.C.

The battalion was here, where I had left it, and I found that my fine quarters had still been reserved for me. So all is well.

September 16, 1915. *Lumbres.*

This morning Lord Cavan,[2] who commands the newly-formed Guards Division, reviewed the 2nd Brigade. Although he is a "dug-out," he has a tremendous vogue, and induces quite extraordinary confidence among all ranks. We formed up in mass in a flat meadow by the brook here, and John Ponsonby, who is now Brigadier, sat on his horse in front and gave the order for the General Salute to the whole Brigade, which was very effective. We then marched past in column of half-companies, to the Divisional Band, the Coldstream in rear.

It was a memorable occasion. Two out of the four

[1] Now Earl Ámherst, M.C.
[2] Earl of Cavan, K.P., G.C.B., G.C.M.G., G.C.V.O., G.B.E.

battalions, as you know, have been right through the war, and might almost have been excused had they got rusty in ceremonial: yet Cavan said he had often seen ceremonial in London after months of practice done not half so well; and he ought to know.

The Prince of Wales was there.

Yesterday, the Corps Commander (General Haking[1]) came over and met the officers and some of the N.C.O.'s of the Brigade, and told them about some stirring events which are about to happen. The meeting took place in my Company's drill field.

He spoke very confidently, comparing the German line to the crust of a pie, behind which, once broken, he said, there is not much resistance to be expected. He ended up by saying, "I don't tell you this to cheer you up. I tell it you because I really believe it."

As he spoke of "pie-crust" I looked at the faces around me, and noticed a significant smile on those of some of the older campaigners who have already "been through it."

September 23, 1915. *Delette.*

We left Lumbres last evening and arrived here about ten o'clock. It is a nice little village, with a brook running through it, and an old church.

My parting with my hosts at Lumbres was quite touching. Madame Avot gave me a box of grapes and apples and strawberries to take away, and the little girl held up her cheek to be kissed. She was half in tears.

The night before we left I dined with the family and met the new C.R.A. and his two Staff Officers. After dinner Madame Avot played the piano, which she does divinely. While she played her husband whispered to me of her accomplishments. "Am I not lucky to have such a wife?" he said. And indeed he is. She is full of genius and charm, and has learnt to speak quite a lot of English since our troops came to France.

As the battalion marched past their house last night, the father and mother and the two children stood outside the

[1] Gen. Sir Richard Haking, G.B.E., K.C.B., K.C.M.G.

37

gate, again to say Good-bye. It made me feel quite home-sick.

Digby left No. 4 Company yesterday to take over the command of No. 3, and Charles Noel [1] has come to me in his place. So now I have Noel, Philipson, and Heathcote.

September 24, 1915. *Rely.*

The whole Brigade [2] marched to this area last night through pouring rain which soaked everybody. To-day it has been fine and the men have had a chance to get dry. As I write the sun is setting a gorgeous red.

Sometime after midnight we shall continue the march. We are moving only by night, hiding during daylight in the villages.

The French and British artillery for several days have been bombarding the enemy furiously. Even here, though we are 18 miles behind the line, we hear the roar of the guns.

September 25, 1915. *Houchin.*

By the time you get this you will have heard that a great combined French and British attack was launched to-day. The weather yesterday was fine, but during the night a drizzle set in which continued till the morning. The sun then made a feeble effort to assert itself, but the clouds soon covered it up, and rain has since been falling almost continuously.

Our bombardment of the German trenches continued through the night, reaching its climax in the morning as the moment of assault approached. Then did the fire become so violent that even at Rely, where we slept, though 18 miles behind the line, the ground shook, and my iron bedstead at the "Mairie" rattled at the heavier bursts.

We expected to march shortly after midnight, but this order was cancelled, and we fell in instead at 5.45 in the morning, reaching the first long halt (Allouagne) at 9.30.

[1] Now Major Hon. Charles H. F. Noel, O.B.E.
[2] The newly-formed 2nd Guards Brigade, consisting of 3rd Grenadiers, 1st Coldstream, 1st Scots Guards and 2nd Irish Guards.

At two o'clock we marched again, and arrived here, very wet, after many halts, at 9 p.m.

As we came within sight of the drifting battle smoke and looked upon the familiar flat landscape and the great cone-shaped spoil-heaps of the coal-mines which stand up like the Pyramids against the sky, a message from Lord Cavan was passed round. It said "that we were on the eve of the greatest battle in history"—"that future generations depended on the result of it"—and "that great things are expected from the Guards Division." Later, we received the splendid news that our troops had broken through the German line and taken Hulloch, Loos, and Cité de St. Elie; all places that we have looked towards so long from the trenches in front of Vermelles.

The road was frequently blocked, and halts were numerous. We met many ambulances returning with wounded, and once I had to halt my Company to allow a party of English and Indian troops to pass who had succumbed to our own gas. The 1st Cavalry Brigade [1] overtook us at the trot on their way towards the break. It is really exciting, this wild rush towards the enemy, to exploit to-day's advantage.

The roads were very muddy, the rain heavy, and the day has been a hard one; but the men are in fine spirit. A private of my Company, when asked if he could manage the last few miles, said: "If we can't do it on our feet, we'll do it on our hands and knees." They are looking forward to a scrap in the open, when they know, man for man, that they can beat the Germans.

October 2, 1915.   *Verquineul.*

My silence during the greater part of the past week will, I am afraid, have caused you anxiety, but it has been quite impossible to write. Our experiences during these days have been wonderfully exciting, and the results have been to some extent satisfactory: but we have seen much of the ghastly side of war, and our losses have been heavy

---

[1] The 15th and 19th Hussars and the Bedfordshire Yeomanry.

—about 300 out of the battalion, including 13 officers, seven of whom are dead.

We are now taking a "breather," with so few officers that Company messes have been dispensed with, and those of us that are left mess together.

I am fit and well, my only "adventure," apart from a blackened toe-nail caused by a splinter of shell, having been a shrapnel bullet, which, after passing through a fat bundle of letters which I luckily had in my pocket, made a hole through the book containing my Company roll, and actually lodged in one of your letters to myself! I did not discover it, or know that this bullet had hit me, till the next day, when I was clearing out my pockets. I will send you the letter with the bullet in it when I get a chance.

Well—to tell you the story! On the night of September 25, after some long marches in the rain, we arrived at Houchin, and spent the night there, the men of my Company packed like sardines in cow-sheds, and the officers on the floor and one bed in a tiny cottage, where, nevertheless, we were very happy, as the owner and his wife were untiring in their efforts to serve us, cooking us eggs and coffee in large quantities.

The following morning (Sunday) we were awake and about at 3.45, but got no order to move till the afternoon; so we had plenty of time to look about.

The village we were in occupies an elevated position, and the sun being bright and the day clear, a splendid panorama was spread out before us. We sat and picked out the familiar landmarks: the famous "pylon" or "Tower-bridge" of Loos; Fosse Eight; the slag-heaps, and other places, and among them and around them we watched the concentrated shelling of the battle—begun the day before —with the anticipatory feeling that we should soon be in it.

At 2 p.m. the battalion marched to Le Rutoire, the ruined farm buildings in front of Vermelles, where we had previously spent so many weeks in the trenches.

In the meantime, "Bing" Hopwood and I had been sent on in advance to reconnoitre, by daylight, the German trenches which our troops had captured the day before and that very morning. It was the first time I had seen a battlefield after an attack, and it was an ugly sight.

The first person I recognized at Le Rutoire was Geoffrey Feilding. The road and ruined courtyard of the farm were crammed with wounded and dead men. No one seemed to know what was happening in front. Some people were optimistic. Others, the reverse.

Hopwood and I crossed our old front line and Noman's Land—here about 500 yards wide—past the Lone Tree to the German trenches. The ground was strewn with our dead, and in all directions were wounded men crawling on their hands and knees. It was piteous, and it is a dreadful thought that there are occasions when one must resist the entreaties of men in such condition, and leave them to get in as best they can, or lie out in the cold and wet, without food, and under fire, as they often have to do for days and nights together. We had some timbers thrown over a trench as a bridge for some of them who said they had been trying all day to find a way across; but we had our own work to do, and we also had to get back and report to the battalion, so we could not do much;—indeed, it would have been a never-ending job had we attempted it.

The German trenches, which for so many weeks we have looked at only from the other side of Noman's Land, were very like our own. The barbed-wire entanglements in front of them were, however, far more formidable than ours. These formed a regular maze, and how our men got past them is a mystery. The ground was littered with German rifles, and bayonets, and bombs, and equipment of every sort. The air still reeked of gas, which clung to the ground and made our eyes smart; and every now and then a shell came crashing over from the other side, or a flight of machine-gun bullets made us bob.

The battalion arrived about nine o'clock, and we spent the night—till 3 a.m.—lying in the open. We then marched to the German trenches, which we manned, and proceeded to convert for our own use.

At four in the afternoon the Colonel gave us orders for an attack which he explained was to be made half an hour later upon the Chalk Pit and Wood, a mile and a quarter in front of our position;—the 2nd Irish Guards in front, the 1st Coldstream supporting.

This attack was launched punctually, but the Irish Guards met with heavy opposition, and though the 1st Scots Guards, who were on their right, came to the rescue, it was some hours before the position had been forced.

Meanwhile, I with my Company waited for the order to advance, which, since we were momentarily expecting it, and were moreover in complete ignorance as to the progress of the operation in front, seemed all the slower in arriving. A certain number of shells were falling around us, but beyond wounding Captain Guy Darell (then second in command of the battalion) who was with me, these did very little damage.

At last our turn came. Since it was already getting dark, I went out in advance to keep touch with the leading Companies. As I did so I met a stream of battle stragglers. Many were wounded, but with them there was also a liberal accompaniment of unwounded "friends" and others who obviously should not have been there. In reply to my questioning the latter gave the well-worn excuse that "an officer had given the order to retire." I called on them to turn, but they were in no mood for that: they were surely and sullenly bound for home.

I had no time to waste, so left these men to the tender mercies of young Dermot Browne, who had just then walked up, and who began to deal with them very thoroughly, as they deserved, with a heavy hunting crop which he carried.

By the time No. 4 Company was well launched it was dark and rain was falling. I had warned the men that if they met any stragglers as they went forward they were to sweep them along with them, if possible, or, failing that, to allow them to pass through their ranks, and I am proud to say that they carried out this order literally, not a man turning to right or left; though, as all will understand who have had such an experience, the temptation to some of them must have been considerable.

The darkness was soon like pitch, so that we lost touch with the advanced Companies, and the firing from the front having become very heavy, I decided to leave the men under an officer (Heathcote) behind the wood, in what happened to be more or less sheltered ground. I myself went forward with an orderly to explore. It was impossible to see a yard, but we picked our way step by step, and, after tumbling once or twice painfully into shell-holes, we reached the Chalk Pit Wood and felt our way through it.

All the while, the wounded, who were lying pretty thick on the ground, kept calling to us to fetch them away. I felt a beast for not being able to help them, but we had no stretchers, and after promising to do what I could I pushed along, for from the sound of digging in front it was clear that we were on the track of what we were looking for.

Then, to my relief, a voice called out from the slush, "Hullo, Rowland!" It was Cecil Trafford. There they were—all mixed—Scots Guards, Irish Guards, Grenadiers, digging in for dear life. It was the new front line on Hill 70. I knew then that my people could not be far away, and after following the line a short distance towards the left we came upon them.

Then I returned, having been away about an hour, to fetch up the men I had left behind the wood. During my absence Heathcote—the only officer with this party— had been shot through the spine by a stray bullet and lay paralysed. It was his first time under fire.[1] I sent him back on a ground-sheet, and with the men rejoined the battalion. On the way I met Arthur Egerton, who is now Colonel. He said I had been reported killed and that a stretcher had been sent out to bring in my body!

By this time the Chalk Pit and Wood were well in our

---

[1] After lying paralysed for two years, he died.

hands, but there was no sign of the 1st Guards Brigade, with whom we should have been in contact on the left. Our left, in fact, was "in the air," and as the battalion was on the left of the Brigade, and my Company was on the left of the battalion, I found myself at the danger-point of what was a very precarious situation. I therefore set out with two orderlies, if possible to find the 1st Brigade.

At a point some distance along the road towards La Bassée my attention was attracted by four wounded Englishmen, who, as they heard our steps, called out for water. They had already lain two days in the muddy ditch by the roadside, where they had been left behind when our forces had retreated the previous Saturday. Having lent them our water-bottles, and promised to send for them later, we continued our search for the 1st Brigade, but eventually, having failed to find any trace of it, and having been a long time absent from the Company, I decided to return and report what I had found out—or rather had failed to find out.

As we repassed the wounded men in the ditch they again called to us, but seeing no object in stopping then I was for hurrying on, when their calls became so urgent that I decided to hear what they had to say.

It is typical of the chivalrous character of the British soldier that, in spite of the wretchedness of their position, it was not about themselves, but about us, that these men were concerned. They wished to warn us about a sniper, who, they said, was in a tree in front of us. They had heard him shooting at intervals all the time they had lain there.

Though it was unlikely that any sniper would be perched in a tree on so dark a night, we were proceeding with caution, when from some bushes on the left there came groans as if from a wounded man. My orderlies were convinced it was some enemy device to draw us into a trap, but I thought I would chance that, and following the direction of the groans, I soon came upon a dying German soldier.

He sat propped up in a sniper's pit—a grotesque figure, with his ridiculous pickelhaube tilted over one eye. As I approached he muttered some sort of imprecation. I promised him he should be looked after. He was quite a lad and so frail and light and his face so pale and artless as I lifted him out of the pool of rain-water in which he sat, that it was hard to believe that he had been engaged upon so dirty a trade. He died as I moved him, and I left him lying by the edge of the pit from which he had been sniping English soldiers. He was evidently the man referred to by the wounded men in the ditch.

During the rest of the night we dug in the rain and by morning had got more or less cover. Our position was the most advanced in the new line—a pronounced salient—very exposed but important to hold.

Early in the morning the expected German bombardment began, and during the day—until the late afternoon—we collected the wounded of last Saturday, and otherwise lay in the narrow holes, like shallow graves, which the men had dug during the night.

About 3 p.m., or perhaps rather earlier, our artillery began a bombardment of the enemy lines, and particularly of a house and mine building (Puit 14 bis) some 200 yards in front of us.

At five minutes to four an orderly reported that the Commanding Officer wished to see me, so I went towards a limekiln which did duty as Battalion Headquarters. This consisted of two underground chambers, with a vertical flue at one end, and a staircase leading to the surface at the other end which was nearest to the enemy.

As I walked across the open towards this place the German shelling became intense. A shell pitched within 3 or 4 yards of me, but by a miracle did me no harm. I met Digby hurrying back to his Company. He said things were pressing and I had better run. I found Egerton giving final instructions to young Styles, of No. 1 Company, who fell wounded and was captured a few minutes later while leading his Company to the assault.

45

The Colonel told me that we were to attack the house and mine building (Puit 14 bis) immediately; that Nos. 1 and 2 Companies were to make the attack, and that No. 4 was to occupy the trench vacated by them.

I ran back to my Company and found many of the men dozing after the strenuous work of the past few days and nights. Already, the enemy had spotted what was happening, and a storm of fire had burst out. I swept the men out of the rifle-pits and called to them to follow me to the forward trench. The noise had become so great that no order could be heard; and the men were half dazed by the suddenness of the change in the situation.

Immediately we showed ourselves we were met by a terrific hurricane of machine-gun and rifle fire from Bois Hugo—a wood on our left front—and by shell-fire of every description. All was howling Inferno. The trees were crashing. I ran forward to the trench I had been told to occupy, but found when I reached it that I had got there alone. I went back, but the general din drowned all individual sound. I could not even hear my own voice. I found Charles Noel and young Philipson preparing to make a dash with the Company across the open, and presently in the face of the storm of bullets this was done, and the forward trench was manned.

By this time the assaulting Companies were returning, having lost practically all their officers and over a hundred men apiece during the few minutes they had been out of the trench. Riley, commanding No. 2, came in wounded, and Holmesdale also appeared. He was with the machine-guns. He was on his way back to Battalion Headquarters and offered to take a message for me. He made a dash across the exposed strip of ground that separated the trench from the limekiln; but he had no luck, for just as he reached the other side, he fell, with a bullet through the leg. He is a charming boy, and it gave me a considerable qualm to see him fall, especially as I could not tell from where I was whether his wound was slight or serious.

The attack had failed, but as the Brigadier (General John

Ponsonby) said later, it had been watched from a hill behind, and all who saw it had agreed that the attempt had been beyond praise, and that in the face of the fire which was encountered there was no alternative but for the assaulting Companies to fall back.

In a letter which he has just sent us he says:

"I should like to express to my old battalion my sincerest sympathy and regret at their heavy casualties.

"The battalion was asked to attempt to capture an important strategic point. Casualties in an attack are nowadays bound to be very severe, and although the position attacked was found untenable, the way the battalion responded to the order was worthy of the highest traditions of the Coldstream.

"Lord Cavan commanding the Guards Division has expressed to me his admiration at the way the battalion advanced to the assault on September 28th, and the way in which they continued to advance under a mostly deadly fire till they reached their objective."

We spent the next two nights in improving our newly-dug trenches, during the daytime being subjected to heavy shell-fire, which came from the flanks as well as from the front, and was almost continuous. The strain upon the men was heavy, but they bore it splendidly and cheerfully. To make matters harder, there was a penetrating rain which soaked us all, and the cold was bitter, so that we were not only practically sleepless, but wet and shivering all the time. We never lay down: there was nowhere to lie but the watery trench. Of course we had no hot food or drink, but mercifully a rum ration was got up which was a Godsend to all.

Occasionally, the moon shone out, lighting up the chalk-like snow, and showing up the bodies of the dead that lay in the great pit.

I was visited the first night by the Brigadier, who is always there when he is wanted, and glad I was to see him.

While he was with me a couple of whizz-bangs burst low over our heads, and a few minutes later, when he had gone,

were repeated.   I was still standing at the same spot, talking
to a young sapper officer who had come up to put out some
wire.   He collapsed into the bottom of the trench.   He was
untouched by the shells, but so blinded by the shock that he
was barely conscious of the fact even when I flashed an
electric torch in his eyes.   I confess I began by thinking he
was making too much of it, as the shells had burst as close
to me as to him.   But he was still "hors de combat" two
hours later, and was sent away.[1]

One night a C. of E. Chaplain came up, and I took him
over the ground, and he said a prayer over each group of the
dead—representing many regiments—that lay around the
chalk-pit.   It was a melancholy sight.

Contrary to all expectations and in spite of constant
alarms the enemy never counter-attacked, and early yesterday morning we were relieved and got to billets here, and I
to a bed, at seven o'clock a.m.—after six nights and days my
first real lie-down sleep.

Our crowning tragedy occurred on Wednesday.   During
the morning a message was passed along the front line,
where I was in command, to the effect that some of the
troops on our right were leaving the trench.   I immediately
sent an orderly to report this to the Colonel, who presently
sent for me.

I moved along the trench to a point opposite the limekiln,
which, as I have told you, served as his Headquarters, so
that I could talk to him across the intervening open space.
I reported the situation and mentioned casually that the
enemy's shells were enfilading the trench.   I said this in the
flippant kind of way which people are apt to adopt while a
bombardment is on, though, to be candid, they are feeling
far from flippant.   He laughed and answered, in the same
strain, "It's very unpleasant."   This finished our conversation, and they were the last words he ever spoke.   As he
said them he was killed.

A shell burst.   I knew it was close to him, but direct hits

[1] The writer subsequently heard that a fortnight later he had not
regained his sight.

are rare, and believing him to be safely under cover from splinters (he was standing with Dermot Browne, the Adjutant, in the doorway at the top of the staircase), I thought nothing of it, and returned to my place in the trench.

Soon, a message was passed that some one was calling me. I turned back along the trench, but could hear nothing. Then an agonized voice moaned out something which the men said was my name. I went to the edge of the Chalk Pit just behind the trench and there saw an officer. He said that the entrance to the limekiln had been blocked by a shell, and that the Colonel, Adjutant, Second in Command, and all the Headquarter Staff were buried!

I called for six volunteers with picks and shovels, and we crept across the open to the limekiln. At the back of the kiln I saw the Colonel of the 2nd Irish Guards, who confirmed the bad news. At the rear of the kiln there was the flue or chimney I have mentioned, and through this, by means of a piece of telephone wire which he lowered to the chamber below, he got out Hopwood, who was now acting Second in Command.

I went round to the main entrance.

I found a horrible state of things. The orderly whom I had sent with my message to the Colonel lay buried all but his head and shoulders, his head soaked in blood, and both his legs broken. Egerton and Dermot Browne were dead, and the three were jammed together under a mass of earth and fallen timber. Two of the volunteers—an oldish man named Robins and Murphy, an Irishman—were especially to the fore with the digging. Yet it seemed we should never get them out. For each shovelful of the loose crumbling rubbish dug out another slid in. The living man's feet were hopelessly wedged between a balk of timber and the two dead bodies.

After an hour's ceaseless work, during which the shelling continued, we extricated the living man. The other two were not got out till after dark. We buried them at night behind the wood. I read the burial service over Dermot Browne from your prayer-book which I always carry.

49   E

Rather, I should say that I read half of it, since Father Knapp, of the Irish Guards, came in the middle and relieved me of my task.

I had fifty-five casualties in my Company, including some of my best men. C——, one of the Company wags, got shot through the leg and was last seen hopping towards the rear, with a beaming face, and calling to his friends that he'd got a cushy one at last! I was afterwards told that he had jokingly suggested shooting his Company officers also through the leg, because he did not want to have them killed. You should have seen me when I got back to billets. At the Chalk Pit we were cut off from water (except the rain), so could not even wash our hands. My clothes were torn and caked with clay from head to foot: my face black from powder smoke and brown from the showers of earth which were constantly poured upon us by the bursting shells. I was unshaved. I was shivering in a man's greatcoat which a corporal had brought me, picked up on the battlefield, my own having been lost; as also was my mackintosh, my ground-sheet and my pillow, which I had given to a dying man in the Company.

I hope and believe we shall continue to hold the ground we won. It had previously been taken last Saturday, and lost again. It was strewn with the dead of that attack; and with the wounded, who had been lying out ever since in the cold and rain, without food or water.

This is the most horrible aspect of this horrible war. You hear the wounded calling for help, or blowing whistles; you see them waving their handkerchiefs; doing anything and everything to attract attention; and you have often to ignore their appeals. One's first attentions are due to one's own wounded.

Yet, I am glad to tell you that we were able to collect a large number of last Saturday's wounded—between 100 and 200 I should think, including an immense major of the Buffs who had defied all previous efforts to remove him. Indeed, when our men found him he said: "It's no use unless you have a stretcher; it's been tried several times." In

AFTER THE BATTLE OF LOOS
The Colliery Headgear   (Known by the Soldiers as the Tower Bridge)

spite of the days and nights he had lain out, foodless, and in the rain, he was quite cheerful.

I am sorry to say we lost some good men in this rescue work. Tommy Robartes and Fair were both killed in this way. In fact, it became so dangerous that the Colonel stopped it after a time.

I feel that we are beginning to see daylight now. Goodbye, and God bless you.

October 3, 1915 (*Sunday*). *Vermelles.*

This morning we got sudden orders to move, and for the moment we are back in the old ruins of Vermelles. But the scene is very different from what it used to be. Since the German retirement the place has been quite transformed, and it is now crowded with troops. The ground everywhere is trodden down. Horses, transport, artillery—all the paraphernalia of modern offensive war—surround us.

I felt very proud of the battalion as it marched away this morning, again for the battle line, after its short two nights' rest. One would have thought from the demeanour of the men that they had been in comfortable billets for a month. There can be no troops like them in the world. Even in the British Army they shine supreme, as you well know.

October 4, 1915. *Vermelles.*

Last night we (the Company Commanders) went out to reconnoitre the trenches which we shall have to occupy in the event of certain contingencies. All day and night both the Germans and our people were very noisy. The artillery fire was heavy, and there were loud and prolonged bursts of machine-gun and rifle fire. I was not able to find out what it was all about, and I don't think anyone else, beyond those taking immediate part in it, was much wiser.

They don't tell us much, and all we knew, as we felt our way along the dark trenches, was that showers of dropping bullets, partly spent, from the direction of Hohenzollern Redoubt, were falling around us.

The trenches were packed with troops in course of relief, and walking wounded and wounded on stretchers, all coming away from the firing line, so that it was a very slow and tedious affair working one's way forward. After we had finished our explorations there was a lull, and we were able to get out of the trenches and return across the open without danger.

The weather is very cold, and we lay shivering all last night. To-night we have rigged up a fire. I now have three officers besides myself in the Company—Jackson, Roland Philipson, and Daniell (the last from Windsor).

Father Knapp[1] came here yesterday. There was such a din, however, that it was hardly possible to hear him speak, and he decided not to attempt a service, but gave his blessing.

October 12, 1915.   *Prière de Ste Prie.*

I am writing this from a tiny room at night, at a place called Prière de Ste Prie—a developing coal-mine, now for obvious reasons suspended, where we arrived a couple of hours ago, and where I sincerely hope the battalion will have a rest for a day or two. It deserves it. There has been no rest, and with the exception of two nights no proper sleep, since we left Delette on the evening of September 23.

Nowadays, conditions are greatly changed from what they used to be. Brigades, almost Divisions, are billeted in places which were formerly considered none too commodious for battalions: in short, space is scarce; and, to-night, the only man in the battalion who has a bed is Guy Baring,[2] who is now our Commanding Officer. I, personally, am very well off in that I have a tiny room to myself, a tiny table to write on, and my valise on the floor to sleep upon. As I have said, it is a developing coal-mine. Such few buildings as there are are unfinished. There is no furniture; and one of the Companies has been unable to get in at all, and is sleeping out of doors on the grass.

This morning we marched from Sailly Labourse, which village, after six nights in the fire-trench facing Hohen-zollern Redoubt (a place of which I expect you have read a

[1] Father Francis Knapp, D.S.O., M.C.; died of wounds August 1, 1917.
[2] Lieut.-Col. Hon. G. V. Baring, M.P., killed in action, September 15th, 1916.

good deal lately), I reached only yesterday morning at 4.30, feeling so tired that I went straight to bed and stayed there till 3 p.m. Jackson and I had spent a night longer in the trenches than the battalion, having volunteered to get certain work finished of which I will tell you more fully some day.

The trenches we have left were not in a nice condition, as we took them over. They had been the scene of several bloody attacks. The weather was wet: the place deep in mud and filth. They were strewn with every kind of discarded equipment, rifles and bombs. In front, the dead lay thick. Inside the trenches there were also still a few. There were no dug-outs to speak of. The outlook, altogether, was most undesirable; but, fortunately, the weather cleared up after we got in.

As I look upon such scenes as these it occurs to me what a good thing it would be to bring some of our professional hypochondriacs—male and female—that they might witness the appalling wastage of our best manhood. Could they go back and still worry about their own wretched unhealthy minds and bodies after seeing the prodigality with which these healthy young men have given their lives away?

Nevertheless, I confess that the first sight of the reckless slaughter brings a sense almost of shame. I find myself half wondering if the people at home can possibly realize what is going on here.

"Oh! if I were Queen of France, or, still better, Pope of Rome,
I would have no fighting men abroad and no weeping maids at home;
All the world should be at peace: or if kings must show their might,
Why, let them who make the quarrels be the only ones to fight."

Who was it wrote that?

The dead seem to have a strange and subtle fascination for the living. I noticed that at Loos. When we were advancing over the old fought-over ground the whole Company would turn and look each time we passed a dead body. Perhaps they were thinking that they might soon be looking like that themselves; but they would not touch the bodies. I soon found out that a night burying party would always shirk its job.

As I have said, we spent six nights facing Hohenzollern Redoubt, during which time none of us had any sleep to speak of. Day and night the men worked, getting the trenches into shape, and also making other preparations, of which I cannot speak at present. I give you the following in diary form:—

Last Tuesday, on the way up, your prayers again followed me. We were marching by Companies along the road, before taking to the cover of the communication trench. I was leading my Company, when a German "pip-squeak" shell fell not more than 5 yards in front of me. It failed to explode, and we marched on over it.

On Wednesday we were vigorously bombarded during the afternoon, many heavy shells bursting so near the trench as to cover us with earth. Our artillery, all the night before and that day, shelled Hohenzollern Redoubt in the ratio of about four to one.

On Thursday we had a light day, but the artillery again dropped some heavy stuff on Hohenzollern Redoubt.

On Friday there was a very heavy artillery duel, which lasted for six hours, from noon till 6 p.m. This was the biggest thing of its kind, I think, that I have seen. Most of the shells from both sides passed in a continuous stream over our heads, with the roar of express trains. They were not being aimed at us in the front trenches, but the noise was none the less for that.

Then, for an hour or more the Germans concentrated on my bit of trench. They did a good deal of temporary damage to the earthworks, and caused a lot of inconvenience, but killed only one of my men that afternoon. And, towards evening, they made a bombing attack on the battalion on our right, which looked like being successful till our 3rd Battalion bombers rushed in like tigers and completely outdid them.

During the whole of this heavy shooting my men never stopped work. At one moment, at seven different places, either the trench had been blown in or the recesses we were making beneath the parapet had collapsed through the vibration from the bursting shells. It began to look as though it would be impossible to complete the work we had undertaken.

However, just as I was beginning to feel desperate, one of the men came forward and said: "In private life I am a timberman, sir, and I think I can get it right." Three hours later the damage was repaired: the trench was in apple-pie order; and the work we had been ordered to do was almost completed.

On Saturday we had a quiet day. On Sunday we were moderately shelled in the afternoon; and, in the evening, the battalion was relieved, I staying behind with Jackson, as I have said, for the night, to see the work finished.

After dark, we were shelled again, just when we did not want it; but though a few shells fell close, no harm came of them.

So you will understand that I was very tired and sleepy when at last I got to billets yesterday morning, though I feel quite rested now and "in the pink," as the men say in their letters home.

The battalion had just upon forty casualties, mostly from shell-fire, during the days it was up.

3.15 *p.m.* I have just returned from parade. You may be surprised to hear that I have only learnt to-day from the *Daily Mail* that the heavy bombardment of last Friday was the accompaniment to the big German counter-attack of that day, in which it is claimed that we killed 8,000 men: an estimate upon which, however, personally, I humbly venture to cast doubt. Such is our ignorance of things that are going on even a few hundred yards away from our immediate surroundings!

October 14, 1915. *Prière de Ste Prie.*

Jackson and I bicycled into Bethune yesterday, and arrived at the outskirts to find 15-inch shells plunging at intervals of about a quarter of an hour into the centre of the town. These were something new, and heavier than anything I had experienced before. Certainly, the effect was very shattering, and the pieces were flying wide, and falling several hundreds of yards from the point of impact of the shells.

The population, who had seemed almost to have grown accustomed to their "iron ration," were evidently startled by this ponderous stuff, and were crowding into the streets; and most of the shops, and even the famous "Globe" (where our officers meet and pow-wow over cocktails), were closed for the time being.

Yesterday afternoon, also, the second great British attack was launched—though the Guards took no active part in it; —a sort of repetition of September 25. The news we have received so far is very fragmentary, but they say it has been successful.

The fact that this attack has been made unseals my lips, and I can tell you now of the mysterious work we were doing in the trench opposite Hohenzollern Redoubt, and at which I could only hint before. We were excavating emplacements under the parapet and filling them with cylinders of chlorine gas, in preparation for yesterday's attack. We stored 420 of these cylinders in our bit of trench.

When I said that on the night I stayed behind the Germans started shelling just when we did not want it, I meant that they did so at a time when the trench was packed with cylinders, to say nothing of the men who were bringing them in; and, when I explain that these cylinders are big and heavy and each requires four men to carry it (two carriers and two reliefs), you will be able to picture the congestion that was produced in the narrow trench, and you can imagine what the effect would have been if a chance splinter of shell had happened to puncture a cylinder and let out the gas: and this condition of things continued during two nights.

To repeat, we prepared but did not take an active part in the attack. We did, however, supply a platoon under a subaltern which held the smoke candles, and produced the smoke cloud which concealed the advance of the attackers: —a device which is reported to have been very effective.

Well, we have blazed away a lot of ammunition (would

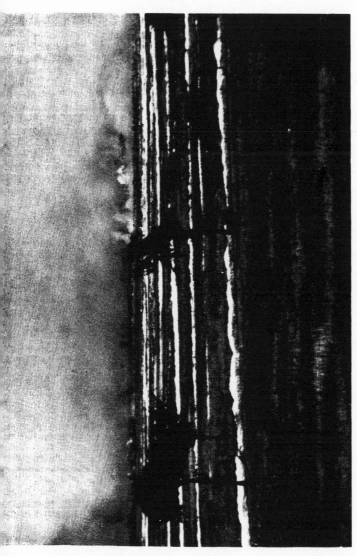

BRITISH ATTACK ON HOHENZOLLERN REDOUBT

13th October, 1915

Clouds of smoke and gas can be seen in the distance, and the British Trenches
can be traced by the chalk which has been excavated

you believe it? An artillery officer told me the other day that some of the shells we have bought from America are *literally* filled with nothing but sand!). The great thing now is to push, and keep on pushing. Frankly, I am surprised that we have not already been sent for; but perhaps they are going to give us a few days more rest. We can do with it.

October 19, 1915. *Reserve Trenches opposite Hohenzollern Redoubt.*

On Friday, the 15th, we got orders at 2 p.m. to be ready in half an hour to march from Prière de Ste Prie to the trenches, and we arrived in position in front of Hohenzollern Redoubt at midnight. ´We found ourselves immediately to the right of the sector we had occupied a few days previously —in the portion which was then held by the Irish Guards.

On our way up we saw the Prince of Wales, who stood by the roadside as we passed.

We found the trenches greatly changed since we had left them. The big attack of Wednesday, the 13th, had been made, and contrary to the first messages that came through, had failed with very heavy losses. Only a part of the trench which had formed the front of Hohenzollern Redoubt was still held by our troops; the rest of the Redoubt was in German hands, with the exception of such part of it as had been transformed into Noman's Land, having been blown sky-high by the artillery.

This bit of trench we proceeded to occupy, as well as the old front line in which we had placed the gas. The cylinders were now empty. The communication trenches —and in many parts the fire-trenches also—had been blown in by the enemy's shells. Both were littered with the sweepings of war—gas-pipes and cylinders, discarded rifles and equipment, bombs, small arm ammunition-boxes, and the dead. On the ground in front lay hundreds of our dead. The narrow communication trenches were also crowded with living men, scrambling in the dark to pass one another.

I suppose there is nothing in the world where theory differs from practice so much as in war. Contrast the practice trenches in Windsor Park with the trenches here.

Since this battle began, Brigades and more have been squeezed in where battalions used to be. The communication trenches are very long and very narrow. They are crossed and re-crossed and threaded by telephone wires—many of them loose and dangling—which trip you up, and catch you by the head; and, during the period which has elapsed since the war began, a perfect maze of trenches has evolved, in which no amount of organization will prevent men losing their way, especially in the dark.

The congestion in the trenches at night, during this time of battle, must be seen to be appreciated. The communication trenches, except where blown in by shells, are generally just wide enough for two men with packs to squeeze past one another with difficulty. Picture what happens when—as is often the case—a Company or Battalion going in takes the wrong turn and meets another coming out! The chaos becomes more bewildering still when they meet in a tunnel; and when, as last night, one is being relieved by people who make such a noise that the relief is spotted and the enemy opens fire with shrapnel, the climax is reached.

Well, on Friday evening, we ran into all these things. As we were getting into position, heavy bombing started in Hohenzollern Redoubt, which was the destination of No. 3 Company, commanded by Charles Noel. This was accompanied by rifle and machine-gun fire, and after the usual pyrotechnical display on the part of the enemy—that is to say, plenty of red and green rockets and white flares, their artillery opened a heavy searching fire over our trenches, as the result of which we were lucky in that only one shell fell among our men, though killing and wounding several.

By midnight we had got more or less settled; that is, we remained stationary from that hour till daylight. As a matter of fact, we could hardly have moved, if we had wanted to. Even in the morning the communication trenches were still packed with troops. One of my platoons was completely blocked up, shut in by a party of Grenadiers at one end and a barricade at the other—the latter caused by the bursting of a shell on the top of a tunnelled part of the trench, underneath which some more Grenadiers lay buried.

On the day that followed (Saturday) there was heavy hostile shelling in the morning; later, moderate shelling at intervals. Night came, and was quiet. About 2 a.m. I visited Charles Noel in the Redoubt, and spent some time with him.

This shambles (you can call it nothing else) is about 200 yards in front of our old fire-trench. The part of it which we hold and the communication trench leading to it have been so shelled that, at the time we took them over, they were no longer trenches but ditches, very wide and shallow, with frequent upheavals in the floor, indicating the positions of dead men, now wholly or partly covered with earth splashed over them by the bursting shells and the passage of troops.

It would, I suppose, be an exaggeration to say that the parapets at this place are built up with dead bodies, but it is true to say that they are dovetailed with them, and everywhere arms and legs and heads protrude.

At one place an arm and hand stuck out and dangled across the trench. On one of the fingers was a solid-looking gold ring, and in spite of the fact that, owing to the narrowness of the passage, each man that passed it had to brush the hand aside, it spoke well for the battalion, I thought, that to my knowledge the ring still remained untouched for more than twenty-four hours; and though in the end it disappeared I am convinced it was not taken by any Coldstreamer.

The artillery certainly did its work well here. The surface of the ground over a large area has been reduced to a shapeless jumble of earth mounds and shell-holes. The formidable wire entanglements have gone. On all sides lie the dead. It is a war picture of the most frightful description; and the fact that the dead are, practically speaking, all *our* dead, arouses in me a wild craving for revenge. Where are the enemy's dead? We hear much of them, but we do not see them. During this fighting I have seen thousands of British dead, but the dead Germans I have seen I could almost count upon my fingers.

At nine in the evening (Saturday the 16th) a joint bombing attack upon Hohenzollern Redoubt by the 3rd Grenadiers and ourselves had been planned to begin. Owing to a hitch in the arrangements it was postponed till five o'clock the following morning, when the Grenadiers were to open the ball.

At 5 a.m., while we were standing to, the Commanding Officer (Guy Baring) came hurrying along my trench. He said the plans had been changed, that we had just been detailed to take the place of the 3rd Grenadiers, and that we were to attack immediately. I asked for instructions. He replied: "There is no time for instructions. You must use your discretion." Thus, as at the Chalk Pit, we had only a few minutes in which to organize our arrangements. Charles Noel's bombers (No. 3 Coy.) and mine (No. 4) made the assault. I immediately reinforced Noel by sending one platoon under Jackson into the Redoubt, another to the communication trench leading to the Redoubt, and my remaining two platoons, under Daniell, to the first support trench. I myself, having seen the men into position, went into the Redoubt.

In spite of the unexpected suddenness of the order, there was no crowding and no vestige of undue hurry or excitement. The orders were obeyed in perfect silence, the men filing steadily along the trenches to their positions. At each end of the main communication tunnel I posted sentries to keep it clear, so that it might be available for further reinforcements should they be needed, and for getting out the wounded.

The bombers went in with dash, and to start with made good progress. They rushed the barricade separating us from the enemy, and bombed their way for a considerable distance beyond it. The trenches were, however, so flattened by shell-fire that they gave very little protection. At this spot they are, moreover, a regular tangle. There came a point where the party should have taken an insig-

nificant-looking turning to the left,[1] but in the darkness they
bombed straight on.   The trench they followed became so
shallow that presently it ceased to give any cover at all.   The
Germans, who are always quick to spot a weakness of this
kind, lost no time in making good their opportunity.   They
brought a machine-gun into position; and that ends the story.

Our losses were not severe, but bad enough.   I do not
know what the casualties amounted to in the battalion.
Those in my Company, since we came up this time, are
twenty-four, all told.   These things begin to tell.   I have
lost, I suppose, ninety men, or half the Company, since we
left Lumbres, and Nos. 1 and 2 Companies have lost considerably more, though the gaps have already been almost,
if not entirely, filled by drafts from home.

I remained some hours in the Redoubt, which, at the
time, was a very lively spot to be in.   Fortunately for us,
though the German shelling was very severe, it was a little
wide of the ground we were fighting upon,—possibly owing
to the proximity of many Germans, whose lives would have
been jeopardized by closer shooting.

A good deal of sniping was indulged in by both sides, in
which—speaking of our own side—most of those present
took a hand.   The opposing troops were, however, so close
to one another that this was a tricky game.   It was impossible to search for a target with a periscope, for so hot was the
sniping that no periscope survived more than a minute or
two.   The only way was to peep over the parapet and snap
from the shoulder, and though anyone exposing himself in
this way for more than a second would most assuredly be
shot, there was plenty of light-hearted rivalry whenever a
target did offer.

Once, a party of the enemy had been spotted digging
among the shell-holes not more than 30 or 40 yards in front
of where I was standing, when one of the men who had
mounted the fire-step to shoot recoiled the very instant he
exposed himself, with a German bullet through his cap
which lifted the latter clean off his head.   The self-con-

[1] This was before the days of trench maps and aeroplane photographs.

scious grin he gave as he stepped back into the trench was very comical to see.

There was a curious report which came from I don't know where—that there were Germans still hiding in the Redoubt, in the deep dug-outs, who were in telephonic communication with their people. It is quite likely that such things have happened, though I hardly think it was so on the present occasion. Anyhow, during the hours I spent in the Redoubt on Sunday morning I bore the rumour in mind.

There was one wonderful dug-out which the men had rather avoided, from a feeling, I think, that there was something uncanny about it. I went down and explored it with an electric torch. It was like an old clothes shop. It was 20 feet or 30 feet deep, excavated in the chalk, with two entrances, and with a chamber quite 30 or 40 feet long at the bottom. In the latter were wooden bunks for sleeping, two deep, ranged along one wall; and the floor was almost knee-deep in clothing, equipment, medicine cases, tinned food, and other stuff.

One dead man also was there; again, not a German, but a British casualty from a previous attack, who either had crept in, or—to give them their due—may have been carried in by the enemy to die.

Our bombing attack brought on the heaviest bombardment I have yet sat under. It was at about its zenith at a quarter to ten a.m. It lasted for over nine hours, and was intense during a great part of that time. The stream of German shells was continuous. They came in "coveys," whistling through the air like a storm at sea. As I heard one of the men say—they came "in close column of platoons." Often they were falling at the rate of quite a hundred a minute.

But our trenches here are like network: they are repeated —parallel after parallel; till not only by their very number are they confusing to the German gunners, but the area over which the fire is distributed is fortunately extended, and therein lies our chance of safety.

It is of course bewildering to be shelled like that. There

is no denying that when such shelling happens to be concentrated on the particular bit of trench you are in, as it often
is for an hour or more together, it is extremely disagreeable;
but, on the whole, the damage done by these huge bombardments is out of all proportion to their cost, and they do not
produce the moral effect—or rather the demoralizing effect
—which is their sole object.

Once it is over you shake yourself and recover, and if you
are healthily minded you soon have forgotten it, just as you
forget the other disturbances of life. Yet, to tell the truth,
I marvel myself sometimes how human nerves can stand the
strain of our existence; day after day, night after night, hour
after hour, being shelled; sometimes, for hours at a time, a
heavy shell falling every few minutes within a few yards of
you, shaking the ground beneath you, half stunning you
with the crash of the explosion, and covering you with
earth.

I wrote you a short letter towards the end of the bombardment of which I have been speaking. Just after I had
finished it a shell burst outside the door of the dug-out
where I was writing, upsetting everything. My telephone
dug-out was blown right in, and my trench was smashed in
over and over again.

On Monday it was quiet until 2.30 in the afternoon, and
we were hoping inwardly for a day of comparative peace,
when our artillery aroused the sleeping lion by opening fire.
Personally, I am all for bombarding the enemy and strafing
him on every possible occasion, and I am sure I speak for the
great majority when I say that, so long as we feel that our
guns are doing him some damage, we are willing to sit and
receive the retaliation which almost certainly follows.

On this occasion, however, our artillery began by dropping shells upon our own support trenches, including my
own. This is a practice for which some of the new
batteries are becoming famous. I have myself reported it
over and over again. It is annoying enough in itself, but
on Monday it was doubly so, as the Germans immediately
took up the challenge, and instead of a restful afternoon, we

had to sit through a heavy hate. The same morning, while I was shaving, I got my face scratched by a splint of shell which drew the blood.

I have mentioned tunnels in this letter. A feature of the communication trenches leading towards Hohenzollern Redoubt is that some of them are in the form of tunnels, burrowed through the chalk—2 or 3 feet below the surface of the ground. These Russian saps—as they are called—are, so far as I know, peculiar to this part of the line. But for the fact that they have been penetrated here and there by German shells they would be pitch-dark; and, as they are only wide enough for men to pass along comfortably in single file, they are apt to produce a very choky feeling when they get crowded—particularly if you are inclined to "claustrophobia."

October 20, 1915. *Reserve Trenches opposite Hohenzollern Redoubt.*

The Colonel told me to-day that we are to be hereabouts till the 26th, when we go back for a rest.

They are beginning to issue steel helmets to our men. They look like that kind of suet pudding which we used, as children, to call "Plough-boy's hat"; and they are painted mottled green to make them unconspicuous. There are not, as yet, enough to go round, so they are doled out to the men in the most forward positions.

You can tell M—— that I do not think the trenches would suit her. They are full of mice and rats, which run about like lap-dogs. Last night, while we were dining, our food being spread upon the floor, a mouse ran about among the plates, and was not at all abashed by the burning candles, or ourselves. They run up and down the earth walls of the dug-outs and at night have violent scuffles overhead, shaking the earth into our eyes and ears as we lie beneath.

The amusing thing is that we all take care not to tread upon them or injure them in any way. In some mysterious way the war, while making one more callous to the sufferings of men, seems to increase one's sympathy with the lower animals. Perhaps it is that in the scheme of creation the animals are coming out so much better than the men.

The days of the old famous dug-outs ("Some Hut," for example) are over. What was not good enough for a Company Headquarters in those happy days is now too good for a Battalion and good enough for a Brigade. We are no longer critical in such matters. We do not look for chairs or tables, but sit and eat and sleep upon the hard ground, with a more or less splinter-proof roof, if we are lucky, just high enough to allow kneeling.

It is cold at nights and more so in the early mornings. Speaking for myself, I lie shivering but exceedingly healthy. Yesterday, I rigged up a coke fire in my dug-out, which is a great boon. I have no clothes other than those I wear, except a man's greatcoat, a man's ground-sheet, and a waterproof cape, all picked up in the trenches since I lost my own at Loos.

Philipson and Daniell have gone home, sick. I remain, and, thank God, stick it wonderfully. I have never felt better in my life.

An officer in the battalion has found the diary of a Bavarian Infantry soldier, Otto Arnesmaier—a wonderfully human document, into which the writer pours his full soul. He was a man of gentle disposition, who was no soldier by choice, and indeed hated everything to do with war; a lover of music, which he describes as "the divine daughter of Heaven, and consoler."

His was one of the bodies that helped to make the parapet of Hohenzollern Redoubt.

October 22, 1915. *Fire-trench* (*Guildford Alley*): *Hohen-zollern Redoubt.*

Nothing more unlike the talk of soldiers as depicted on the stage or in the classics could be imagined than the real thing as we get it here. There are no heroics. In fact, it is rather etiquette to grumble and pretend to be frightened. It is, I imagine, a sort of protective bravado.

A short time ago I was listening to one of our young regular officers and a good one too, talking with another officer who is serving for the period of the war, and who came from China specially for the purpose.

The latter was letting fly about things in general and got the reply: "What have *you* got to grouse about? *I* joined the army to enjoy myself, and I find myself plunged into this —— war. I have some right to complain. You joined the army to fight, and you've got what you came for. You have nothing to grouse about."

The men can be philosophic too. The following is a snatch of conversation between two privates of the Scots Guards which I overheard in the trench the other day. Their talk also was of the war.

"If you gets wounded," said one, "and it's a cushy one, you gets sent 'ome; and if you gets killed, well, it's ——all!"

Last night, we relieved the Worcester Regiment and the Irish Guards in Hohenzollern Redoubt and the front line of trenches. The enemy again shelled us while the relief was in progress, but did no damage. I was up at intervals all through the night, as we had much digging work in hand. The night would have been very quiet on the whole, had it not been for our own artillery, who dropped many shells short, and wounded one of my corporals and tore the pack belonging to another man to ribbons. And the next morning, they put a shell into one of my traverses.

I reported the most flagrant cases as they occurred, and sent back the riddled pack as ocular proof, with the result that Brigade has been roused to a healthy indignation, and is now venting its wrath in the proper quarters.

October 23, 1915.

As a result, during the whole of last night an artillery officer was posted near me, at the end of a telephone wire, with orders to try and spot the offending battery or batteries; but our guns did not fire at all, so his efforts were fruitless.

In any case, seeing that there are some hundreds of guns which can range upon the trench from which I am writing, it is practically impossible to identify the precise location from which any particular shot is fired.

The enemy snipers here are very active. They have killed two of my men and badly wounded a Welsh Guardsman since last night—all practically at the same spot. These snipers are very bold. It is a common sight to see two or three of the enemy exposing themselves in a most reckless way. I have myself seen many, and I must admit that they do not look at all downhearted, but spruce and clean and full of confidence. One cannot but admire their audacity. It is, of course, possible that these men are new to the game, but it is just as likely that they are put up as decoys, to tempt us to expose ourselves.

It is getting colder and colder at nights. Last night a half-starved dog crawled into the trench and slept beside me, and I was glad of his company for the warmth it gave.

We are to be relieved to-night and go out, I believe, for a fortnight's rest, of which we shall be very glad. We have had eight days and nights of the worst in these trenches, which have cost the battalion about a hundred casualties, and my Company twenty-six.

October 24, 1915. *Sailly Labourse.*

I have just been sent for by the Commanding Officer and told that in view of my strenuous duties during the past month I can go home on extra leave on the 29th—in five days' time!

*　　*　　*　　*　　*

November 6, 1915. *St. Hilaire.*

As the result of twelve hundred men having missed the boat of the night before, the one by which I crossed was packed. We were cautioned not to crowd to one side for fear of overbalancing the boat, but this caution was unnecessary as the decks were so blocked with humanity that it was next to impossible to move in any direction. General Maxse was on board with his A.D.C., Fred Montague of this regiment, and I had tea with Montague in the saloon.

I failed to get a lift on a motor-car from Boulogne and was obliged to travel on the "leave" train which, like the boat, was overcrowded. There were nine in my compartment, and I was the ninth, so had to balance on a dividing arm-rest. I travelled with a Captain of the Irish Guards whom I only know under the name of "Nosy." The train crawled and we reached our detraining station—which was Lillers—at 2.30 in the morning, having left Boulogne, after much waiting, at 8 p.m. From Lillers "Nosy" and I walked off together through a thick fog. I had about twice as far to go as he, and reached my billet here about 3.30. I found my bed occupied by one of two new subalterns who have joined the battalion from the London Scottish and had been posted to No. 4 Company during my absence. I had not been expected back as it was so late. However, room was made for me and I managed to get a sleep.

Guy Baring asked me this morning if you would under-take some of the visiting of the men's families about London and I said I was sure you would delight in it. I told him that you were the most unselfish woman on earth—which you are.

November 8, 1915. *La Gorgue.*

We fell in this morning at 6.30 and marched till half-past one, when we reached this place, where we expect to be about six days before going to some trenches which will be new to us. As we are so few officers, Humphrey de Trafford[1] and I have joined up our Company messes.

I rode with Guy Baring to Aires yesterday, and we visited the Cathedral, which I thought rather disappointing.

November 11, 1915. *La Gorgue.*

The trenches—or rather breastworks—which we are to take over have been held by Gurkhas, so that they may be expected, with luck, to reach to our men's waists, and we shall have plenty of work to do in building them up. They are very quiet, I believe.

The bands of the different regiments of the Division are to take it in turn to come to France, and the Grenadiers are already here, and have been playing in the square to-day, just outside my billet.

The joint mess (Nos. 1 and 4 Companies) is a very cheery

[1] Now Sir Humphrey de Trafford, Bart., M.C.

place. Last night we had a dinner party and a crowd in after, and it will be the same every evening till the end of this week.

12.15 (*midnight*).

Our dinner party this evening consisted of Alfred Yorke (an old member of White's; forty-four and an ensign!); Lionel Tennyson, Hylton Philipson, Sam Woods, etc.

November 17, 1915.   *Merville.*

The battalion went into the trenches last night, but a most humiliating thing has happened to me. I have had a fall from a common push-bike and have injured my knee. The day before yesterday Hopwood, Charles Noel and I again went up to reconnoitre our new trenches, Hopwood riding, Noel and I on bicycles.

When we got within view of the Aubers Ridge we took to our feet and saw some very pretty shooting as we made off towards the trenches. The German gunners were firing at a house about 100 yards to the right of our starting-point, and hitting it every time. It was empty! We returned to the spot where we had left the bicycles after dark, and in mounting I missed the pedal—a free-wheel: the miserable machine lurched into some deep mud by the roadside; and I came down with a sickening thud upon my knee on the hard road. When I got home the doctor came to see me and found that I had a temperature of 101½; and the following morning my knee had stiffened and filled, and I could not walk without pain. (I have had this "water on the knee" before and know all about it, as you know.)

In the evening I was sent by ambulance to the Casualty Clearing Station at Merville, and here I am in bed, with an Australian Army doctor suffering from influenza on my left, a padre with a rheumatic knee on my right, and in front of me the same Irish Guards Captain whom I travelled with on the sixth, and who now has a shell-wound in the arm.

I have learnt during the last few days that the most exaggerated stories of Flemish winter mud do not exceed the reality. The mud varies in consistency from the creamy variety to the adhesive kind which holds you fast like bird-lime and would suck off the long india-rubber hip boots with which the troops are now provided were they not strapped to the waistbelt, as they are.

The country we have come to is flat, low-lying, and swampy. So sodden is the surface soil that trench-digging is out of the question, and the defences consist of lines of breastworks built up of sandbags.

These breastworks are irregular in design, and, many shells having burst against them, are ragged and dishevelled in appearance. The older bags have rotted and the earth has slipped and shrunk with the weather. The ground in front and behind is thickly pitted with shell-holes, among which occasional little wooden crosses appear, marking the graves of soldiers.

The prevailing impression is one of chaotic fresh-turned slimy earth, and the general scene is one of desolation such as I tried to describe to you when speaking of Hohenzollern Redoubt.

The communication trenches leading to the front line are half full of mud and water, which generally reaches your knees, and sometimes your waist. They have in fact ceased to be of any practical use, and most people travel to and from the fire-trench across the open, by night, which apparently is not so dangerous as might be supposed.

November 23, 1915.   *La Gorgue.*

We marched here to-day. I managed it by climbing on to my horse from a box on the "off" side.

November 26, 1915.   *Merville.*

I have had to give it up, and am back at the Casualty Clearing Station, in bed, and am to be sent to England.

April 9, 1916.   *Harfleur.*

We got here a little before one yesterday afternoon, after the 5½-mile march from the landing-stage at Havre.

The sea was like glass, and the scene was very picturesque and rather spectral as our ship lay to outside the great submarine net, waiting for darkness before setting out. The sun sank into the horizon a gorgeous red, and was followed by the flashes of signals from the destroyers and other craft which surrounded us, while the searchlights played upon the sky, looking for German aeroplanes.

I was O.C. Troops on board, and was invited by the Captain to sleep in his cabin; so I was very comfortable. He wanted me to take his bed, but I could not do that.

I am in the same camp where I was this month last year. It is now the Guards Divisional Base Depot. There must be nearly twenty officers here, including members of all the regiments of the Division.

April 14, 1916.   *Harfleur.*

I hear I am to go to the Entrenching Battalion, to take over the Coldstream Company. It is a kind of advanced Depot—a stepping-stone to the trenches, where the young officers and soldiers are near enough to the front line to get used to the smell of gunpowder and the noise of shells, before actually joining their battalions.

I have a new servant from the 3rd Battalion called Glover who seems a good fellow. He tells me he had never been a servant till he came to Harfleur: in fact, he had never been allowed to be. "You see, sir," he said, "I'm a dare-devil kind of a chap. I don't care what I do. I'll go out on patrols or anything." And Acland Hood, who shared my hut, says that this description of Glover by himself is correct.

April 19, 1916.   *Bois des Tailles (near Bray-sur-Somme).*

We left Rouen at half-past three yesterday afternoon with 1,400 troops on board. I was O.C. train, so had a reserved compartment, which I shared with one of my subalterns. I had never seen Rouen before and was greatly impressed by the Cathedral. I visited the "Place du

71

vieux Marché," where Joan of Arc was burned, the spot
— a couple of yards or so from a butcher's stall—being
marked by a slab over which people walk;—no more.

I reached the Entrenching Battalion this afternoon,
about forty-four hours after leaving Harfleur, after a wet
and muddy march of 6½ miles through comparatively
treeless country of the dreariest variety. The day has
been horrible, and the cheerless aspect of the camp upon
our arrival was most dispiriting. My servant describes it
as a "wash-out," and it is! Perhaps it will improve when
the weather gets better. It is 3½ to 4 miles behind the
firing line, from the direction of which the rumble of the
guns can be heard.

The battalion is commanded by Major Kirby Ellice, of
the Grenadiers, who is extremely nice and kind to me, and
I hope my first jaundiced impression of the place will prove
to have been influenced—more than I can bring myself to
believe at present—by the disgusting weather and the long
and tiring journey;—to say nothing of my disappointment
at not having been sent straight back to the 1st Battalion,
as I had hoped.

April 26, 1916. *Bois des Tailles*

The horrible weather—rainy and cold—which I encountered on my first arrival has gone, after some vicissitudes, and given place to a period of glorious sunshine
What a difference it makes!

This Camp is pitched a few hundred yards from the
Somme—where lie the gun-boats, on the top of the high
escarpment which rises abruptly from the river on the
north side. It is hidden among trees, many of which—
wild cherries—are now thick with blossom.

The men sleep in canvas huts; the officers in tents; and
the officers' mess and ante-room (in one) are in a wooden
shack—rather like a Newfoundland timberman's rig-out—
furnished with two long plank tables, with forms on either
side. I sleep on a canvas cot, and am sitting on it now, as
I write, since chairs do not exist. Indeed, I have not once
sat on a chair since I came here.

On Easter Sunday I rode with Kemes Lloyd [1] to Albert, which is about 5 miles from here. The town has been well bombarded, though in the outskirts the houses are still mostly standing. The most pronounced devastation is in the Cathedral square, which, with the exception of the Cathedral itself, has been completely flattened.

The greater part of the Cathedral, which is a modern building of extremely solid construction, still stands precariously, though seamed with cracks and fissures. But what immediately arrests the eye is a colossal gilded statue of the Blessed Virgin and Child which crowns the summit of the tower. This great effigy has been hit and knocked over, and though it lies poised horizontally in mid-air, in the attitude of diving, it still clings to its pedestal and continues to defy all efforts of the German gunners to dislodge it.

The sight is a very remarkable one, and it is not surprising that a superstition has grown up among the French that the ultimate fall of this statue will be the signal for the downfall of the enemy.

As with many another religious emblem in the fighting line, the chance action of the shells has rather added to than detracted from the impressiveness of this one, and as one looks up at it to-day, the Child, with its hands outspread, seems to be looking down from the Mother's arms in blessing on our soldiers in the ruined square below.

General Maxse [2] told me that when he first came here the figure leant at an angle of about 45 degrees, and that it has gradually sagged to its present position. So perhaps it will not be so very long before the actual crash comes.

April 28, 1916.   *Bois des Tailles.*

Last Wednesday I dined at General Maxse's headquarters, and sat next to the General.

We had whitebait for dinner, which is caught by a very persevering mess cook, who sits on the bank of the Somme,

---

[1] Capt. M. K. A. Lloyd, Grenadier Guards, killed in action September 15, 1916.

[2] Now Gen. Sir Ivor Maxse, K.C.B., C.V.O., D.S.O.

with a gauze net at the end of a pole. He waits till the minnows and small gudgeon swim over his net; then lifts them out of the water; and it takes several hours to get a plateful. But they are very good, and I shall adopt the idea.

From a spectacular point of view this is probably the most interesting section of the British Front. A succession of rolling hills and ridges—in striking contrast to the flat low-lying lands further north—here permits of close and distant observation, with exceptional facility, and one lives with field-glasses "at the ready."

Montague took me by car yesterday to visit a part of his Divisional Front where the Somme forms a loop, almost completely enclosing a large tract of swampy ground, some 2,000 yards by 1,000 yards in dimension, so water-logged that it cannot be trenched, and which, consequently, has become a sort of neutral territory, where the patrols of both sides wander by night and not infrequently encounter one another.

The sun was shining brightly, and the nightingales were singing for all they were worth, and all seemed very restful as we visited the outposts. One of those silent lulls was on, when both sides seem to have gone to sleep.

One sees here as elsewhere frequent illustrations of the huge divergence between theory and practice in war. For example, one of the things we used to learn was that you should avoid woods and villages on account of the target they offer to the enemy's artillery. Yet here, skirting the fringe of the marsh I have described, are three villages—Frise, Curlu, and Vaux, the two first occupied by the enemy; the last by our troops. As the ground on either side of the river rises precipitately, each army can look down upon the roofs of the other.

Frise was demolished during the great enemy attack on the French last January 28, and Vaux is more or less battered too, though not greatly so; but from what I could see of Curlu, it is still in a good state of preservation.

After all, these villages are small fry, garrisoned perhaps by a Company or less apiece, and though it would be easy to blot them out, they are left alone, comparatively speaking,

probably not being considered worth the risk of bringing
down the inevitable retaliation upon the populous villages
behind the line on either side, where very much greater
numbers of troops might be involved.

We visited the chateau at Suzanne, a large pretentious
building which was much damaged by the bombardment
of January 28.   It presents an extraordinary mixture of
the old and the new;—of marble and gilt and glass of the
most lurid modern French style; and such things as an old
family coach emblazoned with coronets; with heavy velvet
trappings round the coachman's seat, and a footboard
behind for the lackeys.   The little house chapel looks well
cared for still, though it is damaged by shell-fire.

May 8, 1916.   *Bois des Tailles.*

Four parcels arrived from you to-day, containing two
pies, a cake, pâté de foie gras, plovers' eggs and smoked
salmon.   Thank you so much.   We had the plovers' eggs
and smoked salmon at dinner to-night.   Kemes Lloyd,
who returned from leave to-day, began by asking who the
new mess president was, so that he might congratulate him.
I said, in justice to my Lady, that it was she who had
provided these luxuries.   To which he answered: "If only
I could find a woman like that, I'd marry her! !"

So we have conscription at last!   It is about time, too.
The Conscripts have not, of course, reached us as yet, but
some Derby (commonly pronounced "Durby") men have.

It is funny how these latter are despised by the other
men—more so than the conscripts, who are regarded as
having at least shown the courage of their convictions.

To be called or even thought to be a "Durby man" is, in
fact, an insult.   A few days ago I was at Commanding
Officer's "orders" when a man was brought up for giving
an insubordinate reply to a corporal.   He had been told to
dig, but his spade, he said, was broken, and he had replied:
"I ain't no b—— Durby man."

May 16, 1916.   *Bois des Tailles.*

The parcel of ham, two dozen plovers' eggs, and the
children's sweets arrived to-day.   Thank you all.

To-day the weather has completely changed, and has been superb. I have been at my usual occupation, digging trenches in the Suzanne Valley.

I had also to go to a new place to start some work, and took with me one of the sergeants—Deakin, by name. He was working for a fruit-grower and seedsman before he enlisted, and being intelligent besides an excellent N.C.O. I found his conversation very entertaining.

The ground is becoming strewn with a great profusion and variety of wild flowers. Few and far between are wild lilies of the valley in bloom, which are much sought after by officers and men, and are therefore difficult to find.

Another very common flower is a white one to which I cannot give a name. It grows from a bulb and has leaves like a daffodil, but much narrower and with a white stripe. The flower itself is like a star. Sergeant Deakin says he has not seen it before, but thinks it may be what is called "Star of Bethlehem." If only you were in the country I would send you some bulbs.

May 28, 1916.   *Station Hotel, Hazebrouck.*

I left camp yesterday at noon with a mixed draft of Grenadier, Coldstream, and Irish Guards, and marched to the railway. It was the first time I had made the trip since the day I first arrived. Do you remember my description? Then the trees had no leaves; the fields no verdure; the whole horizon was a sea of mud, and sheets of rain were falling.

Yesterday, the whole scene had changed. The fields were green with young corn, or yellow with mustard, or crimson with clover. Woods and plantations, the existence of which before I had not noticed, sprung out in all directions, in masses of luxuriant colour. On the hills and in the valleys villages now peeped out, which before I could not see because of the rain; and the big winding Somme graced all. In fact, I discovered that the country I had been living in for six weeks is really very beautiful in spring.

Our train pushed off at five o'clock, and we crawled to

Abbeville, where we spent most of the night, sitting and standing about in the station amid crowds of troops. At one time it seemed doubtful if we should get on from there —at any rate during last night, since apparently our Army had omitted to notify our coming, and there was no room on the train. However, after much telephoning, three cattle trucks were attached, and at about two in the morning we moved out, to be again transferred to another train at 4 a.m. We reached this place in time for lunch, and I managed to get a shave.

None of the Division are in the immediate locality, and the battalions are very scattered. Consequently, I have seen nobody I know except Guy Darell, who now wears red tabs, and who came buzzing along in a big staff car, but pulled up when he saw me.

The last time I had seen him was at the moment he was bowled over by a shell, just as we were about to start off for our attack on the Chalk Pit Wood on September 27.

He advised me to ring up Divisional Headquarters, which I did, and was answered by his brother—Billy Darell, who is A.A. and Q.M.G., and who arranges the posting of officers. He recommended me to write to Guy Baring, and to ask him to apply for me. Apparently, they make a point that there should always be a Captain of each regiment with the Entrenching Battalion. Consequently, they may not release me till they get some one else.

Anyhow, I wrote to Guy Baring. I have considered the matter as much as I can. I have sometimes felt that I should not add to your anxieties at this time by pressing to be returned to my battalion, but, on the other hand, I have thought that if every married man in my position were content to remain in a safe place, it would be a poor look out for the Army. Finally, if I inspire any confidence in the men, it is certainly right that I should be with them, and I am sure you will agree with me in this.

Do write me your views. God knows how I felt for you in the anxiety you must have endured last autumn, and I dread to repeat that.

I leave here to-morrow morning early, and mean to have a good sleep to-night.

May 29, 1916.   *Grand Hôtel du Rhin, Amiens.*

My little scheme to get back to the 1st Battalion has failed so far, and I return to the Entrenching Battalion to-morrow somehow, either by motor-car or train.

I have been in the train all day.   Last night I slept at Hazebrouck, in an extremely comfortable bed, between sheets—the first time that I have done so since I left Heathfield on April 7.

I visited the Cathedral, here, this evening.   The approaches are barricaded with sandbags, to save them from the fate of Rheims.   It is beautiful—particularly the stained-glass windows, but I still think our English Cathedrals can hold their own against the Continental; and, if the war lasts much longer, they will be the only ones left.

June 4, 1916.   *Bois des Tailles.*

I have just got your letter of the 30th.   I felt sure you would take the high line you have.   Thank you so much. However, judging from Guy Baring's letter, it looks as if I shall have some difficulty in getting back to my battalion, as there is no vacancy for a Captain, at present.

June 6, 1916.   *Bois des Tailles.*

I have been thinking things over to-day, and I feel I should not have worried you by telling you I was bored here, and wanted to get back to my battalion.   I ought to have thought more of you and been contented to stay here. Anyhow, my efforts to get away have failed so far, and I shall not renew them.   I shall wait until they send for me, though, if I see a chance of getting some more interesting job, I shall still take that.

But my anxiety to get a more dangerous job is over.   I had a walk with my C.O. yesterday, and he told me—more or less plainly—that he had heard I was too chancy.   Any-how, that is over for good and all.   I can say, before God, that I have never risked a man's life unless I was ordered, or thought it necessary: and I have never asked an officer

78

or man to do a thing which I was not prepared to do myself. He was good enough to say that I was *too brave* (meaning, I suppose, foolhardy); but, never mind, I won't be brave in future. I shall hate it, but I will take any safe billet they may offer me.

When they say these things it makes me feel I have been unfair to you. But I have tried to act as I have thought you would like me to act. Besides, my inclinations are to be in the swim.

You must be most careful about yourself. Don't tire yourself, and you need not worry about me, because I am absolutely safe here.

June 27, 1916.   *Corbie.*

We (the Coldstream Company)—390 strong—paraded at 7.15 on Sunday morning, and marched 8 miles to this place, which is a town with a big church—almost a Cathedral, and an old hospital, something on the lines of St. Cross at Winchester, established eight hundred years ago.

We are in billets. For the officers' mess we have a room over an ironmonger's shop, with chairs, a big table, a piano, and a stuffed heron. We—the officers—sleep in different houses about the town. The men, too, are very scattered. We are all very comfortable, and, speaking for myself, I have a fine bedroom with a feather bed, in a brewery.

Last Saturday evening I walked out with the Commanding Officer to watch the bombardment of the German trenches which started that day. It was a beautiful clear evening, and the sight was very enthralling. It has continued since, day and night, with ever-increasing violence.

We are now well settled down, and our billets, which, when we took them over, were dirty beyond description, already look spick and span, and the men are all at their very best, and playing up all they know for the credit of the regiment.

I have parties out, day and night, chiefly unloading barges of war material.

When we first marched in, the day being very hot, I received a complaint from a Frenchwoman that a bottle of wine had been stolen from her brewery by one of the men. It was the first complaint of the kind I had experienced since I came to France, and consequently I was much annoyed, and confined all the men concerned to their billet.

Presently, the N.C.O. in charge reported that he thought he had found the culprit, a corporal. He said this man was lying asleep, and he thought drunk. Though I doubted whether one bottle of French light wine would make the merest novice drunk, I ordered the corporal under arrest—provisionally. He was genuinely surprised, on being waked, to be told that he was under arrest, and was obviously perfectly sober. He had come up with a draft the previous day and having spent two nights in a crowded train, was tired out by the hot march. Still, the feeling among the men was strong. They were, I think, as annoyed as I was at the slur upon the regiment.

At that moment—perhaps under the impulse of popular sentiment—the real offender came forward, with the bottle of wine (untouched) under his arm, and gave himself up. He was a recruit—his first day in France, and I do not think he will do it again.

One of our officer's servants is very young indeed, but is married. His master (K——) said to him the other day: "Surely, it is unusual to be married so young."

To which the boy replied: "Yes, sir, it is. It was one of the misfortunes of the war."

June 27, 1916 (*2nd letter*).   *Corbie.*

Yesterday evening I had a bath in the old Convent hospital. While I was still in nothing but my shirt, an old nun walked in, quite unembarrassed, and began to tell me about Ste Collette, whom I confess I had not heard of before. She was born here, in a house still standing a few doors from where I am writing, and the nun explained, has the town, and particularly the hospital, under her special protection.

She added that the Germans were here for fifteen days

at the beginning of the war, and, though they misconducted themselves elsewhere, they behaved like lambs when they came to the Convent, where the nuns were nursing the French wounded.

June 28, 1916.   *Corbie.*

To-day the Trench Mortar officer of the 30th Division (Captain Edwards) invited me to lunch at his Artillery Battle Headquarters, in front of Bray, to see the bombardment.

It was in full swing, as it has been, day and night, since the 24th. It was an impressive sight. Heavy rain was falling, and the sky was cloudy, and—especially opposite the French—the ridge, where the German trenches are, was hidden by a wall of smoke from the bursting shells. The Germans were not replying at all—at any rate on the back areas, though they appeared to be doing so upon our front line.

They (the Germans) must be having a horrible time, I should think. All our valleys are thick with guns and howitzers. In one small valley alone, which I know well, I was told to-day, we have more guns concentrated than were employed by our army in the whole South African War.

Some of our shells were bursting prematurely, which is bad. It reminded me of poor D—— once when we were at Cambrin and the same thing was happening. It was at the time when a good many ladies at home were beginning to take up munition work, amongst them, he said, his mother; and he remarked: "I shouldn't be surprised if those were some of my mother's shells!"

July 1, 1916 (*Saturday*).   *Corbie.*

This has been a great day, as you will have learnt from the newspapers. The battle, for which we have for some months been preparing, has begun, and, thanks to a newly-made friend, Thornhill,[1] and his car, I have been able to see a lot of it.

The culmination of our bombardment—that is the

[1] Major, Royal Engineers.

infantry attack—took place this morning. It was originally planned for Thursday, but was postponed for forty-eight hours owing to the bad weather, which makes most of the roads, which in this part of France are not cobbled, impassable for heavy transport. When the weather is good the roads are good, and the reverse when it rains. The same rule no doubt applies to the roads on the German side.

The weather, yesterday, had become fine. To-day it was perfect. Between 6.30 and 7.30 a.m. our bombardment was intensified. To give you an idea of what it then became I quote Major Watkins, a Coldstream officer attached to the Staff of the XIII Corps, which is in front of us here. He told me that, on his Corps frontage alone (about 3,000 yards), 42,000 shells were sent over by our artillery in sixty-five minutes, or nearly 650 shells per minute. I hear we have 360 guns on this sector, including 8-inch, 12-inch, and 15-inch howitzers. At 7.30 the infantry went over.

Thornhill called for me between 9 and 9.30. We motored to Bronfay Farm, which is just behind Maricourt, opposite Mametz and Montauban. The battle was then in full swing, and the sight was inspiring and magnificent. From right to left, but particularly opposite the French, where the more rugged character of the country is especially adapted to spectacular effects, the whole horizon seemed to be on fire, the bursting shells blending with the smoke from the burning villages. As I have said before, this is essentially a district of long views. Never was there a field better suited for watching military operations, or for conducting them.

As we looked on, the shells from our heavier guns were screaming over our heads, but still, strange to say, the enemy was not replying behind our front line of the morning.

The wounded—those who could walk—were streaming back, some supported by others; crowds of them. Parties of German prisoners too—I counted over seventy in one group—were being marched under escort to the rear.

They were pitiful objects to look upon; some with beards; all unshaven and dirty; some big, some small with spectacles; most with bare heads; a few wounded; all unkempt, dejected, abject, and dazed. Some looked up as they saw us. Most hung their heads and gazed at the ground. As Thornhill said: "Though our ambition is to kill as many of these people as we possibly can, when you see them beaten, like that, with that look in their eyes, you can hardly restrain a feeling of pity. I suppose it is the English sporting instinct asserting itself."

We stayed half an hour or so at Bronfay; then, Thornhill remembering that we were what is here called "joy-riding," and becoming a little anxious about his car, we motored to other parts of the line, passing through Méaulte and Albert, where the statue on the Cathedral is beginning to look very shaky. Here we saw many more wounded, and more German prisoners. I stopped and spoke to some of the former, most of whom looked tired but cheerful. All were smoking the inevitable "fag." Then we came home, stopping at various points along the way to watch the progress of the battle. Our artillery was still busy, and I counted twenty English and French observation balloons up together. Not a single German balloon was to be seen. All had been driven from the sky, for the time being, by our wonderful airmen.

In the evening, once more, Thornhill came with his car, and we went towards the line. The scene had changed. In the morning the weather had been fine and clear. It was still fine, but, owing to the smoke and dust of the battle, there was now a thick haze. The cannonade had, for the time being, died away. With the exception of a little shelling far away to the right, all had become silent as the grave. One could only imagine our men hard at work in the trenches they had captured, converting them to their own use.

The German artillery scarcely replied to our bombardment of the past week, which must have been very exasperating to their infantry. They shelled our front-line trenches and did some damage, but, so far as this part of the line is concerned, they made no effort to silence the artillery or to block the roads. Even when the infantry attack commenced they failed to put up the usual "barrage." Probably, for the first time in the war, our supporting troops, helped by the undulations in the ground, were able to reach their positions without much difficulty.

It is said that the Germans were unprepared for an offensive in this locality; that the last place they expected to be attacked was opposite the point of contact between the French and British armies;—that, in consequence, they had no great concentration of artillery to meet our troops. If so, they must be blind. Our preparations have been so immense that any photograph from the air must have revealed them. We have made new railways and new roads. The whole landscape has been altered, to say nothing of the fact that, for weeks past, every valley has been filled with troops, horses, guns, and transport.

We have been continually surprised at the way in which the enemy has allowed our transport to crowd over roads which are within easy reach of his artillery, and under direct observation from his balloons and even the ground observation posts.

I hope and believe our people have got the best of them this time, but do not expect to get much definite news for a few days yet. The wounded I have seen have mostly been hit by machine-guns. Judging from the numerous loaded ambulances I have passed, there must, I fear, be many casualties.

It has been a wonderful day, and my first experience of a battle as a sightseer. I feel rather a beast for having done it in this way, but shall continue to see all I can of it, nevertheless, for the sake of the experience, which may be useful later.

July 2, 1916 (*Sunday*).   *Corbie.*
The wounded are still pouring into Corbie by ambulance, in French peasant carts whose owners have picked them up on the road, and on foot. The last arrive, straggling

along the road, white with dust, and generally bareheaded.
The town is beginning to reek of iodoform and carbolic acid.

July 4, 1916.   *Corbie.*

Yesterday morning Kirby Ellice came over to visit us,
and after seeing the Company at drill, he made a little
speech. He spoke of the high standard of discipline in the
Guards and the importance attached to drill, and he congratulated the men on their proficiency in both, and upon the
respect they had earned among the French with whom they
are billeted.

As an argument for strict discipline he quoted the
successes of the enemy, and said that, the day before, he had
watched a mixed party of German prisoners being marched
away from one of the "cages." In spite of all they had
gone through these men fell in smartly, he said, dressed,
and numbered, each turning his head as he did so, as our
cavalry do; then were marched off, as though on their own
parade ground, the words of command being given by one
of their own officers.

In the afternoon, with three of my officers, I visited the
battlefield of three days ago. We lorry-jumped to Bray.
From there we struck off on foot along the road towards
Mametz, one of the villages captured by our troops. The
fighting was still continuing in front, but in the ruined
village itself all was quiet. Our heavy guns were firing over
our heads as we walked, but beyond an occasional shrapnel
burst in the distance, the German artillery was quiescent,
and we were able to explore the surface in safety.

After proceeding 3½ miles we reached what last Saturday
was the British front line. It was very battered, and
scarcely recognizable as a fire-trench. Then we crossed
Noman's Land, where we found infantry at work, salving
equipment, and collecting the dead. Of the latter I
counted a hundred in one group—a pitiful sight!

Then we came to what had been the German wire
entanglements. Here our guns had certainly done their
work well. The wire was completely demolished. Not
one square yard had escaped the shells. Then we came to

the German fire-trench. It is difficult to understand how any living creature could have survived such bombardment. The trench was entirely wrecked, and so flattened that it could have given little if any cover at the end. Leigh Bennett,[1] who was with me and who has been fighting in Gallipoli, when he saw this—his first view of a French battlefield—said: "I see now that what we thought was heavy shelling in Gallipoli was mere child's play."

Fifty yards beyond the German fire-trench was their Support trench, and about the same distance further on, their Reserve trench. Both had suffered severely. The ground is strewn with unexploded shells of ours, mostly of heavy calibre.

I went into some of the dug-outs, but, as I had neither electric torch nor matches, it was not possible to see much. They are of varying depths, some being quite 20 feet below the surface, and are well made, the sides and roofs being strongly supported by timber. I saw only one that had more than one entrance, and it was on fire.

After exploring these remains of the German trenches we went on into Mametz village where living man was represented by the Salvage folk and a few infantry making their way up to the new front line. Scarcely a wall stands, and of the trees nothing remains but mangled twisted stumps. The ruins present an appalling and most gruesome picture of the havoc of war, seen fresh, which no pen or picture can describe. You must see it, and smell it, and hear the sounds, to understand. It brings a sort of sickening feeling to me even now, though I consider myself hardened to such sights.

To give an idea of the long period of time through which the line at this point has remained stationary, I may say that in Noman's Land I saw two skeletons, one in German uniform, and the other in the long since discarded red infantry breeches of the French.

July 5, 1916. *Corbie.*

About midday yesterday a thunderstorm burst out, and for a couple of hours there was torrential rain, so that the

[1] 2nd-Lieut. H. W. Leigh-Bennett, Coldstream Guards.

roads became like rivers. Thornhill and I motored to Bronfay Farm, and from there struck out on foot to our old front line. This brought us to the right of where I had been the day before.

The experience was practically a repetition of what I have described to you; the sordid scenes the same. The scaling ladders used by our troops to climb out of the trenches at the moment of assault were still in position—most suggestive to the imagination! The dead in many cases still lay where they had fallen. Less than a mile along the valley a furious fight was going on around Fricourt and Fricourt Wood. On our right the French were hard at it, and continued so throughout the night. For the time, I have seen enough of battlefields. I am "fed up" as a sightseer.

July 6, 1916.   *Bois des Tailles.*

I was up this morning at 5.30, and at 6.45 we marched from Corbie to rejoin the Entrenching Battalion in the Bois des Tailles.

In spite of my feelings of yesterday, after finding that Fellowes[1] (C.G.), who had just returned from conducting a draft to the Guards Division, wanted to see something of the battlefield, I took him to the right of the section I last visited.

We first went to Carnoy: then we followed the German and British trenches of the morning of July 1 past Montauban to the Talus Boisé. This section has been mined considerably, though with one exception—a huge mine which was exploded last Saturday—the craters are comparatively small. The ground, as usual, is vastly mutilated. I examined a good many of the German dug-outs. Many even of the deep ones had been blown in by our artillery fire, but all that I saw continued to demonstrate with what care the enemy had prepared his defences, and how strong was the line of fortifications through which our troops have forced their way.

I came across some officers of the 15th and 11th Hussars, with a party of men, burying Germans, most of whom they

[1] 2nd-Lieut. R. C. B. Fellowes (Coldstream Guards), killed in action August 21, 1918.

had to drag out of the dug-outs, where they lie, crunched up in fantastic attitudes: a very unpleasant duty after so long an interval.   As I looked down the steep staircase of one of the deep dug-outs, and saw a dead German standing on his head at the bottom, I thought: "Imagine if his mother could see him!"   I suppose our enemies, too, have mothers, to whom they are all the world.

I saw a big "minenwerfer" very cunningly concealed in a deep excavation.   A piece of paper was attached to it, with the following words: "Captured by the Minden boys"; i.e. the Suffolk Regiment, a battalion of which attacked at that point.

Our heavy artillery is being pushed forward and you never know where or when you may stumble into a battery.   Often the first intimation that one is there—for they are well concealed as a rule—is the crack of a gun, and the swish of a shell that feels like shattering your ear-drums.

On the way back Fellowes told me that a few days ago he overheard two privates wrangling about rations.   Said one: "Garn!   Do you call yourself a soldier?"   To which the other replied: "Leastways, I draws the pay as such."

One of my Sergeants brought me a message from Percy Clive, saying that he was well and hoped I was the same. He now commands one of the new battalions of the East Yorks Regiment, which attacked last Saturday at Fricourt, I believe.

July 8, 1916.   *Bois des Tailles.*
Yesterday I went off alone to visit Fricourt, which our troops captured last Monday.   There was a picture of the village two or three days ago in the *Daily Mirror*, which I saw yesterday.   The picture showed a church and a street of battered houses.   It was not the Fricourt of to-day, which has no church, nor even a house standing.   There remain just fragments of walls: that is all.

As you enter the village from this side you pass the cemetery.   The tombstones—practically all—have been shattered and scattered broadcast.   Scarcely a grave could be recognized by its nearest and dearest, save through its position. In one case, near the roadside, a shell has fallen upon one of those elaborate and rather pretentious family vaults so much in vogue in France, pulverizing the great black granite slab which covered it, and exposing the coffin shelves below. What a sudden and rude awakening for those sleeping bodies, and how undreamed of when they were laid in their highly respectable bourgeois tomb!

Heavy rain began to fall at midday, and continued in torrents at intervals throughout the afternoon, and all last night. I had gone to Fricourt to look for Percy Clive, but when I reached the place I found that heavy fighting was in progress before Mametz Wood, about a mile in front, and that his battalion was in it. So I had to postpone my visit.

The wounded were being carried back in streams, all covered from head to foot with the mud in which they had been fighting, slimy and glistening like seals. It looks more and more as if Hell cannot be much worse than what our infantry is going through at the present moment.

I mentioned to a machine-gun officer, whom I met, that I might be going on leave in a day or two, and should like a souvenir from Fricourt. Said he, "I think I can help you then," and took me to a place his men had just discovered. I have seen many dug-outs, but this beat them all. It might almost be described as an underground house, where instead of going upstairs you went down, by one flight after another, to the different stories. There were three floors, the deepest being 60 feet or more from the door by which I entered. The entrance hall—so to speak—was the brick cellar of a former house. There were two entrances, one of which, however, could only be recognized from the inside, since the doorway had been blown in. The other door, by which we entered, had been partly closed by a shell, a hole being left just big enough to crawl through on hands and knees.

The German occupants had evidently abandoned the place in a hurry, in the fear—entirely justified—that they might be buried alive if they stayed there. They had left everything behind. The floors were littered with every kind of thing, from heavy trench mortar bombs to grenades,

the size of an egg, and from steel helmets to underclothing.
Many rifles hung from the wooden walls of the first flight
of stairs. The nooks and corners of the rooms were occupied by sleeping-bunks, and from one of these I picked up
the French *Alphabet de Mademoiselle Lili*, par "un papa,"
delightfully illustrated, which I will send home to the
children.

As I returned to camp I passed many fresh troops on
their way up to the line. What a bad start for them in these
deluges of rain!

One meets nowadays on the roads many wagons returning from the direction of the line, loaded with "swab" equipment. The troops of the new army wear pieces of cloth of
different colours to distinguish their Divisions and Brigades.
A battalion—I think of Royal Fusiliers—which I saw
marching up, fresh and clean and full of life and vigour, a
day or two before July 1, had pieces of pink flannel over their
haversacks, displayed in such a way as to be recognizable in
battle by our aeroplanes.

A few days later I passed a wagonload of salved equipment returning from the line. It was interleaved with the
same pink flannel, now no longer fluttering gaily, but
sodden and bedraggled, and caked with sticky clay.

July 10, 1916.   *Bois des Tailles.*

Yesterday I went and explored the line of trenches
captured this week between Mametz and Fricourt. It is
one of the most mined sections of the whole of our front.
For a length of 800 yards a practically continuous line of
huge craters, some 50 feet deep at least, occupies the full
width of Noman's Land from the British to the German
parapet. Most of these contain water, which in some cases
is red with blood, even to-day, a week after the battle.

The contrast between the two front trenches is remarkable. Though the line has remained stationary so long,
ours gives the impression of a temporary halting-place; the
German of a permanent defence. The effect of the suicidal
German practice of having deep dug-outs in their front line
is illustrated here, for most contain dead, who never could

have fought, but must have been killed like rats in their holes. The havoc of our bombardment is wonderful, and greatly in excess of that done to our own trenches by the enemy artillery.

Many French dead—skeletons now—still lie unburied in Noman's Land, dating from the period before our troops took over this part of the line. I saw some even between the German fire and support trenches, which, one would have thought, the enemy would have buried for the sake of their own comfort, if for no other reason.

July 12, 1916.   *Bois des Tailles.*

German prisoners keep coming back all the time in driblets, and most of the cages hold a few. In one I passed to-day there were about a dozen—big, fine-looking, fit men —apparently quite happy, I must say, chatting and laughing among themselves, and smoking cigarettes and eating bully beef supplied to them by our soft-hearted soldiers, who, though fierce enough in action, seem to take delight in feeding their enemy and giving him smokes once they have him safely caged. I even saw one man go to the trouble of opening a tin of beef before handing it through the wires.

July 14, 1916.   *Bois des Tailles.*

In the early hours of this morning a great and, I hear, successful battle was fought in front of here, preceded by a tremendous bombardment which continued throughout the night.

This afternoon I visited the ruins of Montauban, which was captured by our troops on the 1st. The village is set on a hill, with long views in all directions. In front, in the distance, I could see the woods round the Bazentins, in which this morning's battle was fought, and where fighting was still in progress.

As General John Ponsonby used to say: "A battle three or four times as big as Waterloo is fought a few miles away, but nobody thinks it worth while to ring up and tell you the result";—and you, in London, hear much more quickly than we do;—if indeed the *result* can be gauged at all—for, in truth, bloody though they are, these almost daily battles represent but one move apiece in the deadly game. I was, however, told by several officers that some of our cavalry actually rode through the German line to-day, and there can be no doubt but that the enemy is at least considerably rattled, if not worse, and that the fighting of the past fortnight, though expensive, has gone in our favour.

I met the usual streams of wounded returning, but every one seemed optimistic and quite satisfied with the way things were going.

In two cases I saw prisoners being employed as stretcher-bearers, carrying out our wounded, which strikes me as an excellent innovation; and I also saw plenty of Germans in the cages, as well as a few being led in. In one cage I counted seventeen officers, and seven in another!

July 17, 1916. *Bois des Tailles.*

I took a working party to Carnoy to-day. While I was there a Tunnelling Officer asked me if I would like to see one of the German mines. Of course I said "Yes." There were several entrances—mostly blown in by our shell-fire, and we entered by an undamaged one from the enemy support trench.

First, we descended an incline to a vertical depth of about 15 feet below the surface. Then we climbed 60 feet further down a perpendicular ladder, through a shaft, so narrow that it was possible to rest one's back against the wall. From the bottom of this we followed a close-timbered tunnel to the "transversal" gallery, from which other galleries led towards our own front line. The excavation was in chalk, and perfectly dry. An electric cable (an inch in diameter) passed down the shaft, and the officer who escorted me told me that, when the workings were first entered, an electric plant (dynamo, petrol engine, etc.) had been found, which had since been salved.

By the time I saw them the galleries had been surveyed by our engineers, and, to satisfy their curiosity, connected up with our own, so that it was possible to walk from the German support line to ours, or vice versâ, at a depth of 75 or 80 feet below the surface. My guide told me that on

July 1, at a minute or two before zero (the moment of assault), his Company alone had exploded thirteen mines, beneath or near the German trenches!

I got a lift back to camp on an ambulance—with the usual cargo behind. I sat in front, and found myself beside a young private of the South African Brigade, wounded by a shell in the leg and ankle. He was all in a quiver. He had been lying out, waiting for the stretcher-bearers, from eight o'clock last night till this afternoon, and was in great pain. His Brigade had caught it very badly, and he said there were few of his battalion left. He spoke a good deal. His father, he said, had fought in the Matabele and Boer Wars, and is now fighting in East Africa, where also his brother is. He himself had come on to France from the S.W. African campaign. Before the war he was a hunter in the Transvaal and Rhodesia.

But he was very sleepy, having had no rest for three days, and he kept dropping off to sleep in the intervals of his conversation.

July 18, 1916.   *Bois des Tailles.*

We are in the midst of moving camp. So great has been the success of our troops, and so far away has our front line got from us, that, in order to be within reach of our work, we are moving about 4 miles forward from here. We shall then be in about the same position, relative to the front line, that we were in before.

July 19, 1916.   *Bois des Tailles.*

Captain George Lane (Coldstream Guards), who is Camp Commandant to the Guards Division, and Colonel Balfour, turned up to-day, having come over in a car to see this battlefield.

Kemes Lloyd and I went with them. We motored first to Albert; then to Fricourt. Then we walked along the line of craters to Mametz. From there we motored to Mametz Wood, which was the scene of very heavy and wonderful fighting a week or ten days ago. Here we were fortunate enough to come upon two French 75-mm. batteries in action, firing at top speed. I had always wished but never seen this before at close quarters. The 75 is the French field gun, and though it looks almost like a toy, is the best balanced and the most perfect of weapons, the terror of the enemy, and, worked as it is worked by the French gunners, is probably the quickest firing gun of its type in the field.

The Captain, a Frenchman possessing very striking features, after the "cease fire," seeing how interested we were, walked up to us, saluted grandly, then ordered one more round to be fired—"to demonstrate the mechanism"; then, saluting again, he picked up the last shell-case, and, with a bow, offered it to Colonel Balfour. It was a pretty little piece of by-play, and I shall never forget his face, or the grandiloquent manner in which he presented the souvenir.

July 21, 1916.   *Near Fricourt.*

Yesterday, I was at work, all day, on what has now become one of our main lines of communication in these parts, beginning to convert a quagmire into a road fit for transport of the heaviest kind.

The conditions were something like what it would be if one were repairing Piccadilly during the height of the season without being allowed the privilege of roping off half the street in that aggravating way they have in London. In short, traffic innumerable was passing to and fro all the time.

Part of the backward traffic consisted of a unit of a famous New Army Division—the Highland Brigade—in course of relief from the battle. They have an advantage over us in that when they come out they are met by their bagpipes and drums. Each Company is preceded by pipers.

It was a sad sight to watch them yesterday, however, because scarcely a Company was more than 60 or 80 strong—compared probably with the 180 they had taken into action three days previously; but it was inspiring to see these men. On their faces they showed little sign of the appalling ordeal they had undergone.

The weather to-day has been gorgeous, and the enemy aeroplanes have taken advantage of it and become active. Our anti-aircraft gunners are active too, and hundreds of little puffs from their bursting shells speckle the blue sky.

July 24, 1916.   *Near Fricourt.*

How sad the world is! One of my men has just been before me, almost in tears. He handed me a letter, just received, telling him that the eldest of his two little girls has been run over and killed by a motor-car. He has been out here, and has not seen his family since August last year! I luckily struck the Commanding Officer at an opportune moment, and he has promised to forward an application for special leave for this man; but it will probably fail.

There are so many hard cases, and the Higher Authorities are likely to argue, in this one, that, since the child is dead, the father can do no good by going home;—which is logical, if brutal.

There is a heavy bombardment to-night, as usual nowadays.

July 25, 1916.   *Near Fricourt.*

This morning, I walked with two other C.G. Officers to a point opposite Contalmaison and Poziéres, and watched a terrific bombardment of the latter place by the enemy's artillery.

The Australians and some of our Territorials had attacked once more during the night, and, I hear, had gained the remainder of the village. Hence the fury of the enemy, whose heaviest shells were crashing tempestuously against the ruins, sending up great clouds of earth and brickdust, and producing a Gehenna-like impression, which I confess I felt thankful to be clear of.

Then, my companions being bent on sightseeing turned off to the left, while I struck out alone, in the opposite direction, across country, towards Carnoy, where I had some men at work.

I chose the safest route—as I thought! I worked my way to Mametz Wood; then past Bazentin Wood to Flat-iron Copse, and on through Caterpillar Wood.

Then, suddenly, the enemy opened one of those promiscuous hurricane bombardments, and I found myself in the middle of the picture! I was out in the open when it started, but continued in the direction I was going, trying to look dignified, though in reality feeling rather foolish as I walked among the flying pieces towards some heads which I saw silhouetted against the skyline, some 400 yards away.

These I found belonged to two Gunner Officers and about five men who were sheltering in a trench. By the time I reached them the shelling had become heavy. They invited me into an old German observation post which they were using as a telephone dug-out, and which, being covered with a layer of rails and sandbags, was at least splinter-proof.

I went in, expecting to remain perhaps a quarter of an hour. I stayed, marooned, for 3½ hours! Shells of every calibre—thousands of them, often many in the air together, high explosive and shrapnel—burst on the ground and in the air. They plunged all around our little shelter. One burst on the parapet, 3 feet from the door; another (a dud) landed a foot or two short of the dug-out, penetrated deep into the ground, and made the place shiver. Over and over again, bits of steel and a deluge of soil from a bursting shell rattled into the trench outside. I cannot tell you how annoyed I felt with myself for having got caught in so awkward a situation. What folly to get killed sightseeing, and what a fool to have risked it just as I was going home on leave!

At last there was a lull. One of the men suggested that Fritz had "packed up." I climbed out of the trench and made my way onwards, over the surface. Almost immediately the shelling started again (indeed, an hour later, I saw it from the distance, still going strong), but I determined to chance it this time, and in half an hour or less I found myself amid silent surroundings, among the ruins of Mametz. Here a German shell last night blew up one of our ammunition dumps. I came upon the result—a big crater and a sea of blackened shell-cases.

It was very restful to be out of the shelling, which had been really hot, and reminiscent of the worst days of last September and October. At one time I thought the enemy was going to step in and settle once for all the question of my leave, about which I have already had many disappointments. What a rude conclusion to all the official correspondence there has been on this vexed subject!

Shall I analyse my sensations during a long and heavy bombardment? If I tried to do so I think I should say that for the first hour the feeling is one of apprehension: for the second, of indifference; and, for the third and after, of sleepiness. The soporific effect of a bombardment is very strange.

I reached Carnoy all right, just as my men were being marched away, and got back to camp to find that I had struck the one bad "patch" of that afternoon, outside Poziéres, and that Kirby Ellice from a distant eminence had been making a sketch of the bombardment in which I had so unwillingly figured.

It is quite obvious that the Germans have brought up more artillery since this battle began on July 1.

July 26, 1916.   *Near Fricourt.*

My servant is always asking me to take him with me, "in case," as he puts it, "anything should happen to me." So to-day I took him to Carnoy. He is like a wild man, and is always thirsting to "pop over the sandbags." He assured me this morning that if ever I have to do so (which it begins to seem doubtful if I ever shall) he would like to be by my side; and this, I think, is not mere talk.

He is a very gallant fellow, and last year I believe was recommended for a decoration, though it was refused (he says) because of his previous character. He has not always been a paragon of virtue. But what a reason, if true, to refuse a man recognition of his bravery! He has been out ever since August, 1914, and was at Landrecies in the 3rd Battalion. He has never been more than a private, though he has soldiered all his life, having enlisted at sixteen under a fictitious age. His father claimed him back on that occasion. He is now twenty-six. He told me to-day that he would never be a corporal. Knowing that many men refuse the stripes for various reasons, I asked him—what was his? He answered, characteristically,—that it was because he would never then be able to ask even his best friend, if the latter were a private, to go into a pub with him and have a drink!

He describes to me his "crimes," which, according to him, were mere peccadilloes, such as "Looking contemptuously at the sergeant-major"! but I have little doubt that he has given much trouble on occasion.

His conversation is sometimes, but not always, entertaining. He rattles on, scarcely ever remaining silent for more than a minute or two. A few days ago I sent him into Corbie to buy some things. On his return I asked him if he had seen the people with whom I had been billeted while there.

"Yes," he said, "he had seen the daughter" (who, by the way, has something wrong with her eyes), and that "three R.A.M.C. doctors were just arriving to be billeted in the house."

I asked him how the girl liked the idea of that.

"Oh," she said, "it'll be very bon for me," replied he.

I gathered that she (or rather he, because I am quite sure he did not understand a word of what she really said) intended to imply that the advent of the doctors might mean free treatment for her eyes!

This morning I took him along the old German front line, past the craters, where the whole surface has been so violently distorted by the mining operations and the shell-fire of nearly two years, and where the trenches are battered almost flat.

"They seem to have caught it badly here," I said.

"Yes, sir," he replied. "They've certainly had something to go on with."

We passed a tunnelling company encamped. He said that some of our transferred men were there, so I told him to go and find out if there were any of my old Company of the 1st Battalion among them.

He immediately beckoned to a man with bright red hair, calling out, "Hey, Ginger." This man, by luck, turned out to be an old No. 4 Company man, who had been transferred from us on the road to Loos.

As we walked away, since he appeared to be on such

intimate terms with this man, I asked him his name, which I had forgotten.

He said, "he did not know," never having met him before. "I had to call him something, sir," he said, "so I called him Ginger."

We passed a group of four French skeletons—or rather what had been skeletons till the receding tide of war left them exposed to the traffic in the "fairway." Till July 1 they had lain undisturbed in Noman's Land, in their old uniforms of two years ago. To-day, after the passage of many troops, their bones are scattered, though identifiable by the scarlet rags which still adhere. To-morrow I shall send my servant to bury them, as well as any others he can find. I know of many.

July 28, 1916. *Near Fricourt.*

A message came this evening, saying that I have been granted seven days' leave;—papers arriving to-morrow. So I shall leave here on Sunday morning.

I have a German rifle in my tent which I thought of bringing home, in spite of the regulations to the contrary, but I abandoned the idea on account of its bulkiness. Upon telling my servant this to-day, he offered to take the rifle home for me, when he goes on leave. I asked him how he proposed to do it, adding that he would certainly be stopped.

"I should carry it instead of my own rifle, sir," he said.

"And how would you account for not having a rifle on landing in France again, after your leave?" I asked.

"Oh," said he, with a grin, "you've got to risk something in this world if you are going to have any success";—"You should just see me play nap, sir!"

* * * * *

August 9, 1916. *Near Fricourt.*

I left Boulogne at nine o'clock on Monday evening, and spent most of the night in a crowded train, carrying French troops. The latter filled even the 1st-class carriages,— "poilus"—rather merry—returning to the trenches after six days' "permission"—but very nice.

The train was very late. At 3 a.m. I made the unfortunate mistake of getting out in the dark at a station the name of which sounded to my British ear like Heilly—which would have suited me well—and which had almost the same spelling. But it was not my station! Fortunately, however, a goods train came along a few minutes later, so I climbed on to that, and reached Amiens, where I managed to get a bed, though it was then nearly four o'clock.

Yesterday, I worked my way back here—about 25 miles—by road, getting lifts on sundry motor-cars and an ambulance, and walking a mile or two of the way. To finish up with I was picked up by the Camp Commandant of Rollo's Division, who sent me right up to this camp on his car.

August 13, 1916.   *Near Fricourt.*

Yesterday afternoon I visited the Guards Division, which lately moved to this area.

Just as I was arriving in a Staff car on which I had been given a lift, I passed Humphrey de Trafford and Hugh Kennedy.[1] They were just going out riding. Humphrey is leaving to take over the Adjutancy of the Machine-gun School at Grantham, and had been left out of the trenches, where the rest of the 1st Battalion were.

He walked with me to Divisional Headquarters, where I saw Geoffrey Feilding, and several of his staff.

Geoffrey was in the best of form. He lent me his car to go and see General John Ponsonby, inviting me to return to dinner at 8.15. It was the first of three invitations I had to dine. So I motored off to John Ponsonby's Headquarters and had a great welcome from the General and several others who were there—Guy Baring, who still commands the 1st Battalion, Sherrard Godman, commanding the 1st Scots Guards, "Boy" Brooke,[2] now commanding the 3rd Grenadiers, "Bart" Bartholomew,[3] and others.

They were just sitting down to a Commanding Officers'

---

[1] Lord Hugh Kennedy, M.C., Coldstream Guards.

[2] Now Brigadier B. N. Sergison-Brooke, C.M.G., D.S.O.

[3] Captain Claude Bartholomew, M.C., Scots Guards, killed in action September 15, 1916.

Conference, so I did not stay long.   Then I went back to Divisional Headquarters, where I sat with Geoffrey, in his hut, for half an hour before going into dinner.

After dinner Geoffrey sent me home in his car.   No headlights are allowed, so, as a heavy bombardment was in progress all along the front, the flashes of the guns were very vivid and imposing.   To-night is quiet.   It is a night of flares—white and coloured, and we have been sitting out since dinner, watching what might almost have been a professional firework show.

August 18, 1916. *Near Fricourt.*

This afternoon I watched a huge battle between Martin-puich and Guillemont.   I watched from the high ground just south-east of Fricourt, which commands a wonderful view of the country for a long distance in front—from a spot which was visited by the King when he was here, and is now known as King George's Hill.

The preliminary bombardment, which had continued all through last night and this morning, was greatly intensified, and smoke clouds were turned loose shortly before 2.45 p.m., which was the time appointed for the infantry assault. The latter took place punctually, as was very evident from the simultaneous and sudden crowding of the sky with the bursting shrapnel of the German barrage.   Then Hell pre-vailed till the horizon became blotted out by smoke and dust. It was a terrible sight.   To the onlooker on these occa-sions, as I have said before, it seems almost impossible that any living creature can be in it and survive.   But that is not so.

After half an hour the shelling subsided to some extent, though it was renewed about five o'clock on another section of the front.

It was a big show—far bigger, I daresay, than anyone might suppose from reading the newspaper reports of it which will no doubt appear to-morrow.

Later.   I hope to-day was a success.   Anyhow, I have already seen a batch of prisoners (wounded) in the cage below this camp.

Unwounded German prisoners are employed on the

roads in safe places several miles behind the line. I saw a good many the other day at Corbie. It was funny to see parties of them—great big fellows, including Prussian Guards—being shepherded by our "Bantams." The latter, with their top-heavy rifles and fixed bayonets, look very businesslike, all the same, in spite of their small stature.

August 21, 1916. *Near Fricourt.*

The following are the British and German accounts of the battle which, as I described to you, I watched last Friday, the 18th. You have probably read them in the paper, but may not have recognized them as descriptions of the same battle. Indeed, it is difficult to do so, having regard to the great divergence between the two points of view.

August 19, 1916. *Saturday.*

BRITISH OFFICIAL

3.7 p.m.—Our success reported last night has been maintained and extended.

During the night the enemy delivered several very determined counter-attacks against the positions which we had captured. Except on our extreme right, where the enemy regained a little ground, these counter-attacks were everywhere repulsed.

From High Wood to the point where we join up with the French we have advanced our line over a frontage of more than 2 miles for a distance varying between 200 yards and 600 yards.

We now hold the western outskirts of Guillemont, and a line thence northwards to midway between Delville Wood and Ginchy; also the Orchards north of Longueval.

Between High Wood and the Albert-Bapaume Road we have captured some hundreds of yards of enemy trench.

East and south-east of Mouquet Farm we have advanced our line by some 300 yards.

Between Ovillers and Thiepval we have pushed forward on a front of over half a mile. As a result of these operations several hundred prisoners have been taken by us.

August 19, 1916.   *Berlin, Saturday Afternoon.*
GERMAN OFFICIAL

Our brave troops yesterday victoriously resisted with self-sacrificing tenacity a stupendous effort on the part of our combined enemy.

At about the same time in the afternoon, after artillery preparation, which increased to the utmost violence, Anglo-French masses advanced to the assault to the north of the Somme on the Ovillers-Fleury front over a section of about 20 kilometres, whilst very considerable French forces advanced on the right bank of the Meuse against the Thiaumont-Fleury section and against our positions in the Chapitre and Berg Woods.

North of the Somme the battle raged far into the night. At several points the enemy penetrated into our first line of trenches and was driven out again.

Trench sections captured on both sides of Guillemont—which remains firmly in our hands—were occupied. Between Guillemont and Maurepas we have somewhat shortened during the night our salient line in accordance with our plans.

The enemy has paid with tremendous sanguinary losses for his efforts, which, on the whole, have failed. Our Guards—Rhenish, Bavarian, Saxon, and Wurtemberg troops—maintained their positions unshaken.

On the right bank of the Meuse the repeated French assaults broke down with heavy losses to the enemy after bitter fighting at certain points.

At Fleury village fighting still continues. In the eastern sector of Chapitre Wood over 100 prisoners were taken during a counter-attack.

In the Berg Wood we left some completely destroyed advanced trench sections in possession of the enemy.—*Wireless Press.*

August 21, 1916.   *Near Fricourt.*

I met on the road and rode back yesterday with a major commanding a Horse Artillery (6-gun) battery. He told me he fired 4,000 rounds in eighteen hours;—which gives some idea of the shooting that is going on at present.

I saw the Prince of Wales to-day.

August 23, 1916.   *Near Fricourt.*

This evening, to my joy, I have received orders to rejoin the Guards Division (starting at seven to-morrow morning).

August 25, 1916.   *Naours.*

I was up at 5.45 yesterday morning, to catch the train at Méricourt—the railhead of the Entrenching Battalion—at 8.12 a.m.

Five other officers were with me, including, however, only one Coldstreamer (Walpole). We had an early lunch at Amiens, and afterwards, there being no immediate train out, we managed luckily to find a Flying Corps tender going our way, which brought Walpole, myself, our servants and kits to the Guards Divisional Headquarters at Vignacourt, where we found Geoffrey Feilding and his Staff having lunch.

They invited us in, and I was told that an application had been forwarded for me to go through a course, with a view to my becoming Divisional Trench Mortar Officer. I met Colonel "Billy" Darell, George Lane, Dalkeith, Seymour, Jack Stirling[1] (who was passing), and others. Darell afterwards motored me viâ the different Brigade Headquarters, which he was visiting, and finally dropped me here with the 1st Battalion.

I have met so many friends that it would bore you if I named them all. I had tea with Colonel Skeffington Smith (4th Battalion), and in the evening met General John Ponsonby, who took me along with him for a walk. He said he had heard about the Trench Mortar proposal, and gave me some advice as to the duties it would entail.

The battalion moves at two o'clock this afternoon, and at 7 p.m. we detrain at the same station where I entrained yesterday; so that I shall have done about thirty-six hours' travelling and hanging about, to reach the exact spot I started from!

I saw Father Knapp (you will remember he comes from the Carmelites in Church Street). He has the Military Cross now. He is a splendid fellow, and has been with the 2nd Irish

[1] Now Lieut.-Col. J. A. Stirling, D.S.O., M.C. (late Scots Guards).

Guards ever since Loos. He said he was going to give Benediction at seven o'clock (last night) at the village church. So I went. It is a beautiful church—inside and out;—I think almost the prettiest *small* church I have seen in France. But perhaps I say that because I am in such a happy mood at getting back to the Division.

August 26, 1916.   *Morlancourt.*

We marched 4 miles to the station at Canaples, yesterday, starting at 2 p.m. I marched at the rear of the battalion with Humphrey de Trafford, who, until he leaves for Windsor, is a supernumerary, like myself. He and I stood on the short causeway leading to the village church as the battalion moved off, and, as No. 4 Company went by, I was greeted by broad grins of recognition by the men—that is to say those of them who were with me last year.

All through the day I kept meeting old friends—officers, N.C.O.'s and men. It is surprising what a change eight months have made in some of the younger ones. I left them boys, and return to find them men.

We had a fearful railway journey—I think we could have marched as quickly—but in the end, after a final wait of some hours in the dark a few miles short of our destination, we reached Méricourt, and arrived at our billets here, after a march of 3½ to 4 miles, at 11.30 p.m. It was very dark. It was nice to march with the battalion again, and gave me quite a "homey" feeling, bringing back many recollections of last year.

August 29, 1916.   *Morlancourt.*

Yesterday morning I went to early Communion. Crowds of soldiers of the Division were there, as also had been the case the day before. Father Knapp has certainly succeeded in whipping up his flock. He is now assisted by another priest. He is a very successful Chaplain, has a very pleasing manner, and is very popular with the men. His brother was with me in Matabeleland, but was killed afterwards, in the Boer War.

Last night I dined with the Brigadier (General John Ponsonby). His latest joke is that if anyone makes a "faux pas" in conversation he has to stand on a chair, the unfortunate remark being recorded against him in a book which is kept for the purpose. Most people fall into the trap. I did not escape. I said I had just read a splendid novel—referring to the *Turnstile*, by Mason. They asked me where it was. I said I had sent it to you. The Brigadier at once said this was a case for "the chair." I explained, by way of excuse, that you were "in the wilds" of England, thirsting for literature, which you could not get. I was asked to explain what I meant by "in the wilds." I said Leicestershire. This just put the lid on it. Of course, John Ponsonby was delighted with his joke.

I sat next to him and told him how I had got side-tracked in the Entrenching Battalion. He said he had no idea that I was in France till he saw me a fortnight ago,—which shows how little people know of one another's movements here. He suggested that I ought to get command of one of the New Army battalions, and asked me to come round this morning to talk it over. This I did. I feel I cannot decide upon this point myself. I do not want to leave the Division. But it was arranged that he should discuss the whole thing with Geoffrey, whom he was going to see to-day.

August 30, 1916. *Morlancourt.*

I told you in my letter of yesterday how things stood with regard to myself. This afternoon I got a message to go and see the Brigadier as soon as possible. He told me he had had a talk with Geoffrey, and also with Guy Baring. Geoffrey, apparently, had approved of the idea of a battalion for me, and thought it would be much to my advantage, and that I would do it well. The Brigadier added that it is practically certain that I shall be offered the job of Divisional Trench Mortar Officer, but they are now also going to write up and recommend me for the command of a battalion, which, in any case, even if the recommendation succeeds, will involve a delay of a few weeks—which will give us time to decide.

So you see things are going well with me. Moreover, you need have no anxiety, because it is hardly likely that my new battalion (if I get it) will have to make any more attacks this year. Indeed, it is extremely unlikely, because the attacking season will be practically over by the time I get there.

This battalion went out to practise open fighting this morning. I rode with the Colonel, but it poured with rain, and, when we were all wet through, it was decided to give it up.

I wonder what you will think of my news to-day. I have always said before that I would rather command a Coldstream Company than a battalion elsewhere. But the difficulty is my age. There is no getting away from the fact that, although physically I am well fitted for the strain and hardships, I am, in years, very old as Company Commanders go. I am double the age of all or nearly all the other Company Commanders of the Division, and there is practically no chance of promotion here.

Do write and tell me what you think.

September 1, 1916. *Morlancourt.*

The air is thick with balloons and aeroplanes nowadays. Yesterday I counted thirty-three English and French, and three German balloons up at once.

In addition, there must have been thirty aeroplanes at least, or sixty-six in all. And, if I had had glasses, I could no doubt have seen more.

September 3, 1916 (*Sunday*). *Morlancourt.*

Still no orders. Bewicke-Copley[1] has just come out again, and he and I are riding out this afternoon to a place where Geoffrey is inspecting ideas from the different Brigades with a view to determining how best the men can be equipped for the attack.

This morning (Sunday), at ten o'clock, I went to Mass. As I was leaving the Church I met Cecil Trafford, who asked me to his mess (Headquarters—1st Scots Guards).

The latter is a house with a sort of garden or small yard in front of it. As we were crossing this there was a sudden loud explosion, and bits flew through the air about us. We looked round and saw Leach, the bombing officer of the battalion (who had just come from visiting my own mess),

[1] 2nd-Lieut. R. L. C. Bewicke-Copley, killed in action December 21, 1916.

on the ground, 4 or 5 yards away. He lay on his back, in a pool of blood, his arms outstretched and both his hands blown off. His brother officers soon began to collect around him, so I left, but I do not think he then had more than a short time to live.

Later. I have learnt some particulars about poor Leach's accident. He was detonating a bomb in the orderly room, which is a shed opening on to the yard, when the safety-pin slipped. Seeing that it was going to explode, and some of his men being in the shed, after ordering them to lie down, he picked up the bomb and dashed outside to get rid of it. He then had less than four seconds in which to decide what to do. I can only suppose that seeing Cecil and myself in the middle of the yard he came to the conclusion that his one chance of throwing it safely away was gone.

So he turned his back to us, faced the wall, and hugging the bomb in his hands, allowed it to explode between his body and the wall.

It is impossible to speak much of such courage and self-sacrifice. He is since dead. He was only twenty-two.

September 4, 1916 (Later).   *Morlancourt.*

For better or for worse I have some interesting news for you to-day, though I wish I had had an opportunity of talking it over with you beforehand.

This afternoon, after tea with No. 2 Company, Bewicke-Copley and I rode to see the Grenadier Boxing Competitions. I rode a "hairy" on a snaffle, which tried to bolt most of the way. Half-way, we passed in the distance two Staff Officers, one of whom called to me. They turned out to be Colonel "Billy" Darell and Hermon Hodge. The former told me that I had been recommended for the command of one of the New Army battalions, and that to-day, in running through the correspondence, he had seen that I had been appointed to a battalion of the Connaught Rangers. It was not official yet: he had only had time to glance at the papers; and not even Geoffrey knew about it.

After the boxing I called on John Ponsonby and told him what Darell had told me. He is confident—and so, he told me, is Geoffrey, with whom he has again discussed the matter—that I shall do right to accept. Being only a Special Reserve officer, you see, and an amateur soldier at that, I can never rise higher than a Company Commander here.

I then returned to the mess, where I found "Bing" Hopwood, who, in Baring's absence, is commanding the battalion. I told him also what I had heard, and he and I went for an hour's walk, and talked things over. He is an extraordinarily silent fellow, and in the early days of our acquaintanceship I confess I never understood him. But the last fortnight, living with him, I have got to know him, and have acquired great confidence in him, like every one else. He was very congratulatory and said a command was miles better than to be Divisional Trench Mortar Officer (which—he said—is a difficult and rather unsatisfactory job).

As I have said, I do so wish I could have talked it over with you, and got your opinion. It would have been such a help to me could I have done so. As it is, I feel very diffident as to whether I can command a battalion efficiently—let alone a battalion of Irishmen, of whose characteristics I am completely ignorant. You must continue to pray hard for me, and that whatever I may have to do I do it well;—and all will come right, I am sure. It will be a strange feeling, jumping up to find myself a Colonel.

All this is quite unofficial, of course, but I will write again immediately I hear anything definite.

We have, since last night, been under three hours' notice to move.

It is raining hard.

September 5, 1916. *Morlancourt.*

To-night I have been with others to see an exhibition of the "Somme film," which was shown upon a screen, erected in a muddy field under the open sky. Presumably by way of contrast Charlie Chaplin was also to have appeared, and I confess it was chiefly him I went to see. However, I came too late, and saw only the more harrowing part of the entertainment.

This battle film is really a wonderful and most realistic production, but must of necessity be wanting in that the battle is fought in silence, and, moreover, that the most unpleasant part—the machine-gun and rifle fire—is entirely eliminated. Of the actual "frightfulness" of war all that one sees is the bursting shells; and perhaps it is as well. I have said that the battle is fought in silence; but no, on this occasion the roar of real battle was loudly audible in the distance.

I must say that at first the wisdom of showing such a film to soldiers on the brink of a battle in which they are to play the part of attackers struck me as questionable. However, on my way home, my mind was set at rest upon this point by a conversation I overheard between two recruits who were walking behind me.

Said one, "As to reality, now you knows what you've got to fice. If it was left to the imagination you might think all sorts of silly b—— things."

I wonder where his imagination would have led him had he not seen the Cinema. Would it, do you think, have gone beyond the reality? Hell itself could hardly do so. I think sometimes that people who have not seen must find it difficult to comprehend how undisturbed life in the trenches can be on occasion: equally, how terrible can be the battle.

September 6, 1916. *Morlancourt.*

There was Brigade Battle training to-day, and, on my return to billets, I found my orders. I am to assume temporary command of the 6th Connaught Rangers, belonging to the 47th Brigade, 16th (South Irish) Division, who, I find, are not far from here, at Carnoy—a place I knew well when I was with the Entrenching Battalion, as you will remember. It is the only battalion of the Connaught Rangers on the Western Front, and I am to join it this afternoon.

I will write again to-morrow, if I get the chance, and tell you how things are going.

September 7, 1916. *Carnoy.*

I reported to my new Brigadier (47th Brigade) last evening. He is General George Pereira,[1] Grenadier Guards— an elder brother of Cecil Pereira,[2] whom you know.

---

[1] Brig.-Gen. George Pereira, C.B., C.M.G., D.S.O.
[2] Now Maj.-Gen. Sir Cecil Pereira, K.C.B., C.M.G.

I had tea and dinner with him, and found that he knows many of the family well. He has told me to put up a Major's crowns. I am of course on probation, and I have not an easy task before me; therefore, I shall require all your prayers. What would I not give for the opportunity of a few words with you! I have hated having to make this great change without consulting you, and even without your knowledge.

My new battalion is one of the two which captured Guillemont four days ago:—as hard a nut to crack as there has been in this battle, so far. It was the battalion's first attack, so it has not done badly; though the casualties have been heavy, both the Colonel and Second in Command having been killed.

I think we shall very soon be going out for a long rest, which I understand is overdue.

September 7, 1916 (*Evening*).   *Carnoy.*

My new battalion, or rather the remnant of it, was bivouacking when I joined it, on a slope alongside the ruins of Carnoy, amid a plague of flies, reduced (apart from officers) to 365 other ranks, and very tired after the capture of Guillemont, in which it had taken a prominent and successful part, though the toll had been so heavy.

Since General John Ponsonby had first suggested the possibility of my being appointed to the command of a New Army battalion, I had hoped that I should perhaps be allowed a week or two with the officers and men, to get to know something of them before taking them into action: and certainly, in ordinary times, one would not expect a battalion straight out of one exhausting attack, and so punished as was this one, to be ordered back, without rest, into another. Yet such is the case.

To-day, within twenty-four hours of assuming command, I am to move up in front of Ginchy, preparatory to attacking that village the day after to-morrow. My orders are to take 200 fighting men, plus signallers and Battalion Headquarters;—about 250, all told.

The few remaining are to be left behind, as a carrying party, to keep the fighting line supplied with water (a great difficulty nowadays) and ammunition.

September 8, 1916.   *In Trenches, facing Ginchy.*

At 5.50 last evening I paraded my 250 Irishmen, who, before moving off, were addressed by the Senior Chaplain of the Division. Then, kneeling down in the ranks, all received General Absolution:—after which we started to move forward, timing our arrival at Bernafay Wood for 8.20, when it would be dark.

At Bernafay Wood we were met by a guide, who led us through Trones Wood—that evil place of which doubtless you have formed your own conception from the newspaper descriptions of the past two months. Thence, to what once was Guillemont.

All former bombardments are eclipsed by the scene here. Last year, in the villages that had been most heavily bombarded, a few shattered houses still stood, as a rule: last month, occasionally, a wall survived. But to-day, at Guillemont, it is almost literally true to say that not a brick or stone remains intact. Indeed, not a brick or stone is to be seen, except it has been churned up by a bursting shell. Not a tree stands. Not a square foot of surface has escaped mutilation. There is nothing but the mud and the gaping shell-holes;—a chaotic wilderness of shell-holes, rim overlapping rim;—and, in the bottom of many, the bodies of the dead. Having reached this melancholy spot, we left the cover of a battered trench which we had followed since leaving Trones Wood, and took to the open.

The guide was leading. I came next, and was followed by the rest of the party in single file. The moon shone brightly, and, as the enemy kept sending up flares from his trenches at intervals of a minute or less, our surroundings were constantly illuminated, and the meandering line of steel helmets flickered, rather too conspicuously, as it bobbed up and down in crossing the shell-holes.

I do not know if the Germans saw it or not. They soon started shelling, but as the ground we were passing over is

HIGH STREET, GUILLEMONT
September, 1916

commonly being shelled, there was nothing peculiar in that. We plodded on.

The guide soon began to show signs of uncertainty. I asked him if he had lost his bearings—a not uncommon thing on these occasions. He admitted that he had. I crawled past the body of a dead German soldier into the doorway of a shattered dug-out, and with an electric torch studied the map.

As we started off again the shelling increased, and once I was hit by a small splinter on the chest, which stung. The men began to bunch in the shell-holes. They are brave enough, but they are untrained; and 91 of my 200 fighting men were from a new draft, which had only just joined the battalion.

I shall not forget the hours which followed. Remember, I had only the slightest acquaintance with the officers, and as for the rank and file I did not know them at all;—nor they me.

The shells were now dropping very close. One fell into a group of my men, killing seven and wounding about the same number. My guide was hit and dropped a yard or two in front of me. I told him to lie there, and I would have a stretcher sent for him: but he pulled himself together, saying, "It's all right, sir," and struggled on.

About 10.30 p.m. we reached our destination—only to find the rear Company detached and missing, as well as the medical officer and my servant. However, they turned up just before daybreak, having spent the night wandering among the shell-holes.

At the position of assembly, which was at the junction between the Guillemont-Combles road (known officially as Mount Street) and the sunken road leading to Ginchy, we found things in a state of considerable confusion. The battalion we had come to relieve had apparently thought it unnecessary to await our arrival, and as, consequently, there was no one to allot the few shallow trenches that were available, a sort of general scramble was going on, each officer being naturally anxious to get his own men under cover, before the daylight of the morning should reveal them to the enemy.

Luckily, the enemy was now quiet, and before it was light enough to see, the troops were disposed more or less in their "jumping off" positions, where they were to wait some forty hours or more for "Zero"—the moment of attack.

During the night a wounded Saxon crept into the trench close by me and I sent him to the rear.

September 9, 1916.   *In Trenches, facing Ginchy.*

We spent yesterday in getting ready for the attack, and this morning (Saturday), between eight and nine o'clock, our artillery began to bombard the German lines.

This preliminary bombardment, in so far as I have observed it, has, up to the present, been disappointing, a very large proportion (about half) of the shells having failed to explode. Many, too, have fallen short, some upon my parapet, and one has fallen into the trench, wounding four of my men. I have reported these cases to the rear as they have occurred.

The trenches in which we are waiting are very restricted and so irregular in form that it has been possible only by distributing the Companies in scattered portions, and by dovetailing them with another battalion, to fit them in at all. Things have not been made easier by the fact that my adjutant went sick yesterday with trench fever and had to be sent down. In his place I have appointed young Jourdain—a boy of 18½—who seems to be possessed of wisdom far beyond his years.

My headquarters are in a trench which runs alongside the sunken road, and which was German till a few days ago. There is a hole in the side (marked in pencil with the name of a German soldier)—about 4 feet square by 8 feet deep, which serves as a sleeping-place for two or three at a time. The first German trench is some 300 yards in front, and has been reported by the patrols of the battalion that preceded us to be unoccupied, or only lightly held. We shall know more about this to-morrow.

On our left front, some 750 yards away, is the village

of Ginchy: on the right is Leuze Wood (universally known among our people as Lousy Wood).

September 10, 1916. *Happy Valley.*

It is over. After a wait of forty-two hours, the leading Companies of the Brigade went over the parapet yesterday afternoon at forty-seven minutes past four o'clock.

The scheduled moment of "Zero," as a matter of fact, was two minutes earlier, but at the last moment orders came to postpone the assault two minutes, to give time for a final intensive bombardment of the German lines.

Perhaps there were good reasons for this, though it might be thought by the critical, that a bombardment would be as effective during the two minutes preceding, as those following Zero; and, having regard to the difficulty of insuring the delivery of messages to the front line at such times as these, that it would have been wiser to avoid interference with the Infantry Time-table.

The prearranged plan was that the 6th Royal Irish Regiment on the right and the 8th Royal Munster Fusiliers on the left should lead the attack for the 47th Brigade, in four waves, at distances of 50 paces, and that they should be followed, at 15 paces, by two more waves, composed of the 6th Connaught Rangers, with one Company of the 7th Leinster Regiment and two of the 11th Hampshire (Pioneers). The 168th Brigade was to be on our right.

The right battalion of the 48th Brigade—which like ourselves belongs to the Irish Division—to our immediate left, moved forward at 4.45, having, presumably, failed to hear of the postponement.

I cannot say whether this influenced our artillery, and caused them to abandon or to modify the intended last two minutes of "intensive" bombardment, though it certainly had the effect of bringing on the enemy's counter-barrage before its time. I can say that on my immediate front our artillery fire continued to be ineffective, and it is a fact that the Germans seemed very little disturbed by it, their snipers coolly continuing their operations even after the attack had been launched.

The leading wave of the 47th Brigade, as I have said, left the trench at 4.47. It was immediately mowed down, as it crossed the parapet, by a terrific machine-gun and rifle fire, directed from the trench in front and from numerous fortified shell-holes. The succeeding waves, or such as tried it, suffered similarly.

Then Captains Steuart and Bain, who commanded C and D Companies of the Connaught Rangers, observing a check, got out of the trench, and started to rush their men forward: but they had only gone a few yards when both fell wounded.

On the right, there being no suitable jumping-off trench, it had been arranged that the Leinster and Hampshire parties, which were under my command for the day, should cross the open to their starting-point, but before they were able to reach it all the officers but one of the latter battalion had been hit, in addition to many of the rank and file. The officer commanding the Hampshire Companies had already been wounded by a sniper earlier in the day.

The trench in front of us, hidden and believed innocuous, which had in consequence been more or less ignored in the preliminary artillery programme, had—perhaps for this very reason—developed as the enemy's main resistance.

This, in fact, being believed to be the easy section of the attack, had been allotted to the tired and battered 47th Brigade. Such are the surprises of war! Supplemented by machine-gun nests in shell-holes, the trench was found by the few who reached close enough to see into it to be a veritable hornets' nest. Moreover, it had escaped our bombardment altogether, or nearly so. While the battle was in progress one of our aeroplanes, after flying overhead, dropped a map reporting the enemy in force there, but the news came too late to be of value. To the left of the Brigade, where heavy opposition had been expected and provided for, comparatively little was encountered. The artillery had done its work well, and the infantry was able to push forward and enter Ginchy.

In the meantime, the jumping-off trench soon became packed with the returned attacking troops and their wounded. The former were disordered and obviously shaken. Indeed, it was more than ever apparent that—apart altogether from the effects of the ordeal through which they had passed and were still passing (since the enemy artillery was still pounding furiously, while the machine-guns were raking up the parapets of our shallow trench)—they were in no condition for battle of this strenuous order, as I had thought before.

Those that were not raw recruits from the new drafts were worn out and exhausted by their recent fighting, and much more fitted for a rest camp than an attack.

One of the first sights I saw was poor Steuart being carried back on a stretcher. A few minutes before I had been talking and laughing with him, and, as I stopped to speak to him, now, his face wore the same cheery expression. I had known him only two days, but had formed the very highest opinion of his character, and, since our first meeting, had counted much on his help during the trying times that were before us. He was full of life and spirits and daring—the acme of the perfect soldier. But such men are rare: they often die young; and this, I fear, is to be his fate. The bullet that hit him penetrated his hip, and, glancing upwards, is reported to have touched a vital part. He lay some hours in the trench, till his turn came, and the firing had quieted down sufficiently to send him away, never once by word or gesture betraying the pain he must have been enduring.

Later during the afternoon another of my officers—Seppings Wright—was killed in the trench by shrapnel. I came upon his body during one of my rounds, and helped to lift him—he was a big and heavy man—into a shell-hole, beside the place where he had fallen. He had been in charge of the machine-guns.

Heavy shelling continued throughout the rest of the day and during the night—a lurid night of countless rockets and star-shells from the enemy, who was nervous; a night of

wild bursts of machine-gun and rifle fire—delaying our
relief by the 4th Grenadier Guards from 9 p.m. (when it
was due) till 4.40 the following—that is to say—this
morning.

Then, after three practically sleepless nights, under
shell-fire most of the time—often heavy, we marched back
to Carnoy Craters, as the old front line of June 30, at the
point where it is crossed by the Carnoy-Montauban road, is
called.

Here we are bivouacked, and I have just had a good
sleep on the ground, under the canopy of a transport
wagon.

The scene was very weird as we picked our way back this
morning, through the waste of shell-holes with their mourn-
ful contents, accompanied by our wounded, and preceded
by a stretcher on which lay the body of Colonel Curzon,
who had commanded the Royal Irish, and who dined
opposite me with the Brigadier four nights ago—on the
night I joined this Brigade. I found myself following
immediately behind his body.

During the three days my casualties have amounted to
92 (9 officers and 83 other ranks), out of the 16 officers and
250 other ranks with which I started, bringing the total
casualties of the battalion for the past nine days to 23
officers and 407 N.C.O.'s and men. Of the latter, 63
are missing; 54 were killed, and others have since died.

Thanks to my splendid doctor—Knight, a Newfound-
lander—we got away all the wounded.

Later. This afternoon we marched to "Happy Valley,"
where we are bivouacked.

September 13, 1916.   *Corbie.*

The battalion is resting at Vaux, a pretty little village
on the Somme, about a mile from Corbie, into which town
I have ridden to-day, and where I have seized a few minutes
at the Town Major's office to write to you.

My days are spent in reorganizing the battalion, which,
as you may imagine, is not an easy task, since practically all
the old officers, including the Adjutant, have become

THE BATTLE OF GINCHY, 9TH SEPTEMBER, 1916
Supporting Troops moving up to the attack

casualties. The boy Jourdain is still acting Adjutant and is doing it marvellously well, in spite of his extreme youth.

September 16, 1916. *Vaux-sur-Somme.*

The Guards were in action yesterday, and my old battalion has once again suffered badly, and Guy Baring and all four Company Commanders have been killed.

As we came away from the Ginchy attack the other day, I passed the battalion, which was bivouacked near us in Happy Valley. They were then "next for it." I stopped for lunch. The young officers crowded round me afterwards to hear my news, joking and laughing about it all, and asking what it was like "up there." Poor little Dilberoglue, who commanded one of the Companies, clung to the boy next to him, and pretended to shiver with fear at the prospect of what was before him. And the Fates have taken his joke seriously, for to-day he is dead. He was a very competent young officer.

I shall write to Geoffrey Feilding—I feel sure you would have me do this—and ask him, if through this action the Guards Division is short of officers, to consider me available in any capacity.

This afternoon I had a call from Major Willie Redmond—brother of John Redmond and Member for Waterford—such a simple nice fellow. This (16th Irish) Division, on the Staff of which he is, is, very evidently, the apple of his eye. He congratulated me, both on arrival and departure, though whether upon having been appointed to command a battalion in the Division, or upon having come unscathed out of the recent fighting, he did not indicate.

September 17, 1916 (*Sunday*). *Vaux-sur-Somme.*

We were expecting to go back yesterday into the firing line, but we have since got orders to move to-morrow in the opposite direction. This means, perhaps, that the claim of the Division to a rest has been recognized; or more likely, the necessity that an opportunity should be given to replace at any rate some of the recent heavy losses by drafts from home.

We received the melancholy news last night that Steuart

had just died of his wounds.   He is the greatest possible loss.
He was a magnificent smiling type of officer, and I never
saw grander courage than he displayed both before and after
receiving his wound.   I have told you how patiently he
waited to be taken away, and I now add that the manner in
which—without any sign of annoyance—he endured for
several hours the heavy shelling that must be so trying for
the helpless wounded, was remarkable to see.   He makes
the fifth of my officers that has died as the result of that day.

11.30 *a.m.*   I have just had a call from General Hickie [1]
—my new Divisional Commander.   It was the first time
I had seen him.   He seemed very pleased and proud of his
Division.   He asked why I was wearing only a Major's
crowns.   I said I had only authority for that.   He then
told me at once to put up a Lieut.-Colonel's badges, so,
from to-day, I may ask you to address my letters by that
rank!

You have absolutely nothing to worry about now.   I
shall, for a time at any rate, be in the safest of places.

September 19, 1916.   *Huppy.*

We left Vaux yesterday morning, and, after marching a
few miles, "embussed" (as the army language has it).
Then, after 5½ hours on wheels, we finished with a short
march, which brought us here to Huppy where we billeted
for the night, and from where I write.

I forgot to tell you that the battalion has a band of drums
and fifes, and Irish bagpipes.

September 22, 1916.   *Fontainehouck.*

We are in Belgium.

We got to this place about seven o'clock last evening,
after a 3-mile march from Bailleul, the detraining station.
We are in very comfortable billets, *well* behind the line,
and it is a nice sunny day: so all looks rosy.

September 23, 1916.   *Fontainehouck.*

The change in things generally is most gratifying.   The
battalion has made wonderful strides during the last few
days, and everything is getting shipshape now.

[1] Maj.-Gen. Sir William Hickie, K.C.B.

The character of the country we are in is very different to that which we have left. The scenery is beautiful; and the weather fine.

September 24, 1916.   *Locre.*

We moved 6 miles this morning, to this place, where I hear we are likely to remain undisturbed for a week or eight days; after which we are due to go into the trenches in front which are reputed to be very peaceful;—a theory which is certainly supported by the absence of the "angrier" sounds of war.

There is a big convent here, where the nuns provide meals for British officers, and we lunched and dined there to-day, very comfortably.

September 25, 1916.   *Locre.*

The men are living in wooden huts, and so should I be, but that I *must* have a table to write at and something to sit upon, and the huts are devoid of furniture. So I have procured a bedroom at a little convent in the village.

It is like living in a new world to be among these Irishmen, so great is the contrast between their national characteristics and those of the men I have come from. Unlike some Irish battalions, this one is composed, practically entirely, of Irishmen. They are, I should imagine, difficult to drive, but easy to lead. They are intensely religious, loyal to their officers, and, as every man Jack of them is plainly out—to the best of his capacity—to do whatever is required of him, they are an exceedingly satisfactory body of men to deal with, though, as yet, they have comparatively little training.

They are easily made happy. Perhaps they are easily depressed. Perhaps, too, like many others who are not Irish, they are better when things are going well than badly. Most of the officers are Irish, though not all, and I must own that I feel the sincerest gratitude to one and all for the generous and open-hearted manner in which they received me, a stranger amid strange surroundings, upon my first arrival, and the zeal with which they have since supported me.

The losses of the Guards between Ginchy and Les Boeufs on the 15th appear to have been very heavy, and I keep hearing daily of the loss of friends. Pike Pease was killed that day. Do you remember him? I saw him for the last time, I think, last November, at the hospital at Merville. He was a typical specimen of the clean English boy, with a fine brain and a promising career before him, and he was only nineteen.

Claude Bartholomew, too. I saw a good deal of him during the days I was at Morlancourt, his camp being a few yards only from my billet. He was a great little soldier. He was as you know on the Stock Exchange before the war. He was full of resource and ingenuity, and a master in the tactical handling of machine-guns, of which he commanded a Company.

One of the last times I saw him was on the day we first heard of Roumania's entry into the war. He had looked in at the 1st Battalion Headquarter mess, where I was sitting, alone. He took the line that the war *must* now be over in six months. "How damnable," he said, "to think that peace must come so soon, yet it is a moral certainty that, after surviving so many months of it, you and I will both be dead in a fortnight!"

That was three weeks ago, on the eve of the attack. He is a great loss and will be difficult to replace.

This morning the battalion was inspected by General Plumer,[1] who commands the 2nd Army to which we now belong. He was in Matabeleland when I was there, in the rebellion of 1896.

September 26, 1916. *Locre.*

To-day I have been to reconnoitre the trenches, or rather breastworks, which we are to take over. They cross the swampy ground below the Wytschaete Ridge, which, crowned by the ruins of the Hospice and a red pile of brick, or what looks like brick, frowns down upon them. Some 5 miles to the left stands up the skeleton of Ypres, where

[1] Now Field-Marshal Lord Plumer, G.C.B., G.C.M.G., G.B.E., G.C.V.O.

the ruined Cathedral can from our trenches be seen, towering into the sky.

All was very quiet.

The line will be wet and nasty in winter, but to-day the sun was shining, and the whole country seemed smiling. The silence was quite extraordinary. There was no shelling. Moreover, trees are standing, and many of the buildings are only slightly damaged. The fields are green and coloured with wild flowers; and to-day I saw two cows grazing not so very far behind the firing line, while, as I walked along the communication trench, two cackling cock-pheasants flew overhead.

After the Somme it seems like coming from Hell to the Thames Valley in summer-time; and they say it has always been like this lately. Is it bad to say, "long may it continue so"?

After breakfast at the convent, this morning, I was taken to see the room, full of silent girls—mostly refugees from Ypres, where the lace is made. Though so close to the firing line (about 7,000 yards), the atmosphere was the same as that, for example, of the Convent in Kensington Square;—the same well-swept, polished floors; the same clean-looking, sweet-faced nuns, moving quietly and quickly about their business.

They told me that the Germans spent ten days in the Convent and behaved well, but never paid for anything. In the village they seem to have looted considerably.

September 27, 1916.

In Front of Wytschaete (on the Kemmel-Vierstraat Road).

We have come up and are holding the front line, and I write from my headquarters in a farmhouse on the Kemmel-Vierstraat road (known officially as "York House"), some fifteen hundred yards behind the fire-trench, part ruined, yet commodious and comfortable.

The signallers, runners, etc., live, and I and my headquarter officers sleep, in sandbag shelters in what used probably to be the garden. It is as quiet as Gordon Place. Substitute an occasional rifle-shot or a burst of machine-gun fire for the traffic in Church Street, and you have it.

On my way up I saw a German observation balloon that had broken loose and was drifting, half hidden by the clouds. Our anti-aircraft guns were shooting vivaciously, and it soon began to drop, looking more bedraggled each minute as the shrapnel hit it and the gas leaked out. The wind was blowing in our direction, and the balloon was sinking towards the ground our side of the line, therefore there did not seem much point in pounding it; but I suppose the rare temptation of a steady target is over-mastering.

Then aeroplanes hove into sight from all quarters, like vultures round a dying mule, and, circling round, peppered the balloon with their Lewis guns. Suddenly, it took fire, and, burning like a huge candle from the upper end, fell out of my sight, leaving behind it a column of smoke.

Lest you may think this inhuman and brutal behaviour on the part of our "Archies"[1] and airmen, I am sure it is safe to say (though I did not actually see it happen) that the occupants of the balloon had long since made themselves safe and reached the ground with the aid of their parachutes.

September 28, 1916.   *In Front of Wytschaete.*

I have walked—I don't know how many miles—to-day, through our new trenches, well made by Canadian troops, but still requiring an enormous amount of spadework before the winter. I have a big digging party out to-night.

In three days we hand over to another battalion, and move back into support, when my headquarters will be at another farm ("Siege Farm"), some 300 yards behind this one.

The news seems good. As the German papers say: "in the orgy of destruction on the Somme our soldiers are standing in Hell." So are ours, but they take that as part of the day's work, and will continue to do so, with smiling faces.

[1] Anti-aircraft guns.

September 30, 1916. *In Front of Wytschaete.*

I have an orderly named Lavender, who shadows me wherever I go, and when I say that he shadows me I mean it literally. I find from experience that I have only to call quietly "Corporal Lavender," and I immediately get his reply in a deep Irish brogue "Here, sorr." No matter where I may chance to be, he is always *there*. He is a splendid type of faithful Irishman, tall in stature, gentle in manner, and always solemn. Indeed, he never smiles. He has an eye which misses nothing, a memory that rarely fails him, and, altogether, he inspires much confidence.

Being always with me, he is bound sometimes to over-hear things which are not for general knowledge, and I remarked to him upon this fact the other day. To which I got the following reply: "When I was in the Royal Irish Constabulary, sorr, I was taught three things—to keep my eyes and my ears open, and my mouth shut."

Like all Irishmen he is a bit of a politician, and as we pass along the communication trenches on our way to or from the front line, he following me, we sometimes discuss the politics of his native land. A few days ago the subject was the relative aims of the Nationalists and the Sinn Feiners, and I asked his views. Said he: "The Nationalists aim at getting independence by constitutional, the Sinn Feiners by unconstitutional, means":—which, after all, is about as concise a way of putting it as he could have chosen.

October 1, 1916 (*Sunday*). *In Front of Wytschaete.*

This evening a German aeroplane was brought down opposite us, in flames. It fell like a stone, leaving a vertical column of smoke behind it.

This place is as bad as any I have seen—even on this front—for rats. I can walk out any night, at any time, and by switching on a torch, count on seeing several at once. Even during the day they run about, almost as though man were non-existent. The fact is, they have come to be accepted so much as part and parcel of the war that their presence is generally ignored, and they enjoy an immunity that must be very gratifying to them.

The other night I was waiting in the fire-trench for the return of an officer's patrol from examining the German wire. The patrol had been gone a long time, and I was beginning to feel some apprehension regarding its fate, when a huge rat ran along the parapet. Instead of trying to kill it, the men in the trench started calling "puss, puss":—which will show you the terms we are on with the rats!

October 4, 1916.   *Siege Farm.*

We were relieved last evening, and came into support.

Everything is going on well here, and the front continues very peaceful. The battalion is being reinforced up to its establishment—I think more quickly than any other in the Division. Of course, this is luck. But I hope, and expect, soon, to have a very fine battalion.

October 5, 1916.   *Siege Farm.*

We move back into reserve this evening after dark, and are due to remain out for eight days. It will not be too comfortable, since we shall be in tents, amid very muddy surroundings: and, worse, there will be no ground on which to train the Companies.

We are getting plenty of rain, with little peeps of the sun.

3.20 p.m. The Brigadier has just concluded his visit. He expressed himself delighted, and was most complimentary on the work that has been done:—which was very gratifying.

October 9, 1916.   *La Clytte.*

Fresh officers have been joining almost daily, and I now have thirty-eight, including a regular Major of twenty years' service, who is attached for instruction!! And next week two more Captains are expected, including the Nationalist member of Parliament, Stephen Gwynn—who seems very popular with everybody.

So you will understand that I am well occupied. Indeed, I look forward to the trenches for a rest.

We had a battalion concert to-night, when considerable talent came to the surface. An officer named Holloway was

126

responsible for the programme:—a very clever professional, who was at the Gaiety, I think, when the war broke out.

October 12, 1916.   *La Clytte.*

To-day I took my mare—the best I have ridden since I came to France, inherited from poor Lenox-Conyngham [1] —the late Colonel of this battalion, and rode into Ypres. I have long yearned to see the city.   But what a scene of desolation!—truly, a city of the dead; a ghostly solitude. Not a sound unless that of a gun or bursting shell: not a soul to be seen in the long streets of ruins, except rarely, here and there, an English sentry, or a party of English soldiers, with rifle, pick, and shovel, marching to or from the trenches:—not a man, woman, or child of the nation that built and owns the city.   It is indeed a tragic sight.

October 15, 1916.   *In Front of Wytschaete.*

During my rounds this afternoon I met poor Parke (who till a few days ago was acting as my second in command) being carried along the communication trench known as Watling Street, on a stretcher.

He had just been killed by a direct hit from a chance shell.   He was forty-seven years old, and I was just trying to get him a rest behind the line;—which, added to the fact that he was only recently married and had just returned from spending a short leave with his wife, makes it all the sadder.   He was brother to the Parke who was with Stanley in "Darkest Africa."   He was a cheery fellow, and I shall miss him very much.

I hear to-day that the Divisional Commander has recommended me for the permanent command of this battalion, and that the recommendation has been approved, with effect from September 6—the date I took over on the Somme.

It is now the strongest and the show battalion of the Division.

October 17, 1916.   *In Front of Wytschaete.*

I feel, though I have written many letters, that I have told you really very little about the battalion I am commanding.   But now that I have got to know it, and to be

[1] Lieut.-Col. J. S. M. Lenox-Conyngham, killed in action September, 1916.

proud of it, I think I must try and give you some idea of the people I am with, and the atmosphere I live in.

First of all, then, I find both officers and men magnificent—plucky and patient, keen and cheerful. Since I came here I have introduced gradually many innovations —notions I learnt from the Guards. I have tightened up the discipline a lot. Inferior men might have resented it; yet I have not once encountered from any rank anything but the most loyal and whole-hearted co-operation.

These Irishmen have, in fact, shown themselves the easiest of men to lead; though I have an idea, as I said once before, that they would be difficult to drive.

I have heard it said, and have always believed, that there is no such thing as a "bounder" in Scotland, and I think I have learnt here that the same may with truth be said of Ireland. The result is that the officers' messes of the Division, though they include many diamonds in the rough, are pleasant places to live in—full of good will and good cheer. Among my lot I have a successful trainer of race-horses, an M.F.H., an actor, a barrister, a squireen or two, a ranker from the Grenadiers, a banker, a quartermaster from the 9th Lancers, a doctor from Newfoundland;—members, in short, of many professions; a lot of boys too young to have professions:—and a Nationalist M.P. is coming!

I feel particularly pleased with them all to-day. The fact is that the very right and proper policy of the Brigadier, and of the whole Brigade, of tormenting the enemy, is beginning to take effect, with the result that the latter, yesterday, broke away from his previously peaceful habits, and retaliated. Indeed, he seemed considerably annoyed, and pounded our front line severely with heavy trench mortars, etc., and the area, generally, with artillery. He blew in a considerable length of our breastworks, and altogether, for some hours, was very nasty.

But the officers and platoon sergeants handled the men cleverly, with the almost miraculous result that the casualties were so trifling as not to count. As soon as it was dark all

THE CLOTH HALL, YPRES

set to work to repair the damage, and, though the Germans used their machine-guns freely, the men laughed, and went on filling sandbags. One or two wags amused themselves by signalling the "misses" with their shovels—as they do on the range; and by daylight the trenches were again presentable.

This morning all was quiet once more, and the sun was shining. The men were in the best of spirits, with grins on the faces of most of them. They *knew* they had done well; and in spite of a large number of direct hits on the fire-trench, and many more close shaves, the casualty list had totalled only four wounded, three of them slightly. Such is the glorious uncertainty of shell and trench-mortar fire!

This morning one of my corporals killed a German and wounded another in Noman's Land. The latter crawled back towards his line, and, as he neared it, three of his friends came out after him. My men then acted in a manner which would perhaps nowadays be regarded as quixotic, so relaxed—thanks to our opponents—have the rules of this game of war become.

They did not shoot.

October 26, 1916. *Butterfly Farm* (*in Brigade Reserve*).

Stephen Gwynn arrived to-day. He has just been in to lunch. He is the very antithesis of the Irish politician as popularly represented by the Tory School. He is old for a Company Commander—fifty-two. All the more sporting therefore to have come out in that capacity, especially since he seems to have had a hard tussle with the War Office Authorities before they would consent to send him.

October 29, 1916 (*Sunday*). *Butterfly Farm.*

We have our tails up to-day because we have just heard that Private Hughes, of this battalion, has been awarded the V.C. for his behaviour at Guillemont. It is *something* to have a V.C. belonging to your battalion!

October 31, 1916. *In Front of Wytschaete.*

At last, after seven days, M.'s long description has come, and I know something of the new baby I have never seen.

I had a delicious letter from J—— on the subject, in which she said that, so far, she had only seen Pru with her eyes shut. The whole letter radiated with the spirit of the "Little Mother."

We are in the front line till the day after to-morrow, and all is going well. How war alters one's preconceived ideas! You know the sort of impression one is apt to get in England of the Irish Nationalist M.P. Well, ours here!—you should see him—a refined, polished, brave gentleman; adored by his Company, which he commanded before, earlier in the war. Knee-deep in mud and slush; enthusiastically doing the duty of a boy of twenty. I have seldom met a man who, on first acquaintance, took my fancy more. Have you ever read his books, which I am told are very beautiful? My only fear is that the exactions of the trenches during the winter months may prove too much for him.

November 7, 1916.   *Curragh Camp.*

I enclose two newspaper cuttings. They quote what were probably the last writings of Kettle, a talented Nationalist member of Parliament, who belonged to this Brigade and was killed at Ginchy on September 9. I think his ode to his child is very fine.

From the *Weekly Irish Times*, November, 1916.

LIEUTENANT KETTLE AND CONCILIATION

Mrs. Kettle has asked us to publish the following copy of a note which her husband, the late Lieutenant T. M. Kettle, wrote for publication a few days before his death in action:

"Had I lived, I had meant to call my next book on the relations of Ireland and England *The Two Fools: A Tragedy of Errors*. It has needed all the folly of England and all the folly of Ireland to produce the situation in which our unhappy country is now involved.

"I have mixed much with Englishmen and with Protestant Ulstermen, and I know that there is no real or abiding reason for the gulfs, salter than the sea, that now dismember the natural alliance of both of them with us Irish Nationalists. It needs only a Fiat lux! of a kind very easily compassed, to replace the unnatural by the natural.

"In the name, and by the seal, of the blood given in the last two years, I ask for Colonial Home Rule for Ireland, a thing essential in itself, and essential as a prologue to the reconstruction of the Empire. Ulster will agree."

To My Daughter Betty—The Gift of Love

(These are the last verses written by the late Lieutenant Kettle—a few
days before his death in action at Ginchy.)

In wiser days, my darling rosebud, blown
    To beauty proud as was your mother's prime—
    In that desired, delayed, incredible time
You'll ask why I abandoned you, my own,
And the dear breast that was your baby's throne.
    To dice with death, and, oh! they'll give you rhyme
    And reason; one will call the thing sublime,
And one decry it in a knowing tone.
So here, while the mad guns curse overhead,
    And tired men sigh, with mud for couch and floor,
Know that we fools, now with the foolish dead,
    Died not for Flag, nor King, nor Emperor,
But for a dream, born in a herdsman shed
    And for the secret Scripture of the poor.

T. M. Kettle.

In the Field before Guillemont, Somme, September 4, 1916.

November 9, 1916.   *Curragh Camp.*

Paradoxical though it may seem, I have less time for
writing here, while "resting" in the safe surroundings of
Divisional Reserve, than I had when the battalion was
manning the fire-trench. The fact is that while we are
here we are the butt of the Higher Command, whose
attentions while we are behind—I am inclined to think
—are even more trying than those of our enemies when
we are facing them, and are certainly less justified.

To-day we have a plethora of Generals and Staff Officers.
We are occupying a new and model camp which is not quite
finished, and which, being the latest thing of its kind, is
the cynosure which all are brought to see and admire.
Unfortunately, like other places which still have the work-
men in, the camp is untidy. There is much *obvious* refuse
lying about, which clamours to be removed, but there is
besides, here and there, an extraneous item such as a dead
rat, so camouflaged by its protective covering of mud, that
it has escaped my eagle eye; and (such is the way of things)
it seems inevitable that each time a visiting General stops to
question a soldier he does so opposite one of these atrocities;

131

—and, the more critically disposed the General, the more surely does the calamity occur. This is discouraging both to the officers and the men, who have reached a high state of efficiency in the noble art of "cleaning up," and are indeed second to none in this respect.

It has often struck me as extraordinary, seeing the pain which is caused to some Generals by seeing the least spot of dirt about the camp or personnel of a tired trench-worn battalion of infantry, that the same Generals should be so blind to similar defects in their own entourage, where there is no possible excuse for such laxity. Yet, so far as my experience goes, there is generally to be seen in such cases an uncouthness which it would be difficult to match.

Indeed, if I ever meet one of my men on the road, unshaved, or with flowing hair, or otherwise unmilitary, I immediately conclude that he is "detached" from the battalion, and employed on some "Staff" job: and I am hardly ever mistaken.

November 13, 1916. *Curragh Camp.*

Bar accidents, it is arranged that I go on leave on the 23rd (in ten days). I have had over seven months of it this time, with only seven days at home, and though I could not possibly be better in health, I feel I may be getting just a little stale.

We return to the trenches to-morrow.

November 17, 1916. *In Front of Wytschaete.*

The Staff Captain rang me up this morning to say that a Divisional car is going to Boulogne on the 21st, and would I like to go by that? However, I have decided to stick to my original plan, and not to go till the battalion is out of the trenches.

It is freezing hard, and the breastworks are frozen stiff.

* * * * *

December 8, 1916.

Facing Messines—Wytschaete Ridge (Cooker Farm).

After dining together at Boulogne, I travelled up in the train with a Brigade Major of the Ulster Division, whose acquaintance I had made on the boat.

We reached Bailleul, where we detrained, at half-past

seven this morning, and after getting some breakfast, I
called on Eustace Blundell (Coldstream Guards) who is
on the Corps Staff there.   While I was in his office, in
walked the Staff Captain of my own Brigade—Harrison, a
first-rate fellow, and very quickly he arranged for a motor-
car to take me to my battalion.

I learnt, to my surprise, that the Brigade had moved
during my absence, and that the battalion, which was due to
return to the trenches to-day, had been ordered up three
days before its time into a new sector, nearly a mile to the
right of where it had been before.

There I joined it, after lunching at Brigade Headquarters
at Dranoutre on the way, and it is from there that I now
write.   I received a very cordial welcome from every one,
including the Germans, who were shelling heartily as I came
along the communication trench in the side of which my
dug-out is.

I find the battalion happy in having captured three
prisoners in Noman's Land the night before last;—quite
an event in these dull days.

December 12, 1916.
    Facing Messines—Wytschaete Ridge (*Cooker Farm*).
Sleet has been falling more or less continuously, and the
men are wet through.   Yet, I never hear them complain.

December 13, 1916.   *Curragh Camp*.
We came out of the trenches last night, and I took off
my clothes for the first time since I said "good-bye" to
you, last Thursday (the 7th), at Charing Cross.

The night was cold—too cold to sleep comfortably,
although I have a nice hut here—and this morning I was
rather tired and got up late.   Since then I have been
busy, arranging details; visited by the Divisional General;
also by Filson Young (of the *Daily Mail*) and Philip Gibbs
(of the *Daily Chronicle*)—War Correspondents.

Now I am due for Orderly Room: also, I want a bath.

December 14, 1916.   *Curragh Camp*.
I have for many weeks past been working to get some
good company sergeant-majors out from home.   One in

particular I have been trying for—a Sergeant-major McGrath, reputed to have been the best at Kinsale. His Commanding Officer very kindly agreed to send him to me, although he wrote that he regretted parting with him. McGrath arrived the day after I returned from leave, and within half an hour of his reaching the fire-trench was lying dead, a heavy trench-mortar bomb having fallen upon him, killing him and two others, and wounding two more. Now, is not that a case of hard luck "chasing" a man, when you consider how long others of us last? I never even saw him alive.

I visited the fire-trench just after the bomb had fallen. It had dropped into the trench, and the sight was not a pleasant one. It was moreover aggravated by the figure of one of the dead, who had been blown out of the trench on to the parapet, and was silhouetted grotesquely against the then darkening sky.

But what I saw was inspiring, nevertheless. The sentries stood like statues. At the spot where the bomb had burst—within 40 yards of the Germans—officers and men were already hard at work in the rain, quietly repairing the damage done to our trench, and clearing away the remains of the dead; all—to outward appearance—oblivious to the possibility—indeed the probability—of further trouble from the trench-mortar, trained upon this special bit of trench, that had fired the fatal round.

What wonderful people are our infantry! And what a joy it is to be with them! When I am here I feel—well, I can hardly describe it. I feel, if it were possible, that one should never go away from them: and I contrast that scene which I have described (at 1s. 1d. a day) with what I see and hear in England when I go on leave. My God! I can only say: "May the others be forgiven!" How it can be possible that these magnificent fellows, going home for a few days after ten months of this (and practically none get home in less), should be waylaid at Victoria Station, as they are, and exploited, and done out of the hard-earned money they have saved through being in the trenches, and with which they are so lavish, baffles my comprehension. It is unthinkable: and that, I think, is the opinion of most officers who go on leave.

I can never express in writing what I feel about the men in the trenches; and nobody who has not seen them can ever understand. According to the present routine, we stay in the front line eight days and nights; then go out for the same period. Each Company spends four days and four nights in the fire-trench before being relieved. The men are practically without rest. They are wet through much of the time. They are shelled and trench-mortared. They may not be hit, but they are kept in a perpetual state of unrest and strain. They work all night and every night, and a good part of each day, digging and filling sandbags, and repairing the breaches in the breastworks;—that is when they are not on sentry. The temperature is icy. They have not even a blanket. The last two days it has been snowing. They cannot move more than a few feet from their posts: therefore, except when they are actually digging, they cannot keep themselves warm by exercise; and, when they try to sleep, they freeze. At present, they are getting a tablespoon of rum to console them, once in three days.

Think of these things, and compare them with what are considered serious hardships in normal life! Yet these men play their part uncomplainingly. That is to say, they never complain seriously. Freezing, or snowing, or drenching rain; always smothered with mud; you may ask any one of them, any moment of the day or night, "Are you cold?" or "Are you wet?"—and you will get but one answer. The Irishman will reply—always with a smile—"Not too cold, sir," or "Not too wet, sir." It makes me feel sick. It makes me think I never want to see the British Isles again so long as the war lasts. It makes one feel ashamed for those Irishmen, and also of those fellow-countrymen of our own, earning huge wages, yet for ever clamouring for more; striking, or threatening to strike; while the country is engaged upon this murderous struggle.

Why, we ask here, has not the whole nation, civil as well as military, been conscripted?

The curious thing is that all seem so much more contented here than the people at home. The poor Tommy, shivering in the trenches, is happier than the beast who makes capital out of the war. Everybody laughs at everything, here. It is the only way.

December 17, 1916 (*Sunday*).   *Curragh Camp.*

It occurred to me that it would be a nice idea to celebrate the battalion's period in Divisional Reserve by a special Church Parade: so, this morning, we marched with the drums and pipes to the village church of Locre, where High Mass was sung. Three priests officiated. Soldiers, accompanied by a soldier organist, composed the choir; and the battalion bugles sounded the "General Salute" during the Elevation. All was very impressive, and, considering that they are only out of the trenches for a few days' rest, the smart and soldierly appearance of the men was very remarkable. But there is never any difficulty—no matter what the circumstances—in getting a good Irish battalion to turn out well to go to Mass.

I invited the Divisional General and the Brigadier, and both came. The latter stood in the road as we marched to church: the former as we were returning. The men marched past, on both occasions, with plenty of swing, and gave the salutes admirably. Both Generals were delighted. The Major-General was particularly enthusiastic. He said: "By George, you have got some stuff into these men"; then he added: "You should have seen what I had to stand and look at twelve months ago." He ended by saying: "You can congratulate yourself very much indeed. I tell you that."

Christmas Day, 1916.

Facing Messines—Wytschaete Ridge (Cooker Farm).

No letter to-day, but the post has, I know, been hung up by the gale.

Though this is Christmas Day, things have not been as quiet as they might have been, and though we have not

WATERLOGGED SHELL-HOLES ON THE BATTLEFIELD

suffered, I fancy the battalion on our right has done so to some extent. In fact, as I passed along their fire-trench, I saw them at work, digging out some poor fellows who had been buried by a trench-mortar bomb.

This evening since dark, for a couple of hours, the Germans have been bombarding some place behind us with heavy shells. The battery from which the fire is coming is so far away that I cannot even faintly hear the report of the guns while I am in the open trench, though, from the dug-out from which I now write, I can just distinguish it, transmitted through the medium of the ground. I hear the shells at a great altitude overhead rushing through the air. The sound of each continues for nearly a minute, the noise increasing to its maximum, then dying away, till I hear the dull muffled thud of the burst some miles behind our line. The shells are passing over at the rate of more than one a minute.

This morning I was first visited by the Brigadier, who went on to wish the men in the fire-trench "as happy a Christmas as possible under the circumstances." Then the Divisional Commander came, accompanied by his A.D.C., who was carrying round the General's visiting book for signature. This contained many interesting names. I also had several other visitors.

When I had finished with my callers I went out with my little ·45 gun to see if I could kill a pheasant. I got one, which we had for lunch. My servant Glover acts keeper on these occasions. I need scarcely say that I cannot spare time for shooting pheasants, and to-day was my first attempt, but the other officers go out, especially one—a stout Dublin lawyer in private life—who is a very good shot. He went out yesterday, and before starting consulted Glover, who at once brightened up, and said: "If you want a couple of birds for your Christmas dinner, sir, I can put you on to a certainty, if you don't get shot yourself." He took him and they got two.

To-day, Glover took me to the same place:—but it turned out to be no spot to linger in:—a medley of unhealthily new shell-holes, under full view of the Germans. Certainly a good place for pheasants: but imagine what correspondence and courts-martial there would be if a casualty took place under such circumstances, and it became known! I have now put that locality out of bounds, pheasants or no pheasants.

The Chaplain came up and said Mass for the men this morning. I was prevented from going at the last moment by the Divisional Commander's visit, but it must have been an impressive sight. The men manning the fire-trench of course could not attend, but it was not a case of driving the rest;—rather indeed of keeping them away. The intensity of their religion is something quite remarkable, and I had under-estimated it.

The service was held in the open—not more than 500 yards from the German line, in a depression in the ground below the skeleton buildings known as Shamus Farm. Though the place is concealed from the enemy by an intervening ridge, promiscuous bits do come over, and I debated within my mind for some time whether to allow it. In the end, expecting perhaps a hundred men, I consented. But though, like most soldiers, and many others, they will shirk fatigues if they get the chance, these men will not shirk what they consider to be their religious duties, and about 300 turned up.

However, with the exception of a German shrapnel which burst harmlessly about a hundred yards away during the service, all went well, though I imagine Stephen Gwynn, who was the senior officer present, was given some food for thought.

In the evening I went round and wished the men— scarcely a Merry Christmas, but good luck in the New Year, and may they never have to spend another Christmas in the front line! This meant much repetition on my part, passing from one fire-bay to another, but I was amply rewarded. It is a treat to hear these men open out, and their manners are always perfect.

I have a good many recruits just now. Some of them went into the line for the first time last night. I visited them at their posts soon after they had reached the fire-trench, and asked them how they liked it. They are just boys feeling their way. They wore a rather bewildered look. This evening I asked them again. They were already becoming veterans.

They are all going to have their Christmas dinner on the 30th, after we get out.

December 26, 1916.

Facing Messines—Wytschaete Ridge (Cooker Farm).

Every little section of trench here, as elsewhere, is known and labelled by some fancy name, and one of the very worst bits of the fire-trench is called "Happier Moments." He must have been an optimist who thought of that.

As I came out along the communication trench this evening after dark I was spluttered with mud twice by trench-mortar bombs. These things make a horrible noise and mess when they land, but are so big and come so slowly that if you spot them in the air you can generally dodge them, and for this reason the men affect not to mind them much. I, on the other hand, admit that I do not share this feeling of confidence. Frankly, I respect trench-mortar bombs.

December 27, 1916.

Facing Messines—Wytschaete Ridge (Cooker Farm).

There is a sharp salient opposite the centre of the Divisional front, known as Spanbroekmolen—an elevation in the ground—from which we have suffered considerable annoyance. Anyway, the offending spot has, I think, been flattened out this afternoon, with very little loss to our side, and none to this battalion, which figured on the margin of the picture.

Our people sent over *thousands* of heavy trench-mortar bombs, and the artillery supported well from behind. It was a pretty sight. The enemy replied with everything he had, including gas shells, the smoke from which—since there was no wind—hung long upon the ground, like lakes of fog. I watched it all from the communication trench.

After dark I went round the line and found the men cheery, as usual. One of the recruits—a boy—especially took my fancy. It had been his first experience—his baptism of fire. He had picked up a splinter of shrapnel in his bay, which he was treasuring as a souvenir, and showed me delightedly, like a child would a new toy.

When times are quiet, as at present, things which are comparatively insignificant gather importance. A case of "trench feet," for example, will provoke far more correspondence and censure than a heavy casualty list, which provokes none at all. Fortunately, we are free from the former, but is not the principle rather that of "straining at a gnat, while swallowing a camel"?

December 28, 1916. *Derry Huts (near Dranoutre)*

The enemy's retaliation of yesterday turns out to have produced—in the 47th (our) Brigade, no casualties; in the 49th Brigade, which was on the left, one man killed! Is not that marvellous? I almost find it difficult to believe myself, though I know it to be true. Let us hope the Division was as favoured in its aggressive tactics as in the defence! We are naturally getting more cunning, but that cannot account for all.

Do you remember the silly letters that used to appear in the newspapers—I think it was last year—about linnets and pheasants in Norfolk having had their ear-drums broken by the percussion caused by mythical distant battles in the North Sea? Yesterday, while the bombardment was at its height, a robin was hopping playfully about, from sandbag to sandbag, within 10 feet of me: a blackbird was doing the same a few feet further away; and a cat was stalking between the two;—all three unconcerned among their infernal surroundings!

December 30, 1916. *Derry Huts (near Dranoutre)*

To-day, the battalion being out of the trenches, we celebrated Christmas in a sort of way; that is to say, the men had turkey and plum-pudding, and French beer for dinner, and a holiday from "fatigues."

I hope they enjoyed it. The extras—over and above

those contributed by friends at home (whose presents had been very liberal)—cost the battalion funds about £90. But when I went round and saw the dinners I must confess I was disappointed. Our surroundings do not lend themselves to this kind of entertainment; and, as to appliances —tables, plates, cutlery, etc.—well, we have none. The turkeys had to be cut into shreds and dished up in the mess-tins. The beer had to be ladled out of buckets (or rather dixies) later, into the same mess-tins; out of which also the plum-pudding was taken, the men sitting herded about on the floors of the dark huts. It was indeed most unlike a Christmas dinner, but it was the best possible under the circumstances, and the men would have missed it if they had not had it; though, as I say, it seemed to me a dismal affair.

To make the day seem as like Christmas as possible the Chaplain came over in the early morning and said Mass and gave Communion; but as the rain was descending in floods, instead of holding his service in the open, he was obliged to take refuge in a hut, into which only two Companies could be squeezed, and the remainder, who, as usual, had flocked voluntarily to hear him, had to be dismissed. So the day began with a disappointment.

They are a curious crowd. They will report sick pretty readily when they are in Divisional Reserve, and there are drills and fatigues to be done: but when in the line I do not think the average is more than one or two per day for the whole battalion. It seems to be a matter of honour with them:—and where Mass is concerned, they are never too tired to attend. Their devotion is quite amazing.

Although well within range of the daily shell-fire there is a woman with a baby living in the farm where I and my headquarter officers mess. There have, during the past few days, been some heavy bombardments, directed at our batteries in the immediate neighbourhood, in fact in the adjacent fields, some of which are sprinkled like pepper pots with shell-holes. There is a hole through the roof of the hut in which I live, made by shrapnel, and I admit that the thought of the battalion with nothing but galvanized roofing and thin wooden walls between it and the enemy is at times disquieting.

The place is indeed most unsuited for a "Rest" Camp which it is supposed to be, and still less for a nursery.

Still, the woman with the baby clings to her home. I wonder at these women with their babies. They must be possessed of boundless faith. There seems to be a sort of fatalism about them, and, as a matter of fact, they seldom get injured.

December 31, 1916 (*Midnight*).

Derry Huts (near Dranoutre)

It is midnight. As I write all the "heavies" we possess are loosing off their New Year's "Joy" to the Germans making my hut vibrate. The men in their huts are cheering and singing "Old Lang Syne."

The rumpus started at five minutes to twelve. Now, as it strikes the hour, all has stopped, including the singing as suddenly as it began. The guns awakened the men, who clearly approved. The enemy has not replied with a single shot in this direction.

January 1, 1917. *Derry Huts (near Dranoutre).*

We heard Mass again this—New Year's—morning; our third Sunday in three days! The first *our* Christmas Day; the second yesterday, the real Sunday, when Monseigneur Ryan, from Tipperary, preached; the third, to-day.

In spite of the heavy calls for working parties for the front line each day and night, the men off duty roll up always, and march behind the drums to wherever the service may be—in small parties, of course, owing to the proximity of the firing line.

Pray for them as hard as you possibly can.

January 5, 1917.

Facing Messines—Wytschaete Ridge (Cooker Farm).

Most of my officers, as well as I myself, have been suffering from some mild internal complaint while we have been in Reserve. But to-night we came up into the line, and I write from the old dug-out in the side of an alley branching out from the communication trench, at the spot known as Cooker Farm. The dug-out is roofed with steel rails and sandbags, has a fireplace, and is quite a good dug-out, though rather damp, there being an inch or two of water at one end, which gets deeper unless it is pumped periodically.

You may perhaps think it strange that already I begin to feel myself again, but so it is. There is unquestionably some health-producing quality in the effluvia of a trench and the "frowstiness" of a dug-out which is not to be found outside, and, after the war, I quite expect to see "Trench" cures, just as there now are "Open Air" cures!

Night of January 7–8, 1917.

Facing Messines—Wytschaete Ridge (Cooker Farm).

I wonder if I have enough energy left to write. It is nearly 2 a.m., and it has been a heavy day. The enemy declared war upon the battalion this (or I should say yesterday) morning, at the unearthly hour of 4.15, when suddenly he opened an intense concentrated bombardment with heavy trench mortars on a small section of our front line. He kept this up for fifteen minutes, and made a breach,

143

particular I have been trying for—a Sergeant-major McGrath, reputed to have been the best at Kinsale. His Commanding Officer very kindly agreed to send him to me, although he wrote that he regretted parting with him. McGrath arrived the day after I returned from leave, and within half an hour of his reaching the fire-trench was lying dead, a heavy trench-mortar bomb having fallen upon him, killing him and two others, and wounding two more. Now, is not that a case of hard luck "chasing" a man, when you consider how long others of us last? I never even saw him alive.

I visited the fire-trench just after the bomb had fallen. It had dropped into the trench, and the sight was not a pleasant one. It was moreover aggravated by the figure of one of the dead, who had been blown out of the trench on to the parapet, and was silhouetted grotesquely against the then darkening sky.

But what I saw was inspiring, nevertheless. The sentries stood like statues. At the spot where the bomb had burst—within 40 yards of the Germans—officers and men were already hard at work in the rain, quietly repairing the damage done to our trench, and clearing away the remains of the dead; all—to outward appearance—oblivious to the possibility—indeed the probability—of further trouble from the trench-mortar, trained upon this special bit of trench, that had fired the fatal round.

What wonderful people are our infantry! And what a joy it is to be with them! When I am here I feel—well, I can hardly describe it. I feel, if it were possible, that one should never go away from them: and I contrast that scene which I have described (at 1s. 1d. a day) with what I see and hear in England when I go on leave. My God! I can only say: "May the others be forgiven!" How it can be possible that these magnificent fellows, going home for a few days after ten months of this (and practically none get home in less), should be waylaid at Victoria Station, as they are, and exploited, and done out of the hard-earned money they have saved through being in the trenches, battalion had driven it out of my mind. I was in the fire-trench, examining the destruction caused by the bombardment of the early morning, when one of our aeroplanes flew overhead, very low, engaged (as I have since learnt) upon reconnaissance work on my behalf. The enemy of course opened upon it with the usual "Archie" fire. In fact, it was the latter that drew my attention to what was happening, because several "duds" fell close enough to me to be uncomfortable.

I looked up and saw a German aeroplane swoop down upon our man. Then there was a fusillade of machine-gun fire between the two. Then our man's petrol tank was hit and took fire, and the machine became a long streak of streaming flame, making for home, and earth. Every second I thought it must collapse. It seemed impossible that either pilot or observer could be alive, or that the engine could be working. But the rush through the air kept the flames from the canvas, and the aeroplane flew on. It was an inspiring sight;—a magnificent fight between man and death, in which the man won—for the time being.

After a long slanting flight the aeroplane came to ground, a mile or more behind our line. I sent an officer to the spot. Though I could have sworn the occupants were dead, they were not. The aeroplane was a crumpled, shapeless mass, the fire having engulfed it the moment it settled, but both were alive, though one was so severely burned that he is not likely to recover.[1]

January 9, 1917.

Facing Messines—Wytschaete Ridge (Cooker Farm).

After a peaceful day yesterday the enemy is again very vicious (I suppose auxiliary to his peace negotiations), and is plastering the place with thousands of trench-mortar bombs and shells; doing precious little harm;—like a naughty child breaking its toys out of spite, but necessitating a good deal of repair work on our part. We give him back a good deal more than we get, and it must all be very expensive.

[1] He died, but was awarded the V.C.

The whole place is a sea of mud and misery, but I must not grumble at the mud. It saves many thousands of lives by localizing the shell-bursts, and by muffling those very nasty German trench-mortar bombs. "The more dirt the less hurt"—as I think Jorrocks said on one occasion, though speaking of a different subject.

The officers and men stand these poundings like heroes, as they truly are.

January 10, 1917.

Facing Messines—Wytschaete Ridge (Cooker Farm).

A fairly quiet day. In the evening, while I was in the fire-trench, I saw three enemy aeroplanes dash across at one of our "sausage" balloons and set it alight. The occupants of the balloon, which had burned out before it reached the ground, came down by their parachutes.

It was dashingly done, I must admit, and the Germans were back behind their lines almost before our anti-aircraft people had realized what they were at, though I think one of them was winged. It is the third time I have seen this kind of thing since I came into this sector.

January 12, 1917.

Facing Messines—Wytschaete Ridge (Cooker Farm).

I am feeling very fit, though the strain, I think, begins to tell. About 2 p.m. the trench-mortar bombs started to come over, and to-night, commencing at 7.30, we have been bombarding one another hard with artillery. As I write, at a quarter of an hour before midnight, it is still going strong.

They have plumped, I should guess, some hundreds into my small section, but harmlessly—so far as I know at present. They seem to have shells to burn. I have never seen them so prolific, except in battle. I can only suppose they are hoping to awe us into peace. But it is like a big nasty baby battering at a closed door.

P.S. 3 a.m. January 13. I have just returned from the fire-trench, but before going to bed scribble this postscript. After writing the above, having failed to get through to Gwynn by telephone, the wires of which had been twice broken by shell-fire, I got a message by runner which said that his line had been blown in again. So I went down to see, and have just returned.

The shelling had been more effective than I thought when I began this letter. It had been fierce, I knew, but it had been more accurate than I thought then. It is the third time my front line has been badly hammered during these eight days. But no one flinches. They are working like niggers, now, in the snow (or rather sleet), to get a passage through before morning. The fire-trench was blown in in four places to-day. It is uphill work for the garrison, which gets little sleep of any kind, and no real sleep.

Our casualties for the eight days we have been up have been thirty-two, of whom fourteen have been killed. But for a Divine Providence that has shielded us, we should have fared far worse, and I think the men are beginning to believe in the luck of the Connaught Rangers.

January 14, 1917 (*Sunday*).　　　　*Curragh Camp* (*Locre*).

We came out of the trenches last night. I could not describe them if I tried, but they are more wretched-looking than any I have seen since I came to the war.

The most imaginative mind could not conceive an adequate picture of the frail and battered wall of shredded sandbags without actually seeing it, nor the heroic manner in which the men who hold it face its dangers and dis-comforts;—the mud and the slush and the snow; often knee-deep, and deeper still, in water; the foulest of weather; four days and nights (sometimes five) without moving from one spot; pounded incessantly with what the soldiers call "rum-jars"—great canisters of high-explosive, fired from wooden mortars, making monstrous explosions; and often in addition going through an hour or two during the day or night—sometimes two or three times during the twenty-four hours—of intense bombardment by these things as well as by every other sort of atrocity the enemy knows how to use. This when they are in the front line.

From the front line, after eight days, the battalion goes into Brigade Reserve. Even from there the men go up to the front line most nights on working parties, and are pounded again. Then eight days in the front line once more. Then eight days here, in Divisional Reserve, where at least we are free from shell-fire.

The Brigadier goes home on three weeks' leave on the 18th;—a unique event for him!

January 17, 1917.   *Curragh Camp (Locre).*

We woke up to find the ground white with snow, and it has been snowing mildly all day.

I dined with Stephen Gwynn in a private room at the Locre Convent. He had a party comprising, amongst others, Major Willie Redmond, Bishop Cleary of Auckland, New Zealand, General Powell, C.R.A. in the Ulster Division (in peace-time a master of fox-hounds in Co. Cork), Smiley [1] (M.P. for Antrim)—also of the Ulster Division, and Father Brown, who used to be Chaplain to the 1st Irish Guards, and was wounded on September 15 last year, on the Somme.

Afterwards, I walked part of the way home with Willie Redmond. He is a charming fellow, with a gentle and very taking manner.

January 26, 1917.   *Derry Huts (near Dranoutre).*

We were suddenly and unexpectedly relieved to-day:—the reason, a local change. I was not sorry. The weather has been and is *Arctic*, with a biting east wind, and the strain in the front line is considerable. Probably, the enemy gets it worse, since the wind catches him in the back, where—if his breastworks are anything like ours—there is little in the way of parados to screen him. The breastworks are in a horrible state, frozen hard as stone, the ground is white with snow, and the garrison stands four days and nights at a time in the paralysing cold, without exercise, numbed, trench-mortared, and shelled.

January 28, 1917 *(Sunday).*

                    Derry Huts (near Dranoutre).

This evening I rode 5 miles to Corps Headquarters at Bailleul, to dine with the Corps Commander, General Hamilton Gordon. An excellent dinner. Many Generals present, including the G.O.C. Ulster Division (General Nugent).

[1] Peter Kerr-Smiley, M.P. (N. Antrim).

February 1, 1917. *Facing Spanbroekmolen (Fort Victoria).*

The enemy tried again to raid the battalion this morning. At 5.15 he opened a sudden and fierce bombardment with artillery and trench-mortars on the front line and wire, and twenty minutes later the raiders came over the snow, camouflaged in white overalls and head-covers.

The Lewis gun protecting the point which they made for had been put out of action during the bombardment, but the team manned the parapet with their rifles, and two more Lewis guns were brought up, with the result that the Germans were soon put to flight, leaving seven or eight white figures dead in Noman's Land. We shall get these in, or some of them, to-night.

February 2, 1917. *Facing Spanbroekmolen (Fort Victoria).*

We had a lively day yesterday. The raid I described to you was followed at 8.30 a.m. by a second bombardment of equal violence to that of the early morning, and was followed again, at nine o'clock in the evening, by a repetition of the foregoing, less the raid.

We won all round on points. Our casualties were practically nil, though we must have inflicted considerable losses upon the enemy. Our artillery alone put over some 3,000 rounds, independent of the trench-mortars. What an expensive game it is if you work it out in £ s. d.!

We got in some of the spoil last night and shall get in more to-night.

We are being relieved, and shall be out of the trenches for twenty days.

February 4, 1917.   *Wisques.*

We got in another German body after the moon had dropped early yesterday morning. It was dressed only in a thin cellular vest and drawers, besides the tunic and trousers, and was without a shirt. Imagine the cruelty of it this bitter weather, with the thermometer, as it is, registering thirty degrees of frost!

We are burying this man together with one of his comrades in a corner of our own cemetery in Kemmel, and I have given orders for a notice-board to be shown on the

149

parapet, telling the enemy that we have done so; though I am not sure that such a departure from present-day methods will be approved of if it becomes known.

The two dead men are Saxons, and therefore probably R.C., so I have also arranged for our Chaplain to read the burial service over them.

*   *   *   *   *

February 11, 1917.   *Kemmel Shelters.*

I returned to the battalion last evening,[1] and found that the enemy had been shelling my battalion in Camp. It is in Divisional Reserve—training in a *safe* (!) place. Four have been killed and nine wounded, and the huts so badly smashed that two Companies have had to be moved elsewhere.

The place, was properly knocked about, and it was a surprising bit of shelling, too, seeing that the huts were unusually well hidden in a wooded depression, in the lee of Mount Kemmel, and screened by the protection which that steep hill affords. Personally, I could have sworn that these huts, at any rate, would have been safe from bombardment.

But no place is safe.

There seems little doubt but that the trouble was due to some movement which was spotted by a German aeroplane.

February 15, 1917.   *Facing Spanbroekmolen (Fort Victoria).*

Here we are in the trenches again.

This morning, in daylight, a German came running across Noman's Land with his hands up, and was shot by his own people just as he reached our wire. We shall get his body in to-night.

Ivan Garvey, who commands the Company holding the line at the point where it happened, says that three of his men immediately came rushing along the trench to tell him, and that when he went to the spot he found the platoon gazing over the parapet at the dead German. Some of them wanted to go and fetch him in then and there, but Garvey naturally did not allow that.

---

[1] The writer had been to a Battalion Commander's Course at Wisques and Cassel (2nd Army Headquarters).

February 16, 19I7.   *Facing Spanbroekmolen (Fort Victoria).*
During the night we got in the German whom I spoke of in my last letter—shot through the back by his own side.

He deserved his fate, of course.   But how fed up he must have been to do as he did!   He was a fine fellow physically; about twenty years of age; and will be buried to-morrow in a corner of the cemetery.   His pocket was stuffed with picture postcards of and from ladies, and photographs of himself and his family.

Four of my men and one trench-mortar man were killed, and two men were wounded, to-day, by one of our own shells, which fell short.

February 18, 19I7.   *"Doctor's House," Kemmel.*
It is late at night, and at half-past three to-morrow morning we set off on a rather desperate enterprise, for the proper conditions for which we have been waiting many weeks; so long, in fact, that the programme has begun to lose its bite.

The intention is to raid the enemy at three points in daylight, in a fog, or, failing a fog, under cover of a smoke cloud, *without* preliminary bombardment.

The weather so far has been entirely and persistently inappropriate to our purpose.   The days have been clear and sunny; the nights bright with stars; and the wind has blown from the east into our faces, so that an artificial fog has been out of the question.   Hence the long delay.

To-night it seems that we may have the conditions we have wished for.

I am not entirely satisfied with the arrangements.   First, Roche, the Trench-Mortar Officer, in whom I have complete faith, was sent away on a fortnight's course, for a rest— much against his own will as well as mine—before the cutting of the enemy's wire, which had been entrusted to the medium mortars, was anything like completed; and without him I do not quite trust the rest, either to make the necessary gaps, or to keep them open, when made, against the enemy's repair work.

Secondly, I have lost two of the principal officers whom I

had detailed for the raid—both leaders of assaulting parties; one wounded; the other away on an officer's course (the curse, often, of us Battalion Commanders, since we have no option in the matter, and are obliged to send away officers when called for, however little we can spare them). I have applied for this officer back again, and have been refused him. Consequently, though the raid has been well practised over a replica of the German trench which I have had prepared behind our line, the training of these two important adjuncts has been thrown away.

Finally, a one-minute's intense lightning Stokes mortar bombardment which I asked for at Zero has been vetoed, Pereira's view being that this would alarm the Germans in the front line and bring them to their posts. It would doubtless bring *him* to *his* post, but he is apt to forget, I think, that all men are not like himself.

However, for better or worse, we tackle the job to-morrow morning, and all preparations having been completed in so far as is feasible under the circumstances, we have been having a game of Bridge; and now I am off for a few hours' sleep before starting.

February 20, 1917.   *"Doctor's House," Kemmel.*

I with my Headquarters officers reached Shamus Farm at about 4 o'clock yesterday morning, in a dense fog. The men of the raiding parties were already filing in and out of the ruins, loading up with Mills grenades and smoke-bombs and all the other paraphernalia necessary for the undertaking. The green oval patches were being stripped from their sleeves, and everything by which the battalion might be identified, such as letters, regimental numerals, and cap badges, were being collected and put away in sandbags. Each man, as he completed these preliminaries, passed silently into the communication trench leading to the firing line, where all was absolutely still—uncannily so.

Michael Sweetman [1] was with me. He had persisted in coming, and I had given way, though I feel that perhaps I

---

[1] Lieut.-Colonel Michael James Sweetman, East Yorks Regt., the writer's brother-in-law, temporarily attached to the 6th Connaught Rangers.

should have refused him, seeing that he is only attached to the battalion and had no duty to perform; and I am devoutly thankful to say that no harm has come of it.

At seven o'clock I passed along the fire-trench, where the raiders were now waiting for the moment of Zero. Most were cheerfully tucking green miniature Irish flags into their caps or buttonholes, and all seemed full of confidence.

At 7.15 the three parties, comprising 9 officers and 190 other ranks, without any preparatory bombardment, scaled the parapet, and made a wild dash across Noman's Land. At the same moment our artillery opened, according to programme, and put a box barrage round the selected section of the enemy trench.

The centre party reached the German wire, but found it uncut, having—perhaps owing to the fog—missed the gap. 2nd Lieut. Williamson, second in command of the party, was killed as he neared the wire, and 2nd Lieut. Kent, commanding, was wounded in the arm but continued firing with his revolver at the enemy, holding up his wounded arm with his free hand. When he had fired off his six rounds he lay down and reloaded. J. White—a private —then stood up and bombed the enemy in the trench. This party found a covering group lying out in front of the German wire, which however fell back into the trench as our men approached.

The right party had no casualties till it reached the wire. Then 2nd Lieut. Bradshaw, second in command, was wounded, and a minute or two later was hit again and killed. 2nd Lieut. Cardwell, commanding the party, was also wounded severely by a stick bomb, which blew away the calf of his leg. His men then threw all the bombs they were carrying across the wire into the German trench, after which, seeing that the party on their left was retiring, and having lost both their officers, they fell back.

The first wave of the left party started off well under 2nd Lieut. Cummins, a very gallant young officer whom I had put in command in place of the original commander, who was the officer I have mentioned as being absent on a course. The Sergeant, Hackett, was almost immediately killed. The party met with heavy opposition, and some of the men behind them faltering, Captain Garvey, who was in charge of the assaulting parties, ran out across Noman's Land to rally them.

He fell wounded, and Lieut. T. Hughes, commanding the left support, ran forward to help rally the waverers. Private John Collins [1] did the same. This man acted with great dash, rushing recklessly towards the German trench, shouting "Come on the Connaughts"—a cry which some of the enemy took up. Sergeant Purcell and Privates Twohig and Elwin also did their best to encourage the others, the latter standing up and firing with his rifle at the Germans, who now began freely to expose themselves, till he fell, shot through the neck.

Hughes showed great gallantry, again and again exposing himself; then, recognizing that the raid had failed, he fell back, and with the aid of Cummins and two privates—King and Healy—carried Garvey back to the shelter of our trench.

In the meantime the enemy had been retaliating violently upon our front line and communication trench with high explosive and shrapnel, as was to be expected.

After some two hours the firing on both sides died away, and by 9.30 all was quiet. An incident then took place which I think was as remarkable as any that this most unchivalrous of wars can have yet produced.

Our dead and many of the wounded still lay out in Noman's Land, when the fog lifted and the German trench became clearly visible. As I stood in the middle of the fire-trench a man came running to me and reported that the enemy had allowed what he called "an armistice," for the purpose of collecting the wounded who were lying in front of the right extremity of the section.

I hurried along the trench and found that this was literally true. Already parties of men were out dressing the

---

[1] Pte. Collins was awarded the D.C.M. a few days later, but was killed the day after he heard of it.

wounded and carrying them back to our line.   One of my
officers and a German were bending together over a
wounded man alongside the enemy wire.   The Germans,
in considerable numbers, were lolling over and even sitting
upon their parapet, watching the proceedings.   My own
men were doing the same.   As the stretcher-bearers started
to move the dead the enemy called out to "leave the dead
alone," but no notice was taken of this.

I asked how this extraordinary state of affairs had
originated.   I was told that the Germans had called out in
English, "Send out your stretchermen," and that a number
of volunteers—stretcher-bearers, real and self-constituted
(the latter of course stretcher-less)—had immediately
climbed over the parapet.

I noticed Private Collins.   He is one of the "wild men"
of the battalion.   He was sauntering about with a pipe in
his mouth, wearing a bomber's waistcoat, the pockets bulg-
ing with bombs.   This was obviously out of order under
the circumstances, and was only asking for trouble;—in fact
the Germans, I had been told, when they issued their
invitation to the stretcher-bearers had stipulated (rather
naturally) that the latter should come unarmed.

I told Collins to put down his bombs, which he did rather
sheepishly, as though he had suddenly remembered for the
first time that he had them on.   Then, after a parting warning, I moved off towards the left section of the trench, to
see how things were faring there.

The "armistice" had spread, and the scene, if possible,
was more remarkable than that which I had left.   The
distance between the enemy's trench and ours is considerably less here than on the right, being not more than 40
yards at the narrowest point.

I found numerous Germans—almost shoulder to shoulder
—leaning over their parapet, exposed from the waist up:
on our side it was the same.   All were interestedly watching
the stretcher-bearers at work in Noman's Land.   A German
officer was walking excitedly up and down along the top
of his parapet, shouting in perfect English to my men to

"get their heads down or he would open fire," at the same time gesticulating vigorously with his arm.

The whole proceeding was of course highly irregular, and the last of our wounded and dead having by this time been recovered, I ordered the men below the parapet, and a second or two later every head on both sides had disappeared: both the German trench and ours had become normal, and the war had re-started.

Thought I to myself, "These people cannot always be so bad as they are painted": then I proceeded to take stock. But the enemy had exacted payment for his generosity. The officer I had seen near the German wire was missing, as were one or two others.

There may be something to be said in the case of the officer. He had foolishly neglected to remove his revolver (or rather revolvers, since he had two) before going out, and having looked into the enemy's trench was perhaps fair game.

At the same time, by what subterfuge he and the others were inveigled into becoming prisoners, I do not know, and shall not know till the war is over; if then.

February 20 (*Night*).

I fly to you when I am in trouble, and I am feeling very sick at heart, to-night. Ivan Garvey—the ideal Company Commander—the bravest, the cheeriest, the most loyal and perfect of men, was reported a few hours ago to be dead of his wounds. How readily he undertook the work when I first proposed it to him!

As I passed the Aid Post yesterday, on my way back from the line, I went in, and found him asleep under morphia, so did not get a chance to speak to him. Nobody thought he would die then.

Priestman, the Brigade Major, who had been by my side during the affair of the morning, had seen him earlier, before I was able to get away from the fire-trench. He told me he was semi-conscious then, and that he had thought he (Priestman) was me. I like to think that he asked for me.

My God! if the people at home could actually see with

their eyes this massacring of the cream of our race, what a terrible shock it would be to them! But we must see it through. All are agreed upon that.

Nine of my best officers went over yesterday. Three of these are left to-day. And, in addition, one more of my Company Commanders (Fitzgerald) is gone, as the result of this enterprise. He was wounded while cutting the gaps through our own wire, preparatory to the raid, so severely that he too may die.

But all this is not unusual. It is the toll to be expected from a raid when it is unsuccessful, and indeed often when it is successful: and the success or failure of a raid is largely a matter of chance.

I was present at the burial of some of the killed this afternoon, including that of two of my most promising young officers. That is the tragedy of the war. The best are taken. The second best are often left in the safe places.

General Pereira came and saw me this morning, and stayed some time. He was more kind and consoling than I can say.

Private Elwin, too, has died.

February 23, 1917. *Curragh Camp (Locre).*

The battalion is out of the trenches for eight days. The weather has completely changed, and there is a dense fog, which is almost constant.

I have applied for twenty-one days' leave, to which I am entitled. I feel I want a little time and opportunity to freshen up.

I found the following poetic effort, the other day, posted up by the gas gong at S.P. 10.[1]

To H.M. Troops

If the German gas you smell,
Bang this gong like blazing hell.
Put on your helmet,
Load your gun,
And prepare to meet
The ruddy Hun.

---

[1] Strong Point.

February 26, 1917.   *Curragh Camp (Locre)*

There is a sequel to the affair of the 19th. It has beer suggested that the so-called "armistice" constituted a breach of the order which forbids fraternization. The inciden unfortunately occurred right on the top of a memorandun dealing with the subject, and worded as follows:

1. A case has recently occurred in another part of the line in which the enemy are reported to have been allowec to approach our lines and remove the bodies of some of thei: dead.

Whilst doing this he was probably able to secure usefu information as to the state of our wire and the ground ir its vicinity, and in any case he was permitted to deprive us of what may have been a valuable identification.

2. The Divisional Commander wishes it to be clearly understood by all ranks that any understanding with the enemy of this or any other description is strictly forbidden

We have to deal with a treacherous and unscrupulous foe, who, from the commencement of the present war, has repeatedly proved himself unworthy of the slightest con- fidence. No communication is to be held with him withou definite instructions from Divisional Headquarters, and any attempts on his part to fraternize with our own troops is to be instantly repressed.

3. Commanding Officers are to take steps to ensure tha all ranks under their command are acquainted with these instructions.

In the event of any infringement of them, disciplinary action is to be taken.

As a matter of fact I had not seen this memorandum which arrived when I was away from the battalion. Goc knows whether I should have acted differently had I done so! Anyway, a Court of Enquiry is to be convened, to decide whether we did fraternize or not, and orders still more stringent than that which I have quoted have been issued

In future, if fifty of our wounded are lying in Noman's Land, they are (as before) to remain there till dark, wher we may get them in if we can; but no assistance, tacit or

otherwise, is to be accepted from the enemy.   Ruthlessness
is to be the order of the day.   Frightfulness is to be our
watchword.   Sportsmanship, chivalry, pity—all the qualities which Englishmen used to pride themselves in possessing—are to be scrapped.

In short, our methods henceforth are to be strictly
Prussian; those very methods to abolish which we claim
to be fighting this war.

And all because the enemy took toll for his generosity
the other day.

It is beautiful and sunny and warm to-day.

February 27, 1917.   *Curragh Camp (Locre).*

I have written to you much of the staying powers of the
men—how they have stood night after night and day after
day—in the wettest or most Arctic weather, behind these
flimsy breastworks.   You cannot dig trenches in this
locality because you get drowned out.   So you bank up
sandbags and stand behind them.   And the enemy flattens
these every day or two with his "rum-jars"; and we do
the same to his.

"Rum-jar" is the soldiers' name for the German canister,
which is their simplest form of heavy trench-mortar bomb.
Picture a cylindrical oil-drum, 15 inches long and about
11 inches in diameter, flat at both ends, and filled with
high explosive.   That is the "rum-jar."   In the dark, if
you spot it coming, you can just distinguish it in the air,
by the fizzling of the fuse.

But it arrives silently, and is not easy to detect, till it
lands with a mighty bang.   I once spoke slightingly of
these things, but I spoke foolishly.   It is true that, as a
rule, they do little if any damage, because the effect is very
local; but if one happens to hit a man or a collection of
men it blows them to bits.   And these things come in
hundreds, and are a perpetual menace to the men in the
front line, day and night, often for four days and nights
together, and more.

The material effect, as I have said, is small, but the constant stress is tiring to the morale, as it is intended to be,

and, added to the other strains of trench life—the artillery strafes and the mines and other horrors which the poor infantry have to undergo, is very tiring to them. Yet, through it all, they stand, frozen and half-paralysed by the cold and wet, with no individual power of retaliation beyond the rifle which each man carries, and which is about as much use against the weapons by which he is tormented as a pop-gun.

I will tell you two stories which may amuse you.

A certain very charming and gallant General, who some-times visits us, is fond of making little speeches to any group of men he may find drilling, or in the huts when we are out of the line. He also—very properly—likes to take an opportunity to shake hands with any man who has been rewarded or mentioned for having performed a gallant action: and he has a way on such occasions of turning suddenly to the senior officer present and asking, "What were the details of the act for which this man was recommended?"

Among so many stirring events, that is not always easy to recall at a moment's notice, especially when some period has elapsed since the recommendation was made.

Some little time ago, I was told to put forward the name of an N.C.O. or man for a certain foreign decoration. In parenthesis, I may say that I am often called upon to do this, but the recommendation so rarely materializes that the pastime is a dull one. On the occasion in question it had been stipulated, as usual, that the recommendation should be for a "specific act." It so happened at the moment that there was no "specific act" outstanding. However, I decided to give the chance to the Lewis gunners, who I thought had not been recognized as well as they might have been.

The Lewis gun officer either did not take sufficient interest in the matter or did not feel himself equal to the task of "writing the necessary story"; at any rate, he said he had nobody to recommend. Immediately, one of the Company Commanders who happened to be in the room,

more alert, said to me: "Why not put forward Sergeant
R——? He has done excellent work ever since the
battalion came to France, and has got nothing."

This was very true, and no other man being forthcoming,
I asked, "What is the specific act?"

The Company Commander said: "Well, I don't quite
know about that."

I said: "Think it over, and if you can recommend Sergeant R—— for a specific act, I shall be glad to put his
name forward."

The Company Commander went away, and later in the
evening I received his recommendation, couched in the
glowing "paint-the-lily" style which is required if these
efforts are to be successful. I sent it forward, and, not long
afterwards, Sergeant R—— was awarded the Military
Medal—a better decoration than that for which he had
been recommended.

Clearly, the Company Commander's word picture of the
"specific act" had been well thought of by the Powers who
decide these things.

Incidentally, Sergeant R—— had received what he
richly deserved, though perhaps would never have had but
for the circumstances I have mentioned.

Weeks passed. I went away on a course. Many
exciting incidents intervened, and I confess that the nature
of Sergeant R——'s "specific act" had entirely escaped my
memory, when—a few days after the enterprise of February 19—the General arrived on the scene while Sergeant
R——'s company was at exercise.

He first made the men a little speech. Then, having
finished, he turned to me and asked: "Is there anyone in
this Company who has received any decoration lately?"

I said: "Yes, sir, Sergeant R—— has received the
Military Medal."

He went on: "What was the act for which Sergeant
R—— received the Military Medal?"

As I have said, the literary effusion which had secured
the well-merited award had gone completely out of my

head. I looked towards the Company Commander. He, too, for a moment, was nonplussed. Then he butted boldly forward, and in glowing language described how one night when the enemy had demolished part of our breastwork Sergeant R—— had collected six bombers and without any orders had taken up a position in the battered breach, etc., etc., etc.

The General then called Sergeant R—— out in front of the Company, and shaking him by the hand said: "I am glad to have this opportunity of congratulating Sergeant R—— for his gallant act on the night of the ——, when in the middle of a heavy trench-mortar bombardment he collected six bombers, etc., etc.";—then, turning to the Company Commander, he asked: "And what were the names of the six bombers? I should like to congratulate them, too."

This time the Company Commander really was defeated. But the most amusing part of the episode was the look of modest surprise which mounted into the face of Sergeant R—— as he heard his "specific act" recounted. He stood like a stolid block, his eyebrows rising higher and higher, while the Company gazed in amazement at their hero.

I fancy the General, who is very wide awake, saw through it: but he was far too wise to show the fact.

Now for a story about General George Pereira:

One of my Captains, accompanied by a new orderly, was walking along the communication trench one day, when he met the Brigadier. The latter, always fond of testing the soldier's knowledge, asked the orderly: "What is the name of your Captain?" To which the man replied: "I don't know, sir."

Pereira then asked: "Do you know who I am?"

"Yes, sir," replied the orderly, with an intelligent look. "You're the Brigadier."

"And what is my name?" asked the Brigadier.

"I don't know, sir," answered the orderly.

George Pereira turned to the Captain.

"Such is fame," he said.

There are many funny stories about these men when they

first joined the army.   It was a common thing for a man to call an officer "Your honour," and one who wished to be particularly respectful is said on a certain occasion to have addressed the Colonel as "Your Reverence."

But that was before my day.

March 3, 1917.   *Derry Huts (near Dranoutre)*

The Battalion Commanders were sent for this morning, to meet General Plumer, the Second (i.e. my) Army Commander, at Brigade Headquarters.   We went in one by one, and had a tête-à-tête conversation with him.

When my turn came I found only Colonel Monck-Mason[1] (temporarily commanding the Brigade during the Brigadier's absence) and the Army Commander in the room.

The latter was very friendly, and very human.   That is one of his many admirable qualities.   He takes the trouble to know even his Battalion Commanders, and for this and other reasons has earned great confidence among the troops of his army.

After shaking hands, he referred to the raid of February 19.   He expressed the opinion that there should have been a preliminary bombardment by artillery, and asked me why this had not been done.   Obviously, I could not enter into explanations, but he quickly turned to Colonel Monck-Mason, who replied that the trenches were too close together for that.

"Then," said the General, "you should have had a trench-mortar bombardment."   Then he turned to me and said: "I know all about your having asked for a Stokesmortar bombardment: General Pereira has told me."

I felt I could see General Pereira telling him this, and explaining that it was he who had refused it; blaming himself, in fact, for the failure of the raid.   Now, that is just Pereira all over, and I repeat it that you may know the man, and understand why every officer and soldier of his Brigade swears by him.

As one of my brother C.O.'s once said to me: "You know, if he trusts you, that he will defend you, and that no

[1] Lieut.-Col. R. H. Monck-Mason, D.S.O., Royal Munster Fusiliers.

one will be allowed to belittle you except across his mangled corpse." And the feeling in regard to Plumer among the fighting troops—I do not speak for his Staff who no doubt feel this also—is much the same.

We came here yesterday, into Brigade Reserve, to find that the enemy had been shelling the place with high explosive and gas, which latter still hangs heavily on the ground. One shell hit the house where my headquarters are, but the family (mother, baby and all) still cling on.

(*Midnight.*) I have just got my leave.

* * * * *

March 28, 1917. *Mont des Cats.*

On returning from leave I spent the night at Boulogne, and my train, which should have left at 9.54 the following morning, failed to appear till after eleven o'clock. It then took five hours to get to Calais (about 20 miles), and reached Hazebrouck, where I was met by my groom, horse, and mess-cart, at 7.30 p.m.

I rode 10 miles to this place, where I found the battalion, quite changed by the arrival of eighteen new officers, and temporarily commanded by Colonel Jourdain,[1] a regular officer of the Connaught Rangers. I also found Michael, who was hard at work playing Bridge at the time.

I am sleeping in a comfortable bed, in a house below the Monastery which caps the Mont des Cats. We move up to the line again in a few days.

April 5, 1917. *Butterfly Farm (near Locre).*

To-morrow I shall have completed exactly seven months in the command of this battalion. The glamour and romance of the war die away after a time, and only the reek of it remains. One's life is dictated by a sense of duty, which is the one and only incentive. It is only latterly I have felt like this. Till recently, the life interested and held me, and I shall always look back upon 1915 and 1916 as a time of extraordinary happiness.

Perhaps it is the apathetic Monday morning feeling which always follows leave, or it may be the bad weather, the mud,

[1] Lieut.-Col. H. F. N. Jourdain, C.M.G.

and the bedraggled appearance of the trenches that are depressing me; and when spring comes things will look rosier.

April 6, 1917 (*Good Friday*).

"*Turnerstown Left*" (*Vierstraat Sector*).

I write from the trenches.

We relieved the 6th Royal Irish Regiment last night after midnight, and I did not lie down till three this morning. They had just concluded a successful raid on the enemy, having captured twenty-one prisoners, though their casualties had been somewhat heavy.[1]

The aftermath of shelling was still going on as we arrived, but did not hurt us. One small shell went through the Battalion Headquarters kitchen dug-out, about 20 yards from where I am writing, and burst inside. But, though nine men were sitting there, no one was hurt;—which may sound impossible; but it is true.

My headquarters are very cramped, and I have been obliged to leave several officers behind. Michael Sweetman is still here, and went round the trenches with me to-day. He always goes with me on my rounds. He is a very faithful friend, besides being—as M—— would say—very calm, cool and collected on all occasions, and the more I see of him the more I am struck with his rare selflessness.

Our trenches are in an appalling state, but the enemy's trenches are reported to be worse.

April 9, 1917.   "*Turnerstown Left*" (*Vierstraat Sector*).

Yesterday (Easter Sunday) was a heavenly day of sunshine —the finest we have had this year.

Moreover, it was so quiet and peaceful that Michael and I, after going round the lines, sat out in the open and read the papers. There was a good deal of aerial activity, as natural on such a day, and as we lolled about the aeroplanes pooped away overhead with their Lewis guns, and the "Archies" spoke from below. During the night following there was but little gunning over our lines, though for some hours in the morning there were the sounds of what seemed like a big battle far away to the right.

---

[1] The casualties were fifty-eight.

This morning we have again been round part of the front line, reserving the remainder for this afternoon. In a muddy extremity of a bit of trench known as Lark Lane, which we are reclaiming, I met the Brigadier, and had a long talk with him. He seemed very pleased with everything, and I think he was pleased with us. He was, in fact, very complimentary about one or two things. I spoke to him about Michael, who still awaits orders, and who is risking his life daily, and needlessly. As a matter of fact I do not encourage Michael's going into the trenches, where at present he has no duties to perform: but there is no keeping him away.

"It is *my* duty," I say. "You are only a spectator for the moment. Therefore, why go through these smelly drains, and chance getting shot for no purpose?"

"Ah well!" he replies, "I think we'll risk it once more to-day." And so it goes on.

The enemy has knocked over the last outstanding fragment of Ypres Cathedral. When I looked yesterday from the fire-trench for this great landmark, it had gone.

April 10, 1917.   *"Turnerstown Left" (Vierstraat Sector)*

The firing on our right which I spoke of yesterday was of course the huge battle raging on the Vimy Ridge, of which I then knew nothing.

The enemy certainly seems to be catching it on all sides, hot and strong. What a mess he has made of the diplomatic side of the war! To have brought in the U.S.A.— quite unnecessarily;—what a blunder from his point of view. Surely, the nation must have gone mad! I think most of us here are sorry that America has come in. We feel we are capable of finishing the job, and we would prefer to do so by ourselves.

Snow and cold strong wind again to-day. Will spring ever come?

April 11, 1917.   *Rossignol Estaminet (near Kemmel)*

We were relieved last night, and are in support, after five days and nights of the front line. We had an exceedingly quiet time. There has been a change in the enemy

AERIAL VIEW OF YPRES

dispositions in front of us, and "our friends over the way" are now Prussians instead of Saxons.

This morning, we three Colonels—Michael, Jourdain and I—were reconnoitring some trenches. A good deal of shelling was going on—some much too close to be pleasant. One shell fell within a few feet of us, in Watling Street, nearly bagging the lot, and covering us with earth. Michael was in the middle and caught the greater part. He was grazed by a bulky thing, which looked to me like a big piece of shell, so I enquired anxiously if he was hurt: but he picked himself up and muttered, "Thank God, it's only a brick!"

April 13, 1917. *Rossignol Estaminet (near Kemmel).*

Before we came up to the trenches the other day we were practising open fighting, according to a new method of organization, whereby the men are divided up and classified under different categories—Lewis gunners, bombers, rifle grenadiers, riflemen, etc.

The Army Commander inspected them, and before his arrival the function of each man in the attack was carefully impressed upon him. It was explained to the riflemen, for example, that, if asked, they were to reply that they were riflemen; the bombers that they were bombers, and so on.

So pat, in fact, had one man of the battalion got his answer on his lips, that when the General asked him unexpectedly, "Are you a Catholic?", he replied, " I am a Rifleman, sir."

April 15, 1917 (*Sunday*).

Rossignol Estaminet (near Kemmel).

This morning (Sunday) the Chaplain has been going round the Companies, which are scattered, saying Mass, and speaking to the men about your miniature crucifixes.

He explained all about these;—how you had arranged to have them blessed by the Pope, specially for this battalion; how Cardinal Bourne had brought them from Rome; and how, next Sunday, when we shall be back behind the trenches, we are to have a Parade Mass, when they will be distributed. And he said many nice things about you.

It is cold and rainy again to-day, and our "Heavies" have

been giving the Germans a rotten time since morning—
occasionally, a very rotten time. But they have replied
very little.

We go back to the front line this afternoon.

April 17, 1917.   *"Turnerstown Left" (Vierstraat Sector)*.
I think this year must be accursed. Never was a fouler
day than to-day. After a wet night it is still raining this
morning, and the wind is howling dismally, but overhead.
There are points, after all, in being in a trench.

The French seem to have made a spectacular re-entry
into the arena yesterday, but they must have been greatly
handicapped by the weather, like our men at Vimy.

Last night we captured two big Prussian Grenadiers
(unwounded) on our wire. They were brought to my dug-
out at 2 a.m., looking frightened—with their hands still
outstretched in the orthodox manner of the surrendered
prisoner who desires to show that he is not armed; coated
with mud; one bleeding from a tear from the wire; but
neither seeming too unhappy.

If one only knew German this would be the proper time
to extract information. They are too scared to lie much.
Later, when they find out how kindly is the British soldier,
they become sly and independent.

April 22, 1917 *(Sunday)*.   *Birr Barracks (Locre)*.
The ceremony of presenting your crucifixes was performed this morning. All of the battalion that was available
—between 600 and 700—marched in sunshine to the Parish
Church of Locre, led by the regimental pipes and drums.
When we reached the gates we found the Divisional band
awaiting us, which, as the drums stopped, struck up and
played the battalion into church. A crowd of soldiers and
civilians was watching, and overhead, high up in the sky,
a German aeroplane was passing, at which the "Archies"
were potting wildly.

Inside, the church was packed. The Divisional Commander and the Brigadier were there, and with myself had
seats in the chancel. Lined up, facing one another along
each side of the chancel, was a Guard of Honour of sixteen,

with fixed bayonets, which presented arms at the Elevation, while the buglers sounded the General Salute.

The Divisional band stood in the doorway of the church, and played at intervals.

The priest (Father O'Connell), from the pulpit, gave an address, in which he described your happy idea. He spoke about you and also myself, and commended the "spirit" of the battalion. He said that to-day's Mass was to be "for Mrs. Feilding's intention," and asked every one present to pray specially for you—that all might go well with you. So you have had a church full of soldiers—there must have been nearly a thousand altogether—straight from the battle line—praying for you this day. I wonder if any other woman has had the same experience.

When Mass was over the priest asked all but the two Generals and the Connaught Rangers to leave the church, and he then presented the crucifixes; first to the Generals; then to the Guard of Honour; then to the officers and men of the battalion, all of whom kissed them as they received them, and have, I believe, since hung them round their necks.

One of my non-Catholic Company Commanders asked if he might take a crucifix. He told me, later, that it was the most impressive ceremony he had ever seen: and I may admit that the devout reverence of these soldiers, redolent of the trenches, as they filed up towards the altar, affected me, too, very deeply.

Then we marched home, again headed by the drums.

May 2, 1917.   *Birr Barracks (Locre).*

The battalion has twice played football lately against battalions of the Carson (36th) Division, and I am sorry to say got beaten both times.

On the second occasion there was a big crowd of soldier spectators—certainly 2,000 or 3,000. The ground was the best that could be found, but was rather "close up," and would not have been chosen had this large attendance been foreseen. Moreover, the day (Sunday) was the clearest of days, as it happened.

When I arrived, the sight of the crowd, I confess, made me anxious. A hostile aeroplane overhead with wireless apparatus; a German battery behind; a sudden hurricane bombardment with shrapnel; and considerable damage might have followed. And I was the senior officer present.

But to stop a match in process of being cleanly fought before a sporting audience between the two great opposing factions of Ireland, in a spirit of friendliness which, so far as I am aware, seems unattainable on Ireland's native soil— even though in sight (or almost in sight) of the enemy— was a serious matter; and I decided to let the game go on.

However, as I was going round, quietly warning the officers at the first sign of an enemy aeroplane to scatter the crowd, a Brigadier rode on to the ground, and I was relieved to find myself no longer responsible. All went well, but I shall not allow my men to play another "International" match on *that* ground.

During the game a wag on the Ulster side was heard to say: "I wonder if we shall get into trouble for fraternizing with the enemy!"

Michael is leaving me, and though I am naturally glad that he has got a good job, I shall be most sorry to lose him. His military training and knowledge of military affairs have been invaluable to me, and I have got into the way of applying to him for advice in every difficulty that arises.

May 4, 1917.   *Birr Barracks* (*Locre*).

The Padre came to me this morning, and said that there were still about fifty men or more in the battalion who have not yet had your crosses, and were longing for them. It seems that on the Sunday, when they were distributed, every one who could possibly claim to be a Connaught Ranger—many men in fact who are detached from the battalion—heard of what was on, and went to church.

On the other hand, some men of the battalion were on fatigue that day, and though I hoped there would be enough crosses to go round, there were not. The question is: What can be done? Anyhow, I have said I will write to you and ask if you can get a hundred more.

Yesterday evening, as I was going into the Convent to dinner, the enemy was shelling the road about a quarter of a mile in front. Presently, he lifted and dropped a five-point-nine into the field alongside, which he immediately followed with two others. The result was a splinter of shell through one of the Convent windows, but it was enough to demonstrate the need of caution.

I went into the Convent and found the nuns and lay-sisters all in a flutter, rounding up the children. I went into the kitchen premises to calm them down. I don't think they had had it so near before. They asked: "Should they take the children into the cellar?" I said I did not think that was necessary; and then we settled down to dinner, and the offence has not been repeated since.

I rode into Bailleul the other day, and met Willie Redmond. He was with another Nationalist Member of Parliament—Captain Esmonde.[1] The latter looks about nineteen. Redmond said that everybody in the House of Commons is determined now to have an Irish settlement, and he seems confident that Ireland is going to get Home Rule at last.

We are still having wonderful weather. It has been almost like jumping out of January into July.

May 5, 1917.   *Birr Barracks (Locre).*

Again a glorious summer day. After breakfast I walked round the Nuns' garden. It was the first time I had been there. In one corner is a shrine to The Bléssèd Virgin—a sort of miniature Grotto of Lourdes. In front of this is a flower-bed, in the centre of which—planted over and surrounded by flowers—is the grave of a Canadian private soldier, beautifully cared for by the Nuns, with his name and number on a polished brass plate, fixed to a cross which marks the head.

Should it be my fate not to survive this war, I cannot imagine a more pleasant resting-place, and, if I get the opportunity, I shall mention this to the Reverend Mother.

May 6, 1917 (Sunday).   *Butterfly Farm (near Locre).*

I am afraid you are having a trying time, what with

[1] Capt. J. L. Esmonde, M.P. (N. Tipperary).

servant troubles and worries about food for the children, and I cannot express how much I feel for you.

Last evening we came into Brigade Reserve, relieving the same battalion that we relieved two nights before the attack on Ginchy. As on that famous occasion we were shelled on the way up, so were some of my men shelled heavily last night—though, as luck had it, with very little damage, considering.

For some reason—along the whole of this Army front, I believe—the enemy last night took upon himself to be highly objectionable, and at intervals bombarded the back areas violently for considerable periods, with hurricane bursts of intense fire. These outbursts took place at nine o'clock: 12.30: 2.30; and about 4.30 a.m.; and, though very few shells came near my camp, the bombardments were so loud and threatening that I got up and went out twice during the night. In the front line, I hear, it was quiet enough.

In the course of the first bout the shelling set fire to a farm where there is (or was) a big dump of R.E. material, and where I had a party of thirty-five men at work, under a young officer, Pope by name.

The flames shot up into the sky, lighting up the surrounding country, and the Germans fairly rained shells upon the blazing mass. I have visited the place since, and have been much impressed by the fine work done under the heavy bombardment by my little party and others in extinguishing the fire, and so preventing what else must have been a disastrous loss of material.

As is the custom here, the owners were still living in this farm, and one of the duties which Pope found thus suddenly thrust upon him was to take care of the old lady of the establishment.

It has been an unfortunate affair for her. Not only has she lost her farm buildings, but in the wrecked stable ten cows lie dead and roasted, still chained to their stalls—a piteous sight! My people did not know of their existence, and nobody else seems to have thought of them—poor beasts!

It is disgusting to think of the successes the Germans are

having with their submarines. What a lot those cranks have to answer for who opposed and defeated the Channel Tunnel idea so long ago!

May 8, 1917. *Butterfly Farm (near Locre).*

The German artillery continues to be very aggressive, shelling our back areas, roads, and billets, at intervals during the nights.

These bombardments have, of course, levied their toll in killed and wounded men, and also in horses. (Michael and I, during a walk yesterday, came upon ten horses, killed by one shell.) In proportion to the expenditure of ammunition the damage has been slight; but this kind of thing is annoying to the back areas, as you may imagine.

Last night, the Germans got a bit of their own back. At 8.45, by pre-arranged order, practically every gun and howitzer in the 2nd Army opened fire simultaneously, and continued at top blast for exactly five minutes, bombarding *their* back areas, roads and billets.

It was an impressive sight to watch the hundreds—perhaps thousands—of guns in action together, flashing intermittently in the darkness. And each time the enemy ventured to retaliate upon any area, he got a double dose.

From eleven o'clock till five minutes past the operation was repeated. After that the enemy was as quiet as a mouse for the rest of the night.

May 9, 1917. *Butterfly Farm (near Locre).*

The Germans persist in aggravating mood, and we have just passed through a third night in succession of disturbed slumber.

At six o'clock this morning I was woken up by some "crumps" falling rather close, and, as I lay ruminating whether it was worth while getting out of bed, the question was decided for me by a covey of splinters crashing against the wooden wall of my hut.

Then the five-point-nines began to come thick and fast, obviously aimed at two 12-inch howitzers which periodically heckle the enemy from a hollow, less than a hundred yards from this camp.

Why they will persist in placing heavy guns so near infantry rest camps, or vice versâ, it is difficult to understand, but the infantry have come to accept these things as they do the other vicissitudes of the war. Anyhow, the situation was so unhealthy this morning that I decided to move the battalion.

It is interesting to watch the self-possessed and almost leisurely fashion in which such a movement is conducted nowadays. This comes from the familiarity of the troops with shell-fire. The sections were scattered in the fields around, and by this means we escaped without casualties, though two or more shells fell actually into the camp. The bombardment went on for over an hour, some three hundred shells falling. Then the battalion returned to its tents and huts, and shaved, and had breakfast.

Before the shelling had finished Pereira came sauntering along, without even his tin hat on, to see what was the matter, approaching from the "danger" side—i.e. the direction of the target.

The guard had been withdrawn with the rest of the battalion, but owing to a misunderstanding no orders had been given to the gas sentry (Private Peter Oprey), and I found him, when I went back, still standing at his post, fortunately unhurt, though the hut against which he stood was perforated with fragments.

May 15, 1917.   *Kemmel Shelters.*

I feel disappointed when I get a letter from you telling me of troubles with servants, whom war and the high wages of the munition works seem to have so thoroughly unsettled. I hate picturing you in the midst of such annoyances, especially as there is nothing I can say or do can help you. Contrariwise, this remark no doubt applies equally to my stories to you of the goings on here, and I often wonder if I am right in keeping the promise I made you when I first came out to hide nothing from you.

The very fact of my being here must cause you intense anxiety, and, as I am helpless in the case of the servant problem, so it is equally true that there is nothing you can do to deter the enemy from any villainy he may contemplate. And I continue writing to you of all the dangers of the war, remembering that you once said that if I hid anything you would know it, and only imagine worse things than were really happening.

I and my battalion are still detached from the Brigade, digging all the time.

The last few weeks there has been rather an epidemic of crime in the battalion, on a small scale;—insubordination among a few men, who are marched in front of me time after time, and who seem equally impervious to leniency and the severest kind of discipline. I have sent some for court-martial and they have received heavy sentences, which, however, the General has commuted to Field Punishment. The result is that instead of having got rid of these men they remain with the battalion, and are a constant source of trouble and annoyance.

I fully appreciate the General's difficulties. During these times a certain kind of scrimshanker, scenting danger ahead, is apt to commit some crime, hoping thereby to get imprisonment, and so be removed from the firing line. (Others will achieve the same object, more safely, by going sick, and they are often taken, on reaching home, for heroes instead of what they really are;—but that is by the way.) In the case of the former the Authorities are fully alive to the trick. Consequently, there is a tendency to commute all sentences of imprisonment, which, for obvious reasons, are served away from the line, to Field Punishment, which is served in it. But, in the latter case, the punishment falls so flat that the hardened offender cares nothing for it.

In 1915 a different method was followed. Sentences of imprisonment were deferred until the end of the war, and this method had a double advantage. First, the bad soldier had a sort of sword of Damocles ever poised above his head, and secondly, the better man, whose trouble had come from some momentary lapse (an ever-present possibility in war, as in peace), had a chance of atoning for his delinquency, and often, by good behaviour or a gallant act on the battle-field, he earned a complete reprieve.

The trouble I have alluded to is in the present case no more than one of those cycles which all bodies of men go through at times, and it will soon pass away; and, apart from the few troublesome ones I have mentioned—perhaps half a dozen—the battalion is in first-rate form and very cheerful, and the work it is doing here is being well and rapidly carried out, and is receiving much praise.

May 18, 1917. *Coulomby.*

Yesterday morning we left Locre, and marched to Haege-doorne (near Bailleul), where we took train to St. Omer. From there we marched along the canal (where the Red Cross barges are moored) to Arques, where we billeted for the night.

The train journey, as usual, was such as would try the patience of anyone unused to French railways in war-time. To sum up, it took us 7¼ hours to do 25 miles; and we travelled—both officers and men—in goods trucks.

This morning (my birthday) we moved on again by foot, doing 15 miles—a trying march, since the day was hot and the men were heavily loaded up, besides being too fresh from the trenches to be in a fit condition for marching. They came along splendidly, nevertheless, with the drums leading, and finished in the evening with plenty of swing at Coulomby, where many officers and men of other battalions of the Brigade stood by the road, watching them pass.

All along the route numerous inhabitants (who are not so blasé about British soldiers hereabouts as they are nearer the line) turned out to have a look at the battalion. Bevies of children ran alongside, and an old Frenchman—evidently a veteran of the Franco-Prussian War—had all his medals ready, and held them up behind his cottage window, at the same time drawing his hand across his throat in signification of his sentiments towards his quondam—and now once more his country's enemies.

The country is looking superb, and it is strange to be away from shell-holes and the sound of guns. We passed by Lumbres, and I and my Headquarters officers were invited by an old woman into her shop to eat our lunch. She told me that her husband had worked forty-five years for the Avots—father and son—the latter my kind host of August and September, 1915, of whom I have so often spoken to you. She promised to take a message this very afternoon to Madame Avot, saying that I am in the neighbourhood. Then she brought up her little granddaughter —Madeleine—who nearly died of shyness, and into whose small hand I placed a "rent" for the use of the room, as we marched away.

When we reached this place, where we are billeted in barns and farms, very scattered, I was visited by the Brigadier, who gave me his usual cheery welcome. He has started calling me "Moltke" since the great sham battle of Locre, performed before the Big Wigs. I was asleep when he came, under a tree in a very green meadow behind my billet;—so quiet and green, and such a peaceful contrast to what we have come from—and may be going to. Pray for us, and continue to do so.

Talking of praying, George Pereira was telling me a story the other day of one of the Chaplains (an excellent one, too). The two were walking together and the Padre was saying, "I am so resigned to the thought of death that I have no fear of shells. I have placed myself in the hands of God, and death——" As he spoke there came the familiar sound—w-r-r-r-r-h-n—bang! The Brigadier looked round and found himself alone. He hunted about and eventually found the Chaplain on his tummy in a "convanient" trench. I ought not perhaps to repeat this story, which was told by the Brigadier with a twinkle in his eye: and, after all, the Chaplain was very wise; and the teller, who is recklessly brave himself, and loves a good yarn, is the last man in the world to speak slightingly of the "Church."

I heard the good priest of whom the story was told in the pulpit the other day. He started his sermon as follows: "I don't claim to know anything about soldiering: indeed, I doubt if I could tell you the difference between a 'five-point-nine' and a 'rum-jar,' but I do flatter myself I know something about the requirements of the Christian religion," etc., etc., etc.

May 20, 1917 (*Sunday*).   *Coulomby.*

The rest is already beginning to work marvels with the men, and although we have so far had only two days of it, the cheered-up look and the renewed freshness in the battalion is surprising to see.

We had a football match this afternoon, and won it: and this morning (Sunday) we had Church Parade in an orchard. I must say I felt very proud of the battalion. The men had all groomed themselves up like new pins. The mud of the trenches had entirely disappeared. The brass was polished: the leather about the drums was well pipe-clayed: even the cookers and water-carts, the harness, chains, and limbers, were shining and resplendent. The spirit is there: of that there is no doubt; and it is wonderful.

This afternoon I rode with Booth, my Adjutant, to Lumbres, and called on the Avots. About five seconds after I had rung the bell the door was opened by Madame Avot herself. She recognized me at once and gave me such a welcome. She called for her husband, and Jean (who used to follow me about on his bicycle), and the little girl. There was a rush along the passage as they all came bounding out to meet me. I might have been the head of the house returning from the war. It was indeed most touching. The last time I had seen them was on that night when they all waited in the road to say good-bye as we marched past their gate on our way to Loos. Jean and his sister were small children then. To-day Jean is dressed like a man, and both he and Edith are as tall as myself. The latter was in white, and her black hair is cut short round the neck, like P.'s.

I was skurried into the drawing-room. Madame Avot began asking me all sorts of questions—about you, and about the children. She remembered everything about all of you. We started in broken French. Then we got into broken English. She asked, "How is the cheeky one?"—

referring to a description I had once given her of A——.
I had forgotten the episode till she reminded me. I had
tried to describe the three children, and incidentally had
said that one of them was a cheeky little thing. She did
not understand, and I searched for a word, but could not
find any appropriate translation for the word "cheeky."
She has since then learned to use the word herself.

While we sat in the drawing-room the little—now big
—girl (what a long time the war must have lasted for her
to have grown like this) handed round chocolates. Then
I reminded her mother of a musical evening she once gave
us when the C.R.A. of the Guards Division dined there.
She is a genius with the piano. She immediately said:
"Would you like some music now?" and sat down and
played. Then she asked: "Would I like some singing—
French or English?" I said "French." So she sang a
French song with such determination and simplicity that
it quite carried me away. Then she called upon Jean, who
played the violin to her accompaniment.

It all reminded me of that evening in August, 1915, when
she did these same things, and her husband, whose English
was *very, very* limited in those days, edged up to me and
kept saying, "Am I not lucky to have such a wife?"

They have invited me to dinner to-morrow, and it was
a nice thought that they asked me to stay the night—"in the
same room I slept in when I was there before"—the "star"
room of the house. So I am going to dine there, but not
to sleep, as we are billeted 5 miles away, and we shall be
hard at work these few days.

One of my Companies has produced an enormous green
flag with a yellow Irish harp upon it, which the men carry
about with them on the march, and fly outside their billets.
It has not got the Crown, and therefore would be ranked by
some people as "Sinn Fein," I feel sure. But it does not
seem to make any difference to their loyalty and devotion.
How times have changed!

I am billeted in a farm. To get to the room where the
Adjutant and I sleep we have to pass through the kitchen,

where our servants and the women of the house do the cooking. As I was writing this afternoon I overheard them talking, through the door. One of the servants—by way of pleasant conversation—asked one of the women what her name was. She said: "Emilie." He replied: "Nice name—bon name—Emily. I like Emily."

That is Soldier French.

May 24, 1917.   *Coulomby.*

I have not written during the last two or three days. We have been training, and this keeps me out from early morning till late afternoon, after which I have the usual routine work to do, and then am tempted to ride out and explore this glorious part of the country, and enjoy the spring scenery. You will understand what a pleasant contrast our present surroundings are to the ear-splitting, war-torn zone from which we have come.

On Tuesday I marched the battalion to Lumbres, where we spent the day on the banks of the brook, in the same field where Lord Cavan inspected the then newly-formed 2nd Guards Brigade in September, 1915, just before Loos. I think every one enjoyed the outing.

I borrowed Jean Avot's rod and fished, but without success (the trout are very wily there, and the water was thick). I dined with his parents the same evening, as I had done the evening before. Their hospitality is unbounded. On the first occasion, the entertainment was to some extent marred for me by the presence of a little "pipsqueak" (a man—not a shell this time) of the most virulent type—a "purchasing officer," aged about twenty-one. He lolled about, dressed in khaki;—"at the front"—almost out of earshot of the guns, and miles out of their range; parading his intimacy with the family; undisciplined; safe; while better men by far than he are being slaughtered further east. However, perhaps I am maligning him. He says his lungs are weak.

The other day I went to St. Omer, where I lunched with G.H.Q. Staff (Gas Department), and afterwards was shown a very interesting exhibition, which Colonel Foulkes (who has control of these eccentricities of modern warfare) had kindly arranged of the latest and most horrible ways of killing our enemies. It was an instructive afternoon, and there is no doubt that we are already miles ahead of the Germans at their own game. But I cannot go into details, as you will understand.

At the rate we are going I think the enemy ought to be beaten very soon.

May 26, 1917.   *Coulomby.*

To-day we had a big practice day over prepared ground, and the Army Commander (General Plumer), the Corps Commander, and other Generals, came to see us perform.

To-morrow (Sunday) I have arranged a battalion day; platoon and section competitions in the morning, and in the afternoon sports:—a nice free-from-the-war day for men and officers, in fact. We have put up jumps, as the programme includes horse-jumping (in which I am going to compete). And all the Brigade has been invited.

But Courts-Martial and Generals' Conferences are intervening, and everything promises to be spoilt. It *may* turn out all right, but it doesn't look hopeful at the moment (11.30 p.m.).

May 27, 1917 (Sunday).   *Coulomby.*

This morning at eight o'clock one of the Padres said Mass in the orchard. He also preached a short sermon, in the course of which he exhorted the men to join in the singing of the hymns. He told them that they ought not to be ashamed of the men on either side hearing them, however badly they did it, and assured us that God didn't mind at all whether we sang in tune or not, so long as we sang.

Then he burst out: "I don't say *you're* so bad. Anyway, you're miles ahead of the Munsters! I'm simply fed up with the Munsters . . . at any rate so far as singing is concerned!!"

In the afternoon we had our sports after all, and many people came. The weather was perfect, and all was a huge success. Moreover, we managed to get some English stout and gave each man—the visitors as well as the men of the battalion—a free drink, which gave great satisfaction to all. I won the horse-jumping competition.

May 29, 1917. *Arques.*

We moved at half-past six this morning, and after a 15-mile march halted here, where we are billeted for the night. We have two more days' marching in front of us before we reach the line.

The weather is cool, and it has been a fine day for marching, and I never saw the battalion look better as it went by the Brigadier, who stood on the road to watch it pass. It is wonderful what a lot of good a few days' rest and the absence of shells can do to troops, and the ten days of change have transformed these men, who, as they marched to-day, seemed to be without a care or trouble in the world. Each time the drums struck up, and each time they stopped, a wild Irish yell went up; and, as "Brian Boru" was played, that cry which marks certain bars in this spirited tune was rendered in a style that would have brought either tears or laughter to your eyes, could you have heard it.

June 1, 1917. *Clare Camp* (2 *miles N. of Bailleul*).

As we marched yesterday into Bailleul we passed refugees —women, children, and others, the women pushing perambulators with their babies and other belongings. They were leaving the place.

The enemy has at last started shelling it. In fact, he has begun to shell all the towns and villages behind our line. I believe we send over quite sixty or a hundred shells for each one of his;—he is, no doubt, holding his fire;—but the effect is being felt, and the more nervous of the civil population are beginning to move; indeed, having regard to the big shell-holes which I saw as we passed through the suburbs, I only marvel at the courage of the mothers in having stayed so long.

Furniture vans were loading up in front of some of the houses, and in Locre, which is of course very much nearer the line, though I have not yet revisited the hospitable Convent there, I hear that the children have already been sent away.

On the other hand, many sturdy inhabitants remain, and in my wanderings to-day I saw a sight which struck me as pathetic. It was that of a *very* old man and a tiny boy of three or four, crouched together in a flimsy dug-out which the old man had made alongside his still more flimsy cottage.

We reached camp in the afternoon, after a 15-mile march, and found that the enemy had been shelling there: then we bivouacked; and, though a few shells came over during the night, these did no harm—to us at any rate. They were just near enough to wake us up, but not to get us out of bed. While we were at dinner a German aeroplane flew over and set fire to one of our captive balloons.

This evening I went with Goode—one of my Company Commanders—to the top of Kemmel Hill, and from one of the artillery observation posts that have been burrowed into the hill watched a fierce bombardment of the German trenches. We looked on for nearly an hour, while the fire increased and intensified till it grew into such an inferno that the whole horizon was obliterated by the smoke and gas and dust. Above the clouds thus created the German S.O.S. rockets played, like lost souls in hell appealing for deliverance. How they stand it, God alone knows!

P.S. Goode's Company marched in front yesterday, and consequently he rode beside me. He is an excellent officer, and comes out frequently with ideas. Now and again he makes a very sage remark. In the course of the day we passed a fat major of the sort one sees behind the line— with plenty of decorations—evidently the happy occupant of some "fat and cushy" job. Goode remarked: "I'll bet the only time *he* gets the wind up is when he thinks the war is going to end."

Cruel, but possibly true! How many are there like that? I wonder.

June 8, 1917.   *Rossignol Wood.*

After a bombardment without equal in history, we attacked the Germans yesterday morning at ten minutes past three, and took the Messines-Wytschaete Ridge.

Our Brigade was allotted what was expected to be the

most formidable task of the day—the capture of Wytschaete Village, which has been held by the enemy since 1914, having been taken by them that year after much bloodshed. So extravagantly had they paid for it, that, according to one after another of the prisoners we have captured lately, the Kaiser had given special injunctions and exhortations regarding the importance of holding it.

The village tops the crest of the Messines Ridge, and the breastworks, which we have occupied since we came from the Somme, last September, run across the swampy fields to the west of and below it, with the hospice (or convent)—represented by a heap of bricks—standing out prominently against the skyline, beyond the Petit Bois.

Now, the whole ridge and much beyond it is ours, and I am writing this letter sitting in the open in a wood, which, the day before yesterday, would not have been a healthy thing to do.

My letters of late have necessarily been short and scrappy, and you may have guessed—from their very brevity and dullness—how much was going on, and how much we had on hand.

It was during the night of June 2 that we came up to the trenches to take our part in the battle. The day had been chiefly occupied with conferences—with my officers, with the Brigadier, and the Divisional General. At noon, Major Keating—a Connaught Ranger officer, now commanding Tanks—had sent his car for me, and after giving me lunch had shown me his Squadron, comprising the latest super-tanks as well as old veterans that had fought on the Somme. All were well "camouflaged," awaiting the order to advance to the attack.

At 9.30 p.m. we left for the trenches. A good deal of shelling was going on, and we had six wounded and a sergeant killed on the way up. When I reached my Headquarters to be, at S.P.12, I found that the enemy had been shelling there. In fact, so hot had the C.O. of the outgoing battalion found it that he had just moved out, and I found him and his Adjutant squatting in the tiny dug-out of his

Regimental Sergeant-major, which was built into the great barricade of sandbags, known as the Chinese wall. The enemy had dropped one shell plumb in the trench between the C.O.'s sleeping and mess dug-outs, blowing the cook to atoms, and wounding four others.

It seemed to me, on consideration, that it was unlikely they would repeat so good a shot, and as these dug-outs happen to be rather comfortable, in striking contrast to the Sergeant-major's dug-out, which is only about 4 feet high, I decided to chance it and go back, and have survived the experiment. The relief was not complete till 2.30 or 3 a.m.

On June 3 I was visited by the Brigadier and many others, and spent a busy day, preparing details and writing orders for a trench raid, which, suddenly and unexpectedly, I had been called upon to make the following night. Our artillery bombarded the German trenches very heavily all that day, the enemy replying wildly and everywhere, on our front line and the back areas. Our artillery and trench-mortar batteries had full-dress and magnificent rehearsals of intense barrage, under Divisional, Corps, and Army arrangements. The latest refinements of chemical warfare were a feature of the day;—incendiary oil shells; thermit— a mixture of aluminium powder and magnetic oxide of iron, which, on the bursting of the shell, combine, producing a temperature high enough to melt steel, and descend in a glittering cascade of white-hot molten metal on to anybody or anything that happens to be below; gas from projectors; flying-pigs (i.e. bombs from the 9·45-inch trench-mortars —otherwise known as Duchesses); footballs (the big spherical bombs attached to 2-inch steel rods which are fired from the medium trench-mortars); and guns and howitzers of all descriptions and calibres.

The heaviest bombardment was about 3 p.m., and Booth —my Adjutant—and I watched it from Van Horn,—a position with a good field of view. When the firing had begun to relax we returned to Battalion Headquarters, and waited in an "Elephant" shelter, known as Harley House, till the retaliation should have died down. Presently, two heavy shells dropped within a few yards of us. Then a third seemed to fall in the doorway where I was standing. Immediately, all was darkness. The shelter was choked with a cloud of dust and debris. From a corner came a wail: "Mother of God, I'm kilt entoirely!" I wondered how many really were killed, and when the dust had cleared away felt around to see. The shell had fallen on a big dump of trench-mortar ammunition about 30 yards along the trench, and exploded it, and there was a hole 50 feet wide and 20 feet deep as evidence of the fact, though I only found this out afterwards.

The damage, otherwise, was slight. Two men had been killed outside, and two slightly wounded in the doorway. As for myself, I got the blast and the dust, broken by the turn in the trench, but otherwise full in the face, and everything looked scarlet. It was a nasty feeling at first. I heard the doctor whispering, and wondered if I was permanently blinded. For the rest of that day I could not open my eyes. My head ached.

I thought I might have to give in, but I went and had a good sleep in my dug-out after the doctor had washed out and fomented my eyes, and next morning I was all right again.

All through the night there was savage firing, during which the enemy retaliated hotly. Both he and we put over many gas shells. We also put over more oil and thermit.

At 10.30 on the night of June 4 I launched my raid—250 officers and men under Captain Tuite. The objective was the third line of the enemy's trenches, in Wytschaete Wood. Tuite was to advance behind a creeping artillery barrage and was given twelve minutes to reach his final objective. The guns were then to form a "box" barrage till the raiders got home again. He was allowed forty-five minutes in which to do the whole business. In such active times it was not possible to interfere with the ordinary work of the artillery for longer than this.

The raid was skilfully led and was entirely successful.

These affairs sometimes seem to go off better when done on the spur of the moment than after long fussy preparation. About sixty Germans were killed and seven prisoners were brought back, including an acting officer wearing the iron cross. The raiders returned in rags, their clothing torn to shreds by the enemy's wire, and to-day, after four more days of fighting, their clothes are in no better condition, as you can imagine.

We lost three officers—two killed, and one blinded for life, I am afraid, by a bullet which penetrated his eye. There were about forty casualties among the men, mostly slight.

I was up most of the night. In the early morning (about 3.45) the enemy once more started shelling my Headquarters with heavy shell—8-inch and over. They were perhaps trying to repeat their success of two days before, and to fire off more of our ammunition for us. They kept it up till nearly noon, putting over some 300 shells, and it was very uncomfortable. At 10 a.m. I went round the front line, and from there could look back and watch the big shells still falling around my "home."

The ultimate result of this bombardment was a big mess, but little material damage. One of the three principal shelters ("Harley House"—the one in which I had received my shaking two days before) was, however, flattened, and Murphy—one of the regimental police who was on sentry duty—was killed. Another man, also, was buried, but was gallantly recovered, after an hour and a half, badly wounded but still alive, by the pioneer corporal (Coleman), while the shells were still falling. Poor Murphy had a photograph of his children in his pocket—a delightful-looking family.

After midnight (June 5–6) we were relieved from the actual front line by the 6th Royal Irish Regiment. It was the beginning of the great battle. The troops were massed during this night for the coming attack, and the process was a slow one. We did not get through it till 4.30 on the morning of the 6th.

During the night a lance-corporal of mine, who had been reported missing on the night of the raid—Fielding by name—was found in Noman's Land, by another regiment, and brought in.   He had been lying there twenty-four hours with six wounds!   His finders were greatly impressed by his stoic behaviour.

That evening (June 6) we tea'd in the open, about half a mile behind the fire-trench, our artillery shooting hard over our heads all the time, but eliciting no reply from the enemy.   The Brigadier called and congratulated us on the success of the raid.   He was in the best of form, and indeed everybody was very cheerful and full of confidence.   It was very edifying to see the almost exhilarated state every one was in, both officers and men, seeing what a colossal business lay immediately before them.   Later, we had dinner in the open, sitting on the ground, and Colonel Monck-Mason, commanding the 1st Munsters, and his Adjutant dined with us.

The 6th Connaught Rangers were to be broken up for the battle in order to provide "mopping up" and carrying parties for the attacking battalions, thus leaving me personally with very little to do, and after dinner I moved to my Battle Headquarters—a deep mined dug-out in Rossignol Wood, above which I am now writing this letter.   The wood reeked of gas shells, to which the enemy further contributed during the night.

Yesterday morning (the great day) I got up and went out at three o'clock.   The exact moment of the assault (known by us as "Zero"; by the French as "l'heure H") which had been withheld by the Higher Command, as is usual, till as late as possible, had been disclosed to us as 3.10 a.m.

I climbed on to the bank of the communication trench, known as Rossignol Avenue, and waited.   Dawn had not yet broken.   The night was very still.   Our artillery was lobbing over an occasional shell; the enemy—oblivious of the doom descending upon him—was leisurely putting back gas shells, which burst in and around my wood with little dull pops, adding to the smell but doing no injury.

The minute hand of my watch crept on to the fatal moment.   Then followed a "tableau" so sudden and dramatic that I cannot hope to describe it.   Out of the

silence and the darkness, along the front, twenty mines[1]
—some of them having waited two years and more for this
occasion—containing hundreds of tons of high explosive,
almost simultaneously, and with a roar to wake the dead,
burst into the sky in great sheets of flame, developing into
mountainous clouds of dust and earth and stones and trees.

For some seconds the earth trembled and swayed. Then
the guns and howitzers in their thousands spoke: the
machine-gun barrage opened; and the infantry on a 10-mile
front left the trenches and advanced behind the barrage
against the enemy.

The battle once launched, all was oblivion. No news
came through for several hours: there was just the roar of
the artillery;—such a roar and such a barrage has never been
before. Our men advanced almost without a check. The
enemy—such of them as were not killed—were paralysed,
and surrendered. In Wytschaete Village they rushed
forward with their hands up, waving handkerchiefs and
things. And no one can blame them. The ordeal through
which they have been passing the last fortnight must have
surpassed the torments of hell itself.

The extent of our advance you will have learnt from the
newspapers, and I hope you and all the world will have learnt
also that the South Irish Division and the Ulster Division
went forward side by side;—that they opened the battle.

I have been thinking to-day of the saying—that the battle
of Waterloo was won on the playing-fields of Eton. That
remark wants revision now. You must for the "playing-
fields of Eton" substitute the "offices of the Empire."
From the offices have been introduced business methods
which are essential to the complicated operations of
nowadays. The Staff work yesterday was perfect. What a
contrast to the time of Loos!

We were inundated with paper beforehand on this
occasion, so much so that it became a saying: "If ink will

---

[1] The writer has since been informed by Brig.-Gen. Sir James Edmonds,
C.B., C.M.G., R.E., of the Historical Department of the War Office, that
the aggregate charge of "High Explosive" employed was 933,200 lbs.

win this war we certainly shall win it"; but no contingency,
so far as I know, was unforeseen, and within six hours of
the first assault parties were already at work, making
roads across the mutilated zone and even laying water-pipes!
All objectives had been reached punctually to scheduled time.

At 10 a.m. our guns were still pounding, though at
reduced pressure, and the enemy had ceased to reply at all.

There was nothing to keep me any longer at the telephone, and I went forward to study results. German
prisoners were carrying back the wounded. Already our
Field Artillery was on the move forward—a stirring sight
which always fascinates me. As I watch them, though I
have nothing to do with them, I feel a kind of pride in them.
I, as everybody else was doing, walked freely over the
surface; past and over the old front line, where we have
spent so many bitter months. How miserable and frail
our wretched breastworks looked! When viewed—as for
the first time I now saw them—from the parapet instead
of from inside—the parapet only a sandbag thick in many
places—what death-traps they seemed!

Then over Noman's Land. As we stepped out there,
my orderly, O'Rourke, remarked: "This is the first time
for two years that anyone has had the privilege of walking
over this ground in daylight, sir." We visited some of the
mine craters made at the Zero hour, and huge indeed they
are. Then we explored Petit Bois and Wytschaete Wood
—blown into space by our fire and non-existent—the scene
of our raid of the night of June 4. We found the bodies
of an officer and a man of ours, missing since that night,
which I have since had fetched out and buried among many
of their comrades.

Our Tanks were now advancing—a dozen or more of
them—going forward to take part in the capture of the fifth
and sixth objectives. Their duty is to reduce local opposition, when it is encountered, and there they were, lumbering
along, picking their way through the honeycomb of shell-
holes and craters, getting into difficulties, getting out again,
sometimes defeated, but generally in the end winning their

way through this area of devastation, where nothing has been left alive, not even a blade of grass.

I cannot hope to describe to you all the details of a battle on this scale. The outstanding feature, I think, was the astounding smallness of our casualties. The contrast in this respect with Loos and the Somme was most remarkable. Scarcely any dead were to be seen. The German dead had been mostly buried by the shell-fire. Our troops, during the advance, so battered and bewildered were the enemy by our fire and so paralysed by the appalling suddenness of the mine explosions, scarcely lost at all.

But, as is always the way, we lost some of our best. A single shell—and a small one at that—knocked out twelve, killing three outright and wounding nine—two of the latter mortally. Among the victims of this shell were Major Stannus, commanding the 7th Leinsters, and his Adjutant (Acton), and Roche, the Brigade trench-mortar officer. I passed the last-named in my wanderings, lying by a dead private on the fire-step. He was, I think, one of the wittiest "raconteurs" I have ever met, and as brave and ready a soldier as I have ever seen. As Brigade trench-mortar officer he was a genius. In conversation he was remarkable. I lifted the sandbag which some one had thrown over his face. It was discoloured by the explosion of the shell that had killed him, but otherwise was quite untouched, and it wore the same slight smile that in life used to precede and follow his wonderful sallies. In peace-time he was a barrister.

Willie Redmond also is dead. Aged fifty-four, he asked to be allowed to go over with his regiment. He should not have been there at all. His duties latterly were far from the fighting line. But, as I say, he asked and was allowed to go—on the condition that he came back directly the first objective was reached; and Fate has decreed that he should come back on a stretcher.

How one's ideas change! And how war makes one loathe the party politics that condone and even approve when his opponents revile such a man as this! I classify

him with Stephen Gwynn and Harrison—all three, MEN—
Irish Nationalists, too, whom you and I, in our Tory school-
ing, have been brought up to regard as anathema! What
effect will his death have in Ireland? I wonder. Will he
be a saint or a traitor? I hope and pray it may teach all
—North as well as South—something of the larger side of
their duty to the Empire.

P.S. My men found a dead German machine-gunner
chained to his gun. This is authentic. We have the
gun, and the fact is vouched for by my men who took the
gun, and is confirmed by their officer, who saw it. I do
not understand the meaning of this:—whether it was done
under orders, or was a voluntary act on the part of the gunner
to insure his sticking to his gun. If the latter, it is a thing
to be admired greatly.

As always seems to be my fate on these occasions I was
reported seriously wounded!!

The following extract is from captured correspondence:

"To-day the 7th the alarm was given. Terrible drum
fire was heard all during the night. . . . A terrible firing
has driven us under cover. To the right and left of me my
friends are all drenched with blood. A drum fire which
no one could ever describe. I pray the Lord will get me
out of this sap. I swear to it I will be the next. While
I am writing He still gives us power and loves us. My
trousers and tunic are drenched in blood, all from my poor
mates. I have prayed to God He might save me, not for
my sake, but for my poor parents. I feel as if I could
cry out, my thoughts are all the time with them.

"The slaughtering takes place behind COMINES,[1] which
place the English have taken.

"I have already twelve months on the Western Front; have
been through hard fighting, but never such slaughter."

June 10, 1917 *(Sunday).*   *Kemmel Shelters.*

I see from the papers that the battle of the 7th is considered to have been the most successful of the war to date.

Of course, I could not even hint this to you, but, while

[1] ? Messines.

THE RUINED VILLAGE OF WYTSCHAETE

8th June, 1917

we were behind "resting"—so-called, we were in reality practising the attack over fascinating "dummy" representations of the Petit Bois, etc., and the German trenches beyond the Wytschaete-Messines Ridge. Nothing was left to chance. We even had a large-scale model, covering about an acre, which represented, to scale, Wytschaete, the woods, and the villages beyond. This latter—which I believe was made by the engineers—was a triumph of skill. It looked like a huge toy village, and would have delighted the children.

We came out yesterday, and I took Chamier—my Intelligence Officer—and we had a good and hearty lunch and a bottle of champagne at the Convent at Locre.

Willie Redmond is buried in the nuns' garden, on almost the very spot I had chosen for myself.

A large number of the men of the battalion are now the proud possessors of wrist watches—trophies of war.

We are refitting.

June 12, 1917.   *Kemmel Shelters.*

We are still where we have been the last three days, and are sending large working parties up towards the new front line, day and night.

Mrs. Glover, apparently, has had a row with her mother-in-law and the neighbours in Yorkshire. Glover says it is because she speaks with a London and not a Yorkshire accent. Also, he says, a girl whom he used to court is making mischief. He has insisted on my reading a "stinker" he has received from this girl.

It begins—"Private Glover" . . . and ends "Yours Respectively."

Perhaps she meant to say "Yours Retro-spectively"!

The heat, to-day, is tropical, and I am afraid it must be worse for you in London.

(*June* 12: *later.*) I am writing this—my second letter —late at night, because I probably shall not write to-morrow. We move in the morning, early, and backwards. So we shall be away from shell-fire for a bit.

To-day and to-night I have men working in the forward

area, making roads through the shell-holes. I went up there this afternoon, and what I saw made me more proud than ever before, if possible, of being British. Roads, water-pipes, and railways are advancing across the wilderness as no such work was ever done before, even across the African Plain: and all is being done under shell-fire.

You see little locomotives puffing where a few days ago no man could show himself and live. I rode most of the way, and my mare—for the first time—annoyed me. She shied at the guns, and the locomotives, and the lorries, and worked herself *and me* into such a lather, that in the end I left her and took to my feet. I have since made amends to her with sugar.

I picked up Brett, who was the Company Commander on duty, and we explored together the ruins of Wytschaete;—the abomination of desolation;—almost another Guillemont!

You can just distinguish where the roads were. You can recognize what was the chief outstanding feature—the church—only by tracing its position from the map. It should be in the middle of the square. But you cannot recognize the square. All is dust and rubble. We visited the famous Hospice, which caps the ridge, and used to be the most prominent landmark during the long months when we occupied the breastworks in the swamp below. The highest bit of wall remaining is 8 or 10 feet high.

The only structures that have resisted our bombardments are the steel and concrete emplacements built by the enemy among the foundations of the village, several of which have withstood the racket fairly well; and if the garrisons had stood their ground they could have given a lot of trouble.

I found a Y.M.C.A. man in one of these emplacements. He had actually established a forward canteen in it, and had a few packets of cigarettes and other things to sell to the troops. Brett took me to this hole. He explained that the man who occupied it was an "ex-parson." I asked him what he meant by an ex-parson. He said: "Oh, he gave up his 'see' to come out here"—(which showed how much Brett knew about ecclesiastical matters!).

It turned out that this fine sportsman was a Nonconformist minister. We shook hands and I congratulated him on his effort. For his cash-box he had a German machine-gun belt box. Directly he was introduced, he began: "Colonel, can you tell me how I can get some water up here?" I said I had noticed a grand pile of petrol cans full of water on my way up. He said, eagerly: "May I take some of them?" I said: "They are nothing to do with me. I merely mentioned that I had seen them."

He replied, with a wink: "Thank you, Colonel, I quite understand." So I imagine he got his water.

Then we passed on, and as the Germans started putting over shrapnel we took cover: and so home.

We shall probably be back quite ten days. The Division has done its job for the time being.

June 14, 1917.   *Oultersteene.*

Yesterday, we marched back here—to safety—in grilling heat. What with their box respirators with extensions, steel helmets, P.H. gas helmets, rifles, ammunition, packs, etc., there is little doubt but that the infantry soldier is getting over-loaded for marching. His equipment grows as the inventions for killing grow.

Already, he must carry between 70 lbs. and 80 lbs. And after a long bout of inactivity in the trenches (I refer only to the lack of exercise), you can well understand that he is not in condition for weight-carrying. Moreover, he does not improve matters by lapping water out of his water-bottle at every halt, as is his habit if not carefully watched. However, the authorities are beginning to appreciate these difficulties, and to provide motor-lorries for carrying the packs, when such are available.

The Corps Commander (General Hamilton Gordon) met us by the way, and called me to his side while the battalion marched by. He has a very lugubrious face, and looked so melancholy that he might have lost a battle instead of having won one. He shook me by the hand and thanked me most generously for the part my "splendid battalion" (as he was good enough to call it) had played in the victory, the moral effect of which, he said, must be tremendous on the German Higher Command, as well as the rank and file.

I am sleeping and messing in a spotless cottage. The Companies are very scattered—I should think well over a mile apart, from extreme to extreme. Many of the men are bivouacked in the open, or under their ground-sheets, as the weather is beautiful. After the fighting they were in rags from the German wire, and as all identification marks had been removed prior to the raid of June 4, much patching up and sewing on has been necessary; but all have pulled themselves together wonderfully.

Did you see that poor Stephen Gwynn went to speak to his constituents at Castlegar, accompanied only by a local newspaper correspondent, and that they refused to hear him? He was mobbed, in fact, by the young bloods of the place, who stoned him. One went so far as to throw a rotten egg in his face from a range of a yard!

I venture to think that the same lad who did that foul thing would be like a lamb if we had him here;—or perhaps like a lion. I am quite sure he would not have felt even inclined to do as he did. No body of troops could be more amenable or better mannered and behaved, under all conditions, or more faithful and patient than the Irishmen in France. Yet, were they in Ireland, I feel pretty certain that some of them would be liable to emulate the hero of Gwynn's political meeting.

They are truly an extraordinary and inexplicable race. They will do anything they are *asked* to do, even to the death. But they become like mules if they think they are being driven. And that is a fact which we English as a nation have not yet appreciated.

Again, why, after committing the most atrocious crimes in Ireland, are they often allowed to go scot-free? That is another mistake. They do not resent punishment, even of the severest kind, when they know they have earned it, as I have found here. However, there it is. Ireland will always be Ireland. It is a land of children with the bodies of men, and, politically, they do not themselves know what they want.   And, God knows, *we* do not.

June 22, 1917.   *Bollezeele (near Zeggers Cappel)*.

I was up a little before four this morning, and at five we marched to a completely new district, where British soldiers have not previously been billeted.   Never was there a more glorious and inspiring morning, or cloud effects more wonderful.   We rejoiced in the prospect of a cool yet cloudless summer day; but, by six o'clock, all had changed. I cannot remember a more complete transfiguration.   All the blue sky had gone, and the white flecks of cloud, and the golden rays of the rising sun: and instead there were floods of rain, which continued nearly the whole day long, and drenched both men and officers to the skin.   Finally, after an 18-mile march, we found the billeting arrangements incomplete, so that all had to wait out another hour and a half, and have their dinners in the rain.

The men have no change of clothes, but they take these "trials" like they do everything else—that is to say, cheerfully and patiently, and sleep herded together on the floors of stables, and with luck get dry before the morning.   I have been trying to get them an issue of rum to-night, but it is not easy, since we are now in a new Corps and Army.

(*Later.*)   I failed to get the rum.

June 28, 1917.   *Bollezeele (near Zeggers Cappel)*.

To show you how shifting is the officer population of a present-day battalion, I may remark that to-day, though I have about forty officers, I am *the only one* who was present at the battle at Ginchy last September.

June 30, 1917.   *Bollezeele (near Zeggers Cappel)*.

I am getting rather bitten with agriculture.   No wonder these peasants get rich;—or, if they do not (and I really do not know), I should say there must be something radically wrong with the whole system of land tenure in this country.

They are the most industrious and the thriftiest people I have ever seen, and though during this time of war the work is done entirely by women, children, old men, wounded men, and men hopelessly unfit for active soldiering—with a few soldiers (very few) released temporarily for the purpose, I am sure it must be impossible for those who have not seen it to realize what cultivation means in France and Belgium, or to picture the seas of corn and potatoes and roots, extending as far as the eye can reach and further; the forests of hops, weedless; without a barren patch or a neglected spot anywhere.

In the farm where I am billeted there is a farm-hand —a girl of about eighteen. She sleeps on the straw, on the floor of a stable. She is up, bursting with life and spirits, each morning at five o'clock; and she works, at top pressure, without ceasing, till dark. Then she returns to her straw. She is slim, but has the strength of an average man. She handles the farm horses with a single rein (attached to one ring of the bit only), and by word of mouth. Apparently, she neither eats nor drinks.

It is the "manure" season. That is to say, it is the time of year when they carry out the loathsome liquid accumulation of the past twelve months and spread it over the fields, and so wrapt up is this girl in the work, that you would think she revelled in it.

She moves always at the double—whether through the chicken run, whence every bird flies scared and panic-stricken at her wild approach, or *through* the manure heap (for she never goes round it). Each time I pass her she looks up with full face and a cheery grin. I don't suppose she ever washes, and she must reek of manure, but she fascinates me because of her extraordinary vitality. It is quite exciting to watch her at her work.

But, as I look upon her, I despair of the English as an agricultural nation.

July 3, 1917.   *No.* 10 *Stationary Hospital, St. Omer.*

To-day I should be one of a party with General Plumer, making a presentation of the bell of Wytschaete Church (which has been dug out of the ruins) to the King of the Belgians; but, instead, I am in bed in the hospital at St. Omer, enduring the torments of the damned each time I am obliged to make the smallest movement.

Briefly, I turned a somersault with my mare over the

sandbag wall at the Royal Munster Sports yesterday, at Zeggers Cappel, straining or tearing some muscles in my back, and breaking a bone or two in my left hand. The last I remember was crawling away from the course, and the soldiers clapping as I picked myself up from the ground. They are always like that.

I came here on an ambulance—19 miles—and arrived after eleven o'clock, last night. I am glad I have had the experience. I think I understand now in a small degree how the wounded must suffer when they are carried back over the bumpy roads.

*　　*　　*　　*　　*

September 20, 1917.　　*Croisilles-Ecoust Railway Cutting.*

We had a fair crossing on the 18th, and as the train did not leave till the next morning I put up for the night at the Louvre Hotel, in Boulogne.

This train was about a quarter of a mile long, and was *packed* with troops, but being O.C. train I was allotted a compartment for myself, which I shared with a Battalion Commander of the Naval Division—a very nice fellow. So, though the train crawled, it was a vast improvement on my previous experiences of "leave trains."

I reached my detraining station at 7 p.m. This was Boisleux-aux-Monts, which, last spring, was some miles inside the enemy's lines. The station orderly told me that when our troops entered it last March, there was not a bit of track left. All the rails had been ripped up and taken away by the Germans. The turn-tables even had been destroyed. But you would not guess that to see the place to-day.

By 4.30 yesterday afternoon we had come into view of that old familiar sight, the line of observation balloons, indicating our line, and later had passed through the shattered town familiarized to you and me by our visit to the Grafton Galleries (Arras).

At Boisleux-aux-Monts I met Esmonde, the Irish M.P., who had come by the same train, and whom I had not seen since that day when he was introduced to me in the street at Bailleul by Willie Redmond. As neither of us found anybody or any conveyance to meet us we had a long and interesting talk about Ireland, and he told me many things about the history of that unhappy country.

Apparently, it is quite untrue to say that Ireland never was a nation, as the scoffers maintain. There were four kingdoms—Ulster, Leinster, Munster and Connaught, and a Head king ruling all. And when the English claim that the King of Ireland invited Strongbow over, they misstate the case. It was one of the four minor kings who did that, and he was in rebellion at the time!

However, I am straying. I got through on the telephone to the Brigade, who borrowed a motor-car from the Division, and I was fetched away, and spent the night at my Transport lines, about 4 miles behind the firing line. I then learnt that they had only heard at seven o'clock that I was coming, and, not knowing where I should leave the train, had sent to two stations, including the one where I actually had alighted, though the mess-cart arrived after I had left.

I found that Praeger, the Quartermaster, had prepared a meal and a bed for me in a hut he had built of sand-bags, and there I spent the night, in the ruined village of Ervillers.

To reach this place I had motored 6 miles, through country which has been reduced to the primeval condition of the African veldt. The newspapers did *not* exaggerate. The Germans in their retreat—as the Swazis would have done—did their work thoroughly. They left nothing living —not even the apple trees, and nothing standing that had been built by man. For miles and miles in every direction the eye meets nothing but rank grass and weed. The villages, though many of them have never seen a shell-burst, are levelled with the plain; all but the churches, whose sites are revealed to-day by cones of rubble. The avenues of trees which lined the roads are sawn off just above the ground and lie prone. Each cross-road is marked by a yawning mine crater, which our people are busily filling in. The desolation, reaching far and wide, would be more ghastly, had one not become accustomed to such sights, and must easily eclipse any previous outrage of the same kind that has been perpetrated throughout the whole course of history.

Pereira is Acting Divisional Commander during General Hickie's absence on leave, and has visited me. He gave me a warm welcome back to the Brigade, and said he had written the moment he heard I was returning, saying that if I rang up through the R.T.O. at Boulogne he would send a car to meet me. Unfortunately, I had not got this letter, which must have arrived after I left home. Was not that good of him?

This evening I have been round the front line with Crofton, acting second in command. It is, in part, that famous line called after one of the most famous German Generals (Hindenburg)—an impregnable line (as the enemy thought), prepared at his leisure and without embarrassment, miles behind his then front line, and so strong that he believed no troops in the world could reach it. Yet our troops managed to do so, and to capture it (or part of it) last spring, and its former glory is represented to-day by the "MEBUS," that is to say the formidable reinforced concrete emplacements, yards thick and massive as the foundations of a great cathedral, and by a tunnelled trench, safe, you would think, from the heaviest shell. Some of these Mebus are shattered by our fire, and their steel skeletons, torn and twisted, stick out of the lacerated earth, like huge decayed teeth; but many are intact, or nearly so, and to have conquered these latter reflects great glory on the troops that did it.

Our own front line is studded with these excrescences, and facing us in the German trench opposite and behind it are more, which latter have been catching it pretty severely from our artillery the last few days.

Still, it is very quiet and peaceful here, and I am wondering how long it will last. This is an aggressive Division, and our artillery has been baiting the eagle, though without much response hitherto.

I found the battalion in support for eight days, of which

three have expired. We go next into the front line for eight days; then out for sixteen.

My Headquarters are in a comfortable set of dug-outs in a railway cutting. The trenches, too, are good. I am at present writing in my sleeping dug-out. The roof is of curved corrugated steel sheeting (known as a "big Elephant" or cupola), covered with sandbags and sods. The floor is boarded and looks like a Pompeian mosaic, since the boards are pieces sawn from what once was the sign-board of an inn or shop, salved from the ruins near by. There is a fireplace with a white enamelled tile floor and a cast-iron grate, burning wood;—all, both fireplace and wood, collected from the said ruins. The fender is beaten out of old biscuit tins; the bed—a canvas stretcher, which took half an hour to make. And the table on which I write has been made to my order by the pioneer corporal—also from salvage—since my arrival, about midday.

Such is the simple life, and indeed it has many advantages over the artificial life at home. I wish you could see this dug-out. It is very nice, the one fault being that the chimney smokes.

The battalion had a bad time in the fighting at Passchen-daele while I was away—after July 31, for four or five days, and again on August 16. Many good men are gone, including one of my two orderly room sergeants, who was killed by a shell. The weather and the fates fought against them, but, though the casualties have been heavy, the battalion has come out well.

In the case of some other battalions—to quote a description that has been given to me—after four or five days waiting in the trenches, the men were so exhausted with the shelling, and their feet so sore and swollen from the wet, that when the time came to attack they were so weak that they could scarcely have blown out a candle.

This is quite a new section of the line to me.

The following extract from a letter written by a German officer (regiment unknown) is from the VI Corps Intelligence Summary:—

"If it were not for the men who have been spared me on this fierce day, and who are lying around me and looking timidly at me, I should shed hot and bitter tears over the errors that have menaced me during these hours. On the morning of September 18, the dug-out, containing seventeen men, was shot to pieces over our heads. I am the only one who withstood the maddening bombardment of three days and still survives. You cannot imagine the frightful mental torments I have undergone in those few hours. After crawling out through the bleeding remnants of my comrades and the smoke and debris, and wandering and fleeing in the midst of the raging artillery fire in search of a refuge, I am now awaiting death at any moment. You do not know what Flanders means. Flanders means endless endurance. Flanders means blood and scraps of human bodies. Flanders means heroic courage and faithfulness, even unto death!"

September 22, 1917.   *Croisilles-Ecoust Railway Cutting.*
The aerial activity increases constantly, and during the last two days, which have been very fine and clear, there has scarcely been a moment when something has not been happening overhead.

Yesterday morning, at 4.30, I was woken by a heavy trench-mortar bombardment, and got up to see what it was. All along the German line was the usual firework display; —coloured rockets and golden rain, soaring up and tumbling down. It turned out to be a half-hour's strafe by the enemy of the Brigade on our left, but as it was nothing to do with me I turned in again and finished my sleep. This afternoon, there has for a short time been very heavy gunning in the same direction, but further away.

This morning I again went all round the front line, and in the afternoon, from an observation post just behind my Headquarters, had a good look at the German lines and the country surrounding us. The surface is undulating and the views are expansive. Every tree and every village having been destroyed, the distances one can see are great. In the middle or thereabouts of each flattened village there

is a pyramidal pile of what looks like rubbish. At firs
—if you did not know—you might think there had been
a mine or quarry there, and that what you saw was the
spoil-heap. But, in reality, it is (or was) the church. I
the heap is white you may take it that the church was buil
of chalk; if grey, of slate.

At intervals, throughout to-day, the enemy has been
pouring an almost continuous stream of heavy shells into
the ruins of Croisilles and Ecoust—the villages on either
side of us. From my observation post I watched for a
time through my glasses a German soldier leisurely walking
along a trail behind his lines. He was about 6,000 yards
away and out of rifle shot, and as the artillery apparently
did not consider him a worthy target, he still remains
unconscious of the interest he aroused—in me, at any
rate. How often, I wonder, am I an object of similar
interest to the people with spy-glasses over there?

It is 11.15 p.m., and the Germans are dropping a heavy
trench-mortar bomb every three or four minutes—aimed
I imagine, at our front line trench. Although. that is
nearly a mile from where I am writing, each burst shakes
the ground under me.

11.20 p.m. An R.E. officer has just walked in to say
that the enemy has attempted a raid.

September 23, 1917 (*Sunday*).
Croisilles-Ecoust Railway Cutting

We moved into the front line to-day, the relief being
completed by about 9 p.m. My new Headquarters are
close to the old ones, but not so good. Glover, in comparing the two (there is no fireplace here), said: "Our last
quarters were so homely!"

September 24, 1917. *Croisilles-Ecoust Railway Cutting*

The weather continues radiant—hot during the day
and rather cold at night: aeroplanes very active so long as
there is light.

The whole of this morning and part of the afternoon I
spent going round the trenches. I have over a mile of
frontage to look after, which is quite an exceptionally long

tretch, and it takes four or five hours to visit all the
posts.

The scene is that of some of the fiercest fighting of this
year's spring: you do not have to go far for proof of that.
Indeed, the fire-trench itself is more or less of a graveyard.
In one part, particularly, it is lined with tin discs with
numbers on them, indicating where soldiers have been
buried in the parapet; and, wherever you dig, you are liable
to come upon these poor remains.   It is not even necessary
to dig, for they outcrop in places.

We are top-dog here, so far at any rate as position goes,
and altogether better off than we have been since I first
took over the command of this battalion.   Our line is a
patchwork meandering one:—here, a piece of the famous
German *pièce de résistance*, with all its concrete and
tunnelling, now converted to our use; there, one of the
sunken roads, so common in these parts, turned into a
defence;—linked up by other trenches more or less
newly dug.

September 28, 1917.   *Croisilles-Ecoust Railway Cutting.*

Just as I was starting to go round the front line to-day,
the underground listening post reported having intercepted
a German telephone conversation, indicating an impending
bombardment.   I went my usual round, each minute as
I advanced along the communication trench expecting to
walk into something unpleasant.   However, nothing came
of it, and the day, as a matter of fact, was a quiet one.

I wonder if these telephone experts imagine things!

October 1, 1917.   *Croisilles-Ecoust Railway Cutting.*

The infantry gets to look upon the Front Line as its
Special Preserve—which it indeed is, more particularly
during the attacking season, when it becomes a sort of
"Holy of Holies" to the infantry.

We do not resent visitors, but I think we are apt to
regard them something like trespassers.   That is because
we get so few.

The popularity of the infantry seems to vary with the
section of line which it is holding.   At Wytschaete, which

205

was a boisterous place, we were left severely alone. Here on the contrary, where we are in what is—for the time being at any rate—a sort of haven of rest, our privacy is frequently invaded. Perhaps it is a coincidence but Red tabs of high degree are a common sight in the trenches here Even Corps Commanders come to see us. They go into our forward saps, and so peaceful do they find their surroundings, that they pull out maps, and, exposing themselves freely, identify the outstanding landmarks.

Then they pass on their way, and, perhaps a quarter of an hour later, the sentry group occupying the sap gets shelled.

In self-defence we have put up a notice or two, worded as follows:

"Visitors are requested not to show themselves, as by doing so they may give away our positions to the enemy. We live here. You don't."

We have visits here, in fact, from all kinds of strangers, and these do not always have the civility to report themselves at Battalion Headquarters before going through the trenches. They might, quite logically, be arrested as spies, and they are, sometimes. And it serves them right.

The other day I came upon a stranger. I asked him who he was. He said he was an officer of the Siege Artillery. Now, we do not see much of the Siege Artillery in the Front Line. They shoot off the map, from behind, and seem to scorn forward observation. One of their majors called upon me not long ago. I asked him if he would like some targets, explaining that the battalion observers were very alert, and could probably put him on to some good ones.

He said: "Oh! it doesn't matter, thank you."

That is the Siege Artillery way—and it is not encouraging to the infantry.

So I gave the officer in the trench a few hints on manners. I said: "We know the Field Artillery well (the 18-pounders). Their officers are always with us. But your people we do not know. Indeed, all that our men know of you is that they occasionally get one of your shells in the small of the back."

Which was perhaps rude, but perfectly true.

October 3, 1917. *Dysart Camp (near Ervillers).*

The night before last, we were relieved from the line, and went to Inniskilling Camp, at Ervillers, which we reached at midnight.

These camps are scattered about, some 4 or 5 miles behind the line, amid the wreckage wrought deliberately by the Germans, presumably that our troops might have no cover.

In many respects this condition of devastation has its advantages. Not a civilian—indeed, not a native of France—lives within many miles of us, to sell poison to the men under the name of "wine." Consequently, crime has ceased to exist, seeing that the only drink obtainable is the beer from our own canteen. That also is French beer, and very weak, and we sell it only when we can get it, and only when the battalion is out of the line. And we have plenty of firewood and bricks—most valuable for our small building operations, which would certainly have been forbidden to us had the villages been standing, or even had the ruins been occupied.

We are self-contained. Officers' clubs have been run up, built of wood or extemporized out of ruins, but still most comfortable.

The Corps runs one cinema and the Division another, and close to where I am sitting is a ruin labelled "The Hippodrome," where variety entertainments are given by soldier artists.

In fact, having nothing but virgin ground to work upon, things have been done better than they would have been had we found standing villages; and, in many other ways, it is advantageous for the army to be so completely cut off as it is from the outside world. . . . Incidentally, we are far more scattered and therefore safer than we should be if we were confined to the villages which offer a certain target for shell-fire. Thus, in some respects, we are not ungrateful to our enemies.

Last evening, I having had my first bath since leaving England, we moved again, to Dysart Camp—a new Rest Camp about a quarter of a mile from the last. I hope we shall continue to come back here when we are again relieved from the line, so that it will be to our interest to make the place comfortable.

You can imagine how discouraging it is to both officers and men to be sent to a different camp each time they come out of the line, and, when at last they do by chance return to some place where they have been before, to find the cook-houses they had made with so much loving care turned into latrines; the men's reading-room employed as an ablution shed; and the linings of the principal huts vanished into thin air, having done duty as firewood;—and then, on the top of that, though the battalion may only have been relieved from the fire-trench the night before, to be ticked off with entire lack of justice for not keeping their house in order by some "eye-wash" General visiting from the back areas.

To-day has been a day of inspections. The Brigadier inspected the Companies at 2.30; and at 5.30 p.m. the Divisional General presented military medals. Both expressed themselves delighted with everything they saw.

October 4, 1917.   *Dysart Camp (near Ervillers).*

I started off at 8.15 this morning to visit the scenes of our fighting during September, last year, returning in the evening; and it has been a wonderfully interesting though a melancholy day.

The notorious villages—Guillemont and Ginchy—are conspicuous by their absence. I can truthfully say that I have never seen a whole brick in the former place, and the latter—which I had not seen before except from a trench—is much the same. I stumbled through the shell-holes this time in broad daylight, and even so lost my position on the map more than once. I thought of that horrible night of September 7—so short a time after I had aken over the command of this battalion, or rather the remnant of it, and it no longer surprised me that the guide had lost his way on that occasion.

I rode past Ligny-Thilloy, Flers, Longueval, and the dead stumps alternating with soldiers' graves which represent the ill-starred Delville Wood (Devil's Wood, as the men called it) and High Wood.

Miles of devastation and deserted ruined villages and shell-holes—all now grown over with weed and grass. Not a living creature but the magpies, which flit silently about the waste. The ground is just as it was left, thickly littered with the debris of battle. Rifles with the bayonets fixed lie as they were dropped; limbers smashed and half-buried by shell-fire; perforated shrapnel helmets—German and British; equipment, boots, ammunition, stretchers, derelict aeroplanes, and tanks; in fact all the accoutrements of war; with here and there a reminder of the pre-war peace days, in the shape of a shredded threshing-machine or the big sugar refinery of Guillemont,—the latter riddled and torn, the steel-work tangled and twisted like crumpled paper.

A land of poisoned wells (the Germans saw to this) with the labels nailed up by our sanitary people marking them so. A land whose loneliness is so great that it is almost frightening. A land of wooden crosses, of which, wherever you may stand, you can count numbers dotted about, each indicating a soldier's grave, and the spot where he fell.

After several miles of this I came upon the first living human beings—parties of the Salvage Corps, working forwards from the old battle line, gathering up all that is worth saving of the relics I have mentioned. These are mostly of coloured men, who have come from all parts of the world. The first party I saw was composed of Burmans from Mandalay, and, dressed as they were, with woollen Balaclava helmets pulled down over their heads and shoulders, cringing from the wet and cold, they looked like the ghosts of the dead.

Further back, I came upon the work of the Graves

Registration Unit, which, behind the Salvage men, follows the Army forward. Its job is to "prospect" for the dead, and, so skilful have its members become at detecting the position of a buried soldier, that their "cuttings" seldom draw blank. Indeed, this is not surprising, for, no matter where they look, they are almost certain to find what they are searching for. Then they dig up the decomposed fragments, to see if they can identify them, which they seldom do;—after which they re-bury them, marking the spot with the universal wooden cross.

I rode on to Montauban, of which I saw so much when I was with the Entrenching Battalion. The famous figure of the Virgin, which stood by the church, and which survived all the bombardments of last year, though all around Her was destroyed, had been blown down by the wind, and, as the head was missing, I suppose somebody must have taken it for a souvenir. The shattered remains lay upon the ground. She was much gilded and painted, and was made of cheap terra-cotta, hollow inside.

I then wandered through one of our cemeteries at Guillemont, and saw Raymond Asquith's grave, and those of one or two Coldstreamers I knew. And above another single grave I read the names of between sixty and seventy N.C.O.'s and men of the Rifle Brigade.

Then I steered for the sunken road to Ginchy. I followed, as nearly as I could through the thick weed which now covers everything, the course I had followed that night of September 7, last year.

Finally, outside what used to be the village of Guillemont, I looked for the only landmark that remains—the old French pre-war cemetery. There is a great tombstone there covering the family vault, I believe, of the people who owned the sugar refinery. This presents a most extraordinary sight. It is strong, being of massive stone. Consequently, on account of the protection which it afforded from shell-fire, the Germans had used it as a dug-out; and, when they left it, some of our signallers had evidently taken over the tenancy. It is unoccupied by living men to-day, though the floor is still strewn with army forms. A stove is fitted in one corner, with a tin chimney to conduct the smoke outside. In one of the bricked recesses of the vault lies a coffin, undisturbed. The other recesses have been used as soldiers' beds, and, as a second coffin occupied a recess which was evidently required as a bedroom, the coffin has been pulled out, and lies on the floor:—and, further—shameful to relate—the zinc lining of this coffin has been torn open, exposing a woman's face and body. Amid such surroundings the occupants of this gruesome dug-out appear to have eaten and worked and slept for many months.

From here I was able to locate my old trench by the Ginchy sunken road, and though all is now fallen in and grown over, I succeeded in re-tracing our positions of September 9.

I advanced across Noman's Land and made for my objective of that day.

I explored the site of Ginchy, and came across a little group of Guards' graves, including several of my old battalion. I found Jackson, Dilberoglue, Pike Pease, and Scott, lying side by side in the order I have named; little "Bunny" Pease with his steel hat lying on his grave—a custom which has been largely followed by our troops on the Somme, in imitation of the French habit of hanging the soldier's cap upon the cross over his grave. One away from Pease was Walters'—a machine-gun officer of the Irish Guards, and a splendid type of boy, whom I knew well.

My present sniping officer arrived when I was at home. He is very young, and very keen, and very talkative. He spits out whatever comes into his mind. For a few days, while we were in the line, I had to put him in command of a Company, as the Company Commander was away on leave. He did it very well, and displayed, in a marked degree, what is known in military parlance as the "offensive spirit."

When I inspected his section of the line I was struck

by his audacity, and began in my mind to compare my nerve with his. However, one morning, as he and I were talking together in the trench—whizz—a German shell skimmed close over our heads. It took him unawares. He clutched hold of my arm as one of our children might have done.

That, I confess, rather interested me, since it showed that he doesn't like them, though he faces them;—which, I believe, is the attitude of most of us.

I inspected the clothing of one of the Companies the day it came out of the line. The seat of one lad's trousers was like nothing on earth. It was not there. I said: "You look as if you had been hit by a shell." The Quartermaster muttered from behind: "Yes, sir, a direct hit."

A kit inspection is a dull and tedious affair, and almost anything helps to relieve the monotony.

October 8, 1917.   *Dysart Camp* (*near Ervillers*)·

It is an interesting bit of line that the Division is holding, and the opportunities are excellent for watching the enemy at his little daily avocations. From one of the front line observation posts, the other day, I saw three Germans in the course of a quarter of an hour, casually sauntering along their trench at a point where it had been blown in by a shell, and unconsciously exposing themselves from their knees upwards. With my glasses I could see them so clearly that I could have counted their buttons.

That was when we first went up. But such scenes are daily becoming rarer, since our snipers have got to work. The battalion snipers are very good just at present, and the sniping from both sides is active. It is very necessary, but what a callous business it is! I have to order others to do it, but I cannot say I like the idea.

The section of front line which I hold is, as I have told you, more or less of a graveyard. Many soldiers lie buried in the parapet, and in some cases their feet project into the trench. The positions are marked, where known. We come across others, unmarked, as we dig. On such occasions the men put up little notices, some of which

212

DELVILLE WOOD

combine with the tragedy of it all a certain amount of pathetic and unintended humour. As you may imagine, the names of the dead are generally undiscoverable. On one board is written: "In loving memory of an *unknown* British soldier." On another (in this case the man's pay-book was found on his body and therefore his name is known) the following words appear in chalk: "Sleep on, Beloved Brother; take thy Gentle Rest." In another case somebody has contented himself by just writing piously in chalk on the sole of a projecting foot: "R.I.P." Over another grave a bas-relief of the Head of Christ has been carved with a jack-knife on a piece of the chalk through which the trench is dug. It is embellished with hair and a fine halo drawn in purple indelible pencil.

If you saw it all you wouldn't know whether to laugh or cry.

October 9, 1917.   *Dysart Camp* (*near Ervillers*).

Yesterday, I sat in a chair (any kind of chair) for the first time since I left Boulogne on September 19. Brood on this, and do not ever complain of my round back in future. The explanation is that my Adjutant's brother (who is salving the battle wreckage about 10 miles behind the line) sent us a limber-load of things, including a very comfortable camp chair for myself.

October 12, 1917.   *Dysart Camp* (*near Ervillers*).

We are getting a lot of leave for the men at present, which is splendid:—sixteen a day. They are cleaned up and fitted with good clothes before they leave, so that they do not arrive at Victoria covered with the mud of the trenches. Each man, too, has to have a certificate that he is free from vermin; so I hope they arrive sufficiently pure and spick and span, though I am sure they cannot give half so much satisfaction in the streets of London as they would if they arrived muddy.

October 14, 1917 (*Sunday*). *Dysart Camp* (*near Ervillers*).

To-day is Sunday, and the battalion has been having Sports. Lance-Corporal Pierpoint played clown. I have known him for a year or so, but only as a bombing corporal

—and a good one, too. To-day he showed himself off in a new capacity—that of contortionist, a spineless man, and a buffoon of a high order, which, it seems, was one of various callings which he followed before the war.

He boxed to-day, arriving in the ring with a back somersault. He walked about during the sports on his hands —with his legs twisted under his elbows. He tied himself in knots, placing his head between his legs and one leg round his neck, like A—— used to do when she was a baby. His antics were most ludicrous and most extraordinary.

Amongst other faculties which he possesses, or is believed to possess, is one which is invaluable in the trenches. It is that of being able to judge exactly where a trench-mortar bomb is going to fall. His friends in his platoon collect around him when the German "rum-jars" are flying about, and he advises them what to do to dodge each one as he sees it coming through the air—signalling with his arms whether to move to right or left along the trench, or to stand still.

He was certainly *the* feature at the Sports to-day. "By the Holy St. Patrick, look at that," I heard a man call out, as he watched Pierpoint keeping goal in the football match for the Company championship. He is a great goal-keeper, though more by word of mouth than by virtue of any particular skill at the game. He talks incessantly while the play goes on, claiming in a loud voice "Off-side," or "Hands," or any other foul he can think of, on the principle, I suppose, that it *may* influence the Referee; or, if it does not, that it may at least rattle him.

October 17, 1917.   *Dysart Camp (near Ervillers)*.

Yesterday, I travelled far from here and again visited the scenes of the fighting of last autumn. As I passed through the battered stumps which mark the site of Delville Wood, I thought of the wonderful feat performed by our soldiers in taking that most formidable position, in the face of appalling artillery fire directed from behind ridge after ridge in front of it; from each one of which the enemy had full opportunity for direct observation. My groom's thoughts were evidently running on similar lines, for he suddenly said: "If the Americans can fight as well as they can talk, sir, we ought to be able to do some big things next spring." In this connection I fear there are breakers ahead. He went on to say that the other day he had heard an American ask an Australian: "Do you think the Tommies will be able to hold them (the Germans) back till *we* get in next spring?" He got his answer—good and straight; —so straight, in fact, that both men were presently marched off to the Guard-room!

I again explored the ground where we fought on September 9, and was able this time to trace out all the old trenches, both ours and the German. A baby's shattered perambulator lies in a shell-hole just in front of our jumping-off trench. The sunken road, connecting Ginchy and Guillemont, runs past the spot. I suppose some refugee mother, flying before the Germans in the early days of the war, got tired and left it there.

You will remember what a terrific fire we encountered when we attacked at this place. I have ever since been curious to know where that fire came from, and how so powerful a concentration of machine-guns could have completely escaped our artillery. Now I know. A well-concealed and winding trench, branching into two, and worked in conjunction with nests of shell-holes adapted as machine-gun positions! That is what we ran into, and it was a hopeless task we undertook that day. Indeed, after we had been relieved by the 4th Grenadiers, it continued to hold up the whole advance for four days. I walked over a dead German still lying in the German trench, and I daresay there were many others, but the ground is so overgrown with weed that such sights are hidden from the eye.

Combles is a weird, uncanny sight. It was a large village —almost a town—but our army has advanced far beyond it, and its ruins are deserted. The only living creatures I saw were a white cat, crouching among the bricks, and a wandering soldier. I went on through Morval, Les

Boeufs (where the three Coldstream battalions attacked in line), Gueudecourt, Beaulencourt and Bapaume.

All the villages are so wrecked, and the roads through them so broken up with shell-holes and blocked with fallen trees and ruins, that it is difficult and sometimes impossible to pick one's way along them on horseback.

Bapaume was a large town, and not a house has escaped the deliberate hand of the destroyers. The church, which must have been a fine one, judging from the fragments that are left, has gone with the rest.

October 18, 1917.   *Croisilles-Ecoust Railway Cutting.*

We took over the Front Line to-day.

A successful raid was made on the Tunnel Trench, two days ago, by the 7th Leinsters. They employed a ruse, which was certainly a brain-wave on the part of somebody.

On October 11 a thousand gas bombs were fired from "projectors"—500 at 8 p.m., and 500 at midnight. Judging from intercepted enemy telephone conversations, these did considerable execution.

In parenthesis, I may explain that the projector is a kind of mortar. In appearance, it is a short stumpy steel cylinder, about 9 or 10 inches in diameter and perhaps a couple of feet long. Five hundred or a thousand of these are planted in the ground, with their muzzles pointed upwards. All are directed upon the same chosen spot in the enemy's lines. Each is charged with a gas-container, or bomb. The projectors are fired simultaneously, by electricity, and then the gas-containers soar upwards, making, in their collective flight, a rushing sound, as of a mighty wind. They burst as they reach the ground.

The raid was made on the early morning of October 16. It was preluded by a repetition of the projector bombardment of the 11th, but, on this occasion, the containers held no poison gas.

Immediately upon the discharge of the projectors, the raiders dashed into the German trench. Some of them went down into the tunnel: Major Holbrow, a Sapper officer, was among the latter. He took a tape-measure

THE VILLAGE OF GINCHY

with him, and made measurements. The garrison was found wearing respirators.

The sight of our men raiding in the middle of a gas cloud, without respirators, puzzled the enemy. Indeed, it was quite a little time before the prisoners—then safely on their way to our lines—could be persuaded that there was no gas.

When, at last, they realized how they had been had, they became quite indignant.

October 20, 1917. *Croisilles-Ecoust Railway Cutting.*

The day before yesterday we had a visit from the Mayor of Wexford and a friend of his—a red-hot Sinn Feiner, I was told, from Dublin. They had come to Belgium to visit Willie Redmond's grave, and had got passes to come on to the Irish Division.

They were to have gone up into the firing line, but a relief was in progress, so they were not taken further than Battalion Headquarters. It was the first time I had ever seen a civilian in or near the trenches, and their black coats created great interest amongst all ranks.

Yesterday, from one of the battalion observation posts, I saw six Germans, in twenty minutes, through a telescope. They were well out of rifle range, but I could plainly watch all their movements, which, though the latter were very ordinary, were somehow interesting. There is an unaccountable fascination in watching your enemy in his leisure moments.

October 21, 1917 (*Sunday*). *Croisilles-Ecoust Railway Cutting.*

My young sniping officer tells me he had a shot this morning, but his would-be victim signalled a "miss," raising and lowering a stick above the parapet. I have known them do this before with a shovel. Our enemy evidently has some humour in spite of what people say.

Life in London must be getting more and more deadly. I fear it is becoming daily, more and more, a struggle for existence. I hope you do not have to stand in the queues to get your sugar and tea, and I pray that you are not starving yourself.

October 23, 1917.   *Croisilles-Ecoust Railway Cutting.*
Yesterday, with the doctor, I visited the 2nd Suffolks
on our right.   We were sniped at vigorously by machine-
gun fire as we crossed the Bullecourt-Ecoust road, on the
way home.   It is an exposed spot, and must be a source of
a good deal of amusement to the enemy.

October 25, 1917.   *Croisilles-Ecoust Railway Cutting.*
I did not write yesterday.   My days are fully occupied,
from morning till night, when the battalion is in the front
line.   I have my ordinary rounds to make, and, in addition,
receive endless calls from officers representing Field
Artillery, the various calibres of siege artillery, Stokes guns,
medium trench mortars, heavy trench mortars, machine
guns; Intelligence officers, signalling officers; and Generals.
We also get our full share of paper to attend to.

October 27, 1917.   *Croisilles-Ecoust Railway Cutting.*
Last night I got orders to go back this morning to Dysart
Camp, to meet Cardinal Bourne, who is in France on a
visit to the Army.

I arrived before the General and the "super-padrés,"
and seeing a small group of officers, and among them a
priest *not* in uniform, I asked him if he had come over with
the Cardinal.   He replied that he had, so I asked him if
Monseigneur Jackman had come over, too.   He said:
"I am he."   I then had a short and rather restricted conversation with him, as the Munsters and Leinsters were
already drawn up in front of us, ready for the Cardinal;
but he asked to be remembered to you.   I thanked him for
arranging about the crucifixes from Rome, and he pulled
out a larger one from his pocket and gave it to me.

Afterwards, I had a talk with the Cardinal, who also gave
a short address to those of the troops who are resting.
Then I returned to the line, lunching with the Leinsters on
the way.

I rode, both ways, with Colonel Roche-Kelly,[1] who
commands the 6th Royal Irish.   It was a muddy ride,
and was enlivened by the enemy, who was shelling the

[1] Lieut.-Col. Edmund Roche-Kelly, D.S.O.

valley through which we had to pass. Willie Redmond was in Roche-Kelly's battalion, and I asked him to tell me how he came to go over the top on June 7 at Wytschaete.

He said that the Divisional Commander had kept Redmond back from Guillemont and Ginchy because he thought he was too old (as he certainly was); he said poor Redmond worried about this. To make matters worse, he kept getting anonymous letters from Ireland, accusing him of staying behind because he was afraid. (Can you believe that such beasts exist?) But, in spite of repeated appeals, the G.O.C. would not swerve in his decision. I know that Redmond, during this period, was wont to ask his friends if they thought the men ever felt that he *was* holding back.

Well, when the attack on Wytschaete came, he implored so insistently, that the General at last gave way, and said he might go—on the understanding that he returned immediately the first objective was reached, and reported to Divisional Headquarters how the battle was progressing.

Roche-Kelly says that when Redmond arrived at his Battalion Headquarters, and said he had the General's permission, he at first tried to keep him with him; but no, he wanted to go with his Company:—so, thinking that the first Company to go over (as Redmond's happened to be) would have the easiest time, he allowed him to go as a sort of "liaison" officer.

He was hit in the hand or wrist immediately he crossed the parapet, but continued, and was hit a second time in the leg as he reached the German wire. Neither were serious wounds, but, as the General had said, Redmond was too old for the game, and he died when they got him to the dressing station.

Two nights ago Roche-Kelly's battalion—on my immediate left—caught two German prisoners going the unexpected way. They had escaped from a French prisoners-of-war camp, and, though dressed in German uniform, were trying to make their way through our lines, back to their own.

This, I may say, is an almost impossible thing to do, besides being extremely dangerous, for the adventurer runs the imminent risk of being shot or bayoneted, not only by our people, but by his own.

Therefore, I regard these men as sportsmen. One was very sore at being caught. He said he had been fifteen years in the Army and wanted to go on fighting. The other, I gather, was a lesser kind of man, and did not carry it off with the same bravado.

I have spoken more than once of the excellent opportunities we have here of observing the habits of our enemies. Any day—though naturally some days better than others—we can watch them. Many do not get the opportunity of displaying themselves more than once or twice, but there is one sentry who has his "exemption" card, so to speak. He stands by the Mebu known as "Neptune," and except when he is being relieved we see no movement. He is an exemplary sentry. Unconsciously, he shows his steel helmet—no more—and that rarely stirs.

He is not allowed to be shot at, because that would spoil the picture.

October 30, 1917.   *Croisilles-Ecoust Railway Cutting.*

The variations and vagaries of war are very peculiar. My present acting second in command is T. A. Dillon—aged twenty-two. By the fortune of war he is, as I say, acting second in command; while I have some forty other officers, including lieutenants and 2nd lieutenants—some of them almost brilliant—aged thirty, more or less.

The battalion was never in better form than it is at present. In addition to a good lot of officers I have many excellent N.C.O.'s—mostly old Regulars, who have been joining in large numbers during the last few months.

Acting upon orders, we fired over some leaflets, to-day, to our enemies across the way, telling them in the choicest German about the fate of their Zeppelins which attempted to raid London a few days ago. I rather fancy a note was added, in English, to the effect that Otto Weiss—a German N.C.O. with an iron cross whom we got on our wire three nights ago—has received Christian burial. I am now wondering if this latter will be regarded as "fraternizing" with the enemy.

November 4, 1917 (*Sunday*).   *Dysart Camp* (*near Ervillers*).

We were relieved the night before last, after holding the front line sixteen days, and yesterday and to-day (Sunday) have been devoted to hair-cutting, baths, and overhauling of clothing and equipment.

Father Wrafter, who has been out with the Division since it first came to France, came up with the relieving battalion, and while we were waiting for the completion of the relief—a tedious process which always takes an hour or two, and sometimes more, he talked and told stories.

He said that, a few nights before, he had been watching a working party digging a trench in the dark. There entered a sergeant; after which the following dialogue took place:

Sergeant: Is O'Beirne there?

Voice from the trench: Did you say, Brown, Sergeant?

Sergt.: I said, is O'Beirne there?

V.F.T.T.: Yes, Sergeant, Burns is here.

Sergt. (heatedly): It was O'Beirne I said. Do you want me to be talking French at ye?

Among other things we discussed the origin of various expressions much in vogue here. Nobody seems to know where the word "Boche" comes from. "Alliman," which was largely used by the men in 1915, and is (or was) the sole inscription (in pencil) on many a wooden cross, is, of course, a corruption of the French word, but Father Wrafter says that many of the men used it, thinking it meant "Ally-man"—or a man who belonged to the Allies!

"Jerry" (or Gerry), which is the word nearly all our men use when referring to the people opposite (the word "Fritz" is hardly ever used now), is—so Father Wrafter says—contracted from "German."

" A " frames are wooden structures, the shape of the letter " A," which are fixed in the trenches in the inverted position, the sides acting as supports for the walls, and the cross-pieces for the duck-boards or floor-boards.

The other day a Connaught Ranger was staggering along a communication trench carrying one of these things towards the front line, when he met an old friend, a recruit fresh out from Ireland.

"Well, Mike, and how do you like being a soldier?" asked the friend.

"It isn't a soldier you've got to be in this war," answered the Connaught Ranger, "it's a b—— camel."

On the 1st the enemy indulged in a heavy—though harmless—pounding of the neighbourhood of my Battalion Headquarters, which lasted several hours and cost him quite 500 shells, or more. He was aiming at what he believed to be a battery position a couple of hundred yards behind us, and though he was shooting from the map, without any direct observation, the aim was wonderfully accurate, the shells falling almost one on top of another. Indeed, as they lobbed over our heads it was possible, by concentrating one's eyes on the spot where they were dropping, actually to see the shells passing through the air.

It was All Saints' Day, and a priest was saying Mass in a dug-out when the shelling started. After the fourth shell, Mass then being over, I dispersed the crowd as a precautionary measure. Then came the real "hate"—the usual 5·9's, and also many 8·2-inch shells, which latter make a huge and hideous hole in the ground.

While we were having lunch there was a temporary lull, when only a few whizz-bangs came over. I said: "How nice that sounds after all the noise! It's almost like having roses thrown at you at Charing Cross."

"Yes," chipped in the Lewis gun officer, "it's like roses after a brick."

To switch off to the front line. How brave—before the war—we should have thought a man who sat looking through a periscope, with no protection over his head beyond the "tin-hat," immobile, while high explosive was being dropped around him! That is what our sentries do. The last morning the battalion was up, while I was doing my rounds, I was standing with one of the Company Commanders beside a sentry, trying to make out what some object was in Noman's Land—a heap of tangled wire or something of that kind;—when a faint "swish" sounded above, and with a sudden bang—in great contrast to the silence that prevailed—there exploded a few yards away a granatenwerfer, or aerial dart, or pine-apple, or whatever you like to call it;—one of those triangular fish-tailed things, with a body like a prickly pear.

Our interest in the heap of wire quite suddenly vanishes. We wait for "the next," which we know will follow shortly. Strictly, it is my duty to move away. It is the sentry's duty to continue looking through the periscope. But I cannot leave him like that. Therefore I hang about until the second bomb crashes. Then I say a word or two to the sentry and pass along on my rounds. I give you that by way of a glimpse into the life of the trenches.

Last night I went to the Divisional cinema, which is in a restored barn among the ruins of Ervillers. Charlie Chaplin was there, figuratively, and at his best. I confess I am getting to appreciate him; and if you could see how the soldiers love him you would like him too. When his image appears upon the screen they welcome it with such shouts of approval that it might be the living Charlie. The men all flock to these shows, and hundreds are turned away nightly.

November 6, 1917.   *Dysart Camp (near Ervillers).*

I got your letter to-day, describing the air-raid, which interested me enormously and filled me with pride to think of you all joking at the bottom of the kitchen stairs.

I cannot tell you how much I admire the way in which you have handled this problem, forcing the children to look upon air-raids as a game. It is splendid. The others will inevitably take their cue from you. Had you been a man you would have made an ideal soldier. Above all, I admire the way in which you have never woken the children till,

in your opinion, the danger has become imminent. You
are becoming a veteran now, and I have every faith in your
leadership, and that it will carry you and the household
through.

I am glad to think you are all praying for us. We have
a tame lot opposite, but one never knows how they may
develop.

November 10, 1917.   *Dysart Camp (Ervillers).*

The Italians, like the Russians, seem to be going to let
us down. I have always felt that this war would end in a
duel between ourselves and the Germans, and it looks more
and more like it every day. *We* shall certainly win.
Although the enemy has concentrated all his best troops
against us here on the Western Front, in a preponderance
which far eclipses anything he has attempted elsewhere,
we are undoubtedly "top-dog." It is a compliment to
think he so respects us. And it makes me feel more and
more proud of Britain: for, though we have our individual
rotters in plenty, you can always count on our people,
collectively. They will *not* let you down.

The weather continues to be horrible, and we have been
training and shivering all the morning. As we marched
back to camp we passed a woman, walking with a French
soldier. She was the first woman I had seen since
September 19 (nearly two months ago), and in the case of
the majority of the battalion the gap has been considerably
longer; so you may imagine what interest she aroused.
She had no doubt come to have a look at her ruined home,
or perhaps to dig up treasures which she had buried before
she left it.

Spit and polish is the order of the day, and I am all for it
—in reason. But when the men have just come out, after
sixteen days in the line, where they have been squeezed up
in muddy dug-outs during the few hours in the daytime
when they were not on duty and could get a sleep—for they
stand to all night, I think it is a bit thick when high-placed
officers, who do not share their dangers and discomforts
and indeed never, or scarcely ever, go into the firing line

kick up Hell's delight because the bayonet scabbards are not polished! Yet such is the kind of thing we have sometimes to put up with from our friends behind the front.

Personally, I prefer the attentions of our enemies. These are at least logical, and so think all the front line. Although, during the sixteen days and nights the battalion has been up, the breastworks have been collapsed by the rains—to say nothing of German shells and trench-mortars; though our patrols have nightly explored Noman's Land and the German wire, not a word is said about that. Not a remark. Not a comment. It is *polished* bayonet scabbards that they want. The real business we are here for is not even referred to. Can you believe it?

November 16, 1917.   *Dysart Camp (near Ervillers).*

One of my officers, in censoring his men's letters a day or two ago, came upon the following:

"DEAR BROTHER,—

"I can't tell you where I am, but I am at the place which I left to go to the place where I've come from." I think that should baffle the Censor, don't you?

November 25, 1917.   *Croisilles-Ecoust Railway Cutting.*

I have not written to you much lately, and now that you have read the papers you will know why.

Although we have not been in the centre of the picture (the main objective having been Cambrai), and the business upon which we have been engaged has been a side-show, it has been none the less absorbing for the individuals concerned, and my time and energies have been very fully occupied.

We have fought and won a success which, though insignificant no doubt having regard to the war as a whole, was for all that a very heroic affair, in which many officers and men of this battalion distinguished themselves greatly, having in fact done as good a thing as I have seen up to the present. Nevertheless, other things have happened which I will tell you about some other day, and, though they are washed out now, the pleasure of the success is

washed out too, to a large extent, by the loss of my Brigadier
(General George Pereira), who has left us, and who, after
a few misunderstandings at the beginning of our acquaintanceship, had become a very dear friend to me, as he had
to every officer and man of the Brigade. He is about
fifty-three, but has got to look like an old man. He is,
I think, the most loyal and faithful and brave and unselfish
man I have ever met, and I feel a great personal loss in his
departure.

To tell you the story. I have of course known for long
of these impending operations, but I think you will agree
that even you could not have guessed this from my letters.
I have been obliged to keep my own counsel, without
confiding even in my Adjutant or the Company Commanders.

We came up to the front line on the 18th, having for a
few days previously practised the attack over a prepared
replica of the German trenches which were to be our
objective. This naturally suggested to all ranks what was
before them, and, devout though they always are, in the
best of spirits, the whole battalion flocked to Confession
the last evening—the 17th—in the patched-up barn at
Ervillers which serves as a church when we are resting.

No one who has not seen it can ever realize the intense
devotion of these Irish soldiers who have come to fight in
France. What they are like in their own homes in peace
time I do not know, but here, in the war, it is very impressive to see them. For hours that evening the priests
were engaged, the men crowding up silently, passing one
by one to the canvas Confessionals in the far corners of
the old ruin, which was dimly lighted by a candle or two
for the occasion.

The following morning (Sunday) all went to non-fasting
Communion, since it was late in the day, this being allowed
by the Church before going into action. They are getting
used to non-fasting Communion now, though many of
them in the earlier days could not get over the idea that
they were committing a sin by doing so.

In the evening, after dark, the battalion moved up to the trenches, coming in for a certain amount of shelling by the way. On reaching my old Headquarters in the Croisilles-Ecoust railway cutting, I found that the enemy had been shelling there pretty freely, especially during that afternoon, but, though he had demolished a few dug-outs, the material damage had been small, though five men had been wounded.

During the night a German came over and surrendered himself. He said that three of his comrades had started with him, but our Lewis gunners had got on to them, and they did not reach their destination. Of course, the Lewis gunners could not know, in the dark, what these people were coming for.

Unfortunately, the one man who did arrive reached our line just alongside the point of contact with the battalion on our left. He crept over the parapet at a spot where there happens to be what is known in military language as a latrine (pronounced by the men latt-er-reen). One of my men was in occupation at the time, and seeing a figure appear on the skyline, said, " 'Ere, 'ands up and wait till I've finished." The German, not understanding, and frightened, dropped hastily behind the parapet, and crept along to the first post of the next battalion, a few yards away.

It was thus that the Connaught Rangers failed to obtain the credit of this catch, from which the Intelligence Department claims to have extracted some very useful information.

The German trench opposed to us was the famous Hindenburg line. It is a very elaborate work. The surface trench is (or I should say was) wide and deep, and, at intervals of about 25 yards, stairways descend from the parapet side to a heavily-timbered tunnel, in dimension about 7 feet by $4\frac{1}{2}$ feet, which runs along the whole length of the trench for some miles, at a depth of 25 feet or 30 feet below the surface. Let into the wall of the tunnel at the foot of each stairway were heavy charges of high explosive, connected by wires with an electric battery one or two kilometres behind the German line, and intended to blow up the tunnel if it should ever fall into our hands. On the surface, at intervals along the trench, are "Mebus" ("Pill-boxes," as the newspapers call them)—those massive emplacements or shelters of concrete which I have already described, reinforced with steel, the interiors of which are practically impervious to shell-fire, though the exteriors may be, and in fact have been in almost every case reduced to a mangled skeleton of twisted steel.

This roughly describes the position we were to attack, on a frontage of 350 yards, at 6.20 o'clock on the morning of November 20. I may add that all details regarding the structure of the defences were accurately known to us beforehand from the information collected by the raiding parties, and from prisoners.

My orders were to assault with two Companies, which were to advance on the extreme right of the Division, and as the Brigade on my right was to take no part in the action, it meant that I was to attack with my right flank "in the air."

It was very edifying to watch the officers and men preparing for the attack—all optimistic, full of confidence, and cheery:—a little more silent than usual, perhaps, during dinner the night before, though Brett, commanding the right assaulting Company, celebrated the occasion by getting up a lot of oysters of which he very generously sent me a liberal share.

At about 2 a.m. the assaulting Companies began to get into position, and by an hour before Zero each man was in his appointed place, ready for battle. My Battle Head-quarters were in a mined dug-out which had been allotted to me in one of the main communication trenches known as Queen's Lane, some 250 yards behind the firing-line.

Shortly before Zero I headed for the front to wish the assaulting Companies good luck before they went over, but I was delayed, and found myself still in the fire-trench when, bursting out of almost perfect silence, our barrage started.

My orders to the right Company, which was formed up in Martin Road—a sunken road in front of the fire-trench, and which had only some 75 yards to go to the nearest point of its objective, had been to start at two minutes after Zero, i.e. at 6.22, so as to give our guns time to lift.

The danger on these occasions, if they start too soon, is that the men in the impetuous rush forward may run into our own barrage—a thing, unfortunately, that often happens.

The left Company, which had further to go, had instructions to start a minute earlier. The concentrated artillery was to play upon the German trench for four minutes, commencing at Zero, and then to lift, and I calculated that by the time-table I had given them the assaulting Companies would reach the objective as soon as it was safe to do so. As a precautionary measure I had had the direction of the objective marked out with tape the night before, having learned, from previous experience, the difficulty of keeping direction in the dark.

Absolutely to the tick I watched the men scaling the ladders (which had been brought up during the night) and scrambling over the parapet, the signallers under their sergeant (Rogers) struggling with the coils of telephone wire that was to keep me in touch with the assaulting troops once they had established themselves in the German trench. Those are sights that are very inspiring, and which engrave themselves upon the memory, but I prefer to turn away from them.

I had not time to get back to my proper Headquarters, so remained at the head of the communication trench, where there was an advanced signal station with a telephone. By this time the usual inferno, to which at intervals we have become so accustomed, had worked up to its full fury. The semi-darkness of the early morning was illuminated by the bursts of the shells, trench-mortar bombs, smoke bombs, and the flares and excited S.O.S. rockets of the enemy. The air vibrated with the hurricane of our machine-gun barrage whistling from behind and that of the enemy from the front. The enemy shrapnel was bursting angrily overhead. I met one of my men wandering slowly along the trench, with a hot-food container on his back, and a mess tin in his hand. He seemed quite oblivious of the frenzy around him, but he clearly had something weighing on his mind. So I asked him what was the matter. I had to shout to make myself heard. Said he: "I've lost two men for their breakfasts, sorr." I felt sorry for the two men then sailing over Noman's Land, but I could not help smiling at the predicament of the orderly man thus wandering disconsolate!

I decided to control the attack from the forward telephone, but, no sooner had I made up my mind to do so, than the wounded began to stream back. Prisoners also began to arrive, still holding up their hands and muttering "Kamerade": so that soon the dug-out—roomy though it was—became so packed with bleeding men that it was impossible to function, and I decided to go to my proper Headquarters, where at least I should find room to breathe.

At this moment poor Brett came stumbling back, crimson with blood, having been shot through the face, bringing further confirmation of the news which I had already had from him by runner, that the enemy was furiously counter-attacking our exposed right flank. I left him with Barron, the Intelligence Officer, and made for Queen's Lane. Then the messages began to arrive, thick and fast.

I will now stop for the present, and finish in another letter.

November 27, 1917. *Dysart Camp (near Ervillers).*

We were relieved in the line last night, and have come back to Dysart Camp. I will continue where I left off, at the moment when I had reached my Battle Headquarters in Queen's Lane, and had begun to be inundated with messages. I will not weary you with all of these. They reported fierce and repeated counter-attacks on the exposed right flank, and asked that more bombs and more men might be sent across Noman's Land, which by this time had become practically impassable.

I will return to "Zero." Our smoke barrage had deceived the Germans and led them to believe, as had been intended, that gas was being sent over, so that when our men reached their objective they were found wearing gas masks. They appeared to be in a very dazed condition. There were a few sentries in the saps, and a number of men grouped in the tunnel entrances, who were shot or bayoneted.

Immediately the trench had been occupied, the two "Mebus," known as "Jove" and "Mars," were approached from behind, according to plan, both surrendering after slight resistance. Simultaneously, a sentry was posted at each tunnel entrance, and parties provided with wire-cutters to cut the electric wires leading to the mines at the foot of each stairway were sent into the tunnel to clear it of the enemy. This operation was so skilfully and so quickly carried out that not a single mine exploded.

The left Company Commander (Tuite) established his Headquarters in the Mebu "Mars," in which, in the meantime, the signallers were installing a telephone. The right Company Commander began to make similar arrangements in "Jove," he having himself led the party which stormed that "Mebu" and shot at least one of the garrison with his revolver. The tunnel was cleared, and up to 7.30 a.m., 121 prisoners had been counted and sent to the rear. Further captures subsequently increased this number to 152.

At about 7.10 a.m. the enemy began to counter-attack our right flank, which he was quick to spot was in the air, in a very determined and persistent manner, bringing up an overwhelming superiority in men, bombs, and ammunition through the tunnel from the south. The latter afforded him an uninterrupted communication with his rear, the R.E. tunnellers who had accompanied the assaulting party having unfortunately failed to block the tunnel as had been pre-arranged, their officer having been killed just as he reached the trench.

These counter-attacks were repeated over and over

again, the fighting becoming very furious, and continuing almost hand to hand for some hours. You will appreciate its severity when I tell you that the Commander and twenty-six out of twenty-eight other ranks of the right flank platoon became casualties. The officers and men fought with the most heroic determination in spite of a failing and finally disappearing supply of bombs, supplementing the limited supply which they had carried over with them (two per man) with German bombs which they picked up in the trench.

At a critical moment one of the men, Private K. White, rushed close up to a traverse from behind which the enemy was bombing, and actually catching some of their bombs in the air, threw them back before they had exploded.

After the first hour the right Company Commander, Brett, having been wounded and the bomb supply having given out, the survivors began slowly to fall back upon the Mebu "Mars," continuing to hold the enemy in check by Lewis gun and rifle fire—most unsuitable weapons under such circumstances, yielding their ground only inch by inch, and leaving a trail of dead behind them. All their wounded they withdrew.

During this time I was pushing reinforcements with bombs and ammunition across Noman's Land, losing good men in the process, from the heavy machine-gun and shell-fire which was sweeping it.

At 9.45 a.m. Captain Tuite, then commanding both front Companies, was reported severely wounded; but in spite of this most serious loss the remainder stuck it and held their own at "Mars." Thirty-five lay dead, and 105 had been wounded.

A little after one o'clock I was able to leave the telephone, and crossed Noman's Land to the captured trench. I took one of my orderlies, Private Moran, with me. We made a safe crossing and found that a firm defensive flank had been established at "Mars." The enemy was apparently exhausted for the moment, but was still shelling furiously, though wildly, and therefore rather impotently. It was the end, for the time being, of a fine piece of work. The advance to the attack across Noman's Land had been carried out precisely as rehearsed and according to programme, and the subsequent defence of the exposed right flank had been beyond praise.

As it is late, I will continue in another letter.

November 28, 1917.   *Dysart Camp (near Ervillers).*

In yesterday's letter, I had just reached the captured tunnel trench, after a safe crossing of Noman's Land, with my orderly, Private Moran. I had steered rather for the left, which I judged was not so much under observation as the exposed right, and had struck the trench, as I had intended, a hundred yards or so to the left of the left flank of my battalion. I then followed the trench towards the right, and soon found myself among my own men.

I talked to the men as I passed along the line, and found them in good spirits, and confident in the knowledge of the splendid part they had played that morning.

Captain Eric Norman, who commanded the reinforcing Company, had just arrived with the last of his men, whom he had been able to dribble across only four at a time owing to the stormy condition of Noman's Land. Indeed, he had lost his company sergeant-major (Murphy)—killed as he climbed over the parapet.

We were now well established, and though the shelling was very heavy it was still erratic, and was doing little damage —to us, at any rate.

The familiar scene of desolation confronted me. Each time I see this kind of thing I think it is worse than the last time, and indeed, on this occasion, so churned up was the surface that, but for the line of tunnel entrances and the trodden ground between them, there was little left to indicate where the trench had been. It was just a sea of overlapping craters of huge dimensions—a dismal chaos of fresh-turned earth. Some of the German dead still wore gas masks.

On my return journey I explored the tunnel. Half-way down a stairway I came upon three wounded Connaught

233

Rangers—one slight and two stretcher cases, the latter including a man named Moran, of "A" Company.

These I promised to send for, and then went down into the tunnel. It was littered with German clothing and equipment. Here and there lay a dead man, and a living German sat, smoking a cigarette, while he nursed a dying comrade.

I followed the tunnel for some distance. The same description applies. At the foot of one of the stairways lay a dead officer. At the first alarm, they told me, he had challenged the entry of the storming party, and the young Connaught Ranger officer in charge had thrown down a bomb which had wounded him mortally. Another officer lay dying, his servant attending him. The officer died next morning, when the servant—a delicate-looking, square-headed youth in spectacles—was sent back, a prisoner.

I left the tunnel, and climbed again to the surface. The enemy shell-fire had increased. I chanced it, and over again into the open went my orderly and I. Again we dodged through the shell-holes, and had a lively few minutes as we crossed what had been Noman's Land earlier in the day; but we passed through all right, and, as we dropped into the old front line, we breathed freely once more. I said so to Moran, and he agreed. He is a cool fellow, and though he has been out since the early days of the war, nothing seems to move him much.

It is late and I will finish to-morrow.

P.S. Do not confuse Moran, the orderly, with Moran, the wounded man of "A" Company.

P.P.S. The battalion is cleaning up, and refitting, and having baths. This afternoon we had a football match— Officers *v.* Sergeants.

November 29, 1917.   *Dysart Camp (near Ervillers).*

My last letter ends the story of November 20. Among the loot we collected some fine suits of steel body-armour, a specimen of which I have sent you; numerous letters (of no value); a machine-gun or two; granatenwerfers (aerial dart-throwers); a big trench-mortar, with a pile of shells—2 feet long—beside it; also photographs taken from the ground and from the air: and finally, maps.

The maps show not only all the enemy's private arrangements behind his line, but our own as well, our trenches in many instances being actually described by the names under which we know them! This, I must say, interests me very much. It means either that they have secured some of our secret trench maps, or else have extracted the information from prisoners. It is well known that they have all sorts of dodges. The most stoic and loyal of prisoners may be bamboozled into giving away information. For example, the enemy will dress up an English-speaking German as an English soldier and put him among the prisoners—who think he is one of themselves—to pick up snatches of conversation. As before Wytschaete, my own Headquarters were well marked out, in their true position.

On the 21st, while in the captured trench, I met a stretcher being carried out. I asked who was on it, and the wounded man looked up smiling, and said, "I am Moran, of 'A' Company, sir."

I remembered the man I had found on the tunnel stairway, twenty hours earlier. The stretcher-bearers who had been sent to fetch him had failed to find him, and had neglected to report the fact. It is true that the stretcher-bearers had their hands full, but I felt very indignant that a severely wounded man should have been left so long to suffer, and thought how indignant must *he* be.

But Moran was not at all indignant. On the contrary, he beamed from his stretcher, and just said: "I hope you'll all get out of this, sir."

He must be a good fellow, Moran.

The Germans were still occupying the tunnel underneath our right flank, so, after a consultation with Norman, who was now commanding the front line, and who was most willing, as also were his officers and men, arrangements were made to storm and re-capture the Mebu "Jove" at one o'clock that day, and to block the tunnel.

This, however, was vetoed by the Higher Command, who presumably thought that the battalion had had enough.

On the 22nd, smoke was issuing from the tunnel entrance 40 yards from my right flank, indicating that the enemy was still beneath us. So a party, under Norman, went and dropped a charge of high-explosive down the stairway, which must at least have disconcerted the occupants of the tunnel.

As I walked back from watching this operation I met the Brigadier, who was on his way up to inspect our new position. He shook hands with me, and offered his congratulations on what the battalion had done.

On the 23rd the Brigadier visited me again, to say good-bye. It was a sad parting, and I shall never forget him as he hobbled away along the trench-boards;—the final exit from the fighting line of one of the best men that ever breathed.

The same evening, after dark, we having been relieved in the meantime and gone into support in Railway Reserve, the 7th Leinsters, under Colonel Buckley, were put in to retake "Jove," which they did very thoroughly.

I visited the place an hour or two afterwards. Many of my own dead lay around the Mebu and on the parapet of the trench near by, their positions proving how devotedly they had fought. One of them was locked in grips with a dead German. Among them were many enemy dead, both those that my men had killed on the 20th, and with them and sometimes lying on the top of them were the bayoneted corpses of the second fight.

It was a grand though an ugly sight. As I looked at it my men were hard at work digging to connect up "Jove" with the old front line, having been brought up from support for this purpose.

We recovered all our dead and buried them in a little "war" cemetery behind the embankment near what used to be Croisilles Railway Station, and not a single living man remained in the hands of the enemy.

November 30, 1917.   *Dysart Camp (near Ervillers).*

I have done my best to describe this battalion's part in the capture of the famous Hindenburg Tunnel trench. I have told you the things which I have thought would interest you. But, of course, there are many incidents in a battle of this kind which are impossible to set down, and it would bore you if I attempted it.

On the days following the battle the Germans were very unsettled, and showed signs of going back. There was much movement behind their line, which it was interesting to watch.

On the 25th I made a thorough exploration of the new positions, in daylight. I found it possible to show myself, almost anywhere, without being fired at. The enemy had blown in the tunnel between ourselves and the 3rd Division (on our right) the previous night, and smoke was still coming from the Mebu "Neptune."

I am sending home a German bayonet and scabbard; also a sort of back-handed and rather pathetic souvenir—a Connaught Ranger's shoulder-strap. The Mebu "Jove," which we captured on the 20th, passed back temporarily to the enemy the same day, as I have explained. During the time it remained in their hands they cut the identifications from our dead.

When the Mebu came back to us on the night of the 23rd this shoulder-strap was recovered from a dead German.

I think the enemy must be short of shoe-leather. As I passed along the recaptured piece of trench on the 25th, I noticed the body of a young officer of the Royal Irish Regiment, who had been killed while on a wiring party. The enemy had stripped him of his boots.

December 7, 1917.   *Tincourt.*

My letters have been scrappy the last few days, but we have been having a scrappy time, never knowing our movements for more than an hour or two ahead—the usual thing on these occasions; orders cancelled, then counter-cancelled; rumours galore; marches; huts or tents (bitterly cold); but, on the whole, a very cheerful time, though with little opportunity and *no* inclination for settled writing.

Yesterday we marched viâ Le Transloy, Rocquigny, Manancourt, Moislains and Templeux, to Tincourt, where, at this moment, we are waiting. It is a big deserted village, spared by the enemy—a thing apart amid the orgy of destruction—for the concentration of the civil population before the Germans evacuated these parts.

The village is not intact, I need scarcely say. The church is maimed, and many buildings are destroyed, but there remains plenty of fine accommodation, which for the moment we are enjoying.

The civil population having gone away long ago, our men are occupying the empty houses, stripped of every vestige of furniture, and dilapidated, but to them palaces, with huge fires burning, of wood cut from the trees felled by the enemy in his wanton way. They are easily the best billets they have ever had.

The officers' mess is in a building adjacent to the church, and against the wall (of the mess) is a great crucifix, salved by the enemy from the wreckage he has created, and re-erected—as an inscription in German and French declares—"to the memory of those brave soldiers who died at Tincourt in defence of the Fatherland."

The officers sleep in two houses close by—the curé's house and the school, I should judge by the look of them, while I am in a hut—most comfortable—with a stove.

It is, indeed, all much too good to last more than a day or two.

December 8, 1917.   *Tincourt.*

Further details of the fight of November 20 continue to appear. I enclose a letter written by Lance-Corporal Parle to his platoon commander. He was a Lewis gunner, and a stout fellow, as you will see from the letter.

They got real fighting mad that day, and Roche-Kelly told me that, several days after we had been relieved, he found the body of one of my men lying far inside the enemy lines, with six dead Germans around it.

"FRANCE,

"*Saturday, Nov.* 24/11/17

"DEAR MR. RUSSELL,

"I hope you got out of the Battle Safe.   But my object in writing this letter is to let you know where to get the Lewis gun, as I know you will be uneasy about it. this is the story.   I only had 4 men in the Section going in to battle on Tuesday morning so first Whelan got Shell Shock, then when Coy asked for reingforcements I done my leven best to get what of the Section that was left over nomans land   But McFaddin got killed R.I.P   Cloyne got wounded and Trogers got burried.   So there was no one left only myself.   I had Still about 100 yards to go to where A Coy was.   I tryed to take 4 magazings with the gun as I knew the gun was no good without them But a Shell hit near where I was and I got one bit in my back and one in the left leg, so that done it.   So I took the gun back with me.   I could not see any of the Connaughts to give it to.   I left it with the Leinsters.   I don't know the number of the gun as L/C Lynch had my gun so I must have had Lynch's.

"Dear Sir if there is any more which you wish to know about the gun it will give me the greatest Joy to tell you my address is 3835 L/C Parle 6 Conn. Rangers, No. 2 General Hospital, Qnag. Section B.E.F. France.

"I expect to be with the Connaughts in a few weeks as my wounds are not very bad.

"I remain your humbel servent,

"V. PARLE."

December 9, 1917.   *Tincourt.*

I said it was too good to last, and so it has proved.   Late to-night we have received our marching orders, though the latest information had pointed strongly to our remaining here some days longer.

I am getting an old soldier now, and I *never* count on anything for more than a few hours ahead—leastways when it is something nice.   How severe will be the "Sunday sickness" when, after the war, we have to settle down to the monotony of knowing to a certainty where we are going to be, so far ahead as even the following week! I shall be restless, I know,—perhaps even when I come on leave, and you must make full allowance for any sort of mood I may develop. The tedium of home life after this is bound to produce reaction, just as the old pre-war Sundays used to do after a hard week in the City. Don't misunderstand my use of the word "tedium." God knows how we all long for it sometimes!

Yesterday, the four Battalion Commanders of the Brigade rode out with the new Brigadier (Gregorie)[1] to reconnoitre the back areas of the line in front of us. It was a nasty day. We visited the Divisional General, who has been ill, but is nearly well again. He had sent an invitation for the Brigadier and myself to lunch at his Headquarters near Villers Faucon. So we did this, and rode home together afterwards.

P.S. In the old churchyard, close by the hut from which I write, two German soldiers, killed in the Franco-Prussian War, lie buried. Over them their compatriots have, during their recent occupation of this village, put up an expensive granite tombstone—"to their comrades of 1870–1"!

In the German graveyards which I have seen lately, many of the crosses are of elaborate stonework. But there do not seem to be the thousands of graves which our cemeteries with their wooden crosses represent. Can it be that we are not doing them as much damage as we think, or that they have other cemeteries, on a larger scale, further back?

We are now in the VII Corps, and this afternoon, on parade, I read out the farewell letter from General Haldane, commanding the VI Corps which we have left. It is as follows:

"I desire to place on record the good service of the 16th (Irish) Division which is about to leave the VI Corps after serving with it for 3½ months.

"The work of the Division, both in the trenches and behind

---

[1] Brig.-Gen. H. G. Gregorie, D.S.O.

the Line, has been admirable and might well serve as a model of how such duties should be performed.

"In carrying out the capture of the German trenches on the 20th November and their rapid consolidation—an exploit which had defeated the efforts of other Divisions—the Division showed once again what a splendid fighting machine it is.

"It is with great regret that I am forced to part with the Irish Division. I desire to express to Major-General Hickie and all ranks under him my warmest wishes for their future welfare and the hope that I may at another time be so fortunate as to have the Irish Division under my command."

December 10, 1917.   *Tincourt.*

The Divisional General called this morning. He was full of praise and compliments and told me—what we had imagined—that when we left Ervillers on Sunday, December 2, we were destined for Bourlon Wood, but were switched off, owing to contingencies which intervened, to come to the area in which we now find ourselves.

Thus, though all ranks were nerved up and ready for the worst that might happen—indeed were almost eager for it—we were spared what was at that time probably the most damnable spot on God's earth;—a veritable hell; so drenched with gas that the troops holding it had practically to live in their box respirators;—a salient so sharp and so shelled that it was untenable.

Indeed, it has since been evacuated, as you have no doubt learnt from the newspapers.

December 12, 1917.   *Ronssoy.*

We came up into support yesterday. We are in one of a group of large villages which, judging from the ruins, and from the foundations, gates and gardens (which in many cases are all that is left), must before the war have been prosperous sugar manufacturing centres, containing plenty of modern mansions of a rather pretentious kind.

I sleep in a mined dug-out, 30 or 40 feet below the surface, which is comfortable and safe, but, strange to say,

cold. It is when I emerge into the open to visit my
platoons—a job that takes several hours since they are very
scattered—that I have to dodge the shells, and I got well
sprinkled yesterday, almost immediately after my arrival,
by one which crashed into a garden wall less than the width
of the road from where I was walking.

Across the way, some of my officers and men are living
in the cellar of the ancient château—a ruin surrounded by
a moat, which before the war must have been quite an
imposing building. It is pitiful to see it now: no form
or semblance of its former glory, but the great double staircase of stone leading to where once the front-door stood,
and which, being on the side facing away from the enemy,
has so far escaped complete obliteration.

The cellar with its stone walls and arched roofs suggests
Guy Fawkes and the dungeons of the Tower of London,
and it makes a fair dug-out, though, owing to the shell-
shattered condition of the building above it, it is necessary
to crawl on hands and knees to get into it.

When I visited it yesterday I found that a German shell
had just killed a battery sergeant-major near the doorway.

December 15, 1917. *Ronssoy*

The Brigadier has just rung up to say that the Major-
General will not allow two C.O.'s away at the same time;
and as Roche-Kelly was the first for leave, he has been
allowed to go. This is as it should be, but it is rather a
blow. Still, if I am not home for Christmas, I shall hope
to be there a few days later, but I feel I cannot ask the
children to postpone their Christmas tree.

The line we are holding is different to any I have seen
before. It consists of a string of outposts traversing country
which is very undulating. In my sector a road cuts our
trenches at right angles; then, crossing Noman's Land,
continues through the German line. A ridge obscures the
approach, and the only indication that you are nearing the
front is a barricade of wire, which has been thrown across
the road to prevent accidents.

There is a story that, before this barrier was erected,

the doctor of one of the battalions which preceded us, having returned with a mess-cart full of provisions, collected from a certain famous town in our rear, failed to recognize his bearings, and, passing between two outposts, entered the enemy's domain.

The enemy kept everything but the mess-cart and the driver, whom they sent back with a note to the English Colonel.

"Thank you very much," the note said, "for all the good things you have sent us. They will be most useful."

Then the note added, "So will the doctor, when he gets sober"!

December 16, 1917 (*Sunday*).   *Ronssoy.*

I was wandering about the ruins of this village this morning, looking for cellars into which to put my men in case of bombardment;—or rather I was being led by one of my Platoon Commanders to some which he had discovered, when we passed the old peace-time cemetery. It is a shocking sight. Practically every grave has been opened by the enemy; why, I cannot guess. Can it have been to look for supposed hidden treasure, or just wanton insult and desecration?

In one case the great stone slab covering a deep vault has been dropped on to three coffins which lie on the floor below, smashing them, and overturning two, which lie upon their sides, so that the crumbling contents are dribbling out. Into another vault a silvered crucifix has been thrown and lies broken at the bottom. What can the enemy think is the good of all this? What result can he expect from it but the creation in the minds of the French of a furious desire for vengeance? I imagine they will stop at nothing if they ever get into Germany. Imagine, if we had experienced such things in England!

A new second in command has come to me to-day—Major R. M. Raynsford, of the Leinster Regiment.

P.S. One of my Company Commanders has just come in to say that he has had a direct hit on one of his platoons —a casual shell.

December 18, 1917.
Left Sub-Section (Tombois Farm to Island Traverse), Lempire.

We are in the front line again, having come up last night, and I think we are safer by the change!

We woke up yesterday to find snow upon the ground. This silenced the guns, on both sides, for a bit, and thus has its advantages! You see, the sweep of the discharge, when snow is on the ground, gives away the position of batteries to the aerial photographers. So the gunners restrain themselves till they have got their white sheets spread out. Last Winter our people had such perfect photographs of the German positions that it was a case of 'embarras de richesses.'' The counter-batteries had so many targets to choose from that they scarcely knew which to pick out first.

When I wrote last—two nights ago—we had just had what had been described to me as a direct hit on one of the platoons in their billet. As a matter of fact, the shell had fallen in the road, just outside the door. It was an unlucky one, and nine times out of ten would have done no damage. It killed three of my men and wounded five; and it killed and wounded some artillery men and horses who happened to be passing along the road, as well. The snow outside is red with their blood to-day. It was a small shell, too.

At the same time, another bigger shell fell on the roof of one of my Company Commander's Headquarters. In his "situation report" (which comes to me twice daily) he remarked: "Though the enemy obtained a direct hit on my Headquarters—thanks to the hard work done by 'D' Company (i.e. himself) on the strengthening of the roofs of these dug-outs, no material damage was sustained!"

It was, all the same, a lucky one, and though he joked about it, if it had not chanced to strike a steel girder, I should be minus some officers. As it is, it has only bent in the dug-out.

Two casual shells, a few nights ago, fell simultaneously, and killed twenty-two and wounded thirty-two men of the South Irish Horse at Ste Emilie—a short way down the road.   But that is not likely to happen again.   The fact is we have only just come to these parts, and it takes time to dig in.   Each day we improve our position.

The Major-General told me, the other day, that the casualties of the Division, up to the time we left the Bulle-court region at the beginning of this month, had totalled 19,580.

December 19, 1917.

Left Sub-Section (Tombois Farm to Island Traverse), Lempire.

The Brigadier has just rung up and said they have granted my leave for the 23rd; so I shall sail on the 24th and should be with you that evening.

January 8, 1918.   *Front Line, Lempire.*

Once more I have vowed that never again if I can help it will I travel by the "leave" train.   I had forgotten to bring a candle, so, the cold being bitter and the windows broken, I shivered in the darkness.

It is beyond my powers adequately to describe the horrors of the "leave" train, the scandal of which still continues after 3½ years of war.   Though timed to arrive at Divisional Railhead in the early morning we did not do so till the afternoon, and, after fifteen hours on the train, I reached my transport lines near Villers Faucon at 2 p.m. in a blizzard, having had nothing to eat since last evening.

At the transport lines I found officers and men still under canvas, and as the ground was deep in snow the appearance of everything was very uninviting and conducive to nostalgia:—I believe that is the word.

The battalion is in new trenches in the front line, and after getting some food I walked to my Headquarters, which are in a sunken road beyond Lempire, calling in at the Headquarters of the 48th and my own Brigade on the way up.

The line is very quiet.

January 9, 1918.   *Front Line, Lempire.*

The terrible weather still holds, the frost having lasted practically since I left here on the 23rd December to go on leave.   The blizzard continues, and the trenches are half full of snow.   I have spent a good deal of to-day and to-night in them, and find that both officers and men retain their usual cheerfulness and patience in spite of their appalling hardships.

January 10, 1918.   *Front Line, Lempire.*

A few minutes before four o'clock this morning the enemy tried to raid one of my Lewis gun posts which is placed, necessarily in an isolated position, well out in Noman's Land, about 150 yards in front of the fire-trench, in a sunken road which crosses both lines of trenches.   The raiders came across the snow in the dark, camouflaged in white overalls.

In parenthesis, I may explain that while I have been away there have been two unfortunate cases of sentries mistaking wiring parties of the Divisional pioneer battalion for the enemy;—whether owing to the failure of the wiring parties to report properly before going out, or to over-eagerness on the part of the sentries, I do not profess to know. No one was hurt on either occasion, but a good deal of fuss was made about it, our new Brigadier blaming the men who did the shooting—his own men—and saying so pretty forcibly.

When I first heard of this I thought that a mistake had been made—if for no other reason than that there would for a time at any rate be a disinclination on the part of sentries to shoot promptly, which might prove dangerous; —and that is what happened this morning.

The double sentries on duty in the sunken road heard, but in the darkness did not see, a movement in front of them. Hesitating to shoot, they challenged. The immediate reply was a volley of hand-grenades. Private Mayne, who had charge of the Lewis gun, was hit "all over," in many parts, including the stomach. His left arm was reduced to pulp. Nevertheless, he struggled up, and leaning against the parapet, with his uninjured hand discharged a full magazine (forty-seven rounds) into the enemy, who broke, not a man reaching our trench. Then he collapsed and fell insensible across his gun.

The second sentry's foot was so badly shattered that it had to be amputated in the trench. The doctor has just told me that he performed this operation without chloroform, which was unnecessary owing to the man's numbed condition, and that while he did it the man himself looked on, smoking a cigarette, and with true Irish courtesy thanked him for his kindness when it was over.

Words cannot express my feelings of admiration for Private Mayne's magnificent act of gallantry, which I consider well worthy of the V.C. It is, however, improbable that he will live to enjoy any decoration that may be conferred upon him.

January 12, 1918.   *Villers Faucon.*

The incident of the morning before last had so filled me with pride of the battalion that I confess I have been aghast at receiving—instead of any acknowledgment of the successful and heroic repulse of the German raiders by Private Mayne and his companion—the following memorandum, which has been circulated in the Division. I quote from memory:

"Another instance has occurred of an enemy patrol reaching within bombing distance of our line. This must not occur again. Our patrols must meet the enemy patrols boldly in Noman's Land," etc., etc., etc.

How simple and how grand it sounds! I think I can see the writer, with his scarlet tabs, seated in his nice office 7 or 8 miles behind the line, penning this pompous admonition.

So Private Mayne, it seems, will go unrecognized and unrewarded. In the meantime he has died, and I can only say, "God rest his soul"![1]

January 25, 1918.   *Ronssoy.*

Things here are very tranquil. Indeed, the whole front seems quieter than it has been for years. Perhaps the weather accounts for it—and the mud of the trenches—which has to be seen to be believed. To-day has been sunny and warm, and I have seen a pansy in blossom in one of the devastated gardens among the ruins. This must have been a village of gardens once upon a time before the war.

January 27, 1918 (*Sunday*).   *Ronssoy.*

To-day is the Kaiser's birthday, and we half expected that things might happen, but there has been a thick fog, and all has been as silent as can be. I am afraid the troops are not so sorry as they ought to be.

"Am I offensive enough?" is one of the questions laid down in a pamphlet that reaches us from an Army School some 30 miles behind the line. It is for the subaltern to ask himself each morning as he rises from his bed.

[1] He received a posthumous mention in despatches.

Most laudable! But, as the Lewis Gun Officer remarked to-day, it is one of the paradoxes of war that the further you get from the battle line the more "offensive" are the people you meet!

The Brigadier called to-day just as I was finishing lunch, and I had a walk with him. He said he had sent in my name for three weeks' attachment to the French Battalion Commanders' School at Vadenay, near Châlons-sur-Marne, which will be an interesting change—if it comes off.

The battalion is getting very weak, and something will have to be done before long.

January 28, 1918. *Left Sub-Section (Right Brigade)*
(Tombois Farm to Island Traverse), Lempire.

We came up into the Front line this evening, relieving the 1st Royal Munster Fusiliers, and this morning, in anticipation, I went round the trenches—the same that I left to go home on leave on the 23rd December.

The change is remarkable. I left the trenches frozen like rock. I find them, to-day, half full of sticky mud; twice as wide and half as deep owing to the caving of the sides; two layers of trench-boards buried 2 feet deep in glutinous mud. It is a labour to walk in them, and to-day being a clear, sunny day it was not an occasion for easy cuts across the open.

Even so, for long stretches of these trenches you are under full view of the enemy—about 500 yards away. But he does not shoot, which suggests that his trenches are no better than ours (which, no doubt, is the case), and that he does not want us to shoot at him.

Indeed, for a few days past I find that the officers on duty on both sides have been making it a practice to walk along the parapet, so as to avoid the quagmire of the trenches. This morning, however, when an officer on our side tried it, the enemy opened with machine-gun fire: so this highly irregular practice is now at an end, which is perhaps as well.

It has been very misty the last few days. The enemy is wonderfully quiet. You scarcely hear a sound. Just a shell or burst of shells, or a bullet now and then, and that is all.

I got my orders to-day and leave for Vadenay on February 2.

February 2, 1918.   *Continental Hotel, Paris.*

I got up at 4.15 this morning and caught a train at Roisel, reaching Amiens about ten o'clock. There I had lunch, bought a few things, and of course visited, the Cathedral.

The contrast between the destruction I have left behind and this wonderfully majestic work of man was quite bewildering. High Mass was being sung as I went in, and as the great organ thundered out again and again, it made the air and even the ground throb.

I reached Paris at 4.30, and leave again to-morrow at noon. I have just been to Gaby Deslys' "Revue" at the Casino, and as it is past midnight I will go to bed.

February 8, 1918.

Cours Supérieure d'Infanterie, Secteur 220, Vadenay.

It is like being at school again. We go to the lecture room at 8.30, or earlier, each morning, and are lectured to—in French, of course—for $3\frac{1}{2}$ hours, or more! Will you believe me when I tell you that I have sat through $4\frac{1}{2}$ hours of it to-day? In the afternoons we are motored to see different Army Schools, etc.

I am much struck with the thoroughness and efficiency of these Frenchmen, and the serious way—in contrast to ours—that they go about the war. I wonder if they overdo it. And the voluminous literature that is handed to us here to digest almost throws our army (which I have always thought held the record in this particular) into the shade.

But it is an interesting and valuable experience, and I am being most hospitably treated, and am already getting into the French ways of eating and living.

The Commandant—Major Lemaire—is a very animated Frenchman of great personality, though small in stature; —a devotee to his profession and to France! He is so full of energy that he seems to be on springs.

A MUDDY COMMUNICATION TRENCH

One evening the talk turned jokingly on to the question as to which would be the best country to live in during these troublous times. One country after another was mentioned, those least affected by the war being chosen. I think I said South Africa, and Gardner (the only English officer besides myself), I think, said Ireland. When it came to Lemaire's turn, he threw his arms out dramatically, and exclaimed: "La France."

That is his serious side, but he is full of jokes on almost all other subjects, and is a very lively companion. Though between his lectures and sometimes during them he laughs and jokes almost incessantly, he has his troubles, and these are serious. For all his property and that of his wife is in the northern part of France, which has been devastated by the enemy, so that he has only his pay—600 francs a month; out of which he supports himself and his wife, and her parents, and I believe his own as well!

He was in the trenches till a month ago and was severely wounded in the chest at Douaumont (Verdun). Hence his presence here. As he said to me when I first came, "I am no embusqué," and threw open his chest to show me the wound as he said it.

The one discomfort is the cold, since this is a woodless and coalless country, and one cannot get a fire very often. The French do not seem to mind, or else have got "habitué" (as they say) to this kind of hardship. Gardner and I have not, and we slink back from our evening walks with any old end of timber we can find, discarded from the Back Area defences, to warm our frigid billet.

Saturday afternoons and Sundays are kept for "repos," and all are heartily glad of it.

P.S. The other day I met Nungesser—the greatest of the French airmen. He walks with a limp, having been wounded many times.

February 17, 1918 (*Sunday*).   *Vadenay*.

After the long interval of a fortnight your letters are now beginning to arrive in droves. Twenty-seven came yesterday, of which fifteen had been opened by the French censor!

In church this morning—to my astonishment—I recognized the priest who officiated as one of the French Captains whom I meet daily. That is how it is in France. There are thousands of priests serving as soldiers and officers in the army. The priest of this morning, who I never dreamt was a priest till I saw him saying mass, is a smart-looking fellow with a well-brushed-up moustache.

I walked to Attila's Camp (so-called) the other day. It is a wonderful earthwork, of Gargantuan size, dug in the dim ages, long ago, though not by Attila. Nevertheless, it was the scene of the final defeat of him and his Huns.

What sad news about poor Vyvyan Harmsworth's[1] death! I saw him last at that luncheon at Miss Capel's house in Park Place, last August, with his father and Eugène Schneider—the head of Creusot.

The father will feel it terribly. To think that two of his three sons are dead! It seems such a short time since our visit to Highcliffe, when they were boys. How times have changed! Poor Bart, too!

Vyvyan was a fine fellow. With his wealth and backing he could have had his pick of the Staff jobs. But he was not built that way. He was always with the fighting portion of his regiment—except during the times when he was recovering from his wounds.

February 20, 1918. *Vadenay*.

Yesterday afternoon I at last satisfied my ambition, and flew in an aeroplane. It was a glorious day, and, piloted by a little French corporal, we mounted to something over 5,000 feet and cruised for three-quarters of an hour at that altitude. It is a wonderful feeling. We were so high above the captive balloons that they looked like peas, or rather beans (which is their shape).

All was going well when, suddenly, a crack and a whizz: something was wrong in front. Bits of metal came flying back, missing the pilot, but making a hole in each of the wings. A piece 2½ feet long caught up in the stays and

[1] Capt. Hon. H. A. Vyvyan St.G. Harmsworth, M.C., Irish Guards; died of wounds, 1917.

fluttered there. The propeller made a hesitating turn or two, then stopped, and I—who was as ignorant as a babe of what was the matter, and knew only that we were 5,000 feet above the ground—began to wonder what would happen next.

I think I should have expected under the circumstances to feel frightened, but my pilot remained so self-possessed, and the aeroplane began to descend so steadily, that a feeling of almost complete confidence came over me, and I do not think my heart beat one pat the faster.

I repeat this as a study in sensations, and because I think the experience (having regard to the fact that it was my first time up) was interesting and peculiar.

The pilot steered the machine round and round in little spiral curves towards the earth, while I sat and watched the landscape getting closer and more defined, and as a precaution fixed the strap which is provided for the purpose around my waist. As we neared the tree-tops we got rather wobbly (my pilot was manœuvring for position and was keeping the aeroplane level), but finally we landed smoothly on the very aerodrome we had started from;—when I felt much relieved.

They tell me it was a rare accident. It was caused by a valve of the engine, which was of the rotary type, blowing loose, and cutting the steel housing of the motor, round the complete circle. It was some pieces of the housing that had come flying back, and the force required for the operation illustrates the immense power of these engines (250 horse-power).

The engine was of course wrecked; but I have had my fly, though I daresay I am not so keen to repeat it just at present, even if I get the opportunity.

It is wretched thinking of you all in London while these beastly raids are going on.

February 28, 1918.   *Villers Faucon.*

I rejoined my battalion last night, finding it in the Front line, but as under a new rule the Colonel and Second in Command are not allowed up at the same time, and the battalion was moreover under orders to move back to-day for a month's training and digging in the back areas,

I returned to my transport lines, where I slept last night.

A few minutes ago a wire was handed to me cancelling the move I have just spoken of *till further orders*, so I cannot say what is to happen. It is extraordinary that the Higher Command seem *never* to be able to get their orders right the first time.

I reached Paris on Saturday, the 23rd. Charles Mendl [1] called on me at my hotel while I was changing into some clean clothes. He is just as usual, in his usual splendid spirits, surrounded by and on intimate terms with all the men and women who count in Paris, and adored by all the latter. I have heard him described as the Uncrowned King of Paris. He enquired much after you, and asked to be remembered to you, and throughout the whole of my stay laid himself out to give me a good time;—with the result that I did not have one single meal except breakfast at my hotel during the three days I was there.

On the evening of my arrival he took me in his car to dinner at his flat in the Avenue Victor Hugo, where amongst others I met Mrs. Addison—wife of the 1st Secretary at our Embassy. She is said by Charles to be the most beautiful woman in Paris—and I do not imagine he is far wrong. She has what I believe is called auburn hair, perfect features and teeth and complexion, and looks like a picture by Rossetti.

After dinner he took me to a party at the Comtesse de la Berandiére, where I met various people, and had an interesting talk with Joseph Addison (Mrs. Addison's husband), who is very ugly but extraordinarily clever.

His view is that we should have made peace with the Germans when they gave us the opportunity at Christmas time, 1916, and that we shall never be offered such terms again! I wonder.

The next morning (Sunday) I went to Notre Dame, and lunched afterwards at Charles' flat. There I met Maurice Brett[2] (Area Commandant of Paris) and his wife (Zena Dare

1 Sir Charles Mendl; later, Press Attaché to the British Embassy in Paris
2 Hon. Maurice Brett, O.B.E., M.V.O.

—the actress); also Conde di Sannazaro (Italian Military Attaché at Madrid); Countess Bottaro Costa (whose father was so kind to you at Cordova), who married the Italian Minister at Buenos Ayres. She is charming. Her daughter was also there—the Duchesse di Rignano. The latter's husband is the eldest son of Prince Colonna, from whose collection one or two of our pictures in the smoking-room came. She is the dearest and most refined little thing.

In the evening I again dined at Charles' flat, and met the Toulmins. They invited me to lunch next day, and I met Margerie (the Assistant Secretary of Foreign Affairs—or its French equivalent), and Mr. and Mrs. Bate (formerly Miss Vera Arkwright, sister of Esmé Arkwright in the Scots Guards, who was master of the Oakley). The latter is very good-looking, and seems blissfully happy with her American husband (who drives a motor ambulance), in spite of the fact that they live in the Latin Quarter. The same afternoon I met the first Madame Caillaux.

I dined with Prince and Princess Michel Murat—friends of Charles. She is American, and the dinner—I was told beforehand—would be good. In fact, I never saw such a dinner, and certainly I could not describe it, or begin to know how to order it, even if I had the money to pay for it. The food was of the most extravagant and elaborate sort, the courses being served in (to me) the most unexpected order, and once the dinner had got well started, one never had less than three different kinds of wine in glasses before one—all of rare vintage. The Prince is half Russian, and the barbaric splendour of it all was Russian, and the butler was Russian, clad picturesquely in Caucasian uniform. It is of course all very wicked in war-time, and though each time my thoughts turned to the trenches I felt ashamed, and almost home-sick for them, I must own that I would not have missed the experience of that dinner for anything.

Vicomtesse de Janzé and her son were there, the former rather upset at finding herself amid such luxury, since she had been assured it was to be quite a small and simple affair. I had dined with her before in Paris. She is one of the most beautiful and fascinating creatures you can imagine, and like a ray of sunshine in a fog after coming from the society of some of the women you meet in Paris in these days.

She is an Irish Catholic. I wish you could see her. Her son is just emerging from the ranks of the French Army and is an "aspirant"—half-way between a private and an officer. He has been fighting as a private in the Artillery since he was 18½. I spoke to him a good deal, and, as she said "Good-bye," his mother said, "Thank you for being so nice to my boy," and invited me to a tête-à-tête luncheon at her house, to which I went next day.

Among the other guests at the Murat dinner were the Marquise de Charette, George Grahame (Councellor at our Embassy) and Amherst Webber, whom Charles describes as "the most knowledgeable musician in Europe." He is, besides, a wonderful pianist, and judges the voices at Covent Garden.

On Tuesday, after lunching with Madame de Janzé, I visited the Invalides, and found Napoleon's tomb in process of being covered with sandbags. Since the last air-raid the Parisians have been feverishly treating all their public monuments in this manner. They are not so philosophic over their air-raids as you are in London, or so self-possessed. And yet it seems improbable that they will be raided again. The French do not admit this, but there is little doubt but that an informal and tacit understanding exists whereby the German open towns will not be bombarded so long as Paris is left alone.

It seems that you can get any luxury in Paris if only you are able to pay the enormous prices that are asked for everything, even the necessaries;—which is all very well for the rich, but must be "hell" for the poor. Apropos of which I one day saw an old woman picking up tiny chips of wood from the street-sweepings and collecting them carefully in her apron to take home as fuel.

The Parisians have their own war-time code. Dancing

s looked upon with horror, but generally speaking, so
far as I could learn, there is little if any self-denial or
submission to the common interest such as there is in
England; and there were many things I saw during my
short visit which surprised me, having regard to the times
we are living in, and the events that are taking place so
close to the spot from which I write.

They say that a Frenchman will willingly sacrifice his
life or his limbs for his country, but he will not give up
his money or his luxuries. Perhaps that is true of him
as of others. It is at least better than risking neither.

I took the train from Paris, yesterday, and, on the whole,
was not sorry to leave it, though I was sorry to part from
Charles, of whom I am very fond.

March 1, 1918. *Ronssoy.*

The battalion is still in the line (in support for the
moment), and our plans are very indefinite.

For me it does not matter. I have had my rest, but the
men are getting tired. This is, I think, their 38th day
up. Indeed, the whole Division sorely needs a rest, and
above all, training, and has needed it for a long time.

General Hickie has gone home sick, and General Hull
temporarily commands the Division. In my Brigade I am
the only Battalion Commander left of those who were with
it on the 20th of last November. Indeed, one battalion
in the Brigade has gone through two new C.O.'s since that
famous day.

The new Brigadier is certainly making things buzz!

March 5, 1918. *Hamel (Tincourt).*

We were unexpectedly relieved and marched back last
night to this village. Our erratic movements are doubtless
due to the expected German attack, of which the papers
have been so full for weeks past. Here, the feeling of
apprehension seems to be in inverse ratio to the distance
you get from the firing line, where things are quiet, and
consequently there is a disposition to pooh-pooh the fears
of the Intelligence Department.

The battalion wants a rest. It had been up for forty-two days when, last night, it was relieved, and even now I doubt if the rest is in sight, since an order has just come in to go up to-morrow for the day, to dig. I leave you to imagine the state of the men's bodies and clothing after so long a time in the line, almost without a wash.

I was glad to get back to the battalion, and found that all had gone well during my absence, and that every one was happy in spite of the tiring and trying time they had gone through. There had not been many casualties, and very few had been killed, though one *splendid* man had lost his life in what I fear was a foolish attempt to explore Noman's Land in daylight.

March 6, 1918.   *Tincourt.*

I went to see an army oculist to-day at a place about 16 miles from here. On my way back, sitting on the box-seat of an ambulance, I met a string of cavalry horses returning from water. I was admiring the boots of the subaltern who was walking in front, and thinking what a pleasant contrast they were to the ill-fitting slipshod things one sees in the trenches, when I glanced up at the officer's yellow woollen waistcoat, and then at his face. Who *do* you think it was?—Osmund,[1] smiling all over, whom I had not seen since that day at Windsor, when he came over from Sandhurst; and who has now grown into a man.

I stopped and was taken off to have tea at his camp at Doingt, with his colonel (Durand), his squadron leader (Whitehead), and Peto—a subaltern—whom I must have met as a child when staying with his father (Basil Peto, M.P.) and his mother, at Guildford.

Afterwards, I walked back here—about 4 miles, and Osmund came part of the way with me. He is just the same delightful enthusiastic boy he always was. He had been doing an infantry spell in the trenches, and had been on patrol, and was bubbling over with his experiences. He is of the sort who sees only the good in people, and all his

[1] Osmund Stapleton Bretherton, 9th Lancers, killed at Hervilly Wood, near Roisel, sixteen days later (March 22, 1918); nephew to the writer.

geese are swans. He ended up by saying, "The family is doing quite well: You've got the D.S.O., and Uncle Vincent has the M.C., and I've got my second pip!"

It is eighteen months to-day since I took over the command of this battalion.

March 11, 1918.   *Villers Faucon.*

The men continue, as always, in spite of what is beginning to seem an almost interminable period of restless hard work and hardship, to be patient and cheerful and magnificent.

The weather is calm and beautiful, almost like summer, but there is a lot of "wind" of the other sort. The expectation of a coming offensive from the enemy still continues, and my life, consequently, is a very busy one.

March 13, 1918.   *Villers Faucon.*

We are going through a hard worrying time. We were said to be due for a great thrust this morning from our friends across the way, but nothing happened.

The weather continues superb and makes one feel happy to be alive.

March 15, 1918.   *Villers Faucon.*

I got up at 2.30 this morning and marched the battalion forward to man the Reserve trenches behind Ronssoy, as counter-attacking party, against the enemy's offensive which is still expected daily. It was very cold—the ground white with frost. At 10 a.m., no attack having been delivered, we marched back to billets.

Our artillery gave the enemy a heavy pounding for about an hour and a half, which I venture to think at least gave him food for thought.

This morning I saw an aeroplane shot down from a great height. It rolled over and over till it reached the ground —a nasty sight.

This evening a German aeroplane dashed over and brought down the Villers Faucon balloon, in flames. We saw the occupants jump safely out with their parachutes, but the enemy, in spite of furious "Archy" and machine-gun fire, also got away.

March 16, 1918.   *Villers Faucon.*

I was up this morning at three o'clock and marched forward with the battalion to man trenches again, as yesterday. At 6.25 one of our S.O.S. rockets went up, and was followed by many others along the front. Immediately, the artillery and machine-guns opened uproariously all along the line.

To-day (as have others which have passed) had been officially mentioned as the likely date for the great German effort, and all naturally thought for a short while that at last the expected had arrived.

However, after half or three-quarters of an hour of deafening din, all became silent, and it was evident that it was a false alarm. Such are the "jumpy" times through which we are passing.

We then marched away to bury telephone cables, and afterwards home.

March 17, 1918.   *Villers Faucon.*

We again marched forward at three o'clock this morning to man Bois switch and the Ronssoy sunken road. It is a wearing life, and all are feeling the strain. We are still the counter-attacking battalion.

Our pyrotechnicians are testing some wonderful new parachute lights, which illuminate the whole country for miles around, and to some extent enliven these early morning watches.

This is St. Patrick's Day, and, as you know, a great feast-day for the Irishmen, which they look forward to all the year round: yet, though their duties to-day kept them from attending Mass (which means much to them), they accept it all cheerfully, as usual.

They have now returned from the daily wait behind Ronssoy and the subsequent cable-burying, and are having an extra good dinner, which they are too tired to enjoy.

I enclose some shamrock which has been sent to the battalion from Ireland.

March 19, 1918.   *Villers Faucon.*

We have had two comparatively restful days;—by which I mean that we have been left to carry out our more or less normal duties undisturbed.   May it continue! but the wind is up—still very much up!

On the road between here and the front line, where every one that passes can see it, some wag has painted a huge clock face on a wall.   Above it is written in large letters—

WATCH OUR WIND-CHART

The dial is something as below, and a pointer is moved, from hour to hour, as fresh intelligence comes forward from the Higher Command.

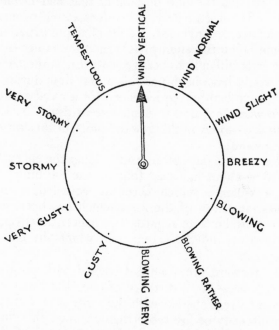

I have invented the dialling as I did not read it carefully, but the gist of it is correct, and I am sure it is not necessary to explain to you the soldier's use of the word "wind."   The thing has caused a lot of amusement.

The weather (using the word in its proper sense) has changed, which is a good thing for many reasons, and particularly that you may be spared air-raids.   Every one here is in good spirits, and I think we have nothing to worry about.

At any rate, so convinced are those that are in a position to know that we are going to be attacked, that they have doubtless made full preparation for our proper support.

March 24, 1918 (*Sunday*). *Bray.*

I have had no opportunity to write during the last three days. As you will have learned, the much advertised offensive crashed upon us last Thursday, since when we have been fighting a rearguard action, almost continuously. A retreat was the one possibility that had never occurred to us, and, unfortunately, it involves a kind of manœuvring in which we are unversed, in spite of all our experience. For the time being the enemy has turned the tables in a manner which it is difficult to realize, so great is the contrast with what would have been possible at any time during last year.

We have had no regular sleep for a week and more, and all are worn out, and to some extent dazed by the fatigue and strain—to say nothing of the shock of this last surprising development.

After several days of uncanny silence the enemy's artillery opened at about half-past four on the morning of the 21st with a violence which certainly equalled, if it did not surpass, anything of the kind which has been seen before in the war, both as regards the concentrated character of the shooting and the extent over which the bombardment was spread.

The forward areas were drenched with poison gas, and the back areas, to a distance of over five miles behind the front line, were shelled with the most savage fury. It was upon intensity of fire more than accurate shooting that the Germans relied, for not only had they refrained from registering beforehand, but there was a dense fog, which entirely prevented any kind of observation. It was, in fact, not until the scheduled moment had arrived for throwing off the mask that the great majority of their thousands of guns—collected silently under cover of darkness during many weeks previously—spoke at all.

Not even our harassing fire had succeeded in drawing a shot in reply, though it had been heavy and persistent during the nights preceding March 21, and even that very morning.

At the opening of the battle two Brigades of this Division were holding the line in front of Ronssoy and Lempire. The third—my own—was in Divisional Reserve, in wooden huts at Villers Faucon, 4 miles behind the firing line. Here we got our full share of the shelling, and at 8.30, after several narrow shaves, my Headquarters were hit.

We were in what—in the far-off days before the war—was perhaps the verger's cottage, on the opposite side of the road to the ruined church. The acting Brigadier (Colonel Weldon[1]) and I and the Headquarters officers—all except two—were standing round a fire on the ground-floor. Major Raynsford—second in command, and Chamier—assistant Adjutant, were in the cellar below, which some of the officers used as a sleeping-room.

The latter was the "safe place" of the establishment. Yet, on this occasion, it served to illustrate the capricious character of shells, for the one which hit the house crashed through into this cellar, blistering the floor and bending the wall of the ground-floor room, yet avoiding those of us who were in it; and, while it buried the officers below under a couple of feet of bricks and mortar, they escaped with nothing worse than a bruising. The cottage, however, was so shaken that another hit would have brought it down, and I decided to leave it.

As soon as the nature of the bombardment became evident the Companies were scattered as much as possible, taking cover by sections in the trenches which formed part of the anti-air bomb defences surrounding the huts, which by a happy inspiration I had had deepened a few days previously in anticipation of such an emergency as this. Sections of men were also distributed wherever the contour of the ground or standing walls provided any sort of cover.

The result, thanks to Providence, was that no casualties were suffered during the morning; and though on one

[1] Lieut.-Col. H. W. Weldon, Leinster Regt.

occasion a shell hit the limber of a field kitchen, throwing down the cook, he picked himself up, and cheerfully continued to cook the men's breakfast.

As things began to look more and more serious Father McShane, the young chaplain, went round the battalion, and gave absolution to all.

While the men were having dinners, Ronssoy was reported lost, and I received instructions to march the battalion forward, and to report for orders to the Brigadier-General commanding the 49th—one of the Front line Brigades.

We were on the move by 12.30. The enemy was still shelling heavily, and we had several casualties as we went forward through the barrage. We passed two huge 12-inch howitzers on the broad-gauge railway, already abandoned, and the adverse trend of the fighting became still more apparent, as we passed the 18-pounder positions, from the vigorous efforts that were being made to get away the guns and howitzers. With their usual dash the Field gunners were struggling to move these guns, but, though they had been pulled out of the pits, they were in many instances destined to go no further, there being no horses left alive to draw them.

As we reached the firing line the trench was being heavily and effectively shelled. A few hours before it had been a Reserve trench—almost our rearmost line of defence; so far behind, in fact, that it was only partly dug. There were considerable gaps; and, as there was no communication trench leading up to it, the only approach was across the open. This trench was between the village of Ste Emilie and Ronssoy Wood, and was known as the Brown line.

We found it occupied by a few living stragglers— remnants of the garrisons of the forward positions, and strewed with the bodies of the dead who had already fallen to the enemy's shell-fire.

Among the severely wounded there lay already one of my Company Commanders (Denys Wickham)—an admirıble officer who has weathered two years of the worst of the war. I stopped a moment with him—long enough to see that he was being looked after, and moved on, the orders I had been given on the way up by the Brigadier of the ₄9th Brigade having been to counter-attack without delay, with the 1st Royal Munster Fusiliers, who, he said, would co-operate on my right flank.

As the Companies assembled for the counter-attack the hostile shelling seemed to increase, and, more than once, there was a direct hit upon a bay, killing or wounding every man in it. A whizz-bang skimmed the parapet and hit the parados where I was standing, splashing my face with earth with such a smack that for a moment I thought my cheek was shot away. I felt and found only a drop of blood. With my usual luck a graze was all there was to show, once the dirt was brushed away.

As I recovered, a recently joined subaltern came to me and reported that Cummins—second in command of his Company—and several men with him had just been killed by a shell, and that the men on either side were shaken; which was indeed scarcely to be wondered at, seeing that many of them (a draft of 180 had joined the battalion only a day or two before) were experiencing their baptism of fire. I told him I was afraid he would have to carry on just the same, and I must say that the plucky and unhesitating manner in which this boy turned back to his job was very admirable.

At the same time, I must confess that the news he had brought was the greatest possible blow. Cummins was one of my most tried and trusted officers: though young, he was, in times of danger and difficulty, always to be relied upon. Moreover, he loved and was loved by his men.

No wonder—with his reputation—that some of his men were shaken! Though he lay dead only a few yards along the trench from where I stood, even I shrank from visiting the spot.

These were the conditions under which the counter-attack was prepared.

It was delivered at 3.45 p.m. by two Companies, with one Company in support and the fourth in reserve. It was pressed with great gallantry, and had it been supported on the right, as had been promised, it is probable that it would at least have resulted in a local set-back to the enemy's advance.

The assaulting Companies (A and D) reached the sunken road bounding the western edge of Ronssoy Wood. As Norman led forward the supporting Company (C) he saw what he at first supposed to be the battalion which should be co-operating on his right, but soon discovered to be the enemy, lining the Factory Ridge to his right front; as well as parties of the enemy approaching along the Ronssoy-Ste Emilie road, evidently with the object of getting round the flank of the leading Companies.

He immediately engaged the enemy, forming a defensive flank along the Ronssoy-Ste Emilie road, but soon fell, wounded in three places. Lieutenant Russell then took command, but fell almost immediately, mortally wounded.

Simultaneously, the only other officer with the Company —McTiernan—was mortally wounded, and, the greater part of the Company having in this short time also become casualties, the remainder were forced to fall back upon the trench they had started from, together with the few that remained of the two attacking Companies, who had suffered equally, the Commander of one (Captain Crofton) having been killed while leading his men forward, while the Commander of the other—Lieutenant Ribbons, who had succeeded Wickham—was made prisoner.

Two tanks took part in this counter-attack, but both were soon knocked out, one receiving a direct hit from a shell which killed all the occupants.

At 5.15 p.m. I was ordered to report at 49th Brigade Headquarters, which were at Ste Emilie, in a deep mined dug-out in the grounds of what once had been the château, and I made my way there between the shell-holes, many of which were so recent that they were still smoking. The bombardment continued violently, though rather wildly, and as I neared my destination the swish of machine-gun bullets mixed with the general din.

Under the circumstances there was a feeling of relief at finding myself underground, at such a depth that even the sound of the shelling was drowned, and I was not sorry to see a cold joint of beef, with pickles, whisky, and a siphon, spread upon a table.

My first duty was to report to the Brigadier the result of the counter-attack. He was apologetic, and explained that his orders for this operation should have been cancelled: they had, he said, been cancelled in the case of the Munsters, but he had been unable to communicate with me. Then he added: "I hope you will not think hardly of me."

There was no answer to this—at least no civil answer. I could see no reason for his having failed to communicate with me; nor, having failed, could I excuse him for having cancelled his orders to the Royal Munster Fusiliers to counter-attack, knowing that we were counting upon their co-operation.

The General then told me that his Brigade was reduced to about sixty men, and that he had been ordered to withdraw; and this he immediately proceeded to do.

I now came back under the orders of my own Brigade, whose Headquarters were in a chalk quarry some 400 yards to the north-west of Ste Emilie. I reported the situation over the telephone, and was instructed to get into personal touch with the officer commanding the Ste Emilie defences (Lieut.-Colonel Crockett, D.S.O.—11th Hants Pioneers), there being no telephonic communication with him.

I had a precarious hunt before at last I found Colonel Crockett in the narrow-gauge railway cutting on the west side of the village. With him I found Colonel Kane of the 1st Munsters, and, considering the location to be more suited for a Battalion Headquarters than the deep dug-out I had just left, and which in spite of its security was much too much like a rat-hole for my liking, I moved there, and notified Brigade to that effect.

The arrangement had the additional advantage that it brought me into close companionship with Colonel Crockett, who is a senior and very level-headed ex-Regular officer, and whose advice on numerous occasions during the trying hours that followed proved invaluable.

Later in the evening the 1st Herts Regt. (Territorial) arrived as a reinforcement, the commanding officer making his Headquarters at the Quarry (H.Q. 47th Inf. Bde.). Three Companies were sent to the Brown line (still the firing line in front of Ste Emilie)—two to the left of the narrow-gauge cutting, and one to the right of the Ste Emilie-Ronssoy road. One Company was kept in reserve in the Quarry.

During the night I visited 47th Brigade H.Q. in the Quarry with Colonel Crockett, who proposed, in view of the probable renewal of the attack by the enemy in the morning, that a preventive counter-attack should be delivered, during the night, on the left of the narrow-gauge cutting. Colonel Weldon had, however, just had orders to move his Headquarters back from the Quarry, and he was leaving as we arrived. Upon my return to my own Headquarters I sent Major Raynsford to visit all the posts occupied by the battalion.

The night and early morning passed quietly.

Throughout the day that followed, owing to our heavy losses in guns the previous day, we were practically without artillery support. At 3.30 a.m. all stood to, but in spite of a thick fog which seemed entirely to favour the enemy, daylight arrived without any sign of further activity on his part.

It was beginning to look as if we might be going to have a restful day, when, at about six o'clock, three German prisoners (an officer and two other ranks) were passed back from the fire-trench. They spoke English fluently, and upon being questioned as to whether it was intended to renew the attack during the morning, replied that it was.

One of these prisoners—a vapid-looking youth with spectacles—was inclined to be talkative. Explaining his capture he said: "To tell you the truth, sir, I lost my way":

but, from the smile on his face, I judged that he was not sorry to be out of it.

The information we had extracted was at once sent back to Brigade, and in less than half an hour, its accuracy was confirmed by the sudden outburst of the enemy's barrage on a similar scale to that of the previous day. This was followed in due course by the German infantry, who swept forward, wave after wave, in overwhelming hordes.

The story of this day is well known;—how our troops, having endured twenty-six hours of the most terrible punishment; largely reduced in numbers; the Lewis guns or their teams (which is the same thing) knocked out, were overcome or surrounded after a stubborn resistance.

In the case of my own Companies, which, as I have described, had already suffered so severely, and had lost three Captains and two seconds in command out of four during the counter-attack of the preceding afternoon, not an officer escaped.

There being no communication trench, the firing line was, from the moment the attack started, cut off from all behind it, and though two of the battalion signallers made a gallant attempt to cross the exposed strip of ground that separated Headquarters from the Companies, they succeeded in delivering their message only at the cost of one of their lives, the other being wounded.

On this occasion it was necessary to employ signallers, as all the runners were out, but I feel I must here—in parenthesis—place on record the wonderful bravery of the runners—both Battalion and Company—at all times, but especially when the conditions have been most exacting and have demanded supreme courage and almost superhuman devotion.

In the course of a battle it is often necessary to send a runner with a message under circumstances which involve almost certain death or wounding, yet never have I seen one of these carefully chosen men waver or hang back. No matter how dangerous the errand—and he well knows what is before him—the runner on duty never wants calling twice. Give him his message, and he will pick up his rifle and be off, often to his death. I have seen so many officers and men go off like that smilingly to their death in this war, and, looking back, it certainly does seem sometimes as though a special buoyancy of spirit animates those about to die.

The Germans continued to shell furiously throughout the morning, and, as our forward areas passed into the hands of their out-numbering infantry, they gradually lifted their guns, and by midday the bombardment of Villers Faucon and the ridges around had become intense.

In the afternoon a general retirement was ordered to a prepared line (the Green line), in front of Tincourt, some miles behind the original front line. We reached it at the cost of a few casualties from shell-fire. I must say I had hoped to find some fresh troops there, but there were none. Indeed, the trench was practically empty.

The battalion was now reduced to the Headquarters Company and thirty-four stragglers.

At dusk I was ordered to line the Tincourt-Templeux La Fosse road (my left on Tincourt Wood), with the 1st Munsters on my left and the 2nd Leinsters on my right; the latter (reduced to the strength of about a Company) having been temporarily placed under my command. My instructions were to cover the retreat of the remnant of the 49th Brigade, which was in front, should it become necessary to withdraw from the Green line, allowing them to pass through my ranks; then to follow after them, and to take up a position on the Doingt-Bois des Flacques line, in front of Peronne.

I made my Headquarters for the night in an exceedingly comfortable three-roomed hut in Tincourt Wood, formerly the abode of an officer of the Divisional Staff, whose Headquarters had been here until the proximity of the enemy during the last two days had driven them further back.

Having in my mind the heroic exhortations which had of late been coming so unsparingly, addressed to us in the Front line from this wood, I confess I was not prepared

270

for the aspect of sudden abandonment which the hut presented.

Its appearance suggested that some sudden and deadly cataclysm had overcome the occupant while he was having his breakfast, the remains of which, together with one or two half-finished cups of tea, still littered the table. The walls were hung with book-shelves and maps (of which latter I have annexed a useful specimen): the floor had a carpet: expensive oil lamps, crockery, and a profusion of knick-knacks lay about: but there was no sign of any effort having been made to save these treasures, so rapid, apparently, had been the owner's exit. Lastly, and to our great satisfaction, there were two camp-beds and a mattress of the softest down.

Think of the exhausting hours through which we had passed, and you will understand that I shall not easily forget that night's rest, the only pity being that we did not get enough of it, and that the few hours we did have were spasmodic and disturbed.

The next morning (yesterday), the 49th Brigade began to fall back soon after daybreak, and the arrangements for the withdrawal to the Bois des Flacques line were carried out without difficulty and in good order. The operation was assisted in its initial stages by a fog, and the retirement was covered by a heavy artillery barrage, as well as by a number of tanks, two or more of which, however, succumbed to engine trouble, and had to be destroyed by their crews, and abandoned.

The position which we now took up was an old line of trenches on the top of a steep ridge. Behind us, in the plain to the west, lay Doingt and Peronne.

As we arrived in sight of these places some buildings were already ablaze, and, as I watched further, I also saw one or two explosions—evidently the work of our own troops—which suggested that preparations were being made for a further retreat.

The sight was not inspiriting. Still, the line we were holding was on the whole well sited, and with the men properly distributed there was not much risk from shell-fire.

Early in the afternoon the enemy's line of skirmishers topped the skyline some 2,000 yards in front of our position. This was followed by the assault troops, who soon had gathered in large numbers in the woods, and wherever the ground gave cover. Simultaneously, a heavy long-range machine-gun fire was opened upon us, which, owing to the steep angle of descent of the bullets, and the shallowness of the trenches we were occupying, was uncomfortable, though the effect was trifling.

The leading skirmishers, pressing forward like hounds on a hot scent, were very bold, and in the face of a fire which was moderate—owing to the necessity of economizing ammunition—persisted in their advance across the exposed valley that separated us.

About this time an enemy aeroplane flew low over our line and dropped a flare. This was mistaken for one of our own signals by our artillery, who immediately put over shrapnel, which killed two of my men, and wounded a third.

At about 1 p.m. I saw the battalion on my immediate left [1] leaving the trenches in a body, and I sent a runner to ask for an explanation. Their second in command returned personally with the runner. He said he had received orders from Brigade to fall back. I suggested that there must be a mistake, and he replied that he would go to Brigade Headquarters and ascertain definitely the acting Brigadier's wishes. I myself went and saw Colonel Crockett, to find out if he knew anything. Then, seeing no reason for a retirement, I ordered two platoons of the 13th Royal Sussex Regiment, which happened to be available, to fill the gap.

As I was returning to the fire-trench I was met by my Adjutant (Captain Ritchie Dickson), who said that during my absence an order had come from Brigade to evacuate

[1] When, later, the writer saw the Officer Commanding this battalion, he told him that, at the time he withdrew, the troops of the Brigade on his left had already vacated the trenches, leaving his left in the air.

the line we were holding, and to fall back upon Biaches. He added that Major Raynsford was making the necessary arrangements.

Major Raynsford had passed the order on, in writing, to the 2nd Leinster Regiment and our own battalion, but when I saw him, a few minutes later, he had just been shot through the body, and was being carried back under considerable difficulty on a ground-sheet. Four men, each holding a corner, were staggering under his weight, and one of these, as he saw me coming up, called out: "It's all right, sir, you can trust us to get him out": and so they did. They carried him under fire a mile or two till they came across a motor machine-gun carriage, and upon this they placed him, and sent him away to safety.

I formed up the few men of the Connaught Rangers at the foot of the hill on the edge of the village of Doingt— the same village where I had taken tea with Osmund so short a time before, and, in conjunction with Colonel Crockett and his men, and Major Whittall's sappers, fire was brought to bear upon the enemy, who were already descending the near side, and whose machine-guns were already shooting from the slopes of the ridge we had just occupied.

We then fell back through Doingt and Peronne, halting parties at convenient points to cover the withdrawal of the remainder. I will not say that the retirement was not ragged. It was. But, though it was followed by the enemy's machine-guns and shell-fire, his advance was sufficiently delayed to enable us to reach an old line of trenches crossing the Herbecourt road, west of Biaches, almost without casualties.

An engineer officer was at each bridge in Peronne, waiting to blow it up after the passage of the infantry, and at the first I left a party, under Ritchie Dickson, to assist in this operation. These rejoined the battalion safely during the evening.

At midnight I received orders to march back to Bray, and at 6.30 this morning we bivouacked in a field a few hundred yards east of the village, where we found Brigade Headquarters, and where I got a couple of hours of much-needed sleep in the Brigadier's tent.

The friends I met expressed surprise at seeing me. For the fourth time during my military career I had been reported killed.

March 30, 1918. *Rouen.*

I hope you got my wire saying that I was safe, in hospital. We have crammed years of life into a week, during which my usual Providence protected me, though the Battalion —indeed the whole Division—is practically gone.

Not one of the officers doing duty with the Companies came out of the second day, and, since then, the small remnant left has suffered still further.

I had to leave them on the evening of the 27th—the seventh day of the battle—just as, with a composite party of stragglers, they were holding up the enemy (locally) rather well. I fell and dislocated my left elbow joint while running forward to get the Lewis guns on to a target of retiring Germans.

I was under chloroform for forty minutes yesterday, while they tried to pull the telescoped bones back into position, but another X-ray photograph, to-day, shows that I have to go through it again this afternoon.

March 31, 1918. *Rouen.*

I concluded my letter of March 24 with our arrival at Bray that same morning. During the day the battered remnants of the battalion were reorganized into two Companies. By the addition of stragglers, and officers and men recalled from courses, leave, etc., our fighting strength had been raised to 7 officers and 180 other ranks.

In the afternoon, the Brigadier (General Gregorie) returned from leave, and the Brigade was detailed for the protection of the bridges over the Somme, it having been reported that hostile cavalry had crossed the river south of Peronne, and were making their way in a westerly direction.

By 10 p.m. I got my men into position at Sailly Lorette the village allotted to me, and, during the night, charge of gun-cotton were laid by the Sappers, preparatory to blowing up the bridges in case of necessity.

Sailly Lorette is an old-fashioned and picturesque village, perched on the slope and summit of the steep escarpment which here forms the northern bank of the Somme, and, in less disturbed times, no more attractive place could be desired for tired troops to billet in.

I set up my mess in a comfortable house owned by an amiable and rather nice-looking woman of the farmer class, and two bedrooms in another house across the way were allotted by the Town-major for the Adjutant and myself to sleep in.

Such beds as those we found awaiting us certainly had not been seen by either of us for many a long day, and, weary as we were, with eyes swollen for want of sleep, it was highly tantalizing to be unable to undress and get between the sheets. That, however, was out of the question: indeed, much of the night was spent in going round the posts.

I was awakened early the following morning by the women of the house, who were rummaging about my bedroom, feverishly sorting out clothes from the wardrobes and dressers, and packing them into trunks which stood on the landing outside.

"Oh! La la! mon Dieu! mon Dieu! Quel malheur la guerre!" they muttered, as they packed. I asked what was up, and they said that the French authorities had ordered the evacuation of the village by the civilian inhabitants.

"How soon did I think the Boches would arrive?"

I did my best to console them, and crossed the road to the mess. I found things much the same there. My hostess—who was, conspicuously, about to become a mother—half hysterical and in tears, rushed into the room where I was having breakfast. In each hand she carried a tumbler of champagne, and one of these she gave to me.

I have never cared much for champagne, and this was no special brand, but the choicest vintage never tasted half so good as this lady's wine tasted to me that morning, and the memory of it will, I hope, stay long after she—poor thing—has come into her own again.

Having finished our glasses, she led me to the cellar, and, throwing open the door, invited me to make what use of it I liked. Then, pointing to three fat pigs in the yard, she cried, "Tuez! Tuez! Keel! keel!"—and she drew her hand across her throat. She supplemented the few English words she knew with graphic gesticulations.

"Give them to your men," she said; "do what you will so long as the Boches do not get them."

Later, I passed her on the road, setting off towards Amiens, with a few cattle and a wagon-load of household things. I stopped and spoke to her. She had, she told me, three farms in the neighbourhood, and was leaving 100,000 francs' worth of property behind to the tender mercy of the Hun.

On the river bank I met a man with two little boys—his sons, he said, whom he had brought in a barge from Peronne. They had been through the bombardment. "Could I tell him how near the Germans were now?"

A frail old man and his wife of seventy or more, trundling in turn a heavy wheelbarrow containing their belongings up the steep ascent which leads from the river towards Amiens, asked if I thought it would be safe for them to rest for a little while. They had travelled all through the night, with nothing to eat. Fortunately, I had a packet of chocolate, so I gave them that.

No words will describe the misery and pathos of these scenes: the sight of poor creatures who only four days ago had been living in what all believed to be perfect safety—many miles behind the battle-line; bundled out of house and home; called upon without warning to abandon all they possessed in the world, and to take the road, dependent upon charity for the very food to keep them alive.

"La guerre, no bon," one of them said to me in the new French; and the thought repeatedly occurred to me—"Thank God, at least, that our people in England have

been spared this!" It was some satisfaction that I was able
to lend a couple of the battalion horses to help some of
the oldest women to get away.

I gratefully took my hostess's three pigs for the battalion,
the only difficulty being to find a man who knew how to kill
them and cut them up. Nevertheless, the battalion (at
any rate the fighting section of it) did not get a chance
of eating them, for reasons which follow.

Concerning the wine cellar, as senior officer in the village
I had to think of the effect of example. I also remembered
that people are apt to criticize Irish troops perhaps more
than others. So—some no doubt thought foolishly—I
decided to deny myself what I confess was a very strong
temptation, that is to make an issue from its very ample
contents to the officers and men.

Unfortunately, the village was full of such cellars, and,
as no arrangement had been made, or if made had not been
put into operation, by the local authorities, for policing
or safeguarding the abandoned houses, it obviously fell to
me to see to this, and I did so, with the gratifying result
that I neither observed nor heard of a single case of looting
or drunkenness throughout the day. I arranged further
that all these stocks of drinkables should be destroyed in
the event of the enemy approaching the village. But this
duty was not to fall to our lot.

We were ordered away during the afternoon to Cérisy,
a mile and a half higher up the Somme, to guard the bridge
there, news having come through that the enemy was now
threatening from the north of the river. As at Sailly
Lorette, arrangements had been made to destroy the bridge
at this village, should the necessity arise.

My sleep was interrupted during the night that followed.
At two o'clock two officers of the Labour Corps burst into
the room where I was sleeping and called out excitedly:
"Do you know that the Germans have broken through on
the north bank of the river, and that you are the last people
left?"

Having delivered this alarming message they disappeared

—I am sorry to say before I had awakened sufficiently from the corpse-like sleep I was so thoroughly enjoying to have them arrested.

Though these officers' fears were obviously genuine enough, there was, during the few days of which I write, too much of this kind of thing. The previous night, for example, two sappers had rushed past the sentries with a similar tale, and there is no doubt but that the enemy inspired many of these incidents. In fact, he made systematic use of his knowledge of human nature, with the object of spreading panic behind our lines. Unhappily, there are always plenty of nervous people in the army, as well as out of it, who can be safely relied upon to spread false news, if only it is bad enough.

I have been told that at this time it had been intended to take out the Division, which, as you now know, had been very badly cut up on the 21st and 22nd. Be this as it may, the fates ruled otherwise. The enemy was pressing hard and with considerable success on the northern side of the river, and during the morning of the 26th the 47th Brigade was ordered to move and take up a line in front of Proyart, a village 3½ miles south-east of Cérisy.

By two o'clock, or shortly after, we were in position, in part lining a railway cutting which happened to be handy, and elsewhere digging in where no natural cover was available. We (the Connaught Rangers) were in the centre, with the 1st Munster Fusiliers and the 2nd Leinsters on our left and right respectively. On the left of the Brigade was the 48th Brigade, and, on the right, the 39th Division.

At 3.50 p.m. it was reported, and it soon also became apparent from the enfilade fire, that the enemy had broken through the 66th Division on the right of the 39th, and this was confirmed shortly afterwards by an officer— 2nd Lieutenant McWeeny—whom I sent to get into touch with the officers commanding the 13th Gloucester (Pioneers) and the 17th King's Royal Rifles.

Later, the position on this flank improved, but it was

then reported to me that the Brigade on our left had withdrawn. This information I passed on to Brigade, and I was ultimately informed that the gap would be filled before dawn.

Nobody slept that night. The battalion frontage was patrolled continuously. Parties of the enemy were observed digging some 800 yards in front of our line, and I sent an officer with a Lewis gun to hamper them.

At 2.30 a.m. I was visited by one of the Staff Officers of the Division, who greeted me with the cheering news that strong French reinforcements were already at Lamote ($5\frac{1}{2}$ miles behind us), and that they would be passing through us to the counter-attack within the next six hours. He added: "So you have only to stick it a short time longer."

This would have been all right if it had been true. Unfortunately it was not.

Not only were there no fresh fighting troops—either French or English—at Lamote, but I saw none when, fifteen hours later, I travelled back to Amiens, and even beyond: and how this Officer came to make so inaccurate a statement is still a mystery to me.

Before daybreak some men were reported to have refilled the gap on the left of the Brigade, but these appear to have gone again almost immediately, and, as soon as it was light enough to see, small parties of the enemy could be observed between our Brigade and the river, making their way towards Mericourt and Morcourt.

When I first saw this movement I sent a message to Captain Goodland (1st R.M.F.), who was on the left, asking him to send a patrol to intercept it, if possible; and I also got a section of Field Artillery and two Vickers guns to sweep the ridge where the enemy were accumulating.

Later, as the movement continued, and the parties of the enemy passing round our flank grew larger and bolder, I sent a Lewis gun under McWeeny to try and get round them.

For several hours the Germans continued to stream through the gap on the left in ever-increasing numbers, and at 10.15 a.m. the position had become so acute that the officer commanding the 1st Munsters reported that he was compelled to accommodate himself to the new situation, and that he was falling back.

A hurried conference was then held, as the result of which Colonel Weldon (2nd Leinsters) ordered a withdrawal in echelon, commencing from the left, to a position on the line Morcourt-Framerville.

The withdrawal, which, so soon as it was observed, drew considerable shell-fire and heavy machine-gun fire from the enemy, was duly carried out, the right covering the retirement of the left during the initial stages. Covering parties were also left temporarily behind as the retirement continued.

That it had become necessary was proved by the machine-gun fire which met us, as we fell back, from the direction of what had been our left rear, in which locality large bodies of the enemy had already collected.

My usual good fortune pursued me on this occasion, though, as we walked back in the face of the gusts of bullets —being pursued in addition from behind by the enemy's shell-fire—the chances of surviving at times seemed very small.

A sight that met us as we passed through Proyart has photographed itself upon my mind. An old man on a high dog-cart, drawn by a crazy-looking horse, rather like the horse Don Quixote used to ride, drove solemnly and reluctantly through the village. He was the last inhabitant to leave. He had a long white beard and wore one of those high black Flemish caps, and the heavy shells falling upon the houses around him, sending up clouds of smoke and brick-dust, left him and his horse apparently quite unconcerned. It looked as though he had clung almost too tenaciously to his home, but I believe he got out all right. At any rate, I watched him pass safely along the first mile or so of the road towards Amiens.

The Colonel of another battalion told me afterwards that, at this same place, he saw an old woman and a little child, stumbling through the fields, hand in hand. The former was too feeble, and perhaps had also been a little too obstinate, to leave her home till the very last moment. Now, perhaps too late, she was devoting her whole energy to saving the child; and, as each shell fell, both threw themselves upon their faces on the ground!

On reaching the new position I occupied an old trench which runs past the junction of the Proyart and the main Amiens roads, and reported to Brigade. I then went back towards Proyart, to look for Colonel Weldon, who, being on my right, had retired after me. Having found him to be safe, I returned to my own men, and, as a general retirement was by this time in progress, I formed them up on the main Amiens road together with the 1st Royal Munster Fusiliers, and a good many battle stragglers from other regiments who had attached themselves to us.

With this force, which must have been close upon 400 strong, I then reported to General Bellingham (commanding the 118th Brigade), whom I met on the road, and waited for a reply from my own Brigade to my message.

At General Bellingham's [1] request I lined up with the 39th Division in three lines of old trenches which cross the Amiens road about 200 yards west of the cross-roads. Here, until I left, some four or five hours later, we held up and inflicted losses on the enemy, who appeared repeatedly in force in the villages of Rainecourt and Framerville, in front of us.

A considerable number of aeroplanes—both German and British—took part in this action, shooting at each other's infantry, and assistance was rendered to us by the artillery, and in particular by a section of 18-pounders, which took up its position immediately behind us, and did good work.

Finally, a counter-attack was delivered by some two fresh Companies which were brought up specially by motor lorry. This proved too much for the Germans who turned and fell back hastily through the now blazing villages.

In doing this, some good targets were exposed and taken full advantage of by our side. It was in running across

[1] Brig.-Gen. Sir Edward Bellingham, Bart., C.M.G., D.S O.

to the Lewis guns to direct their attention to a bunch o
the enemy I had observed, that, at about 4.15 p.m., :
stumbled over some overgrown trip wire, and dislocatec
my left elbow. The men thought I had been hit. So dic
I. And it cost me a good coat, which the stretcher-bearers
ripped open with a knife in their usual reckless fashion
hunting for the wound.

This was the end of the battle, so far as I was concerned
I waited half an hour, feeling very sick, till General Bellingham (who had been away at the telephone) returned. Then
I handed over the command to Ritchie Dickson, the senio:
of the only two officers now left of all we had gone into
battle with on the 21st.

The last sight I saw was that of one of our aeroplanes
crashing vertically to earth from a height of some 400 feet
It fell, head-first, like a stone, and sent the dust flying like
a dud shell. Both pilot and observer must have been killec
instantly.

With my servant, Doyle, I made my way towards Amiens
As we neared Lamote—after a circuitous walk of nearly
4 miles, our troops were falling back in droves across the
road, from the direction of the Somme. I have since
learnt that the enemy had succeeded in crossing at Cérisy
thus getting behind our line on the south side of the river

Our men, as they fell back, were being pursued by a
furious shell-fire. The road, which was being treated as a
special target, was littered with dead horses, and was
horrible to look upon.

We came upon a motor lorry, which was just preparing
to move off. It was filled with wounded, but I got a sea
on the step, while Doyle climbed inside.

For the next few minutes we ran the gauntlet through a
storm of shells. The conductor stood on the step and
bawled encouragement to the driver like a Cockney at a
boat-race. The driver fairly sweated in his efforts to push
the clumsy vehicle along at a faster speed than that for
which it was designed. It was an exciting race, but we got
through, and, after several changes, travelling part of the

way on casual motor-cars which we picked up on the road, and part by ambulance, we eventually reached the Casualty Clearing Station at Nampes. Near Villers Brittoneux (where the line now is), a major of the Heavy Artillery, on whose car we were riding, gave us some port, some chocolate, and a bag of biscuits. These, since we had not had a proper meal for close on thirty hours, Doyle and I devoured ravenously. As we passed through Ameins I noticed marked signs of the heavy bombing the town had received from aeroplanes the night before.

The Casualty Clearing Station which we found at Nampes had moved back with the general retirement, and the tents composing it had barely been pitched when we arrived.

The marquees were faintly lighted by wax candles, and were crowded with herds of wounded. The bad cases lay upon stretchers, which almost hid the ground. So numerous were these that it was often necessary to step over one, and the walking wounded packed the gaps and overflowed outside as well. The doctors and nurses, though they must have been half dead with fatigue, worked cheerfully and unceasingly at the highest pressure.

After being bound up, I was directed to the railway station, to wait for the ambulance train. Here I was fortunate in finding a very generous Railway Transport Officer, who invited me to pass the night in his office, and gave me a meal of eggs and bread and butter, and some rare old rum.

When at last the train arrived, at 3.30 in the morning, it was of so luxurious a type—the latest Red Cross marvel —that the long and tiresome wait was fully compensated for. I was immediately put to bed, and at about 1 p.m. reached Rouen.

And here I am, in No. 2 Stationary Hospital, where I have slept, practically for three days, waking up only to take food or to be chloroformed.

I was chloroformed twice before my elbow, which had then been out of joint for 72 hours, was got right.

*　　*　　*　　*　　*

April 3, 1918.   *Notes made at Dorchester House Hospital.*
                                             Park Lane.

Though the description I have given relates only to
an infinitesimal section of the 50-mile front attacked by
the enemy on March 21 and the following days, it may
give some idea of what an individual experienced, somewhere near the centre of the attack, during this colossal
breakdown of the 5th Army.

To my mind the causes of the failure, in the order of
their importance, were as follows:

1. The tired and untrained condition of the infantry at
the time the battle started.

2. The failure of the machine-gun barrage. This had
been most carefully planned, and looked invincible—on
paper. Theoretically, every yard of the enemy's approach
was to be covered by a rain of bullets, fired over the
heads of our infantry by a line of machine-guns, placed
behind.

3. The new dispositions, introduced less than a fortnight
before the battle, whereby the troops were not to move into
their fighting positions until the alarm was given;—in other
words, the old rule which says that the soldier is to fight
where he stands was abandoned.

4. The fog, which stultified the new system.

5. The absence of reserves behind the front line system.

I have seen criticisms in the Press of the order reducing
Brigades, from four battalions to three. I see nothing in
this. It is surely better to have three strong battalions to
a Brigade than four weak ones, and, if the men are not
procurable, what else is there to do?

No. The primary cause of the collapse was the tired-out
condition of the troops when they went into the battle.

The necessity of rest for fighting troops is well appreciated
by the Germans, but seems often to be disregarded by our
Higher Staff. The British infantry soldier is like the willing horse. He takes his hardships and trials as part of the
day's work. He complains often enough—indeed systematically—but his complaints are not vindictive, and

are not audible outside the trench he is holding, or the stable in which he is billeted.

Consequently, like others of his kind, he is often over-driven, sometimes beyond the limits of human endurance.

When the battle opened on March 21 my battalion had already manned and dug in the Front line system of trenches for fifty-eight days. During this time the men had had no rest or recreation. Sundays, weekdays, even on St. Patrick's Day (the Irishman's greatest holiday) they had toiled alike;—always liable to shell-fire, and frequently enduring it.

It is true that on one occasion we marched back to Tincourt—about eight kilometres behind the line—for $3\frac{1}{2}$ days, but as the men were sent forward on certainly two out of these $3\frac{1}{2}$ days to dig trenches and bury telephone cables (destined never to be used) in the forward area, there was not much rest in that. Indeed, they would have preferred to have remained in the line. Under such conditions training is out of the question. There is neither time nor opportunity.

And so it happened that the attenuated front line of the 5th Army was not in a fit condition to meet the overwhelming hordes that fell upon it on March 21, when forty divisions, which for two months had been training like gladiators behind the German lines, reinforced by eight or ten more divisions on March 22 and 23, were thrust against fourteen Divisions of tired, overstrained, under-trained trench-diggers and cable-buriers![1]

[1] As to the attitude of the men during the retreat the writer cannot do better than quote a private letter—written by another officer who took part in it —which was subsequently sent by Professor Spenser Wilkinson to the *Sunday Times*. The letter describes exactly what he himself saw.

"I wish," the letter says, "you could have been out to see the army during this hard fighting—the men wonderful in their phlegm and humour and incapacity for self-pity. Sometimes, when I have seen them stumping back along a road with the enemy only about two miles behind, after no end of fighting and marching, they were exactly the same in bearing as when advancing last year, and I have never seen anywhere, along the whole line of the retiring battles, any patches of disorganization. I feel sure of our wearing the enemy to pieces before he can do it to us, though, of course, it is bad to lose so many good men."

The Germans were of course favoured by the weather, which must have been almost unique for the time of year. The ground was dry and hard, so that artillery could be moved anywhere, and each morning—but particularly on the morning of March 21—there was a heavy fog, which hid the attacking troops, and masked the machine-guns at the strong points upon whose cross-fire our newly adopted system entirely depended.

So impregnable had these defences been regarded that the possibility of their collapse had not been provided for, and not only was there no organized line behind them, but there were, practically speaking, no troops.

Consequently, once the defence broke down, the remnants from the front line had solely themselves to rely upon. They were compelled to fall back, stage by stage, taking up one position after another, becoming more exhausted each hour, without even the encouragement which the sight of a line of fresh troops, however thin, would have inspired.

Only a miracle kept the Germans from reaching Amiens on March 27.[1] There was nothing to stop them had they pressed forward with cavalry or armoured cars that day, but, fortunately, they used neither.

The casualties suffered by my battalion, almost entirely on March 21 and 22, amounted to 22 officers and 618 other ranks, out of a total of rather more than 700.[2]

[1] The Germans say that their men got drunk on the liquor they found in our Expeditionary Force canteens, and that this is what saved Amiens. And it is more than probable.

[2] The 6th Battalion Connaught Rangers was disbanded during the summer of 1918.

August 14, 1918.   *Boulogne.*

I spent last night at the Louvres Hotel, at this place, and came in for an air-raid, which started just as I had settled down to write after dinner, and continued, with intervals, for a couple of hours, during which time the town was kept in darkness.   I am just leaving for Etaples.

August 15, 1918.   *"J" Infantry Base Depot, Etaples.*

I am in the land of the W.A.A.C.'s, who drive the motor ambulances and do much other useful work.   But, I am told, they are quite adamant on the question of giving "lifts" on their cars, and I may tell you it was an unexpected shock when I got my first rebuff yesterday from a lady who was driving a lorry up a steep hill which I was toiling in the hot sun.   The free and easy methods of the man-infested regions nearer the line, where anyone—however humble his rank—is (or considers himself) entitled by the unwritten law to hail anything on wheels that may be going his way has—as I now learn—spoilt me for this kind of thing.

On reporting to the officer who directs the disposal of reinforcements I was posted to "J" Infantry Depot, the Commandant of which is Lord Douglas Compton (formerly 9th Lancers).

August 16, 1918.   *Etaples.*

I picnicked to-day with Mrs. Worswick and her sister (they are running a soldiers' club), and Lady Sinclair (Marigold Forbes, daughter of Lady Angela), who is just turning twenty-one, has been married six weeks, and whose husband is in the 2nd Life Guards.   Afterwards we bicycled to Paris Plage, and bathed.

While I was drying myself (about 4.15 p.m.) an orderly discovered me (how, I do not know, since I had not thought of leaving any message behind at the Depot to say where I was going), and handed me orders to report at Etaples Station at 5.40, to "proceed and assume command" of the 15th London Regiment—the 1st Civil Service Rifles.

This, to say the least of it, was unexpected, since officers

287

are usually kept waiting for weeks, and sometimes months, in the Commanding Officers' pool, as they call it.

Anyhow, the order was obviously impossible to obey, having regard to the time I received it, so I have asked for, and obtained, a postponement until to-morrow.

August 20, 1918.   140*th Infantry Brigade Headquarters.*

I left the base at 2.20 on the afternoon of Sunday— the day before yesterday—and as I was O.C. train was given a compartment to myself, which I shared with a Colonel Walsh, who was going up to join the III Corps, like myself.

At Canapes, where we detrained, Walsh introduced me to a friend of his, Colonel Chamberlain (formerly 5th Lancers), who is Commandant of the V Corps Rest Camp, and who asked us both to dine and stay the night with him.   He insisted upon my sleeping in his bed, because, as he said, I was going up to the line and he was not.   He is a charming fellow.

In the early morning a car was sent for us, and after a drive of 12 or 15 miles I was dropped at my new Divisional Headquarters at Heilly, which, in 1916, used to be railhead for this section of the line, and which of course I knew well.

The Divisional Commander, General Sir G. F. Gorringe,[1] was just starting off in his car to visit General H. B. Kennedy[2] (60th Rifles), my new Brigadier, and took me along with him.   I found that my new battalion was in the front line, but as it was coming out to-night the Brigadier asked me to sleep at his Headquarters.

I went up in the afternoon, with the Brigade Major, who turns out to be Captain L. C. Gibbs, Coldstream Guards ("Laggs" Gibbs), to visit the battalion, and was introduced to the officers.   This was in the "Bois des Tailles," on the opposite side of the Bray-Corbie road to the spot where I was encamped with the Guards Entrenching Battalion in 1916. At that time it was a very safe place.   It has now lost that reputation, and the inadvisability of hanging about in it is

---

[1] Lieut.-Gen. Sir George Gorringe, K.C.B., K.C.M.G., D.S.O.
[2] Brig.-Gen. H. B. P. L. Kennedy, C.M.G., D.S.O.

reflected in the name given to it by the soldiers, which is "Tout de Suite" Valley.

I still write from Brigade Headquarters, which are in tents, on the battlefield of twelve days ago. They are about a mile from Sailly Lorette, ever memorable to me on account of its associations with the retreat of last March. Last evening, after visiting the battalion, I walked into that once beautiful village, and revisited my old Headquarters of March 24. Much fighting has since taken place there, and the village and church are completely destroyed, and the houses where I slept and messed are gutted.

The country around this camp is still littered with the residue of the battle of August 8. The dead have not yet all been collected, and, I judge, from what I have seen, that our people killed many Germans.

August 21, 1918.

Support Headquarters, near Marett Wood, Mericourt.

I dined again with General Kennedy last night, as the battalion was not due to arrive back from the trenches till 2 or 3 a.m. The "family feeling," which I have always told you is so necessary for successful war, is certainly strong in the Brigade.

As for the Brigadier—I never met a more companionable man. There is nothing whatever of the Staff Officer about him. In fact, though he himself has to wear red tabs as a Brigadier-General, he has a saying that—as a rule—"once a man has put on red tabs it is only a matter of time before he becomes a ——," which is a view not uncommonly held in the fighting line.

This is the 1st Prince of Wales' Own Civil Service Rifles (1/15th London Regiment)—one of the 1st line London Territorial battalions. The Brigade is the 140th—the same that relieved us (1st C.G.) on June 1, 1915, at Le Rutoire. The Division is the 47th. The Corps the III.

I find that I am succeeding Eric Segrave, who has got a Brigade. Strange coincidence, isn't it, that I should find myself thus unconsciously filling the shoes of one of my best and oldest friends? It makes things very much easier, as not only am I sure to get a good name in advance from Eric, but you may be sure that he has left a good battalion behind him.

August 26, 1918.   *Bonnay.*

We have been at it, hammer and tongs, the last few days, but I got out last night for a breather, having been on my feet—which are very sore—almost continuously for four days and nights.   Things have gone well, and there is no doubt but that we are killing a lot of Germans— considerably more than they are killing of us.   Besides, we are capturing large numbers of prisoners.   I am with a splendid crowd.   They are like little lions—these London men.

I have a new second in command, who joined last night —Major Desmond Young, of the 6oth.   That is how I was able at last to get a sleep.

August 29, 1918.   *Carnoy Craters.*

We pushed on forward again this afternoon, and I am writing from what was, on July 1, 1916, the German front line:—a place of desolation; a place where many of our countrymen have died, and where, during the great battle that started that day, I often was.   So, it is familiar ground to me.

We have already come across two "booby traps" this evening, one of which killed two good men—not of mine. The padre has just told me that one of them had been sentenced to seven years for stealing pearls, but was let out when the war came, to join the Army.   He got a D.C.M. and a M.M.   So he made good.

The enemy is moving fast, and is miles away, and will take a bit of catching, I fancy.

September 3, 1918.
              B. 11.   C. 9. 2.   Behind St. Pierre Vaast Wood.

We are up, day and night, at it hell for leather, without rest, and there is no time for letters.   How I long for the despised sheets; and a bath; and a roof; and a few hours of undisturbed sleep!   The racket is as great as ever, yet

I feel well, and remarkably robust. When I get an opportunity I will write you a description of these days.

We had a day yesterday which will be unforgettable—one which showed me once again the best side of these most wonderful men.

By a miracle, again, I am untouched, and I wonder more and more how it is that I can go on like this. I certainly do not feel worthy of it; nor do I see how I can possibly justify my existence if I am still spared after the war is over.

Oh! I am so tired of it all: but you would be proud, nevertheless, if you could hear the compliments the Brigade has been receiving. Even the Army Commander himself hunted us up to-day and thanked us.

September 4, 1918.   *Behind St. Pierre Vaast Wood.*

To-morrow morning we are off again after the enemy. Let us hope he will go back kindly.

The standard of courage among these London lads is so high that men who would be considered brave elsewhere do not seem particularly brave here. In fact, they would look like shivering rabbits beside some of them.

We are very fortunate in our padres. The R.C. Chaplain is Father Benedict Williamson. His real name is, however, known to few, since he is invariably spoken of as "Happy Days," a nickname he has earned from his incurable optimism. Formerly, he was an architect. He is a Catholic by adoption—not heredity. He is a remarkable character. He carries the Host with him always, and administers it to any of the troops whenever they may desire it. The shell-holes serve him as chapels. He is, so he has told me, a believer in "religion by print," on the principle that print does not argue with the reader, and the reader cannot argue with print. Each time the words are read, the same thing is repeated—over and over again—till, at last, the most determined sceptic may be brought to admit that there is something in it after all.

The C. of E. Padre—Farebrother—messes with the battalion. He is not so long from Eton, and is quite charming.

The weather is fine, but cold at nights. I had such a sleep last night—eleven hours without stirring!

September 7, 1918.   *Heilly.*

I had the great satisfaction yesterday of seeing my battalion drive the Germans back to within a little more than a mile and a half of Villers Faucon, the village from which—so far as I was concerned—our retreat of last March commenced.

It has been a wonderful fortnight, though our losses have been heavy, even for this war.

We were relieved during the small hours of this morning, and are now well back, and shall, I hope, get some sorely needed rest and sleep.

September 8, 1918 (*Sunday*).   *Heilly.*

So much has happened since I said Good-bye to you at Charing Cross that the sequence of my letters has got out of joint, and it will be difficult to pick up the thread unless I start again almost from the beginning.

I will, therefore, go back to August 21, on which day I actually took over the command of this battalion. The following morning, at 4.40, the Division was to take part in the 4th Army offensive, to be resumed that day. It seems to be my fate to be ordered into action the very moment I have taken command of a new battalion!

My programme for the first day was to march forward at 6.10 a.m., to take up position in the sunken road leading from Morlancourt to Etineham, near the Bois des Tailles, and to wait until wanted.

The battle opened with a roar at the appointed moment, and by the time we had got under way visibility had been reduced to a minimum by the dust and smoke from the bursting shells;—which was perhaps just as well, since we had 3 miles to go, with the sun low and facing us—the most favourable conditions for observation possible for the enemy.

As we advanced towards the rendezvous we crossed the

round fought over on August 8 and since. Some of the dead still lay where they had fallen, and the debris of battle was scattered everywhere. Here and there was an aeroplane, derelict, where it had crashed. But we had nothing much to worry us as we went forward. A few high velocity shells, fired at random from well behind the enemy's line, skimmed over our heads and burst close by. That was all; and these did us no injury.

By 7.50 a.m. we were in position, the Companies scattered about in shell-holes, and I with my Headquarters personnel in the sunken road, already rather crowded by a squadron of the 1/1st Northumberland Hussars and several whippet tanks which were waiting their turn to advance to the attack. Five minutes later both were off, but they came dribbling back about an hour afterwards, having met with serious opposition.

In parenthesis, I may say that for a tank to be of much use you want a superman inside it, and supermen are hard to find. It is difficult for any man to co-operate efficiently with infantry when he is locked up inside a safe. Nevertheless, tanks are good things to have with you, so long as you do not count too much on them. On no account trust a tank, by itself, to guard your flank. If you do you will almost certainly regret it. The Guards Division knows that from its experience the first time tanks were tried, on the Somme, in 1916.

During the afternoon I got my instructions for an attack to be delivered by the Brigade at 4.45 the following morning. These, however, were subsequently cancelled, owing to the retirement of the Brigade in front of us under pressure from the enemy. The latter had regained the line captured by our troops during the morning, as well as "Happy Valley," a place well known to all those of us who were in these parts in 1916.

During the afternoon the position had become threatening, and at 7 p.m. I was ordered to take the battalion forward and to fill a gap on the right of our Division.

When I reached the front line I found the situation

obscure and unsatisfactory, and I spent the whole night o
my feet, going from one place to another, reconnoitrin
and arranging for the defence of my sector.   Everywher
lay the dead of previous encounters, and, incidentally, w
came across the bodies of a patrol of my own battalior
which—a night or two before—had been caught b
machine-gun fire in what was then "Noman's Land."

There was a good deal of shelling and machine-gun fir
during the early part of the night, which suggested that th
enemy might be contemplating a counter-attack, but sul
sequently all quieted down, and by morning (we stood t
from 4.30 till daylight) we felt ourselves more or less in
position to meet him if he came.

We had to put up with a good deal of shelling the nex
day (the 23rd), which, however, was more noisy tha
harmful.   The men of the advanced Companies were we
scattered in shell-holes, and the Company in reserve wit
Battalion Headquarters stood at the foot of a steep ban
which gave protection.

Behind this bank also were the wounded and a dead office
of another battalion, left from the attack of the previou
day.

Among the wounded was a stoic German sergeant.   H
lay, motionless, throughout the day, apparently obliviou
of the shells which his countrymen kept pouring into th
valley.   He may have been given morphia by the docto
I do not know.   If not, he typically exemplified the stoicis
which has always struck me as so remarkable in th
wounded.   When asked if he minded the shelling he sai
—in his own way—"Good Lord! this is nothing to wha
your people do to us!"

In the evening I was ordered to take part in an attack t
be delivered by the Brigade during the night, at 1 a.m
in conjunction with the 175th Brigade on the right an
the 12th Division on the left, with the object of recoverin
the ground lost the previous afternoon.   The rôle allotte
to the Civil Service Rifles was the "mopping up" of "Happ
Valley," a strongly defended position, honeycombed wit

A TANK IN ACTION

dug-outs;—where, therefore, it was expected to get a good haul of prisoners.

The battalion assembled for the attack shortly before Zero, and I moved my Headquarters to a dug-out on the railway, north of the Bois des Tailles, which had been allotted to me by Brigade. From the railway embankment I watched the opening of the barrage.

How often have I tried to describe to you that grandest and most spectacular of all the shows ever staged by man! the crash of a thousand guns bursting suddenly out of the silence of the night: the continued roar: the rapid intermittent flicker on the clouds: the trembling earth beneath you:—while you listen anxiously for the rattle of the enemy's machine-guns—that nasty sickening sound which you are just able to distinguish amid the din, and which tells you that he is not taking it lying down.

After a few minutes the enemy artillery began to put it back on us, some of his shells bursting unpleasantly close to where I stood. All went well on this occasion. Although there was considerable reply from the machine-guns the operation was entirely successful, and by 2 a.m. parties of prisoners, chattering like monkeys, began to reach my Headquarters.

Some 300 were captured, including two very dapper-looking unwounded officers, one of whom knew a little French. As he spoke he smiled amiably, occasionally appealing to his friend—when asked a question—and laying his hand caressingly on his shoulder. A finicky kind of creature he looked, and mighty glad to be out of it! No fool either, you will perhaps say. Possibly that is so. We also captured a number of machine-guns and some trench mortars.

At 4.45 in the morning, I went forward to the Companies. With my guide—a runner named French—I led off along the railway cutting. Presently we stepped out across the open. It was all right until we got to within 300 yards of the Bray-Albert road. Then the stuff began to fly. An S.O.S. alarm rocket went up from some of our troops in front, signifying a counter-attack by the enemy. It was a false alarm but, none the less, the machine-guns began to rattle, and soon we found ourselves advancing through quite a storm of bullets which whistled past or sent up little spurts of dust as they spattered the ground around us. What a fool I am, thought I, to have followed this boy's short cut across the open instead of practising ordinary discretion and sticking to the railway! He was unimposing to look at, with spectacles and a smile:—in peace-time a clerk in some office: but I never saw anyone more callous to danger than he. *He* won't last long, I decided, and sure enough he has been hit since, though I hope and believe not seriously.

We walked on. As we neared the road a wounded man lying on the grass, a hundred yards away, called out for help. My runner, Lewington, and Private Wells—a servant—went out from the road and brought him in a few minutes later, still under heavy machine-gun fire. I helped them to lift him on to a stretcher. He had been hit badly in the stomach, so that his vitals were protruding. But, as he lay, he muttered plaintively, "Oh, if I could only come across the man as did that." He was carried off to the Aid Post.

On the road I found Major Bates, acting second in command, who had commanded the "mopping up" party. He had made his Headquarters in a drainage sump beside the road, having wisely made some prisoners first deepen it before sending them to the rear.

I found things none too grand. The Brigade on our left had been held up, with the result that a dangerous gap existed between their right and ourselves. For some hours the situation at this point remained critical, and, several times, it was reported that enemy counter-attacks were threatened.

My own personal view was that nothing was further from the enemy's mind than counter-attack. The viciousness of his shelling—all from heavy artillery and trench mortars—though it was by some taken to be in preparation for an attack, suggested to me that it was more likely to be covering a withdrawal;—indeed, that he had already withdrawn his field guns; and I reported over the telephone to this effect.

Throughout the day the enemy continued to pound our lines, but though the men were only lightly dug in they stuck it, and well before midday the situation was soundly in hand.

Shortly after noon I received orders from the Brigadier concerning an advance to be made during the coming night, to a line some 2,500 yards further forward. The Civil Service Rifles were to attack on the right of the Brigade. I went forward with the Adjutant (Captain Paul Davenport, M.C.) to pass these orders on to the Company Commanders, and arrived at Bates' pit on the Bray-Albert road just in time for a regular orgy of "frightfulness" from the "Heavies." The calibre of the shells and the profusion and recklessness with which they were scattered was very suggestive, and to my mind strengthened the theory that the enemy had already withdrawn his field guns, and was now getting rid of surplus accumulations of heavy ammunition, preparatory to complete withdrawal.

Owing to a misunderstanding, two of the Company Commanders had mistaken the rendezvous, so Davenport and I spent an hour and a half or more, waiting with the remaining Company Commanders and Bates, under furious bombardment all the time.

It is a good thing that Battalion Commanders and Adjutants should have their share of this sort of thing to remind them of the troubles of the firing line, and it is a pity that the experience does not more often go higher. As usual, however, the damage done on this occasion was trivial in proportion to the expenditure of ammunition, though one direct hit was obtained a few yards down the road from where we stood, killing and wounding some good men, including a sergeant who was due to go home for a commission, and who, unfortunately, was killed.

General Kennedy sent me a couple of bottles of Veuve Cliquot, 1906, with his final orders for the attack that evening. He is the most thoughtful and generous of Brigadiers, and the act was typical of him. I felt, however, that the Company Commanders deserved it more than I, and so sent the champagne on to them. When I saw them later, I asked how they had enjoyed it, and was told that they had given it to the sergeants:—at which I was not greatly pleased, as that was not what I had intended.

· This wine was some of the last remaining of a priceless collection which the General had bought from the French during the retreat last March. I do not think there is anyone else in the army who would have had the wit to think of such a thing at such a time. When the enemy was advancing on Epernay it occurred to him that there ought to be some good wine going cheap, and he actually sent a motor lorry, in the midst of all the confusion, to buy up what could be got for his Brigade.

To return to the attack of the night of the 24th/25th. Zero hour was to be 2.30 a.m. The battalion assembled for the attack on the Bray-Fricourt road. Near to the assembly position lay many of our men, killed during the previous day or two. Here was a group of ten, evidently all mown down by the same sweep of some machine-gun. There, individual dead and groups of two or three, and, thankfully to say, there were German dead as well.

Both officers and men were naturally tired after the heavy pounding they had undergone during the last twenty-four hours, but with their usual goodwill they stepped off at the appointed time behind a creeping barrage, and reached the neighbourhood of their objective practically without opposition.

The casualties, nevertheless, amounted to some thirty-five, including two officers—one of whom had his foot blown off, and most, if not all, were caused by our own barrage. It is surprising how calmly such accidents have come to be regarded, even by the infantry who are the sufferers. But the sense of comradeship and understanding between the two arms is almost perfect nowadays. Each appreciates the difficulties of the other's job, and the

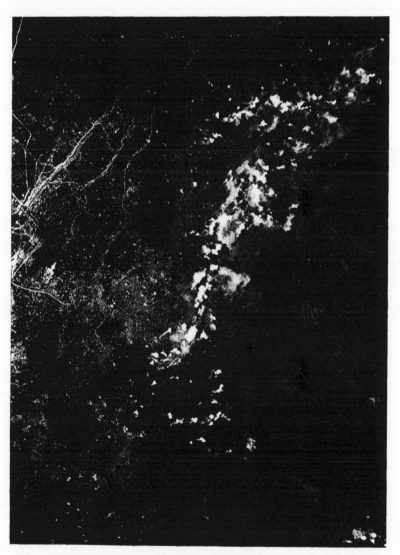

A CREEPING BARRAGE

Infantry Commander has often to resist a strong temptation to complain of too close shooting for fear that, next time, the artillery-man in his anxiety to avoid accidents may lift his guns too much. It is generally better economy to risk a few casualties from our own fire than that the artillery should shoot too much for safety. More casualties may easily be caused in the attack by the machine-guns of the enemy remaining in action between our infantry and our barrage than are ever likely to result from accidents through closer shooting. From the infantry point of view the task of following closely behind the barrage is not the easy matter that it sounds in the lecture rooms behind the line. Owing to the "error" of each gun the so-called barrage "line" is in reality an irregular and varying belt, perhaps 150 yards in width, and it requires much individual judgment on the part of the men to advance at exactly the proper speed—neither too fast nor too slow. It is a difficult business in daylight, and much more so in the dark, especially in the heat and turmoil of an engagement.

At half-past four in the morning I left Happy Valley to visit the Companies. A thick fog had settled down which completely blotted out the landscape. It was obvious directly I came across my men that the battalion had not reached its objective: but how to find the objective in the fog,—that was the trouble. I knew that Bronfay Farm—a famous landmark well known to me in 1916—stood close in front; but as it was impossible to see further than 20 yards, it was difficult to find the place.

With one or two others I struck out right and left and forward; probing into the fog in every direction, and this was not without its interest, for we had advanced over a mile and a half already into the unknown from the position we had fought over the day before, and we had not the least notion where the enemy now was, nor how soon we might walk into his rear-guard. However, all went well, and after a time the sun burst through the fog, and to my delight revealed Bronfay, and I was able to direct the battalion to its proper position.

Then I returned to Happy Valley, where my Head-quarters were, passing on the way a wounded German officer who spoke some English and who told me he had lain out through two of our bombardments. He was lucky to be alive. Others belonging to his side were lying about, less fortunate than he. I imagine they were mostly men left behind by the retiring enemy to do destruction work. Hand charges of high explosive lay beside some of them. There were also machine-gunners, those brave picked men whom the enemy leaves behind to cover his armies in retreat.

At 9 a.m. I slept for an hour in the sun. For three nights in succession I had not lain down, and I had begun to long exceedingly for a few hours of undisturbed sleep. When I woke I took the opportunity of examining "Happy Valley" (what a misnomer!), and, truly, it presented a grim spectacle.

It is a long narrow valley, and small: yet, I actually counted twenty-one German machine-guns that had swept it, and, since my search was superficial, it is probable there were more—to say nothing of those the enemy had taken away. I also saw three minenwerfers (trench mortars). Beside the guns lay many of the gunners, dead; and wherever I looked—whether on the banks or among the dug-outs, or among the bushes, I saw dead Germans—boys many of them, lying singly and in groups. There were also a number of German wounded. God knows how long they had lain there! They had crept into the dug-outs, some of them: others were still in the open. They were quite exhausted. One scarcely breathed at all. Another—very young—whose sufferings had clearly reached the limit of endurance, muttered prayers that the end might come quickly. Between us we got them collected, including the English-speaking officer I mentioned earlier, and a doctor having dressed their wounds, they were sent to the rear.

Again, the patience and dog-like resignation of the wounded—one of the miracles of the war as I think—was most striking.

In the afternoon General Kennedy brought up Major Desmond Young, my new second in command, and at the

Brigadier's urgent wish I left him in charge of the battalion, which was withdrawn from the front line the same night and bivouacked; while I, after an excellent dinner with Wyndham Portal,[1] had a perfectly splendid sleep in a wooden hut, with three others of my officers, at the battalion transport lines near Bonnay.

The next three nights—August 26, 27, 28—the battalion rested in the same trenches and dug-outs, near Marett Wood, that we had started from on August 22, and on the evening of the 28th the Divisional "Follies" gave an open-air show on the slope opposite my Headquarters.

On August 29 we were again on the move forward. The Companies took up a line in front of the Briqueterie —some ruined Brickworks which were General George Pereira's Brigade Headquarters during the battle of September 9, 1916.

I have already mentioned the booby traps at the Carnoy Craters. The amount of trouble and forethought which the enemy expends upon this puerile form of warfare in my opinion indicates the existence of a degenerate strain in his character, which, judging from the experience gained from end to end of our line, is not confined to the few but is general, and organized. Fortunately, it is only rarely that these ruses come off, since all ranks are on the look out for them, and on the few occasions that they do succeed they more often mutilate than kill. It is impossible to picture one of our people descending to such tricks.

At 7 a.m. on the morning of the 30th, we marched to Maurepas Ravine, where we halted, and scattered in shell-holes. The German "Heavies" were busy all that day, and it was necessary to change position more than once, though we were still a long way behind the firing line. At 3.15 p.m. a big shell burst on the further slope of the ravine—quite half a mile away—and a piece hit Davenport, who at the time was walking between myself

[1] Lieut.-Colonel Wyndham Portal, M.V.O., D.S.O., late Life Guards, who commanded the Household Battalion before it was disbanded, but was now commanding the 47th Machine Gun Battalion.

and Knox, the American doctor. So I lost my Adjutant. He is now in England, and a great loss he is, since he is a most able, courageous and valuable officer.

The matter is of interest as indicating the enormous spread caused by the instantaneous—the so-called 106—fuse, which is so much used nowadays both by the enemy and ourselves. Such shells burst instantaneously—as the nose touches the ground, and the pieces fly horizontally to a great distance. They make scarcely any crater at all, and, consequently, it is unlikely that there will be much cover for advancing infantry on the battlefields of the future.

We spent the night and the following day and night in the Ravine, sleeping and feeding comfortably in musty-smelling huts provided by the enemy. These were built of wood, of which he seems to have had a plentiful supply, and showed every sign of hasty abandonment. The musty smell of the German huts and dug-outs is very peculiar, and will, I feel sure, remain familiar to my nostrils till my dying day.

At 3 p.m. on August 31, I got orders for an attack to be delivered by the Brigade at 5.30 the following morning, in conjunction with the 141st Brigade on the right and the 55th Brigade (18th Division) on the left. The objective was to be an old line of trenches skirting the south-west edge of St. Pierre Vaast Wood. The Headquarters allotted to me were in a shelter at the cross-roads, north-east of le Forest. At 2.45 a.m. the battalion moved to its assembly position.

I watched the opening of the battle from outside the door of my shelter with Colonel Kaye, commanding the 17th London Regiment, which forms part of the Brigade, and having stood there some ten minutes we parted, I stepping down into my dug-out, he into his which was immediately opposite. Two seconds later a shell fell on the exact spot where we had been standing, crashing in both doorways. The lights went out and for a few moments all was dust and darkness. Then, when the candles had been relit, we counted the cost. Colonel Kaye's American doctor was the first to be dragged into my dug-out. His face and clothes were white from the chalk dust raised by the explosion, and one of his legs was blown off. It was the first time he had ever been under fire. As he lay he gave instructions as to how he should be handled. He was got away to the rear, but he did not survive more than a few hours. The same shell killed the gas sentry outright, hit my signalling sergeant (Moore) so badly that he died after a short interval, and wounded several runners.

In the meantime, the attack was going well, and prisoners began to come back within five to ten minutes after Zero. One of my Company Commanders (Lieut. Lascelles) and another officer (a South African—2nd Lieut. Kirk), whose first day in action in France it was, were killed early during the advance, but otherwise losses were slight, and by 7.30 a.m. all objectives had been reached and were being consolidated.

Large numbers of prisoners and machine-guns were captured, the battalion's share amounting to from 150 to 200 prisoners, and some ten machine-guns. Included among the former were two doctors, whom we impressed, while others were as usual made to act as stretcher-bearers. A motor ambulance was also captured.

Later in the morning, after visiting the new line, I moved my Headquarters forward to near the road which runs just south of the ruins of Rancourt. There, at 6.5 p.m., I got orders to the effect that the battalion would be relieved during the night and would take part in an operation the following morning, in support to the 74th (dismounted Yeomanry) Division. This relief took place at about half-past eleven, and the battalion marched to its position of assembly on the Rancourt-Peronne road, a few hundred yards south-west of the ruined village of Bouchavesnes.

The plan, which was complicated and ambitious, was that the 74th Division should attack, their objective being Nurlu. The same Division was also to be responsible for the capture and mopping up of Moislains. Our Brigade was to follow in close support, the Civil Service Rifles on the left. After crossing the Canal du Nord the Brigade was to wheel to the left, forming a defensive flank on the high ground to the north-east of Moislains. Zero hour was to be 5.30 a.m.; but as our Brigade had further to go than some of the others, it was to move at five o'clock, so as to get well up behind the assaulting Division.

The battalion was in position at the place of assembly at 3 a.m. The Brigade was to pass Moislains on the south, and the formation of the defensive flank therefore presupposed the capture of the village by the 74th Division.

The battalion advanced in two waves, Desmond Young, second in command, leading. I with my acting Adjutant, Captain Whiteley, followed with the rear Companies. From the start we came under heavy artillery and machine-gun fire, and, as we moved down the slope to the south-west of Moislains, under still heavier machine-gun fire, directed from the village and the rising ground beyond, as well as from both flanks.

In spite of casualties amounting to over half its fighting strength, the battalion—or what was left of it—succeeded in establishing itself in a trench close up to and immediately to the west of the village, with some men of other battalions of the Brigade and a few Yeomanry. The enemy was found to be occupying the continuation of this trench to our left and also another old trench to our left rear, while their men could clearly be seen moving in Moislains, and assembling in the village and in huts immediately to the south of it. Simultaneous counter-attacks were in fact attempted on our left rear and our right front, while the enemy at the same time tried to bomb up the trench on our left.

Both the parados and parapet were manned, and the attacks across the open were beaten off, but the bombing attacks continued all the morning, and, owing to scarcity of bombs, were with difficulty held up.

It was at once obvious that there were no British troops on our front, though men of the 74th Division could be seen in the distance to the right, on a level with the trench we were in.

In the face of the very heavy flank and frontal machine-gun fire, of the heavy casualties already incurred, and of

ιe fact that one flank at least was in the air, it did not
ɔpear practicable either to myself or to Colonel Dawes,
ɔmmanding the 21st London Regiment, for our battalions
ɔ assume the rôle allotted to the 74th Division, and to
:tempt, without a barrage, to capture the village, which,
ɜ a result of the failure of the operation as planned, was
:ill firmly held by the enemy.

A small local attack by about two Companies was
: elivered by the 74th Division on our right, but though it
ɩ ɩade some little progress, and at one point crossed the canal,
ɩ: hardly did more than establish our right flank.   With this
ɛxception, there was no indication of any attack having been
ɕelivered by the 74th Division in the vicinity of Moislains.

For some four hours a German field battery was im-
pudently in action in the open, east of the village, and not
ɩnore than 2,000 yards away, firing over open sights upon
ɩhe trench we were holding.   For a long time we could
ɩnly reply with rifles; feebly, owing to the long range; but,
ɩn the end, our artillery getting on to them in reply to a
ɩequest which I sent by runner, I watched this battery
ɩimber up and gallop away.

What precisely was the cause of the breakdown of the
ɔrogramme is at present unknown to me, but the fact is
ɩhat we advanced from the starting-point on the Rancourt-
Peronne road under orders to support, and under the
ɩmpression that we were doing so, but soon found ourselves
to be leading the attack, though the mistake was not discovered until some considerable distance had been covered.
Indeed, seeing no troops in front, and noticing that the
barrage was too far ahead of us to be of any value, our
first impression was that either the assaulting troops were
before their time, or we behind ours, and we therefore
accelerated our pace in order to catch up with them.

Heavily, however, though this cost us, the mistake gave
the Brigade an opportunity of adding to its laurels, of
which every man took advantage.   I will try and picture
what I saw.   Speaking of my own battalion, most of the
men are very young—in fact, quite boys.   They wear

khaki shorts with grey hose-tops turned down over thei·
puttees.   On their sleeves they have canary yellow heart;
as a distinguishing badge.

The sun began to rise very brightly, shortly after we had
started, and gave us our direction, which was due eastwards.
Almost immediately the enemy opened with a heav·
artillery barrage which he soon supplemented with machine-
gun fire.   In all directions among the advancing battalion
the shells started to burst and the casualties very soon
began to accumulate.   Knox, the American doctor, opened
an aid-post in an open trench which we passed over, where
he dressed the wounded throughout the day under shell-
fire.   The battalion continued its advance.   The machine-
gun fire grew heavier and heavier.   It came from the front
and from both flanks.   With their khaki " shorts" showing
about 4 inches of bare knee the men went forward, looking,
as Desmond Young said, like a lot of boys going to a
football match.   The runners pushed their bicycles.

It was a truly wonderful sight:—each man with his
shoulders squared to the objective, walking with bayonet
fixed, apparently unconcerned, through the deadly fire;
many dropping; the remainder carrying on; needing no
pushing or exhorting; each individual acting as a host in
himself.   The stretcher-bearers went about coolly, at the
walk, from one wounded man to another.   I remember one
stretcher-bearer in particular—a boy of about nineteen,
who was wounded later in the day—and who was really
admirable in his utter sang-froid and disregard of self.

The last hundred-yard lap was the worst, and had it not
been that the ground was pitted with shell-holes, not one
of us could have got across it alive.   Towards the end two
men fell beside me—not more than a couple of feet away,—
one so badly wounded that he died almost immediately.
Then we reached the trench I have spoken of, and, though
the enemy tried hard to throw us out by every means at
his disposal, we managed to stay there, though some
bombers got behind us whom we were unable to tackle
properly owing to our having run out of bombs.

For a time the situation looked precarious.   The shelling,
too, was very furious for some hours; but in the end things
settled down, and though we were a small party and semi-
isolated, we became more or less established.

At about 9 a.m., having failed in our efforts to get
communication with the rear, Colonel Dawes, commanding
the 21st Battalion, went back, and, at 1 p.m., still having
been unable to secure communication, I went back myself,
leaving Desmond Young in charge of the men of the
brigade that still held the forward trench.

I made my way to the nearest telephone which was in
an old limestone quarry on the Rancourt-Peronne road.
There was a sort of communication trench that I was able
to follow, which, however, being only a foot deep in places,
afforded little if any cover.   But the enemy machine-guns
had quieted down, and I got to the telephone without trouble.

At intervals along the forward trench and the communication trench lay the dead and wounded, many of
them.   I passed a group of five signallers, evidently killed
by the same shell, and another of seven or eight men swept
down together by machine-gun fire.

I saw Knox as I passed his aid-post, and told him of the
wounded, and he and Farebrother, the Chaplain, went out
later with a party and fetched them in.

I reported the situation over the telephone to General
Kennedy, and was returning to the front line, when a
messenger came running after me with orders to remain
near the telephone and collate the information.   Later, I
was ordered to withdraw the battalion at 10.30 p.m. to
their old trenches at St. Pierre Vaast Wood.

On the 3rd and 4th September the battalion rested, but
on the 5th we were at it again.   At 5.30 that morning the
141st Brigade passed through the 142nd.   At eight
o'clock the 140th Brigade followed, the Civil Service
Rifles, plus one Company of the 21st Londons, which
battalion had otherwise been withdrawn, being in support.

At my position of assembly (in Pallas Trench), in
addition to the usual dead horses, there was an abandoned

German field battery—the whizz-bang that we have learned
to know so well—with two gunners, dead, beside it
Speaking of horses, I have never seen so many dead horses
as during this recent semi-open fighting, and we, too, have
paid our toll in this respect, the battalion having on one
single day (September 1) lost seven horses killed and three
wounded. Dead horses and derelict tanks have been a
feature, and I have counted as many as nine or ten of the
latter without changing my position.

At noon I moved my Headquarters forward to the
sunken road that crosses Sorrowitz Trench, 300 yards
north-west of Moislains. The Companies waited in the
trench and in the sunken road itself. The shelling was
very nasty, at intervals. A little later I was ordered to
send forward the battalion—now reduced to two Companies
owing to the losses of September 2.

Considerable opposition had been met with from a huge
limestone quarry in front, and from the road and woods
beyond, and instructions had been sent out for an organized
attack to be delivered at seven o'clock that evening. This
battle took place on the rising ground, and it was possible
to watch it very clearly from the sunken road. It was
fought in a shower of rain, and a double rainbow formed
a very imposing setting to the picture. The attack was
entirely successful. Indeed, the following evening, we
dined in the open on the spot where it was fought.

In the middle of the night I was awakened from a much-
needed sleep. General Kennedy was on the telephone
He gave me directions for a further advance to be made
in the morning, and his way of doing this was characteristic

"Got your map?" he asked.

"Yes, General."

"See line—so and so?"

"Yes, General," said I, hurriedly picking out the map
readings he gave me with the aid of a candle.

"Well, you start from there at 8 a.m. Your objective
is the line ——," and he gave a further line of map readings

Then he switched off.

DISABLED TANKS ON THE BATTLEFIELD

He never fusses, thank God: and he leaves all details to the men whose duty it is to do the job. And that, I venture to think, is the proper way to fight battles.

At 8 a.m. (September 6) the battalion was again formed up for the attack, the objective being a line some 5,000 yards in front of the big quarry, and a little more than a mile and a half west of Villers Faucon, where I was with the 6th Connaught Rangers when the great German offensive began on the 21st of last March.

It looked like a nasty bit of country on account of some thick woods we had to go through, but all went well. Desmond Young and I had been taking it in turn to go forward with the battalion, and it was my turn this day.

I started off at 8.15 a.m. and established my advanced Headquarters near the Nurlu-Peronne road, a little beyond the quarry.

There I was joined by "Laggs" Gibbs, the Brigade Major, and we went on together. We reached the object-ive—immediately south-east of Lieramont—about noon, at the same time as the battalion. The men were about 300 yards to the right of the spot we had struck, and had advanced just a little too far, having passed over the crest of a ridge, where they had come under full view of the enemy. The latter was taking full advantage of the con-spicuous target presented, and was pounding unmercifully with artillery and machine-gun fire. This, however, was only for a minute or two. The battalion, under Captain Eccles, turned and walked some 50 yards back over the crest, and as it reached the reverse slope each man again turned and faced the enemy. Gibbs and I watched the movement, and the coolness and deliberation with which it was carried out was admirable.

We then joined the battalion, which lost no time in digging in. Indeed, this was very necessary. The bat-talion advancing on our left had not yet arrived, and the enemy machine-gun fire from that direction was very vicious.

Having seen the battalion into position I returned to my advanced Headquarters. I was soaked with sweat (it was a sweltering day) and took off all my upper garments, to cool.   In doing so I dropped the gold studs you gave me.

You would have been touched could you have seen the commotion which this loss caused. Officers, N.C.O.'s and men crawled about on all fours—literally for hours—searching behind every blade of grass.   But only one was found.

I found Desmond Young justifiably pleased with himself, having discovered a fine piano in Bois Epinette—one of the woods we had taken—in what had evidently been a German Corps or Divisional Headquarters.   It was the only thing left behind.   It weighs about half a ton, but he got it away in the mess-cart, and we have lugged it about ever since, and have had plenty of music out of it.   It will ultimately help to furnish the Regimental Depot at Somerset House.

During the night we were relieved, and bivouacked, and yesterday we were brought here, by motor-bus, to Heilly, on the Ancre.   Our casualties had amounted to the following:

Aug. 24–30.	Officers.	Wounded –	3
	N.C.O.'s and Men.	Killed and died of wounds–	7
		Wounded –	48
Aug. 31–Sept. 6	Officers.	Killed and died of wounds–	5
		Wounded	8
		Missing –	1
	N.C.O.'s and Men.	Killed and died of wounds–	70
		Wounded –	229
		Missing –	18
			389

P.S. While waiting yesterday morning for the buses to arrive, with some of my officers I explored the village of Moislains, and the battlefield of September 2. The German dead still lay about the village. No British dead lay in it or to the east of the trench we had occupied. In the rear of the trench and inside it lay the dead of our Brigade, and the Germans killed in the counter-attack on our left rear.

We retraced the last lap of the attack, and identified the trenches through which the enemy had tried to outflank us. We found their bombing posts, with the stick-bombs still lying on the fire-step, ready to throw. They had paid their toll. All had indeed gone well, but that last exposed slope was a sorry sight. There were our Lewis guns, many of them still mounted and pointed towards the enemy positions—the gunners beside them. The dead lay thick, their packs opened and the contents scattered; their letters and little souvenirs they had carried, thrown out by the ghouls of the battlefield, littered the ground beside them. Beside one boy lay a black earthenware cat, his mascot, which had not saved him. We had certainly paid heavily for this little scrap of trench.

We buried an officer and twenty-four men of the Civil Service Rifles there and then, and many others of the Brigade were still left lying. There was no time for anything elaborate, so the poor bodies with their blackened faces were just lifted into shell-holes or into the trench, one or two or three or four together, and earth was put over them. Then a rifle, with bayonet fixed, was stuck into the ground, butt uppermost, to mark each grave—with the names on a bit of paper attached to the trigger-guard.

Then, after Farebrother had read the burial service, we left them, and the same afternoon reached the Ancre, in which we bathed.

This evening I had my first opportunity of seeing the battalion quarter guard mounted. It is the practice in the battalion for the band to play at guard-mounting when out of the line, ending up always, as the old guard marches away, with the hymn "Abide with Me." It is a pathetic tune, I think, and always makes a lump come into my throat.

The Germans have left literally millions of machine-gun cartridges behind them in their retirement.

September 9, 1918.   *Heilly.*

My Headquarters are below the old château, with its wonderful red-brick wall, in a house, where, in 1916, a restaurant was kept by some refugee French ladies. We used at that time to come over to it—some 3 or 4 miles— from the Guards Entrenching Battalion in the Bois des Tailles, to get the only good meals which were procurable within range.

It was funny to find myself back in this house—now deserted, after two years, and to find it so changed and wrecked, though still good enough to put up in. My bedroom, which is upstairs, has a shell-hole through the ceiling, and the only bit of furniture in it when we arrived was an iron bedstead, so bent and broken that I had made plans to sleep on the floor.

However, after dark, I noticed something going on outside, and, on enquiry, found that the servants had found a fine French mattress in the village, which they were hauling up through the window for my use. It was entirely their own idea, and was typical of the British soldier.

September 12, 1918.   *Auchel, Pas de Calais.*

We marched from Chocques, this morning, headed by the band—a sadly depleted battalion, less than two Companies strong, in spite of drafts from home that have joined during the last few days.

We have come to Auchel, a big coal-mining village, where there are shops and estaminets and women and children, and where the officers will have sheets, and every N.C.O. will have some sort of a bed to sleep in.

It is a great contrast to the scenes we have left in the shocking wilderness of the Somme. Everybody has his tail well up, and though I question if you would think much of our village if you saw it, both officers and men might easily have arrived in Paris or London, so beaming

312

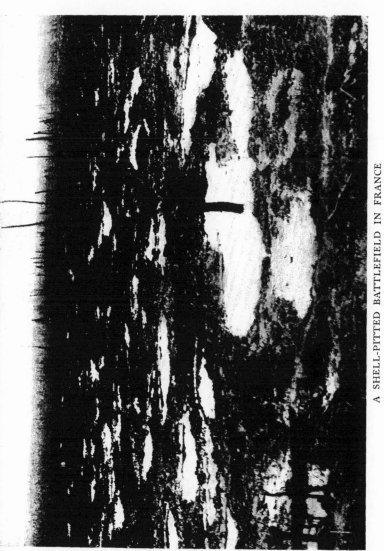

A SHELL-PITTED BATTLEFIELD IN FRANCE

are their faces. We are to remain here a fortnight, to refit and receive reinforcements.

Our band is thirty-three strong. We do not risk it in battle unless we are absolutely tied up for stretcher-bearers.

September 14, 1918. *Auchel, Pas de Calais.*

The men are loving their time here. They sit in the Estaminets—in an atmosphere *you* could hardly breathe in —smoking, and singing, and airing their French. It is just the sort of change they want after all they have gone through—a taste of town life, however remote from the ideal.

September 15, 1918. *Auchel, Pas de Calais.*

This morning General Birdwood[1] attended a Brigade open-air service, held on the Auchel aerodrome. He brought with him Talbot (son of the Bishop of Winchester), who preached. When he had finished, General Birdwood addressed the Brigade; then the battalions marched past him, and the Battalion Commanders were introduced.

The newspapers have always made such a hero of him that I was prepared to be disappointed: but he certainly has a clear eye and a taking manner both with officers and men: and he talked sound common sense in his address to the Brigade, which is more than one always hears on these occasions.

In appearance he is straight and upright, and he has far less "red tab" about him than the most junior member of his staff. He does not even wear a "red hat." Moreover, he is evidently not punctilious about his clothing, for the spikes of the buckle of his belt were missing, and the latter was done up anyhow.

"God helps those who help themselves" was one of the mottoes he pressed home, and he quoted the Bishop of London on the subject of bread, which he said was necessary to life, and yet God provides only 90 per cent. of it, leaving the rest to the farmer and the baker.

So huge is the scale on which this war is being fought that it is a great event to see one's Army Commander.

[1] Now Field-Marshal Sir William Birdwood, Bart., G.C.B., G.C.M.G., K.C.S.I., D.S.O.

I remember once being asked when on leave what the *men* thought of Haig—by a very intelligent man, too. It was during one of the bad times. He asked me this question, and added: "If, by now, they don't look on him as a demi-god, it proves that he is not the right man and ought to go."

You might as well ask what the private soldier thinks of God. He knows about the same amount of each. Though I have been in every army in France even I have never seen the Commander-in-Chief. I have only seen my Army Commander on four occasions in over three years—Plumer twice, and Birdwood twice.

September 16, 1918. *Auchel, Pas de Calais.*

I have just returned from dining with Wyndham Portal. After dinner, we watched a performance by Leslie Henson's concert party, in an aeroplane hangar.

Leslie Henson has come out here from "Theodore & Co.," having been given a commission in the R.A.F., and "does his bit" by entertaining the troops. It is a fine thing for them and goes far to keep them happy. There were, as usual, some good female impersonators, and the show was altogether splendid.

Last night General Kennedy came to dinner in the mess, and the cook made a very successful effort. We had a string trio playing in the next room.

There is some first-class talent in the battalion. Knox, the American doctor, has a voice which is not only, by nature, of extraordinary quality, but is perfectly trained: so, with our captured piano, we have plenty of music. In addition, there are the Divisional "Follies" who are always good.

One of their jokes, which goes down well with a front-line audience, is: "What is a Patriot?"

Answer: "A man who sheds *your* blood for *his* country!"

The orders regarding dress and equipment in the trenches are naturally very rigid, since each man must be ready for action at a moment's notice. Apropos of which there is a story told which is typical of our Brigadier's methods.

One day in the trenches a platoon sergeant was doing

everything he should not do. He had discarded his shrapnel helmet and was wearing a cap. He had thrown down his gas mask. He had taken off his boots and puttees, and left them with his rifle in the dug-out, and, in his socks, was going to get his rum ration; when he looked up and saw the Brigadier coming alone along the trench.

The Brigadier pulled up, and the following dialogue took place:

Brigadier: "So you're not expecting any gas or shrapnel this morning, Sergeant?"

Sergeant: "No, sir."

Brigadier: "I suppose you could run —— fast if they came over, couldn't you?"

Sergeant: "Yes, sir."

Brigadier: "It's —— lucky I haven't seen you, isn't it, Sergeant?"

Sergeant: "Yes, sir."

And the Brigadier continued on his rounds, while the sergeant slunk back and got into his equipment, and, it is said, did not break the rules again.

General Morland, the Corps Commander, visited us this morning and I took him round the battalion, which was out training. It is a sad sight to see it so reduced. To be added to our losses since I joined under four weeks ago, the battalion had already lost 140 men and officers in the trenches during the four days preceding my arrival.

That makes a total of 529, which is nearly equivalent to the fighting strength of a battalion, nowadays.

September 17, 1918.   *Auchel, Pas de Calais.*

This morning was spent in training. In the afternoon I went to Leslie Henson's show again. You never saw a house more packed, or a more enthusiastic audience. I dined with Colonel Dawes, and was given the best dinner of its kind I have had in France. Dawes is only twenty-seven, but has commanded a battalion, except when he was wounded, since August, 1916. He is quite deaf in one ear, having had a bullet through it.

Otherwise, I have spent the day intensively, writing up the official narrative of the recent fighting, which, thankfully, I have now finished, as well as the recommendations for award—that thankless and most difficult of all the duties, apart from the heavy work of rebuilding the battalion, which fall to a Battalion Commander after every battle.

Honours are not, as you might logically suppose, awarded in bulk to a battalion, in proportion to its merit, and left to the Colonel and his Brigadier to distribute in such manner as they think fit. Would that they were! No. They have to be dragged out of the Higher Authorities like back teeth. In each individual recommendation a "specific act" must be cited, which, if there is to be any chance of favourable consideration, must be made to "stand out."

It must be couched in the flamboyant language of the Penny Dreadful, and the result often is that the most deserving cases get cut out by the Authorities, far behind the line, whose function it is to decide these matters, and who, as a rule, have no personal or first-hand knowledge of the men or the conditions upon which they pass judgment.

It has been said that the pen is mightier than the sword, and I can truthfully say that, under our system, if a battalion is to get its proper share of honours, it is essential that its Commander should have at his disposal—not necessarily a truthful but at least a flowery pen. No matter how brilliant the performance, it must be dressed up in language which would startle the performer—generally a modest man—could he see it, so gaudily must the lily be painted.

Apropos of which a story is told of a certain C.O. who once recommended one of his men for a Military Medal. The recommendation was turned down, the "story," presumably, not being considered good enough.

The C.O. was disappointed, since the case was a particularly deserving one, but, nothing daunted, he tried again. He rewrote the story, racking his brains for the

nost extravagant language he could muster. His success
:xceeded his wildest expectations. The man got a V.C.

Indeed, it seems that the most difficult place in which to
vin fighting distinction is the fighting line itself, where,
n my experience, most of the awards that have been given,
is well as *very* many that have not, have been earned several
:imes over, the literary capacity of most C.O.'s having
proved inadequate for the task of writing up the "specific
icts" in language vivid enough to tickle the imagination
of the scrutineers.

Lord! how I hate the system!   I get letters from fathers,
ippealing for their sons.   Mr. McCreery, from Ireland,
points out that Corporal McCreery has been fighting in
:he trenches for two years, and more, and it would do him
so much good when he returns to the R.I.C. to have some-
:hing to wear.   But these things are not for such as he.

I have known men—good men too—eating their hearts
out through want of recognition.   How petty this sounds!
Yet a ribbon is the only prize in war for the ordinary soldier.
[t is the outward visible sign—the ocular proof, to bring
home to his people, that he has done his job well: and, say
what you may, a man's prowess, when the war is over,
will be assessed by the number of his ribbons.

Personally, I often wish that this form of reward did not
exist, seeing that ribbons must be distributed by men, not
gods.   By the way, if they *were* given by God, how many
an iridescent breast would cease to sparkle;—and the
contrary!

Then, think of the Foreign decorations!   These are
handed over to our War Office in batches, at more or less
regular intervals, by all of the Allies.   How many ever
reach the front line?   I have known perhaps half a dozen
to do so in my experience.

Of course, the explanation is that the War Office must
have its pick.   Then G.H.Q.—France must be satisfied.
Then, there are the different Army Headquarters, the Headquarters of all the Corps—not forgetting the Back-area
troops, the Divisions, and the Brigades.   It is not sur-

prising, after so remorseless a filtering, that nothing survives so far forward as the fire-trench, except by accident, and then only if it is very small.

It is a thousand pities that these things should be as they are, since the natural effect is that the high wall of bitter aloofness that too often exists between the fighting and writing sections of the army keeps growing.

Lately, there has been talk of limiting the award of fighting honours for action in face of the enemy. Will the rule be observed rigidly? I wonder. In any case, the decision comes late, since it may be presumed that most if not all those of the Staff that count have already got what they want, though some of them are doubtless hard to satisfy.

As for wound stripes, I don't know who invented *them*. Personally, I think they are un-English, besides being absurd. There are a few people who seem to make a hobby of collecting them. It is not difficult. It is only necessary to be gassed, however slightly, in order to appear in the casualty list. I have even heard of a case where a scratch on a wire entanglement was considered sufficient. But he was a Gilbertian soldier. The absurdity of the whole thing is that a "wound" of such a kind—so far as wound stripes are concerned—ranks equally with the loss of a leg or eye—or two legs and two eyes for the matter of that, so long as they are all lost at the same time.

September 18, 1918.   *Auchel, Pas de Calais.*

I have a surprise for you. We leave for the Italian front on Saturday. I was told this yesterday in confidence. To-day it is official. Of course, if the enemy makes a move between now and then it may be off: otherwise, we go.

I will not disguise the fact that the prospect of a change of climate and "entourage" has caused delight among the troops, as it has to myself. We shall be four days on a troop train. I say I am glad, but, truthfully, I shall feel a little sorry at leaving France. It is a cursed war, and I dislike the whole business as much as anybody. Yet I love it: it has been the breath of life to me, and I shall always look back upon the time I have spent here with great happiness.

Eric Segrave—who is now a Brigadier—motored over to see us to-day. He is just the same as he was nineteen years ago. He got quite sad when it was time to leave. He simply worships this battalion, and looked almost homesick as he went off to rejoin his Brigade, though the latter belongs to the 51st Division, which our enemies reckon to be one of the best in France.

He said: "Won't you change with me and command my Brigade, and let me come and command the battalion again?" Then he said: "To command a battalion is the finest job in the world. It is better than anything in the army or out of it. It is better even than being a Bishop!"— and I agree with him.

He says it is four times more difficult and ten times more interesting than commanding a Brigade. He says: "Of course they un-gum Brigadiers. There are so many Brigadiers and so few Brigades. But good Battalion Commanders are very hard to get."

All the same, a good many Battalion Commanders have been un-gummed, that I know of, and not a few during the last few weeks.

October 1, 1918.   *Foufflin-Ricametz.*

After several orders and counter-orders the move to Italy is off, and we are going back to the line. The transport moves to-day. The rest of us start to-morrow. I feel sorry for myself, but I can tell you I felt ten times more sorry for the men when I inspected the battalion this morning. They have not been told, but they must suspect, and it is, *I know*, a great disappointment to them. But they don't show a sign. Their demeanour is quite unaltered. They are wonderful.

An enemy plane flew very high over us this morning and dropped pamphlets, a specimen of which was picked up by one of my signallers. It is written in very involved and verbose English, and appeals to all who may be concerned to consider favourably the Austrian peace-note. It ends with a request, in large capitals, from "the Imperial and Royal Government," to send delegates to discuss peace in some neutral country.

It looks as though the enemy has traitors in his camp, and supports the theory I have been propounding for the past month—that we shall have peace before Christmas!

October 3, 1918.   *Rue de Tilloy.*

We are again following up the enemy. The battalion entrained last evening at St. Pol. Our destination and the fact that once more the move to the Italian front had been cancelled was known officially only to myself. For all the men knew they might still be bound for the land of their desires.

However, any doubts on the point were dispelled on detraining at two o'clock this morning, for we found ourselves among the ruins of Merville, where, in November, 1915, I spent a week at the Casualty Clearing Station. At that time it was a living town. To-day it is destroyed.

Any disappointment that may have been felt was well hidden. I saw no sign of it, and the only comment I heard was from one of the men who, as he first viewed the scene of desolation by the light of my torch, said to his neighbour: "So, it's to be more mice!"[1]

After leaving the train we marched some miles, and bivouacked in a field a little distance beyond the ruins of Lestrem, at about 4.30 a.m. We were immediately put under half an hour's notice, but did not move till 2.30 p.m., when we got sudden orders to continue the march eastwards, as far as the old British front line in front of Laventie. There, on the "Rue de Tilloy," which runs parallel with and just behind the old line facing the Aubers Ridge, we are spending the night, in shelters constructed by the enemy. We are close to the spot where Robert Filmer was killed in 1916.[2]

Before dining I explored the old trenches with Knox and Farebrother, and watched the sunset, which was very

[1] *Vide* Bairnsfather's picture.
[2] Capt. Sir R. M. Filmer, Bart., Grenadier Guards; died of wounds January 26, 1916.

320

fine, sitting on the edge of a shell-hole in what had been Noman's Land.

October 5, 1918.   *Le Maisnil en-Weppes.*

Yesterday morning, at 8.15, we resumed the advance through country devastated by the enemy, and by twelve (noon) had occupied a position just north of le Maisnil, in front of Lille.

It was an interesting march. The road has been very thoroughly mined by the Germans during their retirement, and great craters block the way at frequent intervals. We passed through the old German front and support lines. Never, in the course of the war, have I seen anything so elaborate. Whether they thought that some day we might make a frontal attack on Lille I do not know, but they have certainly put their best work into the defences here. There are hundreds of miles of barbed wire, and reinforced concrete so massive and so much of it that this portion of the line will remain a monument to the war for all time. All has, however, been blown up and abandoned, and the immensity of the destruction almost rivals that of the construction of this would-have-been impassable barrier—had the enemy chosen to defend it.

I have my Headquarters in a ruined farm stable behind the old German line. The communication trench, or rather breastwork, built up of packing-cases filled with earth, runs past within a hundred yards. We were shelled, sporadically, during the night, one shell falling 6 yards on one side, and another 16 yards on the other of a canvas shelter occupied by one of the cooks, without so much as scratching the canvas.

There are the usual "booby-traps." A few tempting concrete dug-outs have been left undestroyed with little piles of shells inside. These are attached to wires or otherwise arranged so as to explode should anyone enter unwarily: but people are seldom caught by such clumsy devices nowadays.

October 7, 1918.   *Le Maisnil.*

I have just been exploring the old front line, where our

troops and those of the enemy have faced one another, almost without moving, for four years. It is always interesting to revisit these historic places—though this was considered one of the quieter sectors (perhaps the outcome of our intention to spare Lille)—and to think of the many lives that have been laid down among the dreary mudholes.

On this occasion I travelled from east to west—that is from the German side towards ours—and, truly, the contrast between the thorough methods of our enemy and the casual British way is very remarkable. First, I passed through the massive German steel and concrete rear defences—the Mebus or pill-boxes—and the houses that happened to be there, which the enemy has reinforced with concrete (the shell of practically every house about here has been used as a mould for concrete emplacements within): past the support line of breastworks: through acres of barbed wire: past the German front line, stiffened up with more concrete: past more acres of barbed wire. Then, Noman's Land.

Then! a few strands of wire put down anyhow, and behind, a built-up trench of sandbags.

That—will you believe it?—is the British front line: no concrete: no protection: no defences—almost—but the British rifles and quick-firing guns and artillery, which now have gone forward, while the Germans, with all their intricate preparations, are in retreat!

That is the difference between our way and their way. Can you appreciate how good a feeling it gives one to look at it all to-day? And is it not remarkably British?

After all, our way is the best way. Battles are not won by means of deep dug-outs or tunnels—such as the Hindenburg tunnel—under the front line. Such devices can only have the effect of tempting men to cover, and making them disinclined to fight.

We had a little shelling during the night, which wounded two corporals of "A" Company—one of whom, unfortunately, has lost an eye.

October 8, 1918.   *Le Maisnil.*

It has been a very tame affair up to the present.   Indeed,
so far as this battalion has been concerned, we have been
having a very quiet time which seems likely to continue
for a bit at any rate.   I got another draft from home to-
day.   It includes an Italian organ-grinder and a professional violinist from the Imperial Russian Ballet!   The
latter I shall incorporate in the band, but I am at present
doubtful as to what to do with the organ-grinder, who
does not even know English.   Unfortunately, we have no
organ in our band!

I write from the ruined stable I spoke of in my letter of
the 5th.   The floor is brick and caked with horse-dung,
and the walls are bare and ragged.   The roof proper has
been blown away, but the enemy had thoughtfully recovered it with match-boarding and tarred felt before he
left, so that it is more or less rain-proof.   The battalion
pioneers have put in doors and windows, and, this afternoon, have added a huge brick fireplace, so that we shall
enjoy a roaring fire of wood, collected from the ruins.

I feel sure, if you could see us, you would be impressed
by the general appearance of comfort:—though perhaps I
exaggerate the comfort, which is a matter of contrast, after all.

October 8, 1918 (*later*).   *Le Maisnil.*

There is no continuous front line nowadays.   A railway
embankment separates us from the enemy, who has
burrowed into it in parts, and occupies some of the culverts
which run through it.   We hold the line by posts, and so
does he, and the interesting thing is that neither side
knows for certain exactly where the other's posts are.

This afternoon I visited the outpost line with my orderly,
Corporal Douglas.   On the way we passed a little group
of five dead machine-gunners.   An unlucky "whizz-
bang" had hit their emplacement, killing the five and
wounding a sixth, so badly that he is not likely to recover.

October 9, 1918.   *Le Maisnil.*

We are still in support, and during this morning did
some training.   It is odd to contrast the way we do things

now with what would have been possible six months ago
Now, our band plays near enough to be heard in the
front line, and we provide the men with light French beer
when we can get it!

I think that this morning, perhaps, one of the string of
balloons in front may have spotted us. There is always
some idiot who forgets that a party of men doing close
order drill may draw attention on a clear day, and neglects
the ordinary precaution of selecting the site for his exercise
behind a hedge or bunch of trees, or at least where they will
be screened from the enemy's observation.

The result this morning was that three 5·9-inch shells
came tumbling over, in rapid succession.

October 10, 1918. *Le Maisnil.*

I write in a wooden hut, built by the enemy. It is one
of a group which he forgot to burn in his retirement. It is
surrounded by a fence, 12 feet high and composed of
twenty strands of barbed wire. It is provided with a
battery of concrete cauldrons, and I can only suppose was
made for herding prisoners of war. Well, anyhow, we are
in it now, though not as prisoners.

I sent for the piano to-day, and after dinner we had
music. Small, the Intelligence Officer, who is a wonderful
pianist, played, while the doctor sang. It seems funny to
think of first-class music in a wooden hut, 3,000 yards
behind the firing line. That would not have been prudent
six months ago.

October 12, 1918. *Le Maisnil.*

Last evening the enemy threw over a considerable
number of shells, and bits spluttered on the felt roofs and
wooden walls of our huts, causing a very "naked" feeling
inside. One of the shells (a dud) landed on my former
Headquarters (of October 4–9), passing right through the
dining-table. It was a pretty shot.

The shells began to arrive again, this evening, just as
we were sitting down to "bridge," some mustard gas being
mixed with the high-explosive, which is the latest development. I got a good mouthful of the gas, which made me

neeze and cough for half an hour. It is a silly game. We continued our "bridge" with respirators in the "alert" position. How these things do make you slobber when you have to put them on!

October 13, 1918. *Le Maisnil.*

The weather is cold and wet and dismal. I went for a long walk with Farebrother this (Sunday) afternoon, and explored again the old front line. It produces a curious feeling always in me to look at these old lines of breastworks and trenches—500 miles or more in length, every yard of which has been so scrupulously watched all these years by the two lines of infantry; always on the alert, day and night, summer and winter, in sunshine, rain, and snow; at intervals under fierce bombardment; now and then raiding or being raided; occasionally under the utmost stress of war attacking furiously; while their fellows struck at home for higher wages, rattling the sabre like the Germans used to do.

We passed the ancient wall of one of the earliest Carthusian monasteries in France, a hundred yards or less in front of which our old fire-trench runs, while the support line cuts across the great enclosure, and a main communication trench meanders through it. In the middle is the monks' fish-pond, and between the latter and the wall are the graves of some of our soldiers.

We walked on in a south-westerly direction, to where Noman's Land becomes narrow and has been mined. Some Australian dead of perhaps two years ago—or rather their bones, recognizable by the shreds of uniform—still lie there, and we will bury them to-morrow. Beside them lie their rifles, shattered since by shell-fire, and the bombs they carried when they went out to the attack in which they lost their lives.

I will not write more as the cook (who, partitioned off, shares the hut in which I write) is putting over a smoke cloud, compared to which the ordinary German effort is child's play!

October 14, 1918 (*Midnight*). *Estaires.*

Last night, at ten o'clock, the enemy shelled us heavily,

though ineffectually, for twenty minutes (it has become a nightly event), and the dose was repeated at 2 a.m., by which time I was so drowsy and so comfortable in bed that the rattling of the bits against my hut scarcely disturbed me.

Again, we are for Italy. We were relieved by the 57th Division this evening and have marched back well behind the line;—a march which we continue to-morrow. I wonder if this is my exit from the war. The latest "peace" news rather suggests that it may be so. Well, if it is over, how glad we shall all be! Yet, it has been a wonderful experience, and, strange though it may seem, I have enjoyed it. The very frightfulness of it all has punctuated and emphasized the happy intervals. Is it selfish to say this? In doing so I do not forget the long-drawn and weary anxiety that it has meant for you.

The battalion which relieved us was the old 1st Royal Munster Fusiliers, with whom, as you will remember, I was in the 47th Brigade, and whom I last saw on March 27 last, during the retreat towards Amiens. They have again suffered heavily since that day, their Colonel (Kane) and most of the other officers I knew having been killed during the month that has just passed. However, I was glad to find Nightingale and Marsden (second in command and Adjutant) still with them.

We marched away from Le Maisnil in the moonlight, the band playing. In spite of the fact that the distance was long and the men were in heavy marching order, not a man fell out. They were in high spirits and sang as they moved along—a thing they rarely do in this battalion, which, somehow, is very silent on the march as a rule. The latter part of our route was through Estaires—one of the skeleton towns demolished in cold blood by the enemy:— a town, yet not a roof affording shelter.

Farebrother went out this morning with two pioneers and buried the Australians whom we found yesterday. He buried twelve.

October 15, 1918.   *St. Venant.*

I write from St. Venant, devastated by honest shell-fire—

326

stands, more or less. The "structure" of my bedroom survives, and among the rubbish on the floor lies a German cowhide haversack. What was our mess-room has since been used as a Catholic soldiers' chapel, the mantelpiece having served as the altar. On the latter still stand the holy statues and some dead flowers. On the door is an old notice "Out of bounds." The Town Hall, where my Company gave a concert on the 13th November, 1915, is wrecked, though part of the ceiling still remains.

October 16, 1918.   *St. Venant.*

We hang about, at present in perfect safety, amid the ruins of St. Venant. Little groups of two or three women in black—perhaps twenty or thirty all told up to the present —with a few children, keep returning to search among the ruins. Occasionally, they find their home not quite destroyed, and then they set to to clear away the wreckage and scrub the floors, and rig up what bits of furniture they can find. It is wonderful to watch their industry and patience. What a pity that such sights are not always on tap on those occasions when one is worrying about the trivialities that often loom so large in ordinary life! What a tonic it would be!

These women seem to live without sustenance. They cannot have much money and if they have there is nothing to buy. There is no fuel except the rafters of the houses, and food must be exceedingly scarce. Yet they carry on, and show no outward sign of distress. They are doing all this without "man" help, or practically so. I have seen one or two French soldiers on leave, but that is all.

October 17, 1918.   *Fontes.*

We marched again this morning still further back, to Fontes, where I write from an extremely cheerful billet, with electric light, and *such* a bed. I was pleased to find, on arrival, that my Adjutant, Davenport, who you will remember was wounded on August 30, had rejoined the battalion.

Before leaving St. Venant I presented the poor lady with whom I had been billeted with a nice chair which we have been carrying about the last few days, having "salved" it from a German Mebu near Le Maisnil. The battalion pioneers also patched up her windows with pieces cut out of an old sheet, and mended her chimney, which had been hit by a shell, so that she could light a fire.

She had lost most of her belongings—"Volé," she said, "par les soldats Anglais." She took me and showed me her safe, upstairs, which I must confess had been broken open very scientifically, though fortunately, as she explained, without gain to the looter, since only unpaid bills were in it. As I was leaving she came up rather remorsefully and apologized for having said it was "les Anglais" who had done the damage. "She had been mistaken." It was "les Ecossais." She little knew she hit me either way.

Perhaps it may have been true, but you must not judge too harshly. The battle line was immediately in front of the town when the incident must have happened, and the enemy was advancing fast in overwhelming numbers. No doubt some men argued: "If there is anything to be had, it is better that we should have it than the Germans." After all, it is culpable not to destroy valuable material when it appears certain that it must fall into the hands of the enemy, so the individual soldier must not be blamed if he, being human, sometimes applies the rule to his own benefit, though one would prefer that he kept his hands clean.

It is a difficult problem. Assuming the safe to have contained cash, should it be burgled, or left to the enemy? I suppose, strictly, that it should be burgled, and the cash handed to the Higher Authorities.

But it is difficult to arrive at a correct solution of such delicate questions under heavy shell-fire.

October 19, 1918. *Fontes.*

When last I referred to the subject we were *definitely* for Italy. To-day Italy is definitely off. If a private commercial venture were run on these lines, I wonder how long it would last! Well, I am glad to have *something definite*, anyway.

329

There is a joke told about the German evacuation of their line in front of Lille. As soon as they had gone, parties of French civilians came over, bringing coffee and other delicacies for our troops, and considerable fraternization took place. Meanwhile, it is said that the Division in support, which for some reason was unaware of the turn of events, was advancing by "short rushes" to the attack!

I think the war will soon be over, don't you?

October 20, 1918 (*Sunday*). *Fontes.*

In a few days we are to take part in a triumphal march through Lille!

Since I first came to France and was put in the trenches in front of La Bassée I always said: "When the entry into Lille takes place, I hope I shall be there": and, to-day, I find myself detailed for it.

October 25, 1918. *Fontes.*

I have been reading Haig's despatch dealing with the March Retreat. It appears we were in the very centre of the German attack, yet the 16th (Irish) Division is not mentioned, and how the General[1] who commanded the 5th Army at that time could have made the omission is difficult to understand. Nevertheless, the report is intensely interesting to me. Ronssoy, Ste Emilie, and Villers Faucon, which stand out so prominently, were the scenes of our fighting on March 21 and 22, as you will remember, and of our counter-attack at midday on the 21st.

Proyart, which also figures with such importance, was the place where we stood on March 26 and 27. What then remained of the Division was lined up a hundred yards in front of the village. There was no other Division so near as ours; yet another Division, and not ours, is mentioned. Perhaps this is because it was by that time so reduced as to be considered negligible. Yet that is no excuse.

I tried to describe to you at the time how our left was in the air, but, till I read Haig's report, I never realized how critical the position really was during those two days.

From the report I now learn that the Army on our left

[1] Gen. Sir Hubert Gough, G.C.M.G., K.C.B., K.C.V.O.

330

—against whose right flank we had stood—had fallen back 5 miles; and when I saw the Germans (as I described to you) filtering past our left, they were not passing through a gap a few hundred yards wide (as I thought), but through a gap five miles wide! Well! all I can say is that the enemy, on that occasion, threw away a golden opportunity, and how any of us survived was a miracle of God.

October 26, 1918. *Lomme.*

We are in the western outskirts of Lille, having come here by train to-day, and I with my Headquarters am billeted in an imposing—almost baronial—house, which looks as if it ought to be in the centre of a big park, instead of lining a suburban street, as it does. The house is empty except for ourselves and some refugees who live in the kitchen. In normal times it is, no doubt, the home of one of the formerly wealthy manufacturers of this great city, whose practice it is to build the palaces in which they themselves live near their works, and among the more humble habitations of their workpeople, which seem almost squalid by comparison.

Till a few days ago, as you know, these parts were in the hands of the enemy. Till three days ago many of the inhabitants had not tasted fresh meat for twelve months, and had depended for their sustenance on the American Relief Committee, whose white bread, I am assured, was often eaten by the enemy, who substituted black bread in its stead.

A fortnight before the enemy withdrew from his line in front of Lille he appears to have sent away the civilian population—presumably that they might not play the spy on him. These returned, when he had gone, to find their houses spoliated and often wantonly damaged by the men who, for over four years, had been their guests;—enforced, if you like, but still their guests.

The great double room in which I write has suffered in this way. Every panel of the tapestry that covered the walls has been clumsily cut out, and the central curtains which divided the room have been torn and stolen from

the gilded rod which supported them. The broken ends
of the latter dangle from the ceiling. Even the tapestry
backs of the chairs have been cut away.

Coming here, we passed through the old battle lines of
1914 to 1917—as well as the recent ones of autumn of this
year:—past Hazebrouck, Strazeele, Bailleul, and Armen-
tiéres. The sun was setting as we stopped at the last-named
place, and the contrast between the wonderful cloud effects
on one side of the train and the sordid ruins on the other
suggested a new version of "Beauty and the Beast."

From Perenchies, where we detrained, we had a 3-mile
march in the dark. The guns in front—on the far side
of Lille—flashed distantly, and reminded us of our
destination.

As we reached the suburbs our band struck up the
"Marseillaise." It was happy inspiration, and I shall never
forget the scene which it provoked. The people came
running from their houses—old and young, men, women,
and children—carrying lamps and candles. They followed
the battalion, clapping and cheering. It was the first time
for over four years that they had heard troops marching
to that tune. And the "Marseillaise" is a fine tune to
march to, and in spite of not being a Frenchman, I feel the
thrill of it each time I hear it.

To-morrow (Sunday) we devote to "polishing up" for
the great "march-through."

October 27, 1918.   *Lomme.*

To-day, after lunching with Dawes I walked with Farebrother and Knox into Lille—on special pass, since the
town is "out of bounds" for troops. The 5th Army,
represented by our Division, which was opposite the city at
the time of the enemy's withdrawal, will make its official
entry to-morrow. Our preliminary walk, therefore, was
especially interesting—to say no more.

It is a novel and unique experience for most of us to
walk into a town, every inhabitant of which looks at us
like a mother at her sons. Yet, that is what happened to
us three to-day. The ladies welcomed us with smiles.

The children were more demonstrative. They rushed at us and seized our hands. They clung on to us till they had completely satisfied their curiosity—a process which took some time, since many of them can scarcely have been fledged when the war started, and they had certainly never seen an Englishman in uniform before. A little red-haired girl followed us like a lap-dog half-way through the town.

The stories I have heard to-day of how these poor people have for over four years been bullied have aroused in me a bitterness which I have never felt before, and which, somehow, we did not get in the trenches. It is extraordinary, now, to think backwards and to picture the grinding down of the inhabitants of this great city behind the German lines and in front of where we stood during all those years.

To-day, the enemy has gone, and in going has given us some curious illustrations of mentality. He did not dare flatten Lille as he has so many other cities; but, in leaving, presumably as an emblem of his hatred, he has used the upstairs rooms of many of the houses as latrines. In a bedroom of a great house of this suburb of great houses where we are billeted, where the Brigadier has his Headquarters, and where I dined to-night, a certain article was found in a bedside cupboard. It had been used for a purpose for which it was not designed, and on the cupboard door was chalked a notice in German which, translated, read something as follows: "Here is a breakfast for an Englishman, made by a good German."

What do you think of that for "Kultur"?

Can you conceive of the most reckless "enfant terrible" of our race descending to so depraved and childish a revenge as this? It is almost impossible to believe that these things have been done with the knowledge or approval of German officers, but it is not the first time I have heard of such things being done, and, whatever may be said, they suggest an appalling lack of discipline in the German Army.

It is pathetic to see the ecstasy of the inhabitants at their delivery, and I may say that for us also it is a treat to find ourselves among people who do not regard us as milch-cows, as I am bound to say is the case throughout most of the rest of Northern France.

Lille, as you know, is (or was) a city of *huge* factories. So far as I know every single machine has either been removed to Germany or systematically destroyed. One owner of a mill told me to-day that when the destroyers came to break up his plant he asked "for what reason?" They said they wanted iron. Yet they did not take away the iron, which still lies where it formerly stood, blasted to bits! Was it pure lust of destruction, or part of a pre-arranged plot to injure France commercially? Probably, a bit of both.

How the people, and particularly the poor, have lived through it all is the marvel. Meat, to-day, costs 16s. 8d. a pound and has been considerably dearer. Butter, I think, has been and still is 41s. 8d. a pound. I took the doctor into the Hôtel de l'Europe, and gave him a cup of tea, without milk, and four tiny biscuits. I had the same. The bill was 8d. 4d., or 9s. 2d. with the tip. I must say I did not resent it. They had not put up the price for me. It is the normal scale in Lille to-day, owing to the depredations of the enemy. I spoke to the old waiter, who had been in Lille throughout the war. He said that two or three days before they went away the Germans came to the "little lady" who owns the hotel and demanded the key of the cellar. They then proceeded to take £2,000 worth of wine, which they carried away.

I could not help remarking to the doctor: "If they value their wine as they value their tea, that would represent about a case of port."

But, joking apart, it is tragic to look upon these people after all they have gone through. They have temporarily become almost like a race of foreign people, so isolated have they been from the rest of their fellow-countrymen. Why, they hardly know the word "Boche"; and de Caux—our Brigade interpreter—tells me that when he entered Lille the first day wearing his French shrapnel helmet, people asked him "was he a pompier (a fireman)?" They had not seen a French picture paper since the war began. Yet they live in a town as important as Manchester!

Apart from the general brutality of the enemy to the people of Lille, I have heard of cases of kindliness on the part of individual Germans. Nevertheless, I do not think, after what they have seen, that our men will be much disposed to leniency in future.

Desmond Young is running the Battalion Headquarters mess. Not long ago he got some whisky from a well-known firm of wine merchants. It was called "9th hole Whisky," and D.Y. was not at all satisfied with it, and wrote very freely and explicitly to say so.

The firm replied to the following effect: "We have received your letter, which we consider utterly uncalled for —not to say offensive. However, having regard to the circumstances under which, no doubt, it was written, we have decided to take no further notice of it, but to include it in our album of curiosities of the war."

This rather annoyed Young, who for a moment was non-plussed as to what to write back.

However, after a little while he brought me his answer. It was as follows:

"Dear Sirs,—

"I advise you also to include in your collection of curiosities of the war a bottle of your 9th hole Whisky."

October 28, 1918.   *Hellemmes-Lille.*

To-day, in glorious sunshine—the first almost for nearly two months—we marched through Lille.

We billeted last night outside the walls, in the western suburb known as Lomme, and this morning, after passing through Lille from west to east by way of the rue Lequeux, the Canteleu gate, the rue de Turenne, Leon Gambetta, Boulevarde de la Liberté and the Rue Nationale, we passed through the Grande Place—where wooden stands draped in red, white and blue had been erected, and where the Army Commander, General Birdwood, stood:—then, following the rue Carnot, we marched on through and out of the city by the Louis XIV gate, where the bridge has been destroyed and the road mined by the enemy.

We are now billeted in an eastern suburb, *en route* again for the line, whose direction is indicated, it being night-time as I write, by the flashes of the guns.

The day has provided a truly wonderful experience. For miles we marched through decorated streets, through immense crowds of cheering citizens. It is a miracle whence, in so short a space of time, so many flags can have been obtained. I hear that the very morning the in-habitants awoke to find the enemy gone women were to be seen running about the streets waving tricolours which had been hidden during the four years and more that Lille has been held in captivity. But whence the "trappings" of to-day? Can this "curiosity of the war" be attributed to the commercial instinct of the enemy? Some people say so:—that far-seeing as he was in war he had not neglected the smallest details incidental to peace, even should the peace not be *his* peace. But I find it difficult to believe that his patriotism, of which there can be no possible doubt, can leave space for such paltriness as is suggested.

Each battalion was headed by its band to-day, ours play-ing English airs as we passed through the suburbs, and bursting into the "Marseillaise" when we reached the more fashionable parts, with electrical effect upon the people crowded on the pavements. We entered the Grande Place to the tune of the "Sambre et Meuse"—the great French marching song; again changing to the "Marseillaise" as we left it.

The ladies and children gave little souvenir flags to the men, but they fought a little shy of me. Perhaps my rather conspicuous position at the head of the battalion, mounted on a charger which, as you know, is about 17 hands high, put them off. But I was determined not to be outdone, so asked one particular lady if she would give me the flag she was carrying "pour mes enfants." This she not only

lid, but rushed into a house and presently brought out a
)unch of little hand-painted paper flags, so that I have
)een able to send one to each of the children and enclose
)ne herewith, also, for yourself.

On our arrival at Hellemmes-Lille, from where I write,
: received a hearty welcome from my host and hostess—
M. and Madame Paul Lefèvre. The former speaks Eng-
ish, having lived for seven years at Bolton, in Lancashire.
He is a cotton spinner, and is manager of a huge English-
owned factory in which the battalion is billeted. The
:actory has been robbed of every particle of its machinery
·—like the rest. To give you an idea of the size of this
:actory I may say that the whole battalion, including the
:ransport (fifty-seven horses plus vehicles and personnel)
:ire quartered in it. Every man has a bed—that is to say
:i wooden trestle—constructed by the enemy; and we are
:ost in space. Each room would hold a battalion. The
:nachinery has gone to Germany, and the floors it occupied
:iave been refitted as barracks—by British prisoners. It
:s good for our comfort during the day or two we shall
:ipend here, but it is hell for the owners!

During the German occupation my host and hostess
·vere separated by way of reprisal. He was sent to Vilmar,
:n Russia, and she to Holzminden, in Germany. Neither
·vas told where the other was. I asked "why?" They
:iaid they did not know. He said he was told it was because
:ie was an Alsace-Lorrainer, and that he was a hostage. No
)ther reason was given. He was kept in a church at Vilmar
:or seven months, with 50 centimetres in width of ground
:o sleep upon; and he is a fat old man, well on in the fifties.
Think of that!

October 29, 1918.   *Hellemmes-Lille.*

This afternoon I again rode into Lille, entering by the
Louis XIV Gate, by which we left the city yesterday. A
great crater yawns in the roadway opposite this gate, and
a wooden trestle made by our engineers replaces the bridge
over the moat, which, like the other bridges leading eastwards, has been blown up by the enemy.

On reaching the town, as I found no horse or wheeled traffic other than some belonging to our army, I sent my horses home and walked, so as to be in company with the inhabitants, every one of whom was on foot. No, not quite. I saw a hearse drawn by what poor Osmund would have called a "skin": indeed, it was less than a skin. It was a skeleton. That was the only horse or vehicle that I saw in Lille to-day, left behind by the Germans after their merciless occupation of the city.

The buildings have suffered very little. A length of street, here and there, or a block of buildings has gone, but whether as the result of the shelling of 1914 or of fires that have taken place since, I do not know.

There is nothing to buy in the shape of food, and little else, in the shops, either in Lille or its suburbs. In fact, the people, or many of them, seem to be half starving. I put out a "feeler" last night, as the result of a suggestion that was made during dinner, to find out whether all ranks of the battalion would like to forgo part of to-day's rations, so as to give it to the inhabitants of the suburb where we are billeted. They jumped at the idea. The proposal I made was that we should give up a quarter of our rations. They wanted to give half, or all. However, as the battalion is due for the line to-morrow, I decided that a quarter was as much as ought to be given, and this has been done, with eminently satisfactory results.

Knox, the doctor, does quite a large practice among the local inhabitants, as we pass from one place to another, most of their own doctors being away at the war, though I will not say that the fact that our treatment is gratuitous is not also an influencing factor. Anyhow, they come in numbers. Influenza is rampant, though perhaps not so much so as elsewhere, and the people find their way to our aid-post. A few days ago a little boy came along who had blown off two of his fingers and damaged an eye, playing with a detonator which he had picked up somewhere. I fear there will be many more such accidents in Northern France and Belgium.

November 1, 1918.   *Froyennes.*

We left Hellemmes-Lille on Wednesday, the 30th, and
after we had left received a rapacious bill from M. Lefèvre
—for coal briquettes alleged to have been consumed during
our stay in his house! As we had provided him and his
wife with provisions the value of which would have bought
any few briquettes we may have burned many times over,
this was an unpleasant surprise. However, after relieving
our minds by writing a letter to tell him what we thought,
the mess president and I decided to tear it up, and not to
dispute his claim. It is a pity the French cannot throw
off the idea that we are sent to them to be fleeced. He
was entitled to claim for our billeting, and would have got
that in any case.

I with my Headquarters officers then stayed one night
at Chereng, where the battalion billeted in what had been
a fine house before the war. I slept in a big bedroom with
a white up-to-date enamelled bath attached; but, as every
single window throughout the entire building had been
broken by aerial-bomb explosions, it was very cold. A
woman servant who was in charge told me that one of the
bombs (unfortunately ours) had blown off her mistress's
leg, and that she was still in hospital.

Last evening, we came up into the front line, the two
other Battalion Commanders of the Brigade and myself
having, the previous day, reconnoitred the positions we are
to occupy. These are just outside Tournai, which is still
held by the enemy, and in front of the village of Froyennes.

It is really becoming a very interesting—not to say extraordinary—war. The country is well built over and both
the enemy and our own outposts occupy houses, sometimes
not more than a couple of hundred yards apart, from the
windows of which they furtively watch one another's movements, and observe the effect of the hurricane trench-mortar
bombardments in which we both occasionally indulge. I
have been having one this afternoon.

In parenthesis, I may say that it is a style of warfare which
provides plenty of incident, and gives considerable scope

to the adventurously inclined since without actually going into a house it is impossible to find out whether it is, or is not, occupied by the enemy. It seems to suit Desmond Young. When I went my rounds this morning I found him having just advanced one of the posts across a street. He had not been satisfied with the field of fire from the position we had taken over from the outgoing battalion, and had himself crossed over first and crept into the house opposite. He did not feel very happy when the first thing he saw at the top of the stairs was a German helmet. In fact, he said that his heart stood still. But he found it was a false alarm. The house was empty.

In another house a curtain was reported by a sentry to be moving in a suspicious manner. When I arrived on the scene a lively discussion was going on about it. A few minutes later, I heard a hammering sound. It was Young banging at the door of the house with a pick-axe. He got into this house, too, to find it empty, though he was nearly killed by a sniper in the garden, who saw him through the window. He certainly deserves to get something worth having out of this war.

In many of the houses the civilians are still living, sleeping in the cellars, and in one part where the River Scheldt separates the lines, our advanced Divisional party when they first arrived found people actually occupying houses in the space intervening between the enemy and ourselves —in short, in Noman's Land! An order has now been issued prohibiting civilians from remaining within 500 yards of the firing line, though I must confess it is being very tardily obeyed. What do you think of that for up-to-date warfare?

For the most part the houses are not seriously damaged so far, and though the necessity of having to consider such matters is naturally cramping to one's style in war, it is our aim and intention to save them, if possible; and if the enemy also will abstain (which is unlike him), or will retire (which looks very probable), we may succeed in doing so.

It is indeed what you might call "Opéra bouffe" warfare. We are waging it amid charming scenery—the prettiest I have seen in Belgium:—in a rich land of opulent houses and châteaux and great schools and convents; and, incidentally, I may say that every movement we make is observed by the enemy from Mont St. Aubert—a remarkable hill, crowned by a church steeple, that dominates the surrounding country so completely that without going indoors, or behind a wall or hedge, it is practically impossible to get out of sight of it.

My Headquarters are in what was a luxurious house till the tide of battle swept over it, and its owner deserted it, with very pleasant grounds and an imposing entrance hall of white marble. The bedrooms, however, offer no attraction. They have been ransacked and looted in most wanton fashion, before his retirement, by the enemy, who in his childish hate has gone to the extent of tearing open the mattresses, the mohair and down from which, with other rubbish, lie deep upon the floors. But, apart from this, these upper rooms are unattractive, since there is a good deal of shelling at nights, and we eschew the marble hall and the dining "salon" and sleep humbly in the cellar.

The sang-froid of the villagers who have remained is extraordinary. They do not even send away their children, which rather suggests the courage of ignorance, and it is horrifying to see the poor little things playing about, unconscious of the dangers threatening them. It is all so unnecessary. Apart from the "crump" there is a frequent hail of "bits" from the anti-aircraft shells, besides the constant possibility of a bullet fired at or from an aeroplane. Yet not a woman or child has any protection, except the cellar. They go about with bare heads and without gas masks. Yesterday, as my Adjutant (Davenport) and I arrived opposite our new Headquarters, a 5·9-inch shell greeted us, landing in a ploughed field, about 40 yards away. Expecting a second shell we stepped behind a cottage. A woman came out to have a look. I said:

"Ne serait il pas plus sauf pour vous dans la cave." To which she replied: "Et pourquoi pas pour vous?"

As I have said, we are now engaged in "comic opera" warfare. One of my front line Company Commanders has his Headquarters in a château by a lake, surrounded by a green wooded park. Its name is the Château Beauregard. The daughter of the house, Countess Thérèse de Germiny —as charming as her château—is still in residence, her father being dead and her brothers at the war. She is a sort of Lady Bountiful to a large number of villagers, who have congregated and live with her in the cellars. It is inspiring to see this wonderful woman, determined to hang on, as she said to-day, unless or until the evacuation of the village is ordered. Each evening, she and her protégées hold a service in a cellar, while the shells fall in the park and lake, and the enemy (according to his custom as night falls) traverses her shrubberies with machine-guns.

I found her without any protection against gas, so have had my gas sergeant and pioneers at work to-day, making one of her cellars gas-proof; and we have also removed some of the occupants of the cellar, who were down with influenza.

A few minutes' walk from the Countess's château, towards the firing line, is another—a great pretentious and rather grotesque white building—in which Prince Ruprecht of Bavaria, Commander of the German 4th Army Corps, had his headquarters for two years. I have been all over it this afternoon and seen the rooms in which he dined and slept, and the bath in which he washed, till a fortnight or three weeks ago. The building has been pierced several times lately by shells, but on the whole is in good condition.

I dreamed last night that there was an armistice and was woken by the sound of shells.

November 2, 1918.   *Froyennes.*

Last night was very noisy—a night of reciprocal hate; with the result that early this morning the civilians were at last beginning to stream back, pushing hand-carts, carrying bundles, and leading children by the hand. And a good thing too, since many of them—so I am assured by the Countess—are spies. On one hand-cart I saw a baby, two years old or less, which had come practically from the line of outposts. Think of it! After a night, too, that even the old stagers had found distinctly hot.

In the course of my rounds to-day, accompanied by Corporal Douglas, my scout N.C.O.—who, by the way, has just been awarded the D.C.M.—I visited the Countess. Two shells hit her château early this morning, one entering the smoking-room and the other a bedroom above. Both rooms are gutted.

I went down to the cellars to see her and was met with the same smile as yesterday. I asked her when she was going to leave. She said she thought she had better do so to-morrow; not that she feared; but she felt herself superfluous. I advised her strongly, as I had already advised many other women, to go at once—"just for a week or a fortnight, when perhaps the enemy will have retired." I then arranged for a few of my men to carry the best of her furniture into the cellars, where it would be safe from shell-fire.

On the front doorstep, as I was leaving, I met an old woman leading a baby. I asked her why she didn't take the child away. She said she was doing so, but did not explain why she had not done so before. It is inexplicable to me. I can understand a woman clinging to her home for fear it may be pilfered, but I cannot understand her risking her children's lives in a jerry-built cottage, or even in the cellars of a château, when it is possible to get them away. Do they not care for their children? or are they just ignorant of the power of shell-fire or the effect of gas?— against which latter neither they nor their Government on their behalf appear to have made the smallest provision.

I went on to Prince Ruprecht's white château, in the stables of which I have an advanced platoon. This château, like the Countess's, suffered considerably from shell-fire last night. Then, after visiting the outposts, I returned towards Froyennes.

As I was about to visit the support Company Head-quarters in the village I noticed a house with a big fresh shell-hole in the wall, through which some very clean-looking women were shovelling brick-dust. I was rather impressed to see women so punctilious at such a time, so I knocked at the front door and walked in. I found myself in a convent. Just inside the doorway stood a group of nuns. I made some remark about the shell-hole, and was eagerly invited in "to see." They seemed quite delighted that anyone should take an interest in their welfare. Indeed, though it is difficult to believe, they seem to have been left to their fate by whoever the male Belgian authorities were, either in the village or behind it, who were responsible for their safety.

The room I was taken to was the usual convent "parlour" —that is to say what was left of it—with the usual crucifix and the holy pictures: but again I was struck by the fact that this room, though wrecked, was being perfectly swept up, by perfectly clean and starched women, just as you see them in Kensington Square. I was introduced to the Reverend Mother and soon found myself engaged in animated conversation with the nuns, in my appalling French. One of them produced the nosecap of the shell that had done the deed. I said, by way of sheepish con-versation, that it would make a good souvenir. She made a face and said: "C'est Boche," and added that "if it had been one of ours it would have been different"—which I thought was very nicely put.

Then she went on to explain that this was a hospital. You know how bad my French is. All I could see was that a shell had burst on their ground-floor—luckily a shell with an instantaneous fuse, which therefore had not pene-trated the cellar. But I asked her, lamely: "Avez vous des malades, donc?" to which she replied in French: "Come and see."

The Reverend Mother and this nun then led me down into the cellar, and as we reached the entrance the Reverend Mother said: "N'est'ce pas une scéne triste?" And I

looked and saw what I think was the most pathetic sight I
have ever looked upon. There were two cellars, end on
end, lit up by an oil lamp, and in both were packed beds, all
occupied, and in the narrow spaces between the beds were
the sitting "malades."

Directly I entered, the eyes of all lit up as if some deliverer
had come. I was introduced, and they all murmured
"Mon Colonel!" "Bon jour," etc., etc. It was a shock
to me. I was in a hospital for dying nuns. Scarcely one
of them could have been less than seventy, and many must
have been much older. There were two that spoke English.
One had been for some years in a convent at Highgate.
She kept saying, in stilted English: "You will see that
we are in a very unsatisfactory situation."

Another, at the far end of the second cellar, who they
told me had not left her bed for over five years, also knew
a good deal of English and held her thin hand above her
bed for me to shake, calling out over and over again,
"Thank you," "Thank you." I should have broken down
if I had tried to talk much to them. I asked how many
they were. They replied, forty-four. I promised to try
and get ambulances to take them away, and I will do so,
if it is possible, and I hope that no more shells may hit their
cellar in the meantime.

I can still hear their voices as I left them, saying (I cannot
repeat the French): "You will do what you can for us,
won't you; we are in such distress." And the nun from
Highgate, in English: "You see that we are in a very
unsatisfactory situation."

P.S. It is now nearly a quarter to midnight, and I have
already—an hour and a half ago—got a promise of
ambulances sufficient to carry away eight lying-down cases
during this night, and eight more to-morrow morning.
The remainder I will see away somehow, but transport is
very scarce, and those that can walk will probably have to
walk some miles.

Is it not tragic to think of those poor old saints herded
together in their dreary dungeon, with the shells bursting

around them—the one this morning not more than 3 yards above their heads? It has done me good to see them, and I hope the result will be that they will get away.

You should have seen them in their beds:—snow-white linen and starched night-caps, so beautifully washed; as if there wasn't a war within a hundred miles.

My casualties during the night were luckily only twelve, two of whom were killed.

November 3, 1918.   *Froyennes*.

The forty-four aged nuns were got away safely this morning, most by motor ambulance, but some on our battalion stretchers. The latter, loaded with this most unusual freight, each perched on the shoulders of four English soldiers, presented an incongruous sight. How lucky that I noticed the shell-hole in the wall! The Reverend Mother showed her gratitude by leaving us her chickens and rabbits, so to-night the battalion will feed well.

In the course of my rounds this afternoon I still found civilians near the firing line. At the stable of Prince Ruprecht's white château the enemy had been trench-mortaring vigorously with heavy stuff, and one of my men had been killed in the field in front. Yet, the family that lived there, which included several small children, had not gone. They were, however, dressed up to go, in their best clothes, and conspicuous among them was a tiny boy in a vermilion suit.

At last the Belgian authorities are taking steps to evacuate these villages, and two interpreters have belatedly arrived to-day to make the necessary arrangements—or rather, I should say, to ask us to make the necessary arrangements. In consequence, a big cellar at my Headquarters is to-night crowded with a herd of unhappy people, composed in part of a few old and crippled men, but chiefly of women and children. I have just been among them. They look very neglected and dishevelled and hungry, but very patient, and the mother of a small tired child to whom I spoke even forgot her troubles so much as to give it a little motherly lecture as to how to reply politely to a stranger. Our

346

soldiers were feeding the crowd out of their rations. The great number of the children—many under two years of age—is appalling. Isn't it horrible? They may, and I hope they will, get safely away; but why have they been left so long? It is a mistake, too, to move them after dark, since the enemy artillery has a nasty way of searching the roads at night for transport.

The Countess and her protégées left to-day. I am arranging to have her luggage taken out, and also that of a poor old woman who is stopping at my Headquarters to-night—in deathly anxiety lest she should lose her entire worldly belongings, which are packed on a hand-barrow near the firing line—too heavy for her to move. It would all be rather humorous, if it were not so tragic.

The Countess's château had received another direct hit when I visited it to-day, which had gutted the drawing-room.

November 5, 1918.   *Hardie-Planque Farm, Cornet.*

We are in reserve, having been relieved from the line last night. The last four days have been extraordinarily interesting and make me look forward to the line again. Yet, it is anxious work, and very tiring. From moment to moment you don't quite know where you are, and which houses are and which are not occupied by the enemy. There was a lot of trench-mortaring, a lot of machine-gun fire, and occasionally heavy enemy bombardment.

The enemy keeps his back against the wall—in the shape of Tournai, which he well knows we shall not shell, and where therefore he is more or less immune, at least from our artillery. His own hands are not tied by any such considerations. Consequently, we must be ever on the alert, probing here and there, night and day, to find out what he is doing;—whether he is retreating, or, on the contrary, is offensively inclined; since we should look just as foolish if he got away without our knowing it, as if he succeeded in capturing a post.

Yesterday morning, after reporting as the result of the night's patrolling that the enemy was still occupying his

347

normal positions, I was rung up from Divisional Headquarters, some miles behind, and told that everybody but
myself thought the enemy had gone.

I had been up in the line till nearly 2 a.m., but I went up
again. I found one of my advanced posts in the process
of being severely hammered with "pine-apple" darts and
by heavy trench mortars which, as you know, have a range
of only a few hundred yards and therefore are proof positive
that the enemy is near. The men of another post I found
sniping merrily at the German machine-gunners opposed
to them, some of whom were occasionally showing themselves on a railway embankment by the river. No, the
enemy had not gone away yet, so I repeated my report of
the early morning—that the positions were normal.

During the afternoon I was visited at my Headquarters
by Colonel Montgomery, G.S.O. (1) of the Division. He
seemed a little nettled that the Germans should still be there,
so decided was he that they ought to have gone. However,
after dark, the Germans themselves once more demonstrated
their bad taste, and at the same time their presence, by
raiding one of our posts. They did it with determination,
too, employing a heavy covering artillery barrage.

It so happened that the time chosen for this raid was
shortly after the relief of my battalion by the 17th London
Regiment, to whose lot, therefore, it fell to repel it. I
with my Second in Command, Adjutant and Doctor, had
got back about half a mile at the time, the battalion having
preceded us. So our walk to this village was considerably
enlivened.

My new Headquarters are at Cornet, in a quaint old
farmhouse known as Hardie-Planque, and built in 1556.
The women living in it are full of the ghost stories which
are attached to it. It originally belonged, they say, to a
man who sold his soul to the devil, that he might possess
a château. So the devil built him this house in twelve
hours; and then came through a hole in the roof to claim
his victim's soul. If new tiles are put on the roof they fall
off, pulled away, it is believed, by the devil, that his means

of entry may remain; but I may add—parenthetically—that the roof is unusually steep.

One of my officers has gone off to-day to locate the new address of our forty-four nuns, for, though their goats and chickens and rabbits would have starved if we had not eaten some and taken charge of the remainder, we wish to send the Reverend Mother a contribution, and if you or any of your friends would like to add to it, you will receive much gratitude, I am sure. They have not much left.

We have the goats safe at our transport lines, where they are being fed and kept in trust. I saw them this afternoon, thoroughly enjoying themselves, and they are beauties.

November 7, 1918. *Hardie-Planque Farm, Cornet.*

To-day it looks as though we may have peace within a few hours! So near does it seem that we have a sweepstake on the hour when hostilities shall cease! In the meantime, the enemy continues to crash away, night and day, and so do our people, but nothing falls near here.

How strange it will be when the fighting stops. I am already beginning to look back upon the last $4\frac{1}{4}$ years as a sort of dream, in which there outstands a single tall figure in black:—always the last to have been seen by me when leaving for the war, and the first on coming home for leave. I will leave you to guess whose is that faithful, patient figure.

November 10, 1918 (*Sunday*). *Barberie.*

Yesterday morning the enemy was reported actually to have gone back, and it was not long before we received orders to move forward again to Froyennes. I spent the afternoon with Major Yencken, a gunner officer, who is temporarily attached to the battalion, exploring the positions of the machine-guns which had been opposed to us a few days before, when we were in the line in front of the village, and before Tournai.

It is always interesting to learn for certain to what extent the positions of the enemy posts as reported by one's patrols have been accurate or the reverse, and it was gratifying to find these exactly where we expected.

We visited the shell of a building which stood some 200

or 300 yards in front of our outpost line, and which had always been a source of interest because smoke—which it was thought might come from a German field kitchen—issued continually from it. This smoke was so persistent that it was equally probable that it came from some smouldering refuse, but as I knew that the enemy had machine-guns in the immediate vicinity, I had thought it best to give the ruin the benefit of the doubt, and so had had it subjected by Jones—the Stokes Mortar Officer—to a sudden, violent, and very efficient bombardment.

Upon examination yesterday this ruin turned out to have been an ecclesiastical printing establishment. The smoke, which was still rising, came from some smouldering piles of sacred literature and music.

We passed on into the outskirts of Tournai. The streets were already decorated with Belgian flags. (Where *do* they get these flags from?) We had a look at the ancient bridge, which was intact (but well wired by the enemy), and at other bridges which the Germans had destroyed, and at one or two commemorative statues, which—whatever their artistic merit may have been—were certainly inoffensive from a military point of view, and yet had been completely and wantonly broken to bits. Our sappers were busy throwing pontoons and other temporary bridges across the Scheldt, and the advanced troops were already hurrying across the river.

As we passed Prince Ruprecht's château on our return to Froyennes we found six men of the Brigade lying there. They had been killed while on patrol duty;—the last of the Division, and perhaps almost of the Army, to be killed in the war. They belonged to the 17th London Regiment.

At 7.15 this morning the battalion marched forward again. I had a slight fever and slept till about nine o'clock. Captain Kilner, one of my Company Commanders, who had been to Lille to take our contribution to the forty-four nuns, returned during the morning, and he and I rode forward to rejoin the battalion.

The battalion, according to orders, had marched round

Tournai, to the north, avoiding the town. To save time, Kilner and I decided to ride through it. I don't mind also saying that we had a desire to see Tournai. As we reached the boundary of the inner town we were stopped by a sentry and asked for "passes." A very pleasant officer then came up and said he was sorry but we could not go on. He indicated how—at the expense of considerable trouble and delay—passes might be obtained, and we turned off with the intention of following his directions. However, as we came to the next sentry post it happened that a Company of machine-gunners was passing into the town. Thought I to myself, "Why should we be obliged to have passes, and on what grounds should the Brigade that garrisons this town be allowed to put it out of bounds to other troops and so keep all the fun to themselves?" So Kilner and I joined on to the passing Company, and entered Tournai as machine-gunners.

Being Sunday, all the people were in the streets and squares, dressed in their best clothes, and they gave us a great reception. Compared to this, we were comparatively unwanted when we marched through Lille. Here, we were quite fresh from the never never land, and there was not a man we met who did not take off his hat to us, or a woman who did not give us her sweetest smile. Charming ladies and children squandered flags and flowers upon us. We could have collected enough to stock a shop.

November 12, 1918. *Officers' Club (Hôtel Royal), Lille.*

Yesterday, we were to have pushed on and captured another town—Ath—which would have been a bloodless victory, since the enemy was retreating so fast that it was difficult to keep pace with him; and, since my battalion had been detailed as advanced guard, the day would unquestionably have provided plenty of amusement. A screen of cavalry (19th Hussars) was to have advanced in front of us, and this in itself would have been a novel experience, being the first time, I imagine, since 1914, that such a thing has been possible in the war—I mean, of course, on the Western Front.

However, a stop was put to the proceedings by the signing of the Armistice, which took place in the morning, as you know, and my orders were countermanded, and the battalion sent to La Tombe. As we marched away the band played a tune well known to the men, who are accustomed to accompany it with the following words:

> When this ruddy war is over,
> Oh! how happy I shall be!

This, no doubt, was very appropriate, but nevertheless, what a thousand pities that we should have had to draw off at such a moment—just as we had the enemy cold!

The Germans in retiring had, as usual, mined the roads, which were blocked at intervals by huge yawning craters. Our sappers had been very skilful in spotting and disconnecting the unexploded mines, many of which we passed over, and I saw only one go off behind us, and that long after we had passed it.

The railways had, of course, all been torn up;—very artistically too, since this is a kind of work at which our enemy excels. For example, alongside the road by which we marched a railway ran parallel. Here the metals had been ripped from the sleepers, in lengths of some hundreds of yards, and dragged on to the road, along which we found them zigzagging like gigantic serpents. This device, I may say, caused us very little inconvenience, though, as a feat of jugglery, I think it deserves high merit, and reflects great credit on the ingenuity of the people who contrived it. It gave us plenty to talk about, anyhow, and even now I do not feel quite certain how it was done, though there is little doubt but that a heavy locomotive, tearing away the track behind it, was the principal instrument. The German neglects nothing that can be of the smallest use in his scheme of war. I have even seen iron bedsteads, lately, used as frameworks for his barbed wire entanglements.

I woke up again, yesterday, with a temperature, and, as the doctor thought I might be sickening for influenza, he suggested a rest for a few days. So, in the evening, I was

aken in an ambulance to a hospital in the Rue Jean Sans
Peur, Lille. I had eaten nothing for twenty-four hours.
But when I reached the hospital, and found myself in a long
gloomy dormitory with the man in the next bed in delirium,
I felt I was not bad enough for that. It seemed probable
that even if I had not already got influenza I soon should
have it in such surroundings. So I escaped, and got a
comfortable bedroom, with a bath, at the Officers' Club
at the Hôtel Royal, where I slept, and from where I
write.

November 13, 1918.   140 *Brigade H.Q., La Tombe.*

I lorry-jumped to this place to-day, where General
Kennedy has his Headquarters, and has invited me to stay.
It is a suburb of Tournai.

From all I have heard from the French and the Belgians
in the liberated territory through which we have passed—
and when they spoke to me they had not had time to have
been "coached"—our British prisoners must have been
treated very badly.

The Countess de Germiny used surreptitiously to give
them potatoes and other vegetables, but they used also to
pick up rotting cabbages or anything that lay about, and
many people were punished for giving them food. A
woman told me yesterday that a friend of hers had been
imprisoned for eight days for giving food to one of them.
Another story I have been told is of one of our prisoners,
to whom, seeing that he was starving, a girl gave a cabbage.
On this occasion the prisoner was arrested, on a charge of
looting!

The spectacle of the Kaiser and his son flying to Holland,
—after having outraged the world for $4\frac{1}{4}$ years—is the most
humiliating in history, I should think.

November 15, 1918.   *La Tombe.*

Yesterday morning I was sent for by the Major-General
to explain a report—undeniably justified—which he had
received, complaining about my desertion from the hospital
in the Rue Jean Sans Peur. He was very nice about it,
and forgave me.

353   A A

In the afternoon I rode to the top of Mont St. Aubert. It is one of those hills typical of Belgium—like Kemmel, or Mont des Cats, or Monts Noir and Rouge; and, like the Mont des Cats, is capped by a Church.

When we were before Tournai, ten days ago, this wonderful point of vantage was, as I told you, in the hands of the enemy. His artillery observers sat in the point of the steeple, well above the bell, and watched our positions, well knowing from their experience of that period of the war that we should not shell the church. I climbed up into this observation post. The chairs the observers had sat on were still in place in front of the loopholes. It was almost like being in an aeroplane, so steeply and suddenly does the hill rise from the surrounding plain, and so extensive is the view. In front—most conspicuously—stood the great school where one of my posts had been, and to the left, under direct observation through an avenue between the trees, was the Countess's red château.

This morning I attended a "Te Deum" at the Cathedral in thanksgiving for the victory. The Bishop of Tournai officiated, assisted by numerous clergy. The Army Commander, General Birdwood, was there, and he and all the British officers were given seats in the centre of the nave, close up to the altar. The Belgian and our own National Anthems were played, and then, as we British passed out along the length of the Cathedral, the service being ended, the huge congregation which packed the aisles, the galleries, and the organ loft, stood, waving their hats and their handkerchiefs, while "God save the King" was played a second time.

Afterwards, I rode on to call upon Countess Thérèse de Germiny, who had returned to her château immediately the enemy went. She was away in Tournai, but, I am sorry to say, had not found the château as she left it. Some one or other has gone through it since we were relieved, though, fortunately, all the best furniture, which my men had stored in the cellars, was intact.

As for the rest, I am informed that, when she discovered

rhat had happened, she just shrugged her shoulders and
iid "that does not matter. It is a small price to pay for
ich great victories."

Hundreds of refugees and prisoners of war are straggling
ack into Tournai all day long, the latter, after having been
sed to drag the enemy's transport during his last hurried
etreat, having either escaped in the general turmoil, or
een turned loose to find their own way home.

November 16, 1918. *Leuze.*

This morning I again rode round the line of posts of
en days ago—the line of the last stand of the enemy before
is final retirement.

On the right bank of the Scheldt, just in front of the
reat school building, there is a German military cemetery.
The Germans have been much more decorative in these
matters than we. In the middle is an eagle of stone, on
a high pedestal, and at the heads of some of the graves are
carved memorials, also in stone. Even the wooden crosses
are more elaborate than we make them. Sandwiched in
between the German graves, here and there, is an English
grave. Altogether, I saw three, and the name on one was
Fielding—a private of the South Wales Borderers. The
crosses over these English graves are precisely the same as
those on either side of them. But—have I told you this
before?—there is always a distinction between a dead
German and a dead Englishman. The former "rests in
God" (Ruht in Gott); the latter just "rests" (Hier ruht ein
Englander)!

I rode on and called at the Château Beauregard. Mlle
de Germiny was out when I arrived, and I wandered about
the château, looking for her. Just as I was going away I
met her on the doorstep, coming in. She took me round
the rooms and showed me the damage of the shells. She
said she had attended the "Te Deum" at the Cathedral in
Tournai yesterday, and had seen me from the gallery. I
asked her if she would hand on the contribution you are
sending for the poor old nuns, and this she has promised
to do.

In the afternoon I rejoined the battalion at Leuze, 12 miles from Tournai along the Brussels road, and truly glad I am to be with them again. My Headquarters are in a château, belonging to a Baron de Serjeanet. The owner is very old but has a fine spirit. For 4¼ years he has chafed under the Germans. When they first came he asked them to leave him just two rooms to live in, adding that if they would do this they might do as they pleased with the rest. They did. They used nearly all his furniture for firewood, and billeted troops in the château; and Desmond Young tells me that, when he took over, the filth was so appalling that it required a Company of men for two days to clean it out.

I was much touched on arrival to find a room with a spacious view, cleaned and carpeted and furnished for me, and made cheery by a bright red fire. This was the work of my officers. It was like getting home again. When I came down to dinner I found that the baron had sent a present of three bottles of old Burgundy that he had managed to hide from the enemy by burying it;—not an easy thing to do since organized search parties had been constantly on the alert for buried treasure. In Tournai, I am told, a percentage on anything found was paid to the discoverer! But, to return to the Burgundy. The baron said it was worth 25s. to 30s. a bottle, and I am sure he did not exaggerate. It was better than any Burgundy any of us had ever tasted before.

We are on the trunk road to Brussels, and, tramping along this road, from the direction of Germany, we see an almost continuous stream of refugees and men and women deported by the enemy, thousand upon thousand. This has been going on for practically a week now. They push or pull hand-carts, or are harnessed to horse carts and even wagons, which are loaded with their belongings, and all are profusely decorated with the flags of the Allies.

And every motor lorry and indeed every vehicle belonging to our army, going westwards, is also packed to its utmost capacity with Belgians returning to their homes.

November 17, 1918 (*Sunday*).   *Leuze.*

Yes, as you say, the sudden and complete collapse of the Germans is almost bewildering. The feeling among the soldiers here—I speak for those whose duty it has been to do the fighting—was, on November 11, rather one of awe and inability to appreciate the great relief that had so suddenly come to them. There was no visible change in their demeanour. I do not think many—if any—felt much inclined for jubilation, though I will not do them the injustice of saying that had they had the opportunity they would have failed to take advantage of it.

As for the French of Lille and the Belgians of Tournai, the signing of the Armistice meant nothing to them. Peace was proclaimed—so far as they were concerned—on the day the enemy withdrew, and our patrols entered their cities. I cannot help hoping that in the excitement at home no English man or woman has failed to feel humbled by these terrific events, or has forgotten to give proper thanks for the Empire's wonderful escape—indeed, for the escape of all humanity: And I hope that the children—for whom, most of all, the war has been fought, however little they understand these things to-day—may have had the duty of thanksgiving impressed upon them; not just to say 'thank you" once in their prayers, but each morning and evening, again and again, for years to come.

As the padre said to-day: "England has won this tremendous victory after trying for four years to lose the war."

God knows how true that saying is!

Think of the strikes at home, and the bickerings, and the muddles!

P.S. It will probably be asked why our advancing army was called off just as it was on the verge of finally routing the enemy.

I have myself supposed the reason to have been that, as we advanced, we were, each day, putting so many more miles of destroyed roads and railways between our fighting troops and our sources of supply. The German communications were intact, and, had we been lured on a sufficient

357

distance from our base, and then given battle, we might have had a hard nut to crack. However, here is Marshal Foch's own explanation as stated on the occasion of his visit to our Fifth Army Headquarters on the 15th November:

"I have come to offer my congratulations and thanks to you and to the men of your Army for the great works achieved and the glorious results obtained in the last few days. We have won the victory by our tenacity and by the firm resolve of every man to continue fighting until victory was assured. Some of your Divisions were tired Divisions who had fought in great battles on other parts of the front, but, under your leadership they never faltered. They advanced at the side of your fit men. Your soldiers continued to march when they were exhausted, and they fought, and fought well, when they were worn out. It is with such indomitable will that the war has been won. At the moment of ceasing hostilities the enemy troops were demoralized and disorganized, and their lines of communication were in a state of chaos. Had we continued the war for another fortnight we might have won a most wonderful and complete military victory. But it would have been inhuman to risk the life of one of our soldiers unnecessarily. The Germans asked for an armistice—we renounced the certainty of further military glory and gave it to them. I am deeply sensible of the fact that Lille was delivered without damage to the town, and I am grateful for the help given so generously to the inhabitants. This time my visit is short, but I intend to come back. I want to see your men, and I want to speak to them of the glorious deeds that the British Army has achieved."

November 22, 1918.   *Palace Hotel, Brussels.*

To-day, thanks to Major Porteous—Divisional Signals Officer—who provided a car, I was able to motor to Brussels, to search for news of Wilfrid.[1] Porteous himself, and Knox, my American doctor, came with me.

[1] Capt. Wilfrid Stanislaus Stapleton-Bretherton, Royal Fusiliers, the writer's brother-in-law, who was reported "missing" at Gheluveldt on November 8, 1914.

The stream of returning refugees, trekking westwards, still continues, though it is much thinner than it was. Many of them that are bound for the devastated country west of Lille, I fear, are doomed to bitter disappointment. If they can trace even the foundations of their homes they will be fortunate.

As we neared Brussels, having got beyond the area where our troops are known, the inhabitants became more and more enthusiastic. Triumphal arches with messages of welcome had been thrown up, beneath which we passed to the cheers of the villagers. Children held paper streamers across the road, which caught up in the car as we dashed through, and continued the journey with us, fluttering behind.

In Brussels we found all wheeled traffic suspended and the whole population in the streets. King Albert, accompanied by British troops, had this day re-entered the town for the first time after $4\frac{1}{4}$ years of German occupation.

I have never seen Brussels properly before. To-day, in the sunshine, with every monument and building extravagantly decorated with the Belgian colours, it looked more gay than anything I have ever seen. The German occupation seems to have left the place intact, so much so that even the luxuries are obtainable, though at prices so high that it is like eating and drinking gold to partake of them.

We got out of our car in front of the Palace and mixed with the crowd, to whom we immediately became objects of great curiosity. Women and men—mostly women—bunched around us, discussing our nationality and our general appearance, and I must say that their comments were very friendly, and even flattering. They wondered if we were Belgian, or American, or British. Evidently, they did not know even their own soldiers by sight, not having seen them since Belgium adopted the khaki uniform.

I explained that I was English, and at once a lady of the crowd called out, "So am I." She was governess in a Belgian family. She begged us to come and have lunch with her "family," but presently discovered that in her enthusiasm at this reunion with her fellow-countrymen she had lost her "charge." So she had to chase off after the child, though she asked that we would not move till she came back again. We got involved in further conversation with the crowd, every member of which seemed anxious to speak to us: The ladies were particularly ingratiating.

"The Germans hate the Belgians: they hate the French: they hate the Americans":—"mais, ils détestent les Anglais" —said one of our admirers.

"C'est un honneur," agreed the crowd.

An attractive lady, who said she came from Knocke, fed us with sweets from a paper bag. It was all very interesting and remarkable. After some time the King of the Belgians and General Birdwood came out through the Palace gates. I also saw Prince Albert, in R.A.F. uniform. He is a typical clean-looking English boy.

As the evening advanced the crowds started dancing. Old and young together joined in an extravagant orgy of innocent joy such as can seldom if ever have been surpassed. It continued half the night. Parties, led by a few fiddlers, or indeed by any kind of instrument, or none at all; sometimes, each successive file with his or her hands on the hips of the person in front; sometimes, in ranks—fifteen or sixteen abreast—arm in arm; by hundreds and thousands, they danced along the streets—which were brilliantly lighted for the first time for $4\frac{1}{4}$ years—singing the patriotic songs of Belgium. I simply cannot describe it. It was pathetic. It was grand. I have never seen anything like it before, and I am sure I shall never do so again. It was as if a million or more of schoolboys and girls, after $4\frac{1}{4}$ years of dreary term, had suddenly been turned loose and told to enjoy themselves. As for ourselves, each minute as we were recognized the shout went up: "Vivent les Anglais!" or "Vivent les Americains!" or "Vivent les Alliés!"—just as it struck the crowd. But it was generally "Vivent les Anglais!" That was the cry which seemed to come most readily from them.

There were a good many allied prisoners of war roaming

about the streets. The Germans seem to have just turned them loose and told them to "cut along home." And I daresay they would prefer it that way, since they are in a friendly country, rather than be slowly passed back in a more formal way, through "organized channels" involving much red-tape. I know I should.

I stopped three of our own this evening, while I was walking out with the doctor. They were dressed in the grotesque costume with which the enemy has provided them:—black coat with khaki armlet; black—rather baggy —trousers with a broad reddish stripe down the side; and any sort of cap. At once, as has been the case to-day each time I have halted or asked a question (which every one within earshot tries to answer at the same time), a crowd collected. I asked the men if they had any money. They said: "Not at the moment, but they had been told where they could draw some pay to-morrow." So the doctor and I gave them some to carry on with, and the crowd cheered and yelled, "Vivent les Anglais!" which was embarrassing, though well meant. And a gentleman and lady in the crowd invited us to stop the night at their house.

I saw Cardinal Mercier receive a great ovation as he passed through the streets, and a Belgian interpreter—who wore our Military Cross and D.C.M.—came up and introduced his wife to us at the restaurant where we dined. He had just met her for the first time for four years, he said, and she had been imprisoned by the Germans, on one pretext or another, three times during the interval.

I doubt if any officer or man of the Allied armies who has had the luck to be in Brussels to-day has escaped being kissed by at least some of its fair inhabitants.

November 23, 1918.   *Palace Hotel, Brussels.*

This morning I called upon the British Minister, Sir Francis Villiers, at the Legation, which has just reopened. Mr. Gahan, the English Chaplain, was there. We spoke about Nurse Edith Cavell, whom as you will remember, Mr. Gahan attended, and I asked him if she had actually received the brutal treatment that has been described. He said,

"No"—"that was invented by certain of the journalists."
I asked if she had received a fair trial. He replied that she
had. He went on to say that she herself was quite content
with her sentence, and felt no resentment on account of
it. She had expected no other result. The surprising
thing, he said, was that the Germans had left her alone so
long as they did—that she was not arrested earlier for
helping Allied soldiers to escape.

In those early days of the war, he said, the people of
Brussels were very amateurish and did all kinds of reckless
things, not knowing the risks they ran. They were inclined
to look upon the Germans as slow-witted and easily fooled.
Edith Cavell was to a large extent betrayed by the loose,
boastful talk of the people she had helped to get away.
Some Belgians, too, threw her over at the last, and she was
left to bear alone the full brunt of a military offence which
in reality had been shared by many others. But it had
been agreed upon beforehand that it should be so.

Mr. Gahan added that more responsibility had been
placed upon her shoulders by her friends than any woman
should have been allowed to bear. Indeed, after she had
received her sentence, she told him she was relieved that
it was over.

The sentence was carried out quietly and decently in the
early morning. She was accompanied by the German
Chaplain—a good man, he said—and she bore it without
a flinch.

As I returned towards my hotel later in the day I passed
the Cathedral door. It was two o'clock, and the King and
Queen were arriving to attend a service in thanksgiving for
the deliverance of Belgium.

The building was packed to overflowing, even the statues
and plinths of the pillars being hidden by clusters of people
who had swarmed over them to get a view; but, noticing
my uniform, the crowd made way, and I was shown to a
seat well in front, in the centre of the nave.

I was almost the only Englishman there. Presently,
following a procession of priests, the King and Queen

entered with Cardinal Mercier. The "Te Deum" was sung, and was followed by an extraordinary demonstration. Hats and handkerchiefs were waved wildly, and every man, woman and child of the vast congregation broke into shouts of "Vive le Roi!", "Vive la Reine!"

It was a most wonderful and spontaneous outburst of loyalty to the throne. I had never before seen the Cathedral of Brussels, and it was an impressive introduction.

We failed to get away this evening owing to the break-down of the compression gear of the car, so went to a music-hall. I loathe Puritanism, as you well know, but I think a little of it would do that place no harm.

The show ended with the Allied National Anthems, the audience standing up and joining in.

The last turn was the "Star-spangled Banner." Though Knox, who was with me, had been singing energetically enough, this so stimulated his patriotic fervour that he burst into fortissimo. His magnificent voice drowned the singing of the audience. They dropped out gradually, and by the end of the second verse he was singing by himself, accompanied only by the performers who were massed on the stage.

But he was too much even for them, and, one by one, they too gave up, till, in the end, he was performing a solo, the eyes of all riveted wonderingly upon him.

He is a tall, good-looking fellow, and it was a striking finale to the performance.

November 29, 1918.   *Ferfay, Pas de Calais.*

At eight on the morning of the 26th we left Willems and billeted for the night at Haubourdin. The following day we marched 19 miles. This was an intensely interesting day to me. We passed through the battered ruins of La Bassée, in front of which our army stood almost since the war began. We halted for dinners just short of the Cuinchy Railway Triangle. I broke away to visit this famous and formerly most formidable stronghold, which, with my Company of Coldstreamers, I had been detailed to attack on June 15 and 16, 1915. You will remember

363

the occasion. Though I would scarcely have dared at that time to hope that I should ever have the privilege of exploring it—least of all from the German direction, I did so to-day, thoroughly and at my leisure.

I inspected the line of steel trucks, shredded by shell-fire and perforated like pepper-pots, which still stand—as they have stood for nearly 4½ years—upon the triangular siding, at the other side of Noman's Land, behind the German fire-trench.

By the way, I daresay it would interest the many thousands of our soldiers, who have so long peered wistfully at these trucks over the parapet of the Brick-stack trenches, to know what they contain. It is nothing more exciting than coal.

I revisited the Brickstacks (where I received my baptism of shell-fire in May, 1915) and our trenches of that period: and I found little change, excepting the silence. The old listening post and the German crater—15 to 20 yards from our line, and the parapet over which we used to peep, were easily recognizable. The "Guards Club"—that dug-out behind one of the brick-stacks. It was there, too, though smashed in by a shell. Otherwise, the Brickstacks were much as I left them. As we discovered in 1915 they are very enduring.

Then we marched past "Harley Street" and through Cambrin and billeted for the night in Bethune, which, when I last saw it, was a populous town, but has since been evacuated, and is now considerably gutted. The central portion, including the Cathedral, and the market buildings, and the "Globe" restaurant—where our officers used to forgather, is completely demolished.

Yesterday, we marched in rain, viâ Auchel, to Ferfay, where we are likely to remain some time.

December 4, 1918.   *Ferfay.*

The following proclamation of the Mayor of Lille is nicely put, I think, and is a pretty compliment to the 5th Army after its terrible ordeal of last March and April. It is odd to think that I should have been in that Army at the time of its failure as well as of its success.

"To General Sir W. R. Birdwood, K.C.B., etc.,
Comdg. 5th Army.

"General,—The Municipal Council of Lille could not again take up its duties in regaining liberty, after four years of tyranny, without expressing to the chief agents of its deliverance, the Council's inestimable gratitude.

"I owe to my position the honour of transmitting to you the sentiments of the Council, to which I add, General, my personal admiration and respect.

"(Sgd.) C. Delesalle,
"Mayor of Lille."

Extract from the Register of Minutes of the Municipal Council of the Town of Lille, held on Thursday, November 7, 1918, and forwarded under the above letter:

ORDER OF THE DAY.

"The Municipal Council, meeting for the first time since the deliverance of the City, would fail in its first duty if it did not thank its liberators.

"The Council recognizes that it owes its deliverance from the yoke of the Barbarians to the British troops—especially the Fifth Army Commanded by General Sir William Birdwood.

"This freedom has been purchased by the British troops with their blood.

"Generous and chivalrous to the last moment, the Army submitted, with devotion and self-denial, to the fire of the enemy without replying; thereby sparing the City from the inevitable destruction of a second bombardment.

"By consenting to this sacrifice, the importance of which all appreciate, they have further earned the gratitude of the Lillois.

"The people of Lille will not forget, and their Municipal Council declares that the strong ties which bind together the French and British nations shall never be loosed.

"Signed and Sealed
"The Mayor of Lille."

December 12, 1918.   *Ferfay.*

This afternoon, having borrowed a motor ambulance, I undertook to show Knox and another American Army doctor who is visiting us from Paris—over the old Cuinchy-Loos battlefield. It is a melancholy business and I doubt if it is worth the candle, but it is very interesting.

On the way we visited the ruined square of Bethune; thence, viâ Cambrin, we passed along the La Bassée road. We stopped at the point where the latter is (or was) crossed by our front line;—where the Cuinchy Brickstacks and the Railway Triangle stand out on the left, and Etna and Vesuvius and the other famous mine craters, forming a deep-cut valley along Noman's Land, trail away to the right of the road. Do you remember my description of this sector in 1915?

We scrambled over the trenches on either side of the string of craters. It was a new and impressive experience for our visitor, who now saw this kind of landscape for the first time. And this is a fair specimen. The surface, formerly flat, to-day is as the sea would look if it froze suddenly during a hurricane.

Again, I had no difficulty in tracing the old positions, which indeed have scarcely changed during the war. The old listening posts remain, and the advanced line—where you stood so close to the enemy that you had to creep like a mouse—looks almost as I left it in 1915.

Then we went on, through the ruins of La Bassée, past the remains of Haines, Cité St. Elie, and Hulloch, to the Chalk Pit of Loos. So destroyed is this portion of the Lens-La Bassée road that we had to take to our feet. The ground around the Chalk Pit has been much disfigured by shell-fire, and the wood that grew beside it, as well as Bois Hugo—from which we met such heavy fire on September 28, 1915, have completely disappeared. So also has the building alongside the Chalk Pit, in the cellar of which our wounded lay.

Puis 14 (bis), where Harold Cuthbert was killed, is recognizable by the shreds of shell-torn machinery that lie about. But the trench we dug during the night of September 27, and held the following days, is still conspicuous, having been maintained and held by our troops till the enemy's final retirement. Hohenzollern Redoubt is gone, blown into the sky. It is represented, to-day, by some huge mine craters.

I began to feel sorry that I had undertaken to bear-lead the American sightseer. He is a good enough fellow, but was too entirely absorbed in the collection of souvenirs. I remember one of my officers—Barron, during the battle at Croisilles, telling a private whom he found relieving a German prisoner in a dug-out of his watch—if he wanted souvenirs—to go and get them in the firing line. How much less right has a mere sightseer to souvenirs? It is horrifying to see this sacred ground desecrated in this way, and still more so to think of what will happen when the cheap tripper is let loose. With his spit he will saturate the ground that has been soaked with the blood of our soldiers.

This particular man, not knowing what he was doing, would pick up a bone (it is lucky he did not notice any of the boots that still lie about with the broken off foot inside) and would call out, "Oh, look, a human tibia!"—or whatever kind of bone it might happen to be. Like a veterinary man I took round the trenches at Fricourt in September, 1916, he would pick up a battered British helmet—the owner of which had obviously been killed; or a shattered rifle butt—as likely as not that had belonged to one of the men of my own Coldstream battalion of 1915, so decayed was it.

I could overhear Knox whispering to him behind my back to put these things down. *He* knows. It is the way of the world, no doubt, but I pray I may see no more of it. I know that these things will be collected, and hoarded, and no doubt boasted of, by tourists,—things that no one who has fought would have in his possession. Fortunately, the Salvage Corps is busy at work, collecting and burying such trophies.

The entry to the old limekiln, where Arthur Egerton and Dermot Browne were killed, is entirely obliterated, but I found the vertical flue, through which, by means of a piece of telephone wire, we extricated "Bing" Hopwood and the rest of the Headquarters Company, who had been buried at the same time. I looked for the grave in which we buried Egerton and Dermot but could not find it.

Before we left I thought I would give our visitor a *respectable* souvenir, and picked up a German hand grenade. It had been lying about so long that I did not think it could possibly have any sting left. However, I pulled the safety cord to make sure, and immediately there followed a hissing sound. I called to the two doctors to take cover and threw the bomb, which a second or two later went off with a loud explosion.

A splinter drew a spot of blood from our visitor's hand, at which he said, jokingly, "Anyhow, I shall be able to tell them at home that I've had a wound."

Then we went on, through the ruins of Loos, past the great "crassier" upon which the famous pylon (the Tower Bridge as it was called) now lies flat.

It was then getting dark, so we came home.

January 17, 1919.   *Ferfay, Pas de Calais.*

I arrived here yesterday, from leave, to find demobilization the order of the day.

January 18, 1919.   *Ferfay, Pas de Calais.*

We sent off an officer and 26 men again to-day.   The
party for demobilization is paraded each day at 2 p.m.,
when I say good-bye and shake hands with the men, and
the band plays them down the road.

A crowd of the undemobilized waits about to see them
start.

January 22, 1919.   *Ferfay, Pas de Calais.*

It is a depressing process—this watching the melting
away of the battalion.

The cold, too, is very trying, and one is never warm
except in bed: but it can't go on for ever.

January 23, 1919.   *Ferfay, Pas de Calais.*

I was sent for, to-day, to Divisional Headquarters, and
told to bring a certain junior officer of mine, upon whom
my confidential report had not been so favourable as it might
have been.

In parenthesis, I may explain that the Battalion Commanders of this Division have to compose monthly reports
on each individual officer under their command.   The
following questions, amongst others, have to be answered:

(1) Do you recommend this officer for a Staff appointment?

(2) Do you recommend him for promotion?

The reports are marked "confidential," but in the case
of an unfavourable report the officer concerned is entitled
to see it.

However:—to proceed.   I was directed to bring the
junior officer into the Major-General's room, when something like the following dialogue took place:

Maj.-Gen.: I have been sorry to see that your Commanding Officer has not reported favourably of you.

Junior Officer (diffidently): I am surprised to hear that,
sir.   I have always done my best; (then, more diffidently),
I was considered rather a success, sir, before the war.

M.G. (ignoring the J.O.'s reply): I am sorry to see also that your Commanding Officer does not feel justified in recommending you for a Staff appointment.

J.O.: But I have never wished for or expected a Staff appointment, sir.

M.G.: Your Commanding Officer does not recommend you for promotion.

J.O.: I am not due for promotion, sir.

M.G.: Where were you educated?

J.O.: At the Board School, sir.

M.G.: What was your business before the war?

J.O.: I was in a Bank, sir.

M.G.: What was your position?

J.O.: Manager, sir.

After this very naïve interview, which once more illustrated the great divergence between the civilian and the military standpoint, we went and had luncheon.

January 25, 1919.   *Ferfay, Pas de Calais.*

Last night the Major-General came to our "Revue," and stayed to dinner. He is an extreme example of what a man may become who, shielded by his rank, has for years had nobody to stand up to him.

We had a quarter of an hour to wait in the ante-room before dinner, during which I inadvertently, but very successfully, put my foot into it.

By way of making conversation during the interval I said: "I am afraid we shall have to dine off bully beef to-night, General: there has been no fresh meat ration."

The General replied: "Oh! I understood that the rations had been very much better lately."

Then, seeing Praeger, the Quartermaster, standing near, and thinking it might do him some good to meet the General, I called him up, and drew him into the conversation.

I said: "I've just been telling the General, Praeger, that there is no fresh meat ration to-day."

Praeger: That is true, General. The rations have been very poor lately.

Maj.-Gen. (bridling up): That is not at all what I have

been told.   They tell me at the Divisional train that, on the contrary, the rations have been extra good lately.

Praeger (spiritedly): That's what they tell *you*, sir.

Maj.-Gen. (heatedly): I have been asked here, as a guest, to dine.   I have not come to receive complaints.

Poor Praeger, as an old Regular soldier, has a proper, if rather exaggerated, awe of a General, and was by this time beginning to show marked signs of distress.   Fearing, therefore, that in his anxiety to say the right thing he might blunder into still deeper water, I led the way hastily into dinner, which had, luckily, just been announced.   As I walked in with the General he said: "That fellow has been telling you a lot of damned nonsense."

After that, we passed a very pleasant evening, and when the General finally said good night, his manner was so cordial that I forgot all about the incident in the ante-room.

But the General had not.   He went back to his Head-quarters, and there, apparently, had up the Commander of the Divisional train.   Between them they raked out an old order, according to which every unit must send an officer, at an early hour each morning, to the refilling point, to watch the distribution of the rations.

Personally, I had never even heard of the order, which came out before I joined the Division.   Anyhow, no one has obeyed it, and the fact has been disclosed by my unfortunate attempt at conversation in the ante-room.

A memorandum on the subject has come out to-day.   It begins something like this: "Last night a complaint was made to the Divisional Commander by one of the units of the Division," etc., etc.

There is indeed a storm in a tea-cup, and my popularity is on the wane.   And it all comes from asking a general to dinner and trying to make small talk.

January 27, 1919.   *Ferfay, Pas de Calais.*

From the enclosed cutting it looks as if Madame Foch's Memorial Church will be built almost at our jumping-off place on the "Moislains" day—September 2, 1918.

371

From "*Daily Mail*," 25.1.19.

MME FOCH'S PIOUS TASK.

SOMME BATTLE MEMORIAL.

From our own Correspondent.

PARIS, *Friday.*

Marshal Foch's wife is at the head of a committee which proposes commemorating the French dead of 1916 in the Somme battles by building a church on the rise of the Péronne-Bapaume road near the demolished village of Bouchavesnes.

The spot chosen is near the old junction of the French and British front, and is hallowed by the dead not only of 1916 but also of the glorious British victories of last August and September. The project will particularly interest the 47th, 58th and 74th British Divisions.

January 28, 1919.   *Ferfay.*

What was left of our band played the demobilization draft away to-day. It played for the last time, and was then itself demobilized.

February 1, 1919.   *Ferfay, Pas de Calais.*

... I have the unusual worries as well of demobilization according to a plan which only a fatuist on army forms could have invented. I should not care to guess how many times I sign my name per day. The amount of stationery used is colossal. And the exertion of trying to be *fair*—that is to demobilize people according to their merits—is a great test of endurance.

I am bombarded all day long by officers and other ranks urging their claims, and generally, if I accede to their reasoning, I end in finding myself without the means to carry on some important branch of the business.

The cooks, for example, have greater claims (long service, etc.) than almost anyone to go, but we must be fed. I have fifty-five horses: but the transport men—all of long service (owing, I must admit, to the comparative safeness of their job), have nearly all been demobilized. I have one smith to shoe these horses, plus nine Brigade horses, and scarcely a man left who knows a horse's head from its hock.

Don't think I am trying to make a story of it. I am

quite equal to cope with it all, but I shall be glad when it is over.

The men are happy, though very unsettled. They (we all—in fact) are suffering from "reaction."

February 3, 1919. *Ferfay, Pas de Calais.*

The raging desire still continues to be demobilized quickly. Nevertheless, I feel pretty sure that, for many, there will be pathetic disillusionment.

In the trenches the troops have had plenty of time for thought, and, as "Happy Days" said the other day, there has grown up in their minds a heavenly picture of an England which does not exist, and never did exist, and never will exist so long as men are human.

After all, there was a good deal to be said in favour of the old trench life. There were none of the mean haunting fears of poverty there, and the next meal—if you were alive to take it—was as certain as the rising sun. The rations were the same for the "haves" and the "have nots," and the shells fell, without favour, upon both.

In a life where no money passes the ownership of money counts for nothing. Rich and poor alike stand solely upon their individual merits, without discrimination. You can have no idea, till you have tried it, how much pleasanter life is under such circumstances.

In spite—or partly perhaps because of the gloominess of the surroundings, there was an atmosphere of selflessness and a spirit of camaraderie the like of which has probably not been seen in the world before—at least on so grand a scale. Such is the influence of the shells!

The life was a curious blend of discipline and good-fellowship; wherein men were easily pleased; where there was no gossip; where even a shell when it had just missed you produced a sort of exultation;—a life in the course of which you actually got used to the taste of chloride of lime in tea.

In short, there was no humbug in the trenches, and that is why—with all their disadvantages—the better kind of men who have lived in them will look back upon them hereafter with something like affection.

February 18, 1919.   *Château de Ferfay, Pas de Calais.*

Up to the present, I have been billeted at the house of the caretaker of the château of this village—M. Flament. To-day I came to sleep at the château, in a room which I have furnished roughly.

The officers' mess has been in the château since December 16. It belongs to the Comte d'Hinnisdal, but, so far as I can gather, is not used by the family as a permanent home until after they are dead, when they are brought here and buried in a vault near the house. Over the vault is a chapel, in which a pensioned one-legged priest says daily mass for the dead Hinnisdals below.

The château is one-room thick, and so constructed as to be cut by the wind from whichever side it blows, and I cannot help feeling that the family is well advised in avoiding it during their living days. As the result of the war it is now in a wretched condition, leaky and unkempt, stripped of all furniture, bare and comfortless; reduced, in short, to that indescribable state of dilapidation to which only soldiers can reduce a building in which they have been long billeted.

During the war it has been one of our Corps Headquarters. It has never come within the range of battle, which therefore renders curious a story—which has been repeatedly told to me, and which I think may be true, that, while digging a practice trench not so very long ago, some dead English soldiers were found, their burial-place unmarked and unrecorded.

There has been much speculation as to the meaning of this burial, and the explanation which seems to be generally accepted is that the bodies are those of soldiers who were shot for cowardice.

Though I have never actually come across it, I seem to have been reading all through the war of soldiers being shot for so-called cowardice, and I would like to say to you that I disapprove in almost every case of this method of dealing with a trouble which is generally the result of nervous collapse, and may be uncontrollable. The best of men have their ups and downs in war, as in peace. I will go further and say that there are men who are capable of the bravest actions, and yet whose nerve may break down under certain conditions of strain, especially when they have been kept too long in the battle line.

It may be argued that it is as reasonable to shoot one man for a temporary lapse as it is to give another a V.C. for a momentary heroic impulse. Perhaps it is. Both alternatives, I think, are open to criticism. The true test of a soldier is his average behaviour under the tearing stress of war during a long period. It is the same in all walks of life.

Of course, as you know, the justification for these shootings is believed to be that they deter other soldiers from running away. Surely, that is a poor reason to give in our army!

The most deplorable feature of the business is that the court which tries these soldiers is often composed of men who have not themselves experienced, and therefore cannot visualize the supreme test to which, after all, the culprit —even though he broke down—did once submit himself, and that probably voluntarily. There are many who have not done as much.

I do not fail to appreciate the horror it must cause the judges to give their sentence. There is no blame to them. Under the existing system, it is their duty.

But, when I think of the Great Contrast between the culprit—a front-line soldier, and the Court which sometimes tries him, I am reminded of the hale and hearty men who, in the early days of the war, used to tub-thump about England, exhorting their fellow-countrymen to "join the Army" and "do their bit."

And I call to mind a certain subaltern I once knew—a lawyer in private life—who never did an honest day's work in the trenches; yet who, after four days of scrim-shanking in the front line, managed to get sent home:—and was soon promoted to the rank of major, and told off to prosecute conscientious objectors!

There are many who have dodged the firing line—not openly as deserters—but less honestly, under pretexts specious and sometimes almost plausible. They do not get shot.

February 24, 1919.   *Château de Ferfay, Pas de Calais.*

I have just had a letter from Desmond Young, who is now director of a marine salvage company. He writes: "I hope

.   .   .   .

not to have too much to do with the City. I don't like it. I wish—as I know you do—that the Germans would start another old War"!!

What do you think?

March 31, 1919.   *Château de Ferfay, Pas de Calais.*

We continue to get orders and counter-orders, and the home-coming of the Cadre seems likely to be by the Channel Tunnel!

It is, indeed, a miserable business, and has spoilt the whole war for me. Officers and men slink to their homes, one by one,—as "Happy Days" (who left to-day) used to say— as if they had lost the War instead of won it.

May 11, 1919.   *Felixstowe.*

I got to bed about a quarter to four this morning, in a lodging in a row of houses facing the sea, near Landguard Common, where the cadre is in huts.

We crossed from Havre in a crowded transport, on which we passed the night. Besides ourselves there were about 1,500 Canadian troops. I had, or rather shared, a cabin, but the men had scarcely room to breathe.

We hung about Southampton all yesterday, and finally got away about a quarter to five in the evening.

I might describe our journey from Southampton to beyond London—in fact till it became too dark to see— almost as a triumphal progress. The long train of transport never failed to draw attention to us as troops returning from France, and, in the good old English way, the people turned out of their houses, and thronged the streets as we passed, and cheered and waved their handkerchiefs.

376

Though they represented but a microscopic proportion of the fighting troops, it was nice to think that at last, after all the years of war, these men were getting some personal and first-hand recognition from their fellow-countrymen. And they thoroughly enjoyed their home-coming.

I have sometimes heard soldiers in the trenches speak as though they thought the people at home were callous, and thoughtless of their sufferings. But there was no sign of callousness yesterday.

I had not seen this side of England before—at any rate from my present view-point, and for me, a tinge of sadness was mingled with the joy of home-coming as I looked on.

INDEX

379

7960899R00249

Printed in Great Britain
by Amazon.co.uk, Ltd.,
Marston Gate.